ALBANIAN LITERATURE

A Short History

ROBERT ELSIE

I.B. TAURIS
LONDON · NEW YORK

in association with
THE CENTRE FOR ALBANIAN STUDIES

62131578

Published in 2005 by I.B.Tauris & Co. Ltd.
6 Salem Road, London W2 4BU
175 Fifth Avenue, New York NY 10010
www.ibtauris.com

In association with
The Centre for Albanian Studies

In the United States of America and in Canada distributed by Palgrave
Macmillan, a division of St Martins Press, 175 Fifth Avenue, New York,
NY 10010

ISBN: 1-84511-031-5

A full CIP record for this book is available from the British Library
A full CIP record for this book is available from the Library of Congress

Library of Congress catalog card: available

Printed and bound in Great Britain by Biddles Ltd.

Table of Contents

Preface

Albanian literature is a European literature and yet it has evolved in relative isolation from the mainstream of European culture. The Albanian people, who stem from the indigenous nomadic tribes of the southwestern Balkans, and who are at home in some of the roughest mountain terrain of the whole peninsula, consolidated their settlements far from the major crossroads of European civilization. Theirs was and continues to be a different, and quite unique European culture, and their written literature still reflects many of its particular characteristics. This is indeed one of the factors that make Albanian literature so fascinating.

Unfortunately, very little has been written about Albanian letters, with the exception, of course, of works published in Albanian itself. At the international level, the subject is still largely neglected. This neglect derives primarily from the lack of international specialists with a solid knowledge of literary Albanian and is not due to any lack of creative literature itself.

The present volume, *Albanian literature: a short history*, endeavours to fill the gap by providing a concise overview of the development of creative writing in Albanian. It focusses on the major authors and currents of Albanian literature from the earliest texts in the thirteenth, fifteenth and sixteenth centuries to the beginning of the new millennium, and is designed for the general reader who may not have any particular knowledge of the field. As such, it should serve as a useful reference guide for all those interested in Balkan cultures, in comparative literature and in European cultural history in general.

Albanian literature was late to evolve, and its development, indeed its very existence, was threatened in many periods. The first book published in Albanian that we know of was written in 1555. Despite this and other early works, one can only really speak of a national literature in Albania from the late nineteenth century onwards.

The tender plant of Albanian literature grew in a rocky soil. Time and again it sprouted and blossomed, and, time and again, it was torn out of the earth by the brutal course of political history in the Balkans. The early literature of Christian Albania disappeared under the banners of Islam when the country was forcefully incorporated into the Ottoman Empire. The still little-known literature of Muslim Albania withered in the late nineteenth century when the Albanians turned their backs on the Sublime Porte and strove to become an independent European nation. The solid beginnings of modern literature in the 1930s were weeded out ruthlessly by the Stalinist rulers who took power in 1944 and held onto it until 1990. Finally, the literature of Albanian socialist realism, which the communist regime had created, became outdated, untenable and unwanted the moment the dictatorship collapsed. Over long periods of their history, the Albanians were even forbidden by law to write and publish in their own language. A ban on Albanian-language books and schooling was in force throughout Albania virtually until the end of Ottoman rule in 1912, and a similar ban was maintained in Kosova under Serb rule, officially or unofficially, until the 1960s.

Nonetheless, this tender plant has produced some stunning blossoms in that rocky and legendary soil, many of which merit the attention of the outside world.

Albanian literature: a short history hopes to contribute to an awakening of interest in the field, but it can only be a first step. For further research, the English-speaking reader may consult my earlier, two-volume *History of Albanian literature*, New York 1995, which, with its 1,054 pages, also includes much detailed information on a myriad of minor authors and works up to 1990, and my *Dictionary of Albanian literature*, Westport 1986. Other valuable resources in English include: Arshi Pipa's *Albanian literature: social perspectives*, Munich 1978, and his *Contemporary Albanian literature*, New York 1991; and Stuart Mann's *Albanian literature: an outline of prose, poetry and drama*, London 1955, the latter specifically for the pre-WWII period. Koço Bihiku's monograph, *History of Albanian literature*, Tirana 1980, which was widely distributed abroad during the communist era, should be understood as a work of Stalinist propaganda, i.e. the Party's official view of what Albanian literature was supposed to consist of and the values it was supposed to reflect.

The six to seven million Albanians in the Balkans are now, after a long absence, in the process of regaining their place in Europe, and their vigorously thriving culture deserves greater recognition. It is thus to be hoped that this book will provide stimulus.

It remains for me to express my appreciation to the many people and institutions who have assisted me in the preparation of this book. Particular thanks go to Janice Mathie-Heck of Calgary (Canada) for her kind revision of the final manuscript.

Robert Elsie
Eifel Mountains, Germany
May 2005

ALBANIAN LITERATURE

A SHORT HISTORY

1. Early Albanian Literature (15th-17th cent.)

1.1 The Beginnings of Writing in Albanian

The Albanian people were originally a small herding community in the mountainous terrain of the southwestern Balkans. Much has been written and speculated on their origins, in particular by the Albanians themselves who are passionately interested in tracing their roots and in establishing their autochthony. Despite this, nothing has been proven conclusively. What we can say with reasonable certainty is that there is no evidence indicating the Albanians immigrated to their land from anywhere else. As such, it may be safely assumed that they are indigenous to the region, as opposed to their Slavic neighbours who invaded the Balkans from the north in the sixth and seventh centuries.

In view of this autochthony, it can also be taken for granted that the Albanians are, in some form, descendants of the ancient inhabitants of the southern Balkans. To what extent they are the direct heirs of the Illyrians, the Dardanians, the Thracians, the Bessians, or some lesser known people, or indeed a mixture thereof, is a matter which has been much discussed and to which substantial controversy has been attached from the earliest writings on the subject in the eighteenth century right up to the present day.

Unfortunately, we possess no original documents from the first millennium A.D. which could help us trace the Albanians further back into history. They were nomadic tribes in the interior of the country who seem only rarely to have ventured down onto the marshy and mosquito-infected coastline. As such, they long went unnoticed and their early history is shrouded in mist.

A history of the Albanians and their culture must best depart from the moment they entered the annals of recorded history. The first references to them date from the eleventh century, a period in which these tribes were beginning to expand their settlements and consolidate as a people and nation. It is only in this age that we may speak with any degree of clarity about an Albanian people as we know them today. Their traditional designation, based on a root *alban-* and its rhotacized variants *arban-, *albar-, and *arbar-, appears from the eleventh century onwards in Byzantine chronicles (*Albanoi,*

Arbanitai, Arbanites), and from the fourteenth century onwards in Latin and other Western documents (*Albanenses, Arbanenses*).

As a herding community in an isolated mountainous region, the Albanians did not succeed in creating an independent state of their own until the early twentieth century. Indeed a strong sense of ethnic identity, as we conceive it nowadays, probably only crystallized in the nineteenth century. Thus, there was little need for writing, let alone creative writing in Albanian, until the so-called Rilindja (rebirth) period of national revival in the second half of the nineteenth century. Official documents and correspondence in the late Middle Ages and the early Renaissance were written in languages with an established literary tradition: Greek, Latin, Serbian or Italian, depending in most cases on who ruled the territory in question.

The rise of early writing and literature in Albanian is closely linked to the fortunes of the Catholic Church in the southwestern Balkans and to the spread of Italian, specifically Venetian civilization. The Catholic Church put up much resistance to the Turkish occupation of Albania, which began in 1393 with the conquest of the fortress of Shkodra. Resistance was at its height in the age of Scanderbeg who initially received much support from Venice, the Pope and the Kingdom of Naples, and who was widely admired in the Christian world for his fight against the Turks. After Scanderbeg's death in 1468 and the collapse of organised Albanian resistance to the Turks, however, the position of the Catholic Church in Albania became much more precarious. In the second half of the sixteenth century, northern and central Albania were still Catholic, but by the early decades of the seventeenth century, an estimated half of the population of the north had 'turned Turk,' i.e. had converted to Islam. In 1599 there were no more than 130 Catholic priests left in the country, most of whom had little education.

In the final analysis, it was probably Italian and Catholic interests in converting the Albanian masses and subsequently in combatting the spread of Islam in the Balkans that enabled a modest number of religious books to be published in Albanian. Among these works were Latin and Italian texts translated into an as yet unsophisticated language, but there were also ecclesiastical and other texts written in Albanian itself. The authors of the major works of early Albanian literature seem all to have been clerics trained in Italy, where they came into contact with the values of the Renaissance and with the ideas and ideals of Italian civilization. Their homeland, by contrast, remained an isolated and primitive backwater. Albania had no large urban centres, no adequate system of education and, it would seem, no publishing facilities, which are the usual prerequisites for the development of written literature. It is thus to Catholic Church that we must turn our attention for the birth of a new literature.

4

Translations of religious texts into the vernacular had given and were giving rise to many of the national literatures of Europe. In Albania's case, it was a short-lived, though vibrant phase which ended abruptly with the Ottoman conquest and the rapid decline of Catholicism in the southwestern Balkans.

1.2   Theodor of Shkodra (1210) and Other Early Texts

In 1998, a manuscript was discovered in the Secret Archives of the Vatican which may potentially bring about a modest revolution in Albanian studies, pushing back the date of the first substantial work written in the Albanian language by almost three and a half centuries. The 208-page parchment text in question, discovered by Albanian scholar Musa Ahmeti, was written by one **Theodor of Shkodra**, of whom little is yet known. Written by one hand and embellished with golden miniatures and coloured initials, the manuscript is divided into three parts, which seem to suggest three different works. Pages 1-97 deal with theology, pages 98-146 with philosophy, and pages 147-208 with a history of the known world from 154 A.D. to December 1209. On the final page of the manuscript, we find a note by the author, who writes simply: "With the assistance and great love of the blessed Lord, I finished this in the year 1210 on the 9th day of March."

The work or works of Theodor of Shkodra have not yet been published, even in part, but if and when they are, they will no doubt have a major impact on Albanian studies, not only with regard to the history of Albanian literature, but also to our knowledge of the Albanian language, and indeed our knowledge of the Albanian people in general.

Other records of written Albanian, dating from the second half of the fifteenth century, are less spectacular. They consist mostly of words and short phrases discovered in foreign-language manuscripts.

The first, and perhaps best known of these smaller records, is a baptismal formula dating from 1462 which reads as follows: *Unte paghesont premenit Atit et birit et spertit senit* (I baptize you in the name of the Father and the Son and the Holy Ghost). The author of the formula was **Paulus Angelus** (ca. 1417-1470), Archbishop of Durrës and a close friend and counsellor of Scanderbeg (1405-1468). Paulus Angelus included this Albanian translation of the baptismal formula, much needed for the conversion of non-Latin speakers, in a pastoral letter written on the occasion of a synod held at the church of the

Holy Trinity in Mat on 8 November 1462. It is preserved in the Laurentian Library in Florence[1].

Twenty-one years later, in 1483, we come across another Albanian sentence, and our first curse, in a Renaissance play entitled *Epirota*[2]. In this Plautus-style comedy in Latin written by Thomas Medius (Ital. Tommaso de Mezzo), who was a contemporary and acquaintance of Giovanni Pico della Mirandola (1463-1494), an Epirotic (i.e. Albanian) singer named Damascenus abuses an inn-keeper who dislikes his songs, cursing him in his native language with *Dramburi te clofto goglie* (May your mouth tremble). The curse is Albanian and quite similar to many insults still in use today, "May your mouth be shut," "May your mouth dry up" etc., i.e. "May you lose your voice for your wickedness."

Another text in early Albanian is the so-called Easter Gospel or Pericope, fifteen lines in Greek script translated from the Gospel of St Matthew (27: 62-66). The text[3], whose author and exact date are unknown, is in a Tosk dialect, though not well translated. Estimates as to its antiquity have ranged from the fourteenth to the eighteenth century. A palaeographic analysis of the folio preserved in a Greek manuscript at the Ambrosian Library of Milan points to a fifteenth or sixteenth-century text.

The fifteenth century closes with an intriguing Albanian text preserved in Germany, dating from the year 1497. It is the Albanian lexicon of **Arnold von Harff**[4] (ca. 1471-1505), a German knight, traveller and writer born of a noble family in the lower Rhineland (at Harff on the Erft, northwest of Cologne). In the autumn of 1496, von Harff had set out on a journey, ostensibly a pilgrimage to the Holy Land, which took him to Italy, down the Adriatic coast to Greece, Egypt, Arabia, Palestine, Asia Minor, and then back through central Europe to France and Spain. He returned to Cologne in the autumn of 1498 or 1499 and died in 1505. During his travels, von Harff collected material on the languages he encountered. On a stopover in the port of Durrës in the spring of

---

[1] The text was discovered in manuscript Ashburnham 1167 by the Romanian scholar Nicolae Iorga (1871-1940) and published by him in 1915. cf. N. Iorga 1915, p. 194-197.

[2] cf. T. Medius 1483. Though the play was originally published in 1483, the curse was only recognized as Albanian in 1972. cf. L. Braun & M. Camaj 1972.

[3] Codex 133, f. 63, Martini-Bassi Catalogus Codicum Graecorum. The text was discovered by the Greek historian Spyridôn Lampros (1851-1919) in 1906. cf. S. Lampros 1906; and N. Borgia 1930.

[4] The text was first published in German by E. von Groote 1860, and in English by M. Letts 1946. cf. R. Elsie 1984; and A. Hetzer 1981c.

1497, as he was sailing aboard a merchant galley from Venice to Alexandria, he jotted down twenty-six words, eight phrases, and twelve numbers in Albanian which he recorded in his travel journal with a German translation. The account of his journey is considered one of the best examples of the period of this genre of travel narrative which was very popular at the end of the Middle Ages. Von Harff showed a consistent interest in foreign customs and languages during his travels, giving, in addition to the Albanian material, short lexicons of words and phrases in Croatian, Greek, Arabic, Hebrew, Turkish, Hungarian, Basque and Breton. These constitute what one would now call essential pocket vocabularies for travellers, usually including items of food, household and travel necessities and useful phrases such as: "Good morning," "How much does this cost?" and "Woman, shall I sleep with you?" The latter question is, incidently, missing from the Albanian lexicon for one reason or another. On his arrival in Durrës, von Harff writes as follows:

"From Ulcinj to Durrës we travelled with a very bad wind. This is a great city ruined by the Turks, and now subject to the Venetians. This city lies in Albania where they also have their own language which cannot be written well, as they do not have their own letters in this country. I have noted down several words of this Albanian language, which are written below in our letters:

1.	*boicke*	bread
2.	*vene*	wine
3.	*oie*	water
4.	*mische*	meat
5.	*jat*	cheese
6.	*foeije*	eggs
7.	*oitter*	vinegar
8.	*poylle*	a chicken
9.	*pyske*	fish
10.	*krup*	salt
11.	*myr*	good
12.	*kyckge*	bad
13.	*megarune*	to eat
14.	*pijne*	to drink
15.	*tauerne*	a tavern
16.	*geneyre*	a man
17.	*growa*	a woman
18.	*denarye*	money
19.	*sto*	yes

20.	*jae*	no
21.	*criste*	god
22.	*dreck*	the devil
23.	*kijrij*	a candle
24.	*kale*	a horse
25.	*elbe*	oats
26.	*fijet*	to sleep
27.	*mirenestrasse*	good morning
28.	*myreprama*	good night
29.	*meretzewen*	good day
30.	*ake ja kasse zet ve*	what do you have that I like?
31.	*kess felgen gjo kaffs*	how much does that cost?
32.	*do daple*	I'll buy it
33.	*laff ne kammijss*	wash my shirt
34.	*ne kaffs*	what is that called?[5]
35.	*nea*	one
36.	*dua*	two
37.	*trij*	three
38.	*quater*	four
39.	*pessa*	five
40.	*jast*	six
41.	*statte*	seven
42.	*tette*	eight
43.	*nante*	nine
44.	*dieta*	ten
45.	*nijtgint*	hundred
46.	*nemijgo*	thousand"

Von Harff imposed his native German orthography on Albanian which, of course, could not take account of the Albanian phonemes differing from the German. Nevertheless, his transcription of Albanian is no worse than that of other texts of the period and, indeed, his pocket vocabulary could be used by a foreigner with a certain degree of success even today.

---

[5] This item is a misunderstanding on von Harff's part. The Albanian means literally 'a thing, an animal.' The mediaeval traveller probably pointed to something to elicit the phrase 'What is that called?' and received an answer instead of a question.

1.3   Gjon Buzuku and the First Albanian Book (1555)

The first real book printed in Albanian, at least the first one we know of, is no less fascinating than the manuscript of Theodor of Shkodra 345 years earlier. It is a 188-page Albanian translation of the Catholic missal, i.e. fixed prayers and rites that a priest reads during the year at mass, including many extracts from the Catholic breviary, psalms and litanies. Since the frontispiece and the first sixteen sheets of the only copy of the book we possess are missing, we unfortunately know neither its exact title nor its place of publication. In Albanian it is commonly known as the *Meshari* (The Missal). What we do know is that it was written in 1555 by one **Gjon Buzuku**, a northern Albanian Catholic clergyman.

The Missal of Gjon (or John) Buzuku originally consisted of 110 sheets or 220 pages of printed text, of which 94 sheets or 188 pages now remain. Since the book contains well-known liturgical texts and excerpts from the Old and New Testaments, it is not too difficult to interpret despite the complex orthography, the archaic language and the numerous printing mistakes and omissions. The 188 pages comprise about 154,000 words with a total vocabulary of ca. 1,500 different lexemes[6], and are a veritable goldmine for lexicographers and historical linguists.

Little is known about the author of this old Albanian missal. The scant information we do possess about Gjon Buzuku comes from the colophon (postscript) of the missal which Buzuku wrote himself in Albanian, not unaware of the historic dimensions of his undertaking:

"*U doni Gjoni, biri i Bdek Buzukut, tue u kujtuom shumë herrë se gluha jonë nukë kish gjā të ëndigluom ën së shkruomit shenjëtë, ën së dashunit së botësë s'anë, desha me u fëdigunë, për sā mujta me ditunë, me zhdritunë pak mendetë e atyne qi të ëndiglonjinë, për-se ata të mundë mernë sā i naltë e i mujtunë e i për-mishëriershim anshtë Zot' ynë atyne qi t'a duonë ëm gjithë zemërë. U lus ënbas sodi mā shpesh të uni ëm klishë, për-se ju kini me gjegjunë ordhëninë e t'inë Zot; e ate në ënbarofshi, Zot' ynë të ketë mishërier ënbī jū, e ata qi u monduonë dierje tash, mā mos u mondonjënë. E ju t'ini të zgjiedhunitë e t'inë Zot, e për-herrë Zot' ynë kā me klenë me jū, ju tue ëndiekunë të dërejtënë e tue lanë të shtrenbënënë. E këta ju tue bām, Zot' ynë ka(a) me shtuom ëndër jū, se të korëtë t'aj të ënglatetë dierje ën së vielash e të*

---

[6] On Buzuku's lexicon, cf. K. Ashta, 1964-1966, 1996.

*vielëtë dierje ën së ënbiellash. E u mā duo të ënbaronj vepërënë t'eme,
t'inë Zot tue pëlqyem. Ëndë vietët M.D.L.IV. një-zet dit ëndë mars zuna
ënfill, e ënbarova ëndë vietët një M.D.L.V., ëndë kallënduor V. dit. E
se për fat në keshe kun ënbë ëndonjë vend fëjyem, u duo tuk të jetë
fajtë, ai qi të jetë mā i ditëshim se u, ata faj e lus t'a trajtonjë ënde e
mirë; për-se nukë çuditem se në paça fëjyem, këjo tue klenë mā e para
vepërë e fort e fështirë për të vepëruom ënbë gluhët t'anë. Për-se ata
qi shtanponjinë kishnë të madhe fëdigë, e aqë nukë mundë qëllonjinë
se faj të mos banjinë, për-se për-herrë ëndaj 'ta nukë mundë jeshe, u
tue ënbajtunë një klishë, ënbë të dŷ anët më duhee me sherbyem. E
tash u jam ënfalë gjithëve, e lutëni t'enë Zonë ende për muo."[7]*

(I, Don John, son of Benedict Buzuku, having often considered that our
language had in it nothing intelligible from the Holy Scriptures, wished
for the sake of our people to attempt, as far as I was able, to enlighten
the minds of those who understand, so that they may comprehend how
great and powerful and forgiving our Lord is to those who love him
with all their hearts. I beg of you from today on, to go to church more
often to hear the word of God. If you do this, may our Lord have mercy
upon you. Those who have suffered up to now shall suffer no longer.
May you be the elect of our Lord. He will be with you at all times if
you pursue righteousness and avoid iniquity. By so doing, the Lord
shall give you increase, for your harvest shall last until the vintage and
the vintage shall last until the time of sowing. I, moreover, wish to
finish my work if it please God. I began it in the year 1554 on the 20th
day of March and finished it in the year 1555 on the 5th day of
January. If perchance mistakes have been made in any part, I pray and
beg of those who are more learned than I to correct them. For I should
not be surprised if I have made mistakes, this being the very first work,
great and difficult to render into our language. Those who printed it
had great difficulty and thus could not fail to make mistakes, for I was
not able to be with them all the time. Running a church, I had to serve
in two places. And now I beg of you all to pray to the Lord on my
behalf.)

It has been put forth convincingly that Gjon Buzuku did not live in
Albania itself but rather somewhere on the northern Adriatic in the Republic
of San Marco, perhaps in the Venetian region itself, where families of Albanian

---

[7] Phonetic transcription from N. Ressuli (ed.) 1958, p. 379.

refugees had settled after the Turkish conquest of Shkodra in 1479. In Venice, Buzuku would have had greater access to a literary education and to training as a priest than in Albania itself.

Judging from the traits of the northwestern Gheg dialect used in the text, Gjon Buzuku's family must have stemmed from one of the villages on the western bank of Lake Shkodra, possibly around Shestan, which is now in Montenegro. Elements of other dialects also occur, which would seem to confirm the assumption that Buzuku was born and raised outside of Albania, unless of course he was consciously endeavouring to employ a language more widely intelligible than his native dialect. Not only is Buzuku's language completely devoid of the strong Turkish influence in later Albanian, it also contains many surprisingly archaic features not otherwise recorded in the language. Due to the complexity of the writing system he practised, these features have as yet only been investigated in part.

The general consensus of opinion is that this first Albanian book was published in Venice, although other publishing centres on the Dalmatian coast or in Italy would be equally conceivable. There were no Catholic printing facilities in and around Albania itself at the time, at least none that we know of, although the Orthodox Church had printed Serbian-language books in the region in Cyrillic script on various printing presses imported from Venice: Obod 1483 and Cetinje 1494 in Montenegro, Graçanica in Kosova 1539 and indeed Shkodra 1563.

The Albanian missal was published in a northern Italian semi-Gothic script of Latin characters including five characters of Cyrillic origin for sounds not occurring in Latin or Italian. Buzuku and/or the printers must therefore have had contact with Serbo-Croatian, in particular with the *bukvica* script employed in Bosnia. The typeface of the book is similar to that employed in Venice in 1523 and 1537 where missals in Cyrillic had been published for Bosnian Catholics. French scholar Mario Roques (1875-1961) notes in his study of ancient Albanian texts[8] that Buzuku was indebted to the Catholic Slavs of Bosnia, Dalmatia and Serbia not only for the Cyrillic characters and the Venetian typography but perhaps also for the very thought of providing his fellow countrymen with a missal in their own language. Roques also notes parallels in contents with a Bosnian missal published in 1512, and in particular certain Franciscan elements which may give us more indirect clues about the author and his work.

The mystery of Buzuku's missal is compounded by the fact that only one copy of the book has survived the centuries. It was discovered by chance

---

[8] cf. M. Roques 1932b.

in 1740 in the library of the College of the Propaganda Fide by the Jesuit cleric Johannes Nicolevich Casasi (1702-1752) of Gjakova, known in Albanian as Gjon Nikollë Kazazi, when he was visiting Rome in his capacity as Archbishop of Skopje. He described his discovery as "an old Albanian missal totally frayed with age." Casasi made a copy of fragments of the text which he transmitted to Giorgio Guzzetta (1682-1756), founder of the Albanian seminary in Palermo. At the end of the eighteenth century, the book is known to have been part of the impressive collection of Cardinal Stephan Borgia, which later ended up in the Vatican Library[9]. After long years of oblivion, the missal was brought to light by Msgr Paolo Schirò (1866-1941), an Arbëresh bishop and scholar from Sicily, who photocopied the text in 1909-1910 and prepared a transliteration and transcription. Unfortunately Schirò's extensive research on the missal was only published in part[10]. In 1929, three other photocopies were made for the Franciscan scholar Justin Rrota (1889-1964), who published excerpts of the missal in the following year at the Franciscan Press in Shkodra[11]. The first complete publication of the text was undertaken in 1958 by Namik Ressuli (1908-1985), including a photocopy and a transcription[12]. Ten years later, historical linguist Eqrem Çabej (1908-1980) published another, two-volume critical edition in Tirana[13]. Volume one of Çabej's *Meshari* contains an introductory study with a transliteration of the entire text; volume two contains a facsimile of the original and a phonetic transcription which is of great assistance in view of Buzuku's often erratic orthography.

Many observers have been puzzled by the rarity of Buzuku's Albanian missal and by the lack of Albanian books in the sixteenth century in general. The reason is to be found in Church history. The policies of the Catholic Church with regard to publications, in particular publications in the vernacular, vacillated substantially during the years of the Council of Trent (1545-1563) and thereafter. In the spirit of a much-needed Reformation, the Church initially authorized some translations of ecclesiastical texts into the vernacular, but soon changed its course. In a reaffirmation of the traditional Catholic teachings of the Counter-Reformation, which put an end to the Renaissance in Italy, and in the general atmosphere of intimidation which reigned during the Inquisition, it soon put the very same books onto the Index and suppressed them.

---

[9] It is now catalogued under Ed. Prop. IV. 244.

[10] cf. G. Schirò & G. Petrotta 1932.

[11] cf. J. Rrota 1930.

[12] cf. N. Ressuli (ed.) 1958.

[13] cf. E. Çabej (ed.) 1968, cf. also S. Riza 1996, p. 491-542.

Particularly rigorous were the Index of 1554-1555, i.e. the very year Buzuku finished his missal, and the Index of 1559 under Pope Paul IV (r. 1555-1559). "The Venetian version of the new Index banned the *opera omnia* of about 290 authors, over four times as many as its predecessor, as well as many more individual titles... The 1554-1555 Index having been withdrawn, the Venetian Holy Office resorted to individual decrees... Fifty-seven bookmen appeared before the Holy Office on August 22, 1558 to be informed that they were forbidden to print the Bible in any vernacular... The new Index was printed and promulgated in Rome in January 1559. Paul IV's Index condemned the *opera omnia* of about 550 authors, nearly twice the number listed in the 1554-1555 Index, as well as many more individual titles... Paul IV's index introduced into Italy a feature of earlier northern European Indices; it specifically condemned nearly sixty editions and printings of the Bible. It also banned the printing and possession of Bibles in any vernacular except with the permission of the Inquisition... In Paul IV's Rome, where even the cardinals held their tongue for fear of the Inquisition, the new Index produced consternation and caused large numbers of books to be destroyed."[14]

Not only was Buzuku's missal, which was printed in a language no one in high Church circles could have understood, probably regarded as a heretical threat, it also soon therafter became outdated. In 1563, one of the concluding decrees of the Council of Trent called for a revision of the two most important liturgical manuals used by the Church: the breviary and the missal. The reformed versions of these manuals appeared in 1566, together with a new catechism. "The papacy sent each work forth with a bull that rejoiced in its appearance, prescribed its use throughout Catholic Christendom and banned most older versions."[15]

Thus, even in the unlikely event that Buzuku's missal had escaped the attention of the Inquisition, it would soon have been out of date and unfit for use. Many liturgical and religious works are also known to have been suppressed or withdrawn from circulation in the subsequent thirty year period between 1568 and 1598. Seen in the light of the influence of the Council of Trent and the Inquisition, which was at its height at the time of writing, it is quite miraculous that even one copy of the Albanian missal survived[16].

Subsequent authors of early Albanian literature such as Lekë Matrënga (1567-1619), Pjetër Budi (1566-1622) and Frang Bardhi (1606-1643) do not seem to have known about the missal, although the erudite Pjetër Bogdani (ca.

---

[14] cf. P. Grendler 1977, p. 95, 115-117.

[15] cf. P. Grendler 1977, p. 169.

[16] On this period cf. also I. Zamputi 1988; and V. Kamsi 1997.

1630-1689), in a report to the Propaganda Fide in 1665 in which he refers to the lack of books in Albanian and lists publications of which he had heard, mentions a certain '*Euangelii in Albanese*' (Gospels in Albanian)[17]. This may very well be a reference to Buzuku as well as an indication of the original title of the work.

Gjon Buzuku was not a creator of literature per se. His missal, with the exception of the colophon, is simply a conglomeration of translations of Latin religious texts. But as author of the first real book printed in Albanian, it was he who can be said to have given birth to literary Albanian. Because the missal and other religious texts in Albanian which may have existed in the mid-sixteenth century were suppressed by the Inquisition, an Albanian literary tradition which might have arisen here, based on the astounding achievement of Gjon Buzuku, was nipped in the bud and stifled.

1.4   Lekë Matrënga and the Christian Doctrine (1592)

The second major work of early Albanian literature is entitled *E mbsuame e krështerë*[18], Rome 1592 (Christian Doctrine), a twenty-eight page catechism translated from the Latin catechism of the Spanish Jesuit priest Jacob Ledesma (1516-1575). It was written by Luca Matranga (1567-1619), now known in Albania as **Lekë Matrënga**, an Orthodox cleric of the Arbëresh community of Sicily. The manuscript form of Matrënga's translation survives in three differing versions[19], the first of which is apparently in Matrënga's own handwriting. From the date given in the first version, we know that Matrënga finished his translation on 20 March 1592 in Piana dei Greci (now Piana degli Albanesi) in Sicily. The published version, of which, like Buzuku's missal, only one copy survived, was printed in Rome by Guglielmo Facciotto 'with the permission of the superiors' and discovered by Mario Roques[20]. It is based on

---

[17] cf. Dh. Shuteriqi 1977, p. 58.

[18] cf. M. La Piana 1912; J. Rrota 1939; M. Sciambra 1964; F. Sulejmani 1979; S. Riza 1996, p. 543-552; R. Ismajli 2000, p. 101-108; and M. Mandalà 2000.

[19] cf. S. Riza 1962, 1965b. It is preserved in the Vatican Library and is catalogued under Codex Barberini Latini 3454. Another version of the manuscript, discovered by Giuseppe Schirò in 1909 and used by Marco La Piana in 1912, has apparently since disappeared.

[20] cf. M. Roques 1932b, p. 19. It is preserved as Codex 3518 in the Vatican Library.

one of the badly revised versions of the manuscript and contains many mistakes. The full title of the edition is:

> *"Embsuame e chraesterae. Baeaera per tae Vrtaenae Atae Ladesmae sciochiaeriet Iesusit. E prierrae laetireiet mbae gluchae tae arbaeresciae paer Lecae Matraengnae. Imbsuam i Cullegit Graec tae Romaesae. Dottrina Christiana. Composta dal Reuerendo P. Dottor Ledesma della Compagnia di Giesù. Tradotta di lingua Italiana nell'Albanese per Luca Matranga alumno del Collegio Greco in Roma"*

(Christian Doctrine. Done by the Reverend Father Ledesma of the Society of Jesus. Translated from Italian into the Albanian language by Lekë Matrënga, student of the Greek College in Rome.)

Matrënga's work contains an introduction in Italian, an eight-line poem which constitutes the earliest specimen of written verse in Albanian, and the catechism itself, being religious instruction on church doctrines in the form of questions and answers. In his introduction dedicating the work to Cardinal Ludovico II de Torres, Archbishop of Monreale, Matrënga explains that the translation was for the use of the Arbëresh who could not understand the Italian version of the catechism in circulation, noting that it would be useful for the "hundreds of families in Calabria and Apulia" of Albanian origin.

Lekë Matrënga was born either in Piana dei Greci south of Palermo or in Monreale, scion of an Arbëresh family which had emigrated to Sicily, probably from the Peloponnese, in about 1532-1533. The exact date of his birth is not known[21]. He studied for five years, probably from 1582 to 1587, at the Greek College of Saint Athanasius in Rome, which had been founded in 1577, and then returned to his native Sicily. He is mentioned in the 'Chronicle of all the students of the Greek College from its foundation to the year 1640 which states tersely: "Luca Matragna (sic) of Monreale in Sicily of Albanian nationality was of a mediocre temperament, studied Greek and Latin humanities, then departed due to an indisposition, having been at the college for five years." Not much is known of Matrënga's life except that he was engaged in pastoral duties among the Arbëresh in Piana dei Greci in December 1601 and that he died as an archpriest on 6 May 1619.

---

[21] Marco La Piana 1912, p. 4, gives 1560 which is now considered too early. Dhimitër Shuteriqi 1987, p. 97, has suggested a date of birth as late as 1571-1572.

Lekë Matrënga does not seem to have known Gjon Buzuku's missal which was published thirty-seven years earlier. He was not at any rate influenced by the latter's orthography. He restricted himself to letters from the Latin alphabet whereas the northern Albanian writers from the Balkans made use of Cyrillic additions. Matrënga employed *ae* for the schwa vowel now written as *ë*, the Italian *sc(i)* for *sh* and was first to use *th* for the dental fricative. His Albanian[22] is also strongly flavoured with Greek vocabulary, not only because Greek was the language of the Orthodox church, but also because it was from Greece that the Sicilian Arbëresh had fled sixty years earlier. His own grandparents, if not his parents, must have taken part in that exodus. Matrënga's work comprises a total vocabulary of about 450 lexemes.

Lekë Matrënga is also, as is noted, the author of the first poem to be published in Albanian, a modest work in eight lines of hendecasyllabics (eleven syllables) with an alternating rhyme. It contains a poignant message and is entitled simply 'Spiritual Song':

> "*Cghíthaeue u thaerés cúx dó ndaegliésae,*
> *Tae mírae tae chraextée búra e gráa,*
> *Mbae fiálaet tae tinaezót tae xíchi méxae,*
> *Sé síxtae gneríj néx cciae mcátae scáa,*
> *Elúm cúx e cuitón sé cáa tae vdésae,*
> *E mentae báxcae mbae taenaezónae i cáa,*
> *Sé chríxti ndae parráisit i baen piésae,*
> *E baen paer bijr tae tij e paer vaeláa.*"

(I call upon all of you who wish indulgence,
All good Christians, men and women:
It is the word of God that you go to mass,
For there is no man among us who is without sin;
Happy be he who remembers he is mortal
And who reflects constantly upon God,
For Christ will give him his place in heaven
Together with his children and his brethren.)

Though short in comparison with other works of early Albanian literature, a mere 28 pages, Lekë Matrënga's Christian Doctrine is of historical and literary significance not only as the second oldest publication of Albanian literature, but also as the first work by an Italo-Albanian and the first one

---

[22] cf. K. Ashta 1957, 1965, 1998.

written in the southern Tosk dialect. All other early Albanian authors, Gjon Buzuku, Pjetër Budi, Frang Bardhi and Pjetër Bogdani, wrote in their native northern Gheg dialects.

1.5   The Works of Pjetër Budi (1618-1621)

Two generations after Gjon Buzuku follows the second major figure of early northern Albanian literature. **Pjetër Budi**[23] (1566-1622), known in Italian as Pietro Budi, was the author of four religious works in Albanian. He was born in the village of Gur i Bardhë in the Mati region of the north-central Albanian mountains. He could not have benefited from much formal education in his native region, and trained for the priesthood at the so-called Illyrian College of Loretto (*Collegium Illyricum* of Our Lady of Luria), south of Ancona in Italy, where many Albanians and Dalmatians of renown were to study. At the age of twenty-one he was ordained as a Catholic priest and sent immediately to Macedonia and Kosova, then part of the ecclesiastical province of Serbia under the jurisdiction of the Archbishop of Antivari (Bar), where he served in various parishes for an initial twelve years. In 1610 he is referred to as 'chaplain of Christianity in Skopje' and in 1617 as chaplain of Prokuplje.

It was in Prokuplje in southern Serbia, a year earlier, that a meeting of various national rebel movements had been held to organize a major offensive against the Turks. In Kosova, Budi came into contact with Franciscan Catholics from Bosnia, connections which in later years proved fruitful for his political endeavours to mount support for Albanian resistance to the Porte. In 1599, Budi was appointed vicar general (*vicario generale*) of Serbia, a post he held for seventeen years. As a representative of the Catholic church in the Turkish-occupied Balkans, he lived and worked in what was no doubt a tense political atmosphere. His ecclesiastical position was in many ways only a cover for his political aspirations.

Pjetër Budi was filled with an ardent desire to see his people freed of Turkish bondage and he worked actively to this end. He is known in this period to have had contacts with figures of influence such as Francesco Antonio Bertucci and with Albanian rebels seeking the overthrow of Ottoman rule. But

---

[23] cf. I. Zamputi 1965a, 1985; M. Domi 1966, 1967; H. Lacaj 1966; S. Riza 1979, 1996, p. 553-566; G. Svane 1985a, 1985b, 1986a, 1986b, 1986c, 1986d etc.; P. Budi 1986; R. Ismajli 2000, p. 111-237; and B. Gjoka 2002.

Budi was no narrow-minded nationalist. As far as can be judged, his activities, then and later, were directed towards a general uprising of all the peoples of the Balkans, including his Muslim compatriots.

In 1616, Pjetër Budi travelled to Rome where he resided until 1618 to oversee the publication of his works. From March 1618 until ca. September 1619, he went on an eighteen-month pilgrimage to Santiago de Compostela in Spain. Back in Rome in the autumn of 1619, he endeavoured to draw the attention of the Roman curia to the plight of Albanian Christians and raise support for armed resistance. On 20 July 1621, he was made Bishop of Sapa and Sarda (*Episcopus Sapatensis et Sardensis*), i.e. of the Zadrima region, and returned to Albania the following year. His activities there were often more political than religious in nature. One of his interests was to ensure that foreign clergymen were replaced by native Albanians, a step which could not have made him particularly popular with some of his superiors in Italy. In December 1622, some time before Christmas, Pjetër Budi drowned while crossing the Drin river. It has been alleged that he was the victim of an assassination plot though the evidence to this effect is not conclusive[24].

Much of the biographical information we possess about this author derives from a letter dated 15 September 1621 which Budi addressed to Cardinal Gozzadini in Rome and in which he set forth his plans and strategies for an uprising in the Balkans. In this letter he also noted:

> "... in the space of seventeen years, as far as I was able, I never ceased in my efforts to aid and comfort those peoples, including indeed the priests, with spiritual models, by continually writing spiritual books in their language, both in that of Serbia and in that of Albania, such as are seen in all those countries nowadays."

This would seem to indicate that during his years of service in Kosova and Macedonia, Budi had been devoting his energies to the writing and translation of devotional works now lost. How could one otherwise account for his having published four works in Albanian comprising a total of one thousand pages within the space of five years?

Budi's first work is the *Dottrina Christiana* or *Doktrina e Kërshtenë* (Christian Doctrine), a translation of the catechism of Saint Robert Bellarmine (1542-1621). It was published in Rome in 1618 and is preserved in only one original copy[25]. The title page bears the following information:

---

[24] cf. I. Zamputi 1958, 1985.

[25] This copy is preserved in the Vatican Library and catalogued under R.I.VI.449.

"*Dottrina Christiana. Composta per ordine della fel.me. Di Papa
Clemente VIII. Dal. R. P. Roberto Bellarmino Sacerdote della
Compagnia di Giesv. Adesso Cardinale di Santa Chiesa del Titolo di
S. Maria in Via. Tradotta in lingua albanese. Dal Rever. Don Pietro
Bvdi da Pietra Biancha. In Roma, Per Bartolomeo Zannetti. 1618. Con
Licenza de' Superiori.*"

(Christian Doctrine, composed in honour of the blithe memory of Pope
Clement VIII, by Robert Bellarmine, priest of the Company of Jesus,
now cardinal of the holy church entitled Santa Maria in Via.
Translated into the Albanian language by Reverend Don Pjetër Budi
of Gur i Bardhë. In Rome, by Bartholomew Zannetti 1618. With the
permission of the superiors.)[26]

Saint Robert Bellarmine of Montepulciano was a cardinal and Jesuit,
canonized and declared a doctor of the Church in 1930, whose widely
circulated Christian Doctrine, like his other works, had shown him to be an
able theologian in the conflict with Protestantism. His so-called 'little'
Christian Doctrine, a work which the Counter-Reformation particularly
recommended for missionary use, had been originally published in 1597 and
was subsequently translated into a number of languages including English,
Welsh, Arabic (1613) and Greek (1616). Pjetër Budi's Albanian translation of
the Christian Doctrine (1618) consists of 169 pages.

The Albanian Christian Doctrine was subsequently reprinted by the
Congregation of the Propaganda Fide in Rome in what would seem to be
relatively large editions in 1636, 1664 and in 1868. In 1759, we know that there
were still a total of 960 copies of the book in the depository of the Propaganda
Fide[27].

Of more literary interest than the catechism itself are Budi's fifty-three
pages of religious poetry in Albanian, some 3,000 lines, appended to the
Christian Doctrine. It constitutes the earliest poetry in Gheg dialect. Much of
it was translated from Latin or Italian, though some is original.

Budi's second publication contains his three other works. The
frontispiece bears the title:

---

[26] Noted in handwriting at the bottom of the page is "Autor dono dedit Bibliothecae
Vaticanae. 29 Januari 1622" (The author gave [this copy] as a gift to the Vatican
Library. 29 January 1622).

[27] cf. *Archivo storico della S. Congregazione 'de Propaganda Fide,'* SC Stamperia
2, f. 246.

"Ritvale Romanvm et Specvlvm Confessionis. In Epyroticam linguam a Petro Bvdi Episcopo Sapatense & Sardanense translata. Sanctissimi Domini Nostri Gregorii XV liberalitate typis data. Romae, apud Haeredem Bartholomaei Zannetti. 1621. Svperiorvm permissv."

(Roman Ritual and Mirror of Confession. Translated into the Epirotic (Albanian) language by Pjetër Budi, Bishop of Sapa and Sarda. Given to print by the liberality of our most reverend lord Gregory XV. Rome. Bartholomew Zannetti 1621. With the permission of the superiors.)[28]

This publication contains: 1) the *Rituale Romanum* or *Rituali Roman* (Roman Ritual), a 319-page collection of Latin prayers and sacraments with comments in Albanian; 2) a short work entitled *Cusc zzote mesce keto cafsce i duhete me scerbyem* (Whoever says Mass must serve this thing), a 16-page explanation of mass, and; 3) the *Speculum Confessionis* or *Pasëqyra e t'rrëfyemit* (The Mirror of confession), a 401-page translation or, better, adaptation of the *Specchio di Confessione* of Emerio de Bonis, described by Budi as "some spiritual discourse most useful for those who understand no other language than their Albanian mother tongue." Both the Roman Ritual and the Mirror of Confession are supplemented by verse in Albanian.

The language used by Budi in his works is an archaic form of Gheg preserving many interesting phonetic features[29]. Eqrem Çabej has noted that Budi endeavoured to write in some sort of literary standard rather than purely in his native dialect, which again might be taken as an indication of the existence of a certain literary tradition in northern Albania. The alphabet he employs is similar to that of his predecessor Gjon Buzuku, though at no point does Budi mention having ever heard of Buzuku.

At first glance Pjetër Budi can be regarded as a translator and publisher of Latin and Italian religious texts. His significance as a prose writer, however, goes beyond this. His various prefaces, pastoral letters, additions and postscripts, amounting to over one hundred pages of original prose in Albanian, betray a good deal of style and talent. His language is authentic and refreshingly idiomatic when compared to Gjon Buzuku before him and Pjetër

---

[28] Here, too, in handwriting at the bottom of the page is "Autor dono dedit Bibliothecae Vaticanae. 29 Januari 1622" (The author gave [this copy] as a gift to the Vatican Library. 29 January 1622). The work is indeed still preserved in the Vatican Library under Barberini B VI.56. int. 1.

[29] On Budi's language, cf. K. Cipo 1952; E. Çabej 1966; G. Svane 1980, 1982a, 1982b; and P. Budi 1986.

Bogdani half a century later. For instance, he often endeavours to provide synonyms of Albanian origin for the many foreign terms he uses. Though not as elaborate and abstract as Bogdani, who possessed a greater vocabulary, Budi remains the most spontaneous and prolific writer of the age.

Pjetër Budi is also the first writer from Albania to have devoted himself to poetry. His works include some 3,300 lines of religious verse, almost all in quatrain form with an alternate rhyme. This verse, nineteen poems in all, comprises both poetic translations and original poetry by Budi himself, as well as at least one and probably two poems[30] by one **Pal prej Hasit** (Paul of Hasi). The vast majority of the poetry is octosyllabic, which is the standard in Albanian folk verse. Though Budi's religious verse is not without style, its content, being imitations of Italian and Latin moralist verse of the period, is not excessively original. He prefers Biblical themes, eulogies and universal motifs such as the inevitability of death. Nor are his rhymes always elegant, a fact which derives in part no doubt from his limited vocabulary, calculated at 2,453 lexemes[31].

What is attractive in Pjetër Budi and Pal prej Hasit's verse is the authenticity of feeling and genuine human concern for the sufferings of a misguided world. One poem which conveys this compassion well is that about death and the greatness of man. It begins as follows:

> *"O i paafati njerii,*
> *Gjithë ndë të keq harruom,*
> *I dhani ndë madhështii,*
> *Ndë mkat pshtiellë e ngatëruom;*
>
> *Ndo pak jee, ndo j rii,*
> *Përse s'shtie të kuituom,*
> *I vobeg ndo zotënii,*
> *N ceije iee kriiiuom?*
>
> *Balte e dheu cë zii,*
> *E io ari cë kulluom,*
> *As engjiishi cë tii,*
> *Ndo guri cë paaçmuom;*

---

[30] cf. S. Riza 1979, p. 120.

[31] cf. K. Ashta 1966, 1998.

Kaha të vien n dore tyy,
Mbë të madh me u levduom,
Ndë sqime e ndë madhështii,
Tinëzot me kundrështuom?

Lavdinë tand të levduom,
Ti pa vene ree vetë,
Ame cote idhënuom,
Kuur leve mbë këtë jetë,

Aty s'prune begatii,
As vistaar të levduom,
As urtë a diekëqii,
As gurë të paaçmuom;

Aty s'prune madhështii,
As dinje me ligjëruom,
As vertyt as trimënii,
As vetiu me ndimuom;

Aty s'prune zotënii,
Kual të bukur as të çpeitë,
As dinje gjak e gjeni,
As të mirëtë as të keqtë;

Po leve gjithë mëndryem,
Ame n cote idhënuom,
Tue qaam mallënjyem,
Me një zaa të helmuom..."[32]

(Oh, hapless, luckless man,
Forever lost in evil,
Given over to conceit,
Damned, in sin enveloped.

Be you young or be you old,
Be you lord or be a servant,

---

[32] Transcription adapted by Rexhep Ismajli in P. Budi 1986, p. 64-67.

Why is it you can't fathom
From where you have derived?

Of this black soil you're mud
And not of sparkling gold,
Not of the purest angels
Nor of rich, precious stones.

Where do you find the force
In vanity to revel,
The good Lord to oppose
In his splendour and his glory?

Of your renown alone
Do you take note forever,
Though expelled into this life,
Rejected by your mother.

Here you have brought with you
Neither wealth nor lavish treasures,
Nor wickedness nor wisdom,
Nor values, precious jewels.

Here you have conveyed
No greatness and no knowledge,
No courage and no virtue,
Nought with which to aid you.

Here you've not borne with you
Sleek steeds or noble standing,
Neither family nor relations,
Nothing good nor evil.

You were birthed defiled,
Forsaken by your mother,
And in a wretched voice
Forlorn, ever lamenting...)

1.6   Frang Bardhi and his Latin-Albanian Dictionary (1635)

Frang Bardhi (1606-1643) is the fourth in the sequence of early Albanian writers of note. He is author of the first Albanian dictionary, published in Rome on 30 May 1635, which at the same time constitutes the first work in Albanian not of direct religious content.

Frang Bardhi, known in Latin as *Franciscus Blancus* or *Blanchus*, was born in Kallmet (near Lezha) in northern Albania to a family which had a tradition of furnishing its sons as bishops for the church and as soldiers and officials for the Republic of Venice. His uncle was Bishop of Sapa and Sarda. Bardhi was sent to Italy where he studied theology, as had Pjetër Budi, at the Illyrian College of Loretto, and later at the College of the Propaganda Fide in Rome. On 30 March 1636, no doubt with family influence, he was appointed Bishop of Sapa and Sarda himself, replacing his uncle who became Archbishop of Antivari (Bar). Before his departure for Albania on 8 April of that year, he obtained the requisite 'imprimatur' for the second printing of Budi's Christian Doctrine, which bears the text:

> *"Nos Franciscus Blancus Dei, & Apostolicae Sedis gratiae electus Episcopus Sappatensis, & Sardanensis... vidimus ac studiose considerauimus versionem Doctrinae christianae in Epiroticum idioma olim impressam ac publicatam..."*

> (We Franciscus Blancus, by the grace of God and the Apostolic See, elected Bishop of Sapa and Sarda... have seen and studiously considered the version of the Christian Doctrine in the Epirotic language once printed and published...).

From 1637 onwards, Bardhi submitted reports[33] in Italian and Latin to the Congregation of the Propaganda Fide from Albania, containing a wealth of information about his diocese, about political developments, Albanian customs and the structure and position of the church. Nineteen of these letters and reports are preserved in the archives of the Propaganda Fide. In 1641, two years before his death, he is known to have travelled back to Rome to submit one report personally. After a short but intense life as a writer and ecclesiastical figure, Frang Bardhi died on 9 June 1643 at the age of thirty-seven.

---

[33] cf. I. Zamputi 1956; I. Zamputi (ed.) 1963-1965; and R. Elsie 2003b, p. 178-194.

It was during his last year at the College of the Propaganda Fide when he was twenty-nine years old that Bardhi published the 238-page Latin-Albanian dictionary for which he is remembered[34]. The work, bearing the title *Dictionarium latino-epiroticum, una cum nonnullis usitatioribus loquendi formulis*, Rome 1635 (Latin-Epirotic dictionary with several common expressions), comprises 5,640 Latin entries translated into Albanian, and is supplemented by an appendix of parts of speech, proverbs and dialogues.

In his preface in Albanian entitled "To all those Albanians who take up this book to read and study it," Bardhi explained his intentions:

> "Having considered for some time, my beloved (readers), after I entered the college, with what sort of book I could, on the one hand, help our language which is becoming more and more lost and bastardized as time goes by, and on the other hand, help all those of you who are in the service of the Lord and the holy Catholic church and who do not know the Latin language, without which no one can pay service to the concepts, customs and ceremonies of the holy church of Rome as he should without making great mistakes and errors, I thought it a very good idea to compile and translate a dictionary from the Latin language into the Albanian language which is nothing other than a book containing words and names found in this part of the world. That is, names of people, animals, bodies of water, mountains, plains and other things found in the heavens or under the heavens, as well as of God, of the angels and saints. This book does please me and I believe that it will be of help, however small."

The two objectives of the dictionary were therefore to save the Albanian language from 'bastardization' and to help the Albanian clergy to learn Latin. The first of these goals may be seen within the context of the strong Turkish influence the Albanian language was undergoing in the seventeenth century. How was "Allah, Allah!" which Bardhi gives as an expression of admiration, to be appreciated by a Catholic priest? The second objective is clarified in Bardhi's letters and reports to Rome in which he laments about the standards of the Albanian clergy. In the seventeenth century, the Catholic church in northern Albania was in a state of rapid disintegration.

---

[34] There are two modern editions of the dictionary available, both including photostatic copies of the original: by M. Roques 1932a and by E. Sedaj 1983 (cf. F. Bardhi 1983). For further studies, cf. K. Kamsi 1956; K. Ashta 1962; 1971-1974; P. Geci 1965, 1970; P. Daka 1983; Sh. Demiraj 1986; and R. Ismajli 2000, p. 241-268.

The majority of the episcopates were vacant and many clergymen were illiterate. Most native Albanian churchmen seem to have had only a vague idea of the teachings of the church and many, not to be outdone by their Orthodox counterparts, were married. It was Bardhi's intention to assist them in learning Latin both to improve their standards and to overcome the need for the often unpopular foreign clergy in the country who, in turn, had little or no knowledge of Albanian. In one case it was reported with dismay that Albanian women had to confess through an interpreter. In one of his reports, dated 8 February 1637, Bardhi adds that he had translated other ecclesiastical works[35] into Albanian, evidence that the Latin-Albanian dictionary was not his only work in Albanian. Whether his other translations were ever circulated or published is not known.

Bardhi's dictionary is the first work of Albanian lexicography and by far the most important of the twenty-two Albanian dictionaries to be published subsequently up to 1850. It appears to have been well circulated. In 1759, there were some 360 copies of the book in the depository of the Propaganda Fide in Rome[36]. The *Dictionarium latino-epiroticum* is neither systematic nor compiled with much thought to the practical needs of its user, but as the first work of its kind, we can forgive its author for such shortcomings. Bardhi has no problems rendering concrete terms into Albanian, but his language often falters when he is faced with more abstract concepts: *materia* "a thing from which other things are made," *substantia* "a thing which keeps man alive," *patria* "the land where a person is born."

Of no less interest than the dictionary itself is the thirty-three page appendix, divided into seven chapters (1. nouns and numerals, 2. family designations, 3. cities and castles, 4. adverbs, 5. prepositions, 6. interjections, 7. proverbs, sayings, dialogues and greetings). Much of the appendix is quadrilingual (Latin, Italian, Albanian and Turkish). In ordering his Albanian vocabulary according to parts of speech, Bardhi offers us what can be seen as the skeleton of an Albanian grammar. The 113 proverbs and sayings he includes (the first such collection), and the subsequent dialogues are of prime importance both for historical linguists and for folklorists.

Bardhi also published a seventy-six-page treatise in Latin on Scanderbeg, entitled *Georgius Castriottus Epirensis vulgo Scanderbegh, Epirotarum Princeps fortissimus ac invictissimus suis et Patriae restitutus,*

---

[35] *Professione della fede* (Profession of the faith) and *Ordine del Sinodo posto nel pontif. Romano* (Decrees of the Synod decided upon at the Roman pontificate). cf. Dh. Shuteriqi 1976, p. 73.

[36] cf. *Archivo storico della S. Congregazione 'de Propaganda Fide,'* SC Stamperia 2, p. 257.

Venice 1636 (George Castrioti of Epirus, commonly called Scanderbeg, the very mighty and invincible Prince of Epirus, restored to his people and his country), in which he refuted the assertion of the Bosnian bishop, Tomeus Marnavitius, that the Albanian national hero was of Bosnian origin. It is a work of erudition and patriotic sentiment, not dissimilar to polemics still conducted and appreciated in the Balkans today.

Frang Bardhi's contribution to Albanian literature per se, his six-page preface to the first Albanian dictionary, is a modest one. In view of the continuing dearth of Albanian writing in the first half of the seventeenth century, however, his work is not without major significance. As a humanist with a strong attachment to the advancement of his people and as a scholar with a broad cultural horizon, he occupies a key position in the development of early Albanian culture.

1.7   Pjetër Bogdani and the *Cuneus Prophetarum* (1685)

Pjetër Bogdani (ca. 1630-1689), known in Italian as *Pietro Bogdano*, is the last and by far the most original writer of early literature in Albania, author of the *Cuneus prophetarum* (The Band of the prophets), the first prose work of substance written originally in Albanian (i.e. not a translation)[37].

Born in Gur i Hasit near Prizren about 1630[38], Bogdani was educated in the traditions of the Catholic church to which he devoted all his energy. His uncle Andrea Bogdani (ca. 1600-1683) was Archbishop of Skopje and author of a Latin-Albanian grammar, now lost. Bogdani is said to have received his initial schooling from the Franciscans at Čiprovac in northwestern Bulgaria and then studied at the Illyrian College of Loretto near Ancona, as had his predecessors Pjetër Budi and Frang Bardhi. From 1651 to 1654 he served as a parish priest in Pult and from 1654 to 1656 studied at the College of the Propaganda Fide in Rome where he graduated as a doctor of philosophy and

---

[37] The most thorough studies of Bogdani to date are by M. Sciambra 1965 and I. Rugova 1982. See also G. Weigand 1927; I. Zamputi 1954, 1963; V. Kamsi 1962; S. Riza 1965a; Z. Xholi 1986a, 1986b, 1990; L. Marlekaj 1989; Dh. Shuteriqi 1977, 1989; O. Marquet 1989, 1991; O. Marquet (ed.) 1997; A. Kostallari, S. Mansaku, Xh. Ylli (ed.) 1991; and Sh. Osmani 1996.

[38] Some authors prefer to date his birth 1625, but 1630 would, nevertheless, seem more likely.

theology. In 1656, he was named Bishop of Shkodra, a post he held for twenty-one years, and was also appointed Administrator of the Archdiocese of Antivari (Bar) until 1671. During the most troubled years of the Turkish-Austrian war, 1664-1669, he hid out in the villages of Barbullush and Rjoll near Shkodra. A cave near Rjoll, in which he took refuge, still bears his name. In 1677, he succeeded his uncle as Archbishop of Skopje and Administrator of the Kingdom of Serbia. His religious zeal and patriotic fervour kept him at odds with Turkish forces, and in the atmosphere of war and confusion which reigned, he was obliged to flee to Ragusa (Dubrovnik), from where he continued on to Venice and Padua, taking his manuscripts with him. In Padua he was cordially received by Cardinal Gregorio Barbarigo (1622-1697), whom he had served in Rome. Cardinal Barbarigo, Bishop of Padua, was responsible for church affairs in the East and had taken a keen interest in the cultures of the orient, including Albania. He had also founded a printing press in Padua, the *Tipografia del Seminario*[39], which served the needs of oriental languages and had fonts for Hebrew, Arabic and Armenian. Barbarigo was thus well disposed, willing and able to assist Bogdani in the latter's historic undertaking.

After arranging for the publication of the *Cuneus prophetarum*, Bogdani returned to the Balkans in March 1686 and spent the next years promoting resistance to the armies of the Ottoman Empire, in particular in Kosova. He contributed a force of 6,000 Albanian soldiers to the Austrian army which had arrived in Prishtina, and accompanied it to capture Prizren. There, however, he and much of his army were met by another equally formidable adversary, the plague. Bogdani returned to Prishtina but succumbed to the disease there in December 1689. His nephew Gjergj reported in 1698 that his uncle's remains were later exhumed by Turkish and Tartar soldiers and fed to the dogs in the middle of the square in Prishtina. So ended one of the great figures of early Albanian culture, the writer often referred to as the father of Albanian prose.

It was in Padua in 1685 that the *Cuneus prophetarum*, his vast treatise on theology, was published in Albanian and Italian with the assistance of Cardinal Barbarigo. Bogdani had finished the Albanian version ten years earlier but was refused permission to publish it by the Propaganda Fide which ordered that the manuscript be translated first[40], no doubt to facilitate the work of the censor. The full title of the published version is:

---

[39] cf. G. Bellini 1938.

[40] "*Compositio de qua fit mentio, translatetur.*" cf. I. Zamputi 1954; V. Kamsi 1962; S. Riza 1965a; and I. Rugova 1982, p. 46.

"Cvnevs prophetarvm de Christo salvatore mvndi et eivs evangelica veritate, italice et epirotice contexta, et in duas partes diuisa a Petro Bogdano Macedone, Sacr. Congr. de Prop. Fide alvmno, Philosophiae & Sacrae Theologiae Doctore, olim Episcopo Scodrensi & Administratore Antibarensi, nunc vero Archiepiscopo Scvporvm ac totivs regni Serviae Administratore"

(The Band of the Prophets concerning Christ, saviour of the world and his gospel truth, edited in Italian and Epirotic and divided into two parts by Pjetër Bogdani of Macedonia, student of the Holy Congregation of the Propaganda Fide, doctor of philosophy and holy theology, formerly Bishop of Shkodra and Administrator of Antivari and now Archbishop of Skopje and Administrator of all the Kingdom of Serbia).

The *Cuneus prophetarum* was printed in the Latin alphabet as used in Italian, with the addition of the same Cyrillic characters employed by Pjetër Budi and Frang Bardhi. Bogdani seems therefore to have had access to their works. During his studies at the College of the Propaganda Fide, he is known to have requested Albanian books from the college printer: "five copies of the Christian Doctrine and five Albanian dictionaries," most probably the works of Budi and Bardhi. In a report to the Propaganda Fide in 1665, he also mentions a certain '*Euangelii in Albanese*' (Gospels in Albanian)[41] of which he had heard, a possible reference to Buzuku's missal of 1555.

The *Cuneus prophetarum* was published in two parallel columns, one in Albanian and one in Italian, and is divided into two volumes, each with four sections (*scala*). The first volume, which is preceded by dedications and eulogies in Latin, Albanian, Serbian and Italian, and includes two eight-line poems in Albanian, one by his cousin Luca Bogdani and one by Luca Summa, deals primarily with themes from the Old Testament: i) How God created man, ii) The prophets and their metaphors concerning the coming of the Messiah, iii) The lives of the prophets and their prophecies, iv) The lives of the ten Sibyls. The second volume, entitled *De vita Jesu Christi salvatoris mundi* (On the life of Jesus Christ, saviour of the world), is devoted mostly to the New Testament: i) The life of Jesus Christ, ii) The miracles of Jesus Christ, iii) The suffering and death of Jesus Christ, iv) The resurrection and second coming of Christ. This section includes a translation from the Book of Daniel, 9. 24-26, in eight languages: Latin, Greek, Armenian, Syriac, Hebrew, Arabic, Italian

---

[41] cf. Dh. Shuteriqi 1977, p. 58.

and Albanian, and is followed by a chapter on the life of the Antichrist, by indices in Italian and Albanian and by a three-page appendix on the *Antichità della Casa Bogdana* (Antiquity of the House of the Bogdanis).

The work was reprinted twice under the title *L 'infallibile verità della cattolica fede*, Venice 1691 and 1702 (The Infallible truth of the Catholic faith)[42].

The *Cuneus prophetarum* is considered to be the masterpiece of early Albanian literature and is the first work in Albanian of full artistic and literary quality. In scope, it covers philosophy, theology and science (with digressions on geography, astronomy, physics and history). With its poetry and literary prose, it touches on questions of aesthetic and literary theory. It is a humanist work of the Baroque Age steeped in the philosophical traditions of Plato, Aristotle, St Augustine and St Thomas Aquinas. Bogdani's fundamental philosophical aim is a knowledge of God, an unravelling of the problem of existence, for which he strives with reason and intellect.

Though Bogdani's talents are certainly most evident in his prose, his modest religious poetry is not devoid of interest. The basic corpus of his verse are the poems of the ten Sibyls (the Cumaean, Libyan, Delphic, Persian, Erythraean, Samian, Cumanian, Hellespontic, Phrygian and Tiburtine), which are imbued with the Baroque penchant for religious themes and classical allusions.

It is Bogdani's use of the Albanian language which sets him apart from all other early Albanian writers. He has a conscious interest in old and forgotten words and a much richer vocabulary which he skilfully employs to form new abstract concepts. Bogdani philosophizes on scholasticism and theology with confidence and elegance whereas his predecessor, Frang Bardhi, fifty years before him, had experienced obvious difficulties in expressing abstractions of any kind. In Bogdani's work we encounter for the first time what may be considered a literary language. As such, he may justly bear the title of father of Albanian prose.

---

[42] The *Cuneus prophetarum* is also available in modern reprints, cf. P. Bogdani 1977, 1990, 1997.

1.8   The Demise of Early Albanian Literature

Other works of Albanian letters in the seventeenth century are few and far between, like the occasional palm tree on the horizon of a literary desert. None of these works is of particular literary value, though great cultural, linguistic and historical significance must be attached to anything written in Albanian in this period[43].

At any rate, the five Albanian writers of the sixteenth and seventeenth centuries: Gjon Buzuku, Lekë Matrënga, Pjetër Budi, Frang Bardhi and Pjetër Bogdani, form the core of early Albanian literature. They bestowed upon it an initial breath of creative genius and a modicum of refinement and sophistication. Together with a small number of minor authors and no doubt others who have been lost to the annals of literary history, they gave birth to a rapidly evolving literature which was to be nipped in the bud, so to speak, by the tempestuous course of Albanian history. What might have been the solid roots of a dynamic national literature such as those which grew in the more fortunate regions of Europe in the seventeenth century were severed by the Turkish conquest and consequently by the decline and fall of Albania's somewhat ambivalent patron, the Catholic Church.

The Turkish invasion and colonisation of the country which had begun as early as 1385 split Albania into three spheres of culture, all virtually independent of one another: the cosmopolitan culture of the Islamic Orient using initially Turkish, Persian and Arabic as its media of expression; the lingering Byzantine heritage of Greek Orthodoxy in southern Albania; and a declining Italian-oriented culture of the Albanian Catholics of the North. Of greater significance to the eighteenth and early nineteenth centuries, as we will see, was the awakening culture of the Arbëresh in southern Italy, nourished by a more favourable social, political and economic climate and by the fertile intellectual soil of Italian civilization.

With the Ottoman conquest of the Balkans, early Albanian literature suddenly withers and the first notable chapter of Albanian literary history

---

[43] It may be assumed that most works of the period were lost, having no doubt been confiscated and destroyed by the Inquisition. We do know, for instance, of an Albanian catechism from 1584. In Codex Ottob. Lat. 1941 in the Vatican Library, we are informed that "in 1584, Apostolic Visitor Alessandro Cumuleo, together with the rector of the Illyrian College of Loretto, Thomae Radius, ordered the printing of 500 catechisms in the Albanian language, which he took with him and distributed during the apostolic visit he made that year, accompanied by an Albanian priest Armanno Duca, pupil of the Illyrian College of Loretto."

comes to a rapid and definitive close. Not until the so-called Rilindja movement of national rebirth in the second half of the nineteenth century was literature in Albania to regain the vitality it experienced in the sixteenth and seventeenth centuries. The national literature had once again to start afresh.

2. Muslim Literature in Albania (18th-19th cent.)

2.1 The Rise of Islam

On 28 June 1389, the Muslim Turks defeated a coalition of Balkan forces under Serbian leadership at Kosovo Polje, the Plain of the Blackbirds, and established themselves as masters of the Balkans. By 1393 they had overrun Shkodra, although the Venetians were soon able to recover the city and its imposing citadel. The conquest of Albania continued into the early years of the fifteenth century. The mountain fortress of Kruja was taken in 1415 and the equally strategic towns of Vlora, Berat and Kanina in southern Albania fell in 1417. By 1431, the Turks had incorporated southern Albania into the Ottoman Empire and set up a 'sanjak' administration with its capital in Gjirokastra, captured in 1419. Mountainous northern Albania remained under the control of its autonomous tribal leaders, though now subject to suzerain power of the Sultan.

The Turkish conquest did not meet without resistance on the part of the Albanians, notably under George Castrioti, known as Scanderbeg (1405-1468), and also known in Albanian as *Gjergj Kastrioti (Skënderbeu)*, prince and now national hero. Sent by his father as a hostage to Sultan Murad II (r. 1421-1451), the young Castrioti was converted to Islam and given a Muslim education in Edirne (Adrianople). The Turks called him Iskender and gave him the rank of bey, hence the name Scanderbeg.

Much legendry has been attached to the name of Scanderbeg. According to popular tradition, based on embellishments by historian Marinus Barletius, Scanderbeg took advantage of the Turkish defeat at Nish in 1443 at the hands of Hungarian commander John Hunyadi to abandon the Ottoman army, return to Albania and re-embrace Christianity. Thereafter, he united the feudal and independent-minded tribes of northern Albania into the so-called League of Lezha in 1444. By a ruse, he took over the fortress of Kruja and was proclaimed commander-in-chief of an Albanian army which, though independent, would prove to be no match for the huge military potential of the Turks.

The facts of history show that Scanderbeg had already served as an Ottoman official in Albania in the 1430s and was governor of Kruja in 1438. Although he was chosen to lead the forces of the feudal families of the north in 1444, the so-called League of Lezha broke down almost immediately and Scanderbeg allied himself with the Serb despots, George Branković and Stephen Crnojević.

In the following years, again according to legendry, Scanderbeg successfully repulsed thirteen Ottoman incursions, including three major Ottoman sieges of the citadel of Kruja led by the Sultans themselves (Murad II in 1450 and Mehmet II in 1466 and 1467). In fact, this period was more of an Albanian civil war between rival families, in particular between Scanderbeg and the Lekë Dukagjini.

Scanderbeg was, nonetheless, widely admired in the Christian world for his resistance to the Turks and was given the title 'Athleta Christi' by Pope Calixtus III (r. 1455-1458). Albanian resistance held out until after Scanderbeg's death on 17 January 1468 at Lezha (Alessio), but in 1478 the fortress at Kruja was finally taken by Turkish troops. Shkodra capitulated in 1479 and Durrës finally fell in 1501. By the end of the sixteenth century the Ottoman Empire had reached its political zenith and Albania was firmly encompassed within it. The coming four centuries of Ottoman colonization changed the face of the country radically. The new religion, Islam[44], had wedged itself between the Catholic north and the Orthodox south of Albania and, in time, was to become the dominant faith of the country.

During the first decades of Ottoman rule there were few Muslims among the Albanians themselves. In 1577, we know that northern and central Albania were still staunchly Catholic, but by the early decades of the seventeenth century, things had changed. An estimated 30-50 per cent of the population of northern Albania had converted to Islam. By 1634, most of Kosova had also converted. Of the inhabitants of the town of Prizren at the time, for instance, there were 12,000 Muslims, 200 Catholics and 600 Orthodox. By the close of the seventeenth century, Muslims began to outnumber Christians throughout much of the country. Roman Catholicism and Greek and Serbian Orthodoxy had, after all, been the vehicles of foreign cultures in Albania, propelled by foreign languages. They were religions to which the Albanians, as opposed to their Serb, Bulgarian and Greek

---

[44] On the Islamisation of Albania, cf. T. Arnold 1896; E. Jacques 1938, 1995 p. 213-240; E. Rossi 1942; G. Stadtmüller 1955; S. Skendi 1956b, p. 285-299; H. Inalcik 1960; P. Bartl 1968; H. Kaleshi 1975; S. Rizaj 1985; A. Popovic 1986; R. Elsie 1992b, 2001b; H. Norris 1993; N. Ibrahimi 1997; and R. Zekaj 1997.

neighbours, had only been superficially converted and with which they could not so easily identify. The mass conversion of the Albanian population to Islam is all the more understandable in view of the heavy *haraç* or poll taxes imposed on the *rayah* - the Christian inhabitants of the Empire. Many Albanian Catholics retained their Christian faith in the privacy of their homes but adopted Muslim names and customs for use in public. This Crypto-Christianity proved to be a pragmatic and very Albanian solution to the existential problem faced by Catholics living in the Ottoman-occupied Balkans. Characteristic of the Albanian attitude to matters of religion was the motto: "Where the sword is, there lies religion," Alb. *Ku është shpata, është feja.*

Modern Albanian scholars tend to view the consequences of these centuries of Turkish rule as completely negative, in terms of wild Asiatic hordes ravaging and plundering a country which might otherwise have flourished in the cradle of European civilization. This rather one-sided view is determined to a large extent by the experience of the Albanian nationalist movement in the late nineteenth century when the Ottoman Empire was in a period of profound decay. Although the Turkish occupation and, one must say, neglect of Albania brought untold suffering to the inhabitants of the country, it also introduced elements of a new and refined culture which was later to become an integral part of the Albanian identity.

Scholar Hasan Kaleshi[45] (1922-1976) has convincingly suggested that the Turkish occupation of the Balkans had at least the one positive consequence. It saved the Albanians from ethnic assimilation by the Slavs, just as the Slavic invasion of the Balkans in the sixth century had put an end to the process of Romanization which had threatened to assimilate the non-Latin-speaking ancestors of the Albanians a thousand years earlier. Although not recognized by the Turks as an ethnic minority (the population of the Ottoman Empire was divided according to religion, not according to nationality), the Albanians managed to survive as a people and indeed substantially expand their areas of settlement under Turkish rule. Shkodra and the other urban centres along the Albanian coast became truly Albanian cities with an Albanian population for the first time.

While the Turkish Empire, with its centralistic organization and power base focussed on Istanbul, left Albania the cultural and political backwater it had been from the start, Ottoman Turkish culture, which was to reach its zenith during the Tulip Age of the eighteenth century, penetrated the country thoroughly. Southern and central Albanian cities like Berat and Elbasan with their newly constructed fortifications, mosques and medresas became

---

[45] cf. H. Kaleshi 1975.

provincial centres of oriental learning and indeed experienced something of a cultural renascence under Islam, as did Shkodra and Gjakova in the north. Wandering poets, artists and scholars began to enjoy the patronage of local governors and pashas as they did throughout Asia Minor.

2.2 The Literature of the *Bejtexhinj*

Just as early authors of Christian Albania had started by writing in Latin, Italian or Greek, the first writers from Muslim Albania used the literary vehicles of the Ottoman Empire: Turkish and Persian, many of them with notable success. **Mesîhî (Messiah) of Prishtina**[46] (ca. 1470-1512), known in Turkish as *Priştineli Mesihi*, was the pleasure-loving author of love poetry which became the prototype for a new literary genre in Ottoman verse. Another sixteenth-century writer of Albanian origin was **Jahja bej Dukagjini**[47] (d. 1575), known in Turkish as *Dukagin-zâde Yahyâ bey* or *Taşlicali Yahyâ*, and who is remembered for five romantic *mesnevî* and a *divan* of love lyrics written in the Ottoman Turkish of the period.

The transition from Turkish, Persian and Arabic to Albanian as a means of literary expression resulted in an example of what is known as *Aljamiado* literature, a Spanish term denoting a vernacular literature written in Arabic script and strongly influenced by Islamic culture. *Aljamiado* literatures arose notably in Spain and Portugal during the Moorish period and in Bosnia and Albania under Turkish rule. The first attempts in the early eighteenth century by Albanian writers, who had been raised in an Islamic culture, to express themselves not in the languages of the Orient, but in their own native tongue, were just as decisive and momentous as the transition from Latin to Albanian had been for the creation of early (sixteenth and seventeenth century) Albanian literature.

---

[46] cf. E. Gibb 1900-1909, vol. 2, p. 226-256; H. Kaleshi 1964, 1991, p. 22-24; A. Bombaci 1969, p. 330-333; and I. Morina 1987.

[47] cf. E. Gibb 1900-1909, vol. 3, p. 116-132; H. Kaleshi 1964, 1991, p. 19-22; and A. Bombaci 1969, p. 345-346.

The literature of the *Bejtexhinj*[48] as this period of Albanian writing is often called, consists almost exclusively of verse composed in Arabic script. The Arabic writing system had already been adapted, albeit rather awkwardly, to the needs of Ottoman Turkish[49] and was now being moulded to fit the more elaborate phonetic system of Albanian, or more precisely, of the Albanian dialects in question. It proved to be just as unsatisfactory for Albanian as it had been for Turkish. But not only was the script oriental. The language of the *Bejtexhinj* was an Albanian so laden with Turkish, Arabic and Persian vocabulary that it is quite tedious for Albanians today to read without a lexicon. Indeed it is likely that the reader of classical Turkish not knowing Albanian would understand more of many texts than the reader of Albanian not knowing any oriental languages. The stratum of foreign vocabulary that penetrated the Albanian language in this period was used firstly to express the attributes of a new religion and new culture which were initially quite foreign to the Albanians. Secondly and equally important in verse production at least, the use of traditional Arabic and Persian vocabulary greatly facilitated composition in the classical meters and rhymes to be adhered to.

The poetry of the *Bejtexhinj* was strongly influenced by Turkish, Persian and Arabic literary models in fashion at the time both in Istanbul and the Middle East. Most of the genres and forms prevalent in Turkish and Persian verse are to be encountered in Albanian. Here we find, either as isolated poems or within the *divans*: the *murabba'*, quatrain; the *ilâhî*, religious hymns; the *qasîde*, the longer panegyric odes favoured by the Arabs; and the *ghazal*, shorter poems, often love lyrics which were favoured by the Turks and Persians. The metrical system was basically syllabic although occasional attempts were made to introduce quantitative meters. The subject matter was often religious, either meditatively intimate or openly didactic, serving to spread the faith. The speculative character of much of this verse derived its inspiration from the currents of Islam: from authoritative Sunnite spirituality to the intense mystical spheres of Shi'ite Sufism and later, to the more liberal, though equally mystical reflections of Bektashi pantheism. Some secular verse does occur too: love lyrics, nature poetry and historical and philosophical verse in which we encounter the occasional ironic pondering on the vacillations of

---

[48] Alb. *bejtexhi*, pl. *bejtexhinj*, is a term for a popular poet in the Muslim tradition, literally 'couplet maker,' from the Turkish *beyit* 'couplet.' Alternative terms for these wandering minstrels were *ashik*, literally 'lover,' and Turkish *saz şairleri* 'musical poets.' For general sources of this literature, cf. H. Kaleshi 1956, 1958, 1964, 1966-1967, 1975, 1991; O. Myderrizi 1955b, 1955c, 1959, 1965, 1996; Dh. Shuteriqi 1976; M. Pirraku 1979-1980, 1988; H. Salihu 1987; and M. Hysa 1996, 2000.

[49] Turkish was written in Arabic script until 1928.

existence from a world which is easily as exotic to the modern Albanians themselves as it is to the Western reader.

The literature of the *Bejtexhinj* was recorded in manuscripts, most of which are now lost or, at best, still impossible to trace. A few late copies of manuscripts (alas, not the originals) are preserved in the State Archives in Tirana, but most of the surviving manuscript material is still in the hands of private owners, in particular in the former Yugoslavia. Of the manuscripts which have been preserved, very few have been published. As such, the writing of the *Bejtexhinj* constitutes one of the least known chapters of Albanian literature.

The oldest Albanian poem in Arabic script is a light-hearted prayer in praise of coffee, dated 1725 [1137 A.H.], which was written by one **Muçi Zade**, son of Muçi, whom we learn was an old man at the time of composition. Its refrain, *Imzot, mos na lerë pa kahve* (Lord, do not leave us without coffee), will no doubt have a familiar ring to many coffee addicts. Discovered in a manuscript from Korça which is now preserved in Tirana, this poem consists of seventeen quatrains with an AAAB rhyme. It is the oldest piece of literature in the southern Tosk dialect we know to have been written in Albania itself.

The first major poet among the *Bejtexhinj* was **Nezim Frakulla**[50] (ca. 1680-1760), alternatively known as *Nezim Berati* or *Ibrahim Nezimi*. He was born in the village of Frakull near Fier and lived a good deal of his life in Berat, a flourishing centre of Muslim culture at the time. Frakulla studied in Istanbul where he wrote his first poetry in Turkish, Persian and perhaps Arabic, including two *divans*. About 1731, he returned to Berat where he is known to have been involved in literary rivalry with other poets of the period, notably with Mulla Ali, mufti of Berat. Between 1731 and 1735 he composed a *divan* and various other poetry in Albanian, as well as an Albanian-Turkish dictionary in verse form. Although we do not possess the whole of the original divan, we do have copies of ca. 110 poems from it. Some of his verse was put to music and survived the centuries orally. Nezim Frakulla tells us himself that he was the first person to compose a *divan* in Albanian:

> "*Divan kush pat folturë shqip?*
> *Ajan e bëri Nezimi,*
> *Bejan kush pat folturë shqip?*
> *Insan e bëri Nezimi.*

---

[50] cf. E. Rossi 1946; O. Myderrizi 1954; and M. Hysa 1990.

Ky lisan qe bërë harab
Në gussa me shumë hixhab
Shahid mjaft është ky kitab
Handan e bëri Nezimi."

(Who made a *divan* speak in Albanian?
It was Nezim who made it known.
Who made elegance speak in Albanian?
It was Nezim who made it noble.

This language was in ruins,
Veiled in suffering and much shame.
Proof enough is this book
That Nezim made it rejoice.)

Frakulla's *divan* includes verse ranging from panegyrics on local pashas and military campaigns, to odes on friends and patrons, poems on separation from and longing for his friends and (male) lovers, descriptions of nature in the springtime, religious verse and, in particular, love lyrics. The imagery of the latter *ghazal*, some of which are devoted to his nephew, is that of Arabic, Persian and Turkish poetry with many of the classical themes, metaphors and allusions: love as an illness causing the poet to waste away, the cruel lover whose glance could inflict mortal wounds, or the cupbearer whose beauty could reduce his master to submission.

Nezim Frakulla enjoyed the patronage and protection of Sulejman Pasha of Elbasan and of Ismail Pasha Velabishti, the latter a poet himself. At some point after 1747, having returned to Istanbul in search of work, he was sent to Khotin in Bessarabia (now in the Ukraine), probably into exile. There he composed several *qasîde*, one of them celebrating the *firman* authorizing his return home and another on his journey back. Whether due to political intrigue or to the often caustic literary polemics in which he engaged, Frakulla fell into disfavour and left Berat once again to settle in Elbasan for a number of years. On his subsequent return to Berat he seems to have been imprisoned. At any rate, he died in old age as a prisoner in Istanbul in 1760 [1173 A.H.].

Frakulla not only considered himself the first poet to write in Albanian, but also lauded himself as the Sa'dî and Hâfiz of his times. His *qasîde* in Albanian, he tells us, are comparable to those of 'Urfî in Persian and Nef'î in Turkish. Most experts would consider this comparison somewhat exaggerated. While Nezim Frakulla doubtlessly had initiative and talent, his Albanian verse did not by any means reach the level of literary perfection of the Persian classics, nor was the clumsy mixture of Albanian, Turkish and Persian he

39

employed refined enough to enable him to do so. What he did accomplish was to lay the foundations for a new literary tradition in Albania, one which was to last for two centuries.

Hasan Zyko Kamberi[51] was born in the second half of the eighteenth century in Starja, a southern Albanian village near Kolonja at the foot of Mount Grammos. Of his life we know only that he took part in the Turkish-Austrian Battle of Smederevo on the Danube east of Belgrade in 1789 [1203 A.H.] in an army under the command of Ali Pasha Tepelena (1741-1822). He died a dervish, no doubt of the Bektashi sect, in his native village at the beginning of the nineteenth century. His tomb in Starja was turned into a shrine known locally as the *turbeh* of Baba Hasani.

Kamberi is one of the most commanding representatives of the Muslim tradition in Albanian literature, though his main work, a 200-page *mexhmua* (verse collection), has disappeared. A manuscript of this collection is said to have been sent to Monastir (Bitola) in 1908-1910 to be published, but all traces of it have since been lost. Indeed little of his verse has survived and even less has been published. Of the works we do possess are: a short *mevlud*, a religious poem on the birth of the prophet Mohammed[52]; about ten *ilâhî*; and over fifty secular poems.

Kamberi's secular verse covers a wide range of themes. In his octosyllabic *Sefer-i hümâyûn* (The King's campaign) in thirty-three quatrains, he describes his participation in the above-mentioned Battle of Smederevo and gives a realistic account of the suffering it caused. In *Bahti im* (My fortune) and *Vasijetnameja* (The Testament), Kamberi casts an ironic and sometimes bitter glance at the vagaries of fate and in particular at the misfortunes of his own life. *Gjerdeku* (The Bridal chamber) portrays marriage customs in the countryside. It is not a pastoral idyll we encounter here, but a realistic account of the anguish and hardship of young women married off according to custom without being able to choose husbands for themselves, and the suffering of young men forced to go abroad to make a living. In Kamberi's love lyrics, the author laments social conventions that inhibit passion and spontaneity. One shocked Kosova critic described them as 'at times degenerate eroticism'[53]. The most famous of his poems is *Paraja* (Money), a caustic condemnation of feudal corruption and at the same time perhaps the best piece of satirical verse in pre-twentieth-century Albanian literature.

---

[51] cf. O. Myderrizi 1955a.

[52] cf. H. Kaleshi 1958.

[53] cf. M. Hysa 1987, p. 238.

Muhamet Kyçyku[54] (1784-1844) marks the transition between the classical verse of the early *Bejtexhinj* and the Rilindja poets of the second half of the nineteenth century. Kyçyku, who is also known as *Muhamet Çami*, i.e. the Çamian or Çamërian, was from Konispol in what is now the southern tip of Albania. He studied theology for eleven years in Cairo where a sizeable Albanian colony had settled. On his return to his native village he served as a hodja (Muslim priest) and died in 1844 [1260 A.H.].

Kyçyku was a relatively prolific author who wrote in his native Çamian dialect and, as it seems, was the first Albanian author to have written longer poetry. The work for which he is best remembered is a romantic tale in verse form known as *Erveheja* (Ervehe), originally entitled *Ravda* (Garden), written in about 1820. This poetic tale in octosyllabic quatrains with an ABAB rhyme follows the adventures of the fair Ervehe who manages to defend her chastity and virtue through many a trial and tribulation. The motif in this moralistic tale of 'female virtue' occurs widely in both oriental and Western literature. The most likely source for Kyçyku's poetic version of the tale is the Persian *Tûtî-nâme* (Tales of a Parrot) by Ziyâ'uddîn Nakhshabî, inspired by a Sanskrit original, the *Shukasaptati*. The seventeen-page Albanian text consists of 856 lines of verse and is preserved in the National Library in Tirana. It is also one of the rare works of the *Bejtexhinj* to have been published in the nineteenth century, though in an altered version. Rilindja publicist Jani Vreto (1822-1900) not only transliterated and published *Erveheja* in Bucharest in 1888, but adapted it to late nineteenth-century tastes and saw fit to purge it of all its Turkish, Persian and Arabic vocabulary.

Erveheja is not Kyçyku's only surviving work, though it was the only one known for many years. Most of the over 4,000 lines of his verse (ca. 200 pages) which we possess have been discovered within the last seventy years. Kyçyku's other major work is *Jusufi i Zelihaja* (Joseph and Zeliha), a moralistic verse tale in 2,430 lines based on the biblical story recounted in Genesis 39 and in the twelfth Sura of the Koran, of the attempted seduction of the handsome Joseph by the wife of his Egyptian master Potiphar. This 'most beautiful tale,' as the Koran calls it, served as a common motif in Arabic, Persian and Turkish literature. It was adapted, in particular, by the Persian epic poet Firdausî (ca. 935-1020) and later by the mystical writer Jâmî (1414-1492) in *Yûsuf and Zulaykhâ*. The biblical Joseph is in some respects the male counterpart of Ervehe. He, too, suffers much at the hands of his family and enemies and yet steadfastly resists the advances of his master's wife in order

---

[54] cf. F. Fishta 1940b; E. Rossi 1948; O. Myderrizi 1951, 1957; A. Hetzer 1983, 1984; and A. Vehbiu 1989.

to remain chaste and virtuous. Kyçyku's *Jusufi i Zelihaja* evinces a higher level of literary sophistication than *Erveheja*. Its language is more ornate and many of the descriptive passages transcend the constraints of a simple narrative. It also relies more on character analysis as a means of conveying dramatic suspense, in particular with respect to the passions of the enamoured Zeliha.

Among other Muslim authors of note, mention may be made of **Dalip Frashëri**[55], a Bektashi leader from the southern Albanian village of Frashër, who is the author of a literary epic in Albanian. This 65,000-line *Hadikaja* (The Garden), written under the pseudonym of *Hyxhretiu* (The exile), was finished in 1842 [1258 A.H.]. The epic is based on the work with the same title of the Azerbaijan poet Fuzûlî (1494-1556), the greatest representative of Turkish *divan* lyrics. The Albanian *Hadikaja*, divided into ten cantos plus introduction and conclusion, is twice as long as the Azeri Turkish version and constitutes the first real Albanian literary epic. It was composed primarily in octosyllabic quatrains with an ABAB rhyme, though these are interspersed with some six-syllable verse. The manuscript is preserved in the State Archives in Tirana. *Hadikaja* deals not only with the history of the Bektashi sect in Albania, but also, like Fuzûlî's *Hadîqatû as-su'adâ*, with events of Shi'ite Muslim history, notably with the Battle of Kerbela in Iraq in 680 A.D. in which Husein, grandson of the Prophet Mohammed, was killed. Dalip's younger brother **Shahin Bey Frashëri** also tried his hand at a Bektashi epic. His 12,000-line *Myhtarnameja* (The Tale of Myhtar), as yet unpublished, also deals with Shi'ite Muslim history and the aforementioned Battle of Kerbela, of which Myhtar was one of the protagonists. This epic, of which several copies are known, was finished in 1868 and appears to have been based on a Persian original and influenced by an intermediate Turkish version. The two works are often cited by literary historians, but seldom if ever have they actually been read since only very short excerpts of *Hadikaja* have been published so far. A critical edition of these two epics would be of great assistance to their proper evaluation.

The Albanian *Bejtexhinj* were, on the whole, not poets of the calibre of the Persian and Arabic classics, whose literary sophistication sprang from a millennium of refined oriental civilization. They were, however, inventive and talented minstrels who created both a new Albanian literature based on the Islamic traditions of the Orient and a new, but as yet unpolished literary language.

Albanian literature was written in Arabic script for over two centuries in all. It flourished throughout the eighteenth century and the first half of the

---

[55] cf. O. Myderrizi 1955b.

nineteenth century until it was gradually replaced by the romantic nationalist literature of the Rilindja period, written primarily in a number of newly devised versions of the Latin alphabet. In its early stages, the poetry of the *Bejtexhinj*, like much Ottoman *divan* verse, was primarily a literature of erudition and technique. As such, it remained a vehicle directed towards the interests of an elite minority, be it social, clerical or political, and, with time, lost its ability to express the dreams and aspirations of the Albanian people. The waning of the Muslim tradition in Albanian literature was concomitant with the decay of the Ottoman Empire and the rise of the Albanian nationalist movement during which the Albanians began to turn their backs on all things Ottoman and oriental. Turkish was the language of the invader and Arabic script came to be seen by many as an attribute of foreign cultural hegemony amongst a people slowly awakening and striving for self-determination. Only a new Western alphabet, Western ideas and consequently a more European-oriented literature could help Albania resist cultural assimilation by the Turks. The literature of the *Bejtexhinj*, as a result, turned inward upon itself and exhibited an increasingly religious orientation in the second half of the nineteenth century, notably in the cultural wake of the Bektashi. Indeed this literature survived marginally well into the twentieth century. The Muslim tradition was kept up in Kosova in particular, where verse was still being written in Arabic script as late as 1947.

Of all the periods of Albanian writing, that of the *Bejtexhinj* remains the least known, both by scholars and by the Albanian reading public. The manuscripts, as mentioned above, are for the most part lost or inaccessible, and there is a conspicuous dearth of qualified experts able to deal with what might be retrieved. At present, there are very few Albanian specialists with a sufficient command of Ottoman Turkish and of Arabic script, and no foreign Orientalists with a sufficient knowledge of Albanian to be able to deal with this literature on a scholarly basis. Nor did it find much favour among critics and readers in Stalinist Albania because of its fundamentally religious fixation, elitist background, adherence to classical conventions and alien form (the language of the occupant). The modern reader will find the mixture of Albanian, Turkish and Persian taxing, to say the least. The Muslim literature of the eighteenth and nineteenth centuries is nonetheless an integral part of Albania's cultural heritage, a component which remains to be properly appreciated and indeed, to a large extent, to be discovered.

3. Italo-Albanian Literature (18th-19th cent.)

3.1 Albanian Emigration to Italy

One strong branch of Albanian literature to evolve on its own outside the Balkans was that of the Italo-Albanians or Arbëresh of southern Italy. Sporadic groups of Albanians had found their way to Italy as early as 1272, 1388 and 1393, but it was not until the mid-fifteenth century that settlements were established when Albanian troops under the command of Demetrius Reres were summoned to Italy by Alfonso I of Aragon (r. 1435-1458), the King of Naples, to put down a revolt in Calabria. For his assistance, Reres was offered land in Calabria in 1448, and there his soldiers and their families immigrated. His sons, George and Basil, are said later to have made their way to Sicily to establish the first Albanian colonies there. Mass settlement first began, however, with the Turkish invasion of the Balkans which resulted in a great exodus of Albanians to Italy. This exodus became all the more acute after the collapse of Albanian resistance and the death in 1468 of Scanderbeg, who had found a generous patron in the House of Aragon. Between 1468 and 1478 waves of refugees abandoned southern Albania to establish themselves in Basilicata, Molise, Apulia and particularly in Calabria. More Albanians fled Greece in 1532-1533 after Turkish encroachments in the Morea and settled mostly in Sicily. These waves of refugees formed the core of Albanian colonization in southern Italy, although other emigrants followed in later years[56].

All in all, the Albanians founded or repopulated about one hundred towns and villages in southern Italy, over half of which are to be found in the mountains of Calabria. Today, there are about fifty towns scattered throughout the *mezzogiorno* where Albanian is still to be heard. These communities, comprising an estimated Albanian-speaking population of about 20,000

---

[56] On the Albanian colonization of southern Italy, cf. T. Morelli 1842; V. Dorsa 1847; P. Scaglione 1921; D. Zangari 1940; F. Tajani 1969; D. Cassiano 1977a; P. Bartl 1981; C. Rotelli (ed.) 1988; and F. Dessart 1984.

(100,000 fifty years ago), are located in seven regions: Abruzzi, Molise, Campania, Apulia, Basilicata, Calabria and Sicily.

3.2   Early Arbëresh Literature

The first work of Italo-Albanian literature, the *E mbsuame e krështerë* (Christian Doctrine) by the Sicilian archpriest Lekë Matrënga (1567-1619), dates, as we have seen, from the end of the sixteenth century. This religious translation by an Arbëresh cleric with the simple and pragmatic aim of bringing Christianity closer to his people in southern Italy by using their language was, however, destined to remain an isolated instance of vernacular creativity since, as far as we know, it did not suffice to stimulate any other Arbëresh religious leaders or intellectuals of the period to put their mother tongue into written form.

The seventeenth century, which proved comparatively fruitful for the development of writing and literature in Albania itself, saw virtually no signs of literary activity among the Italo-Albanians. Indeed, we must wait a whole century and a half for the seeds of Albanian literature to sprout under the serene Italian sky and in the fecund soil of Italian civilisation.

It is to the mountains of Calabria that we must turn for the first Arbëresh poet of real talent. **Giulio Variboba**[57] (1724-1788), known in Albanian as *Jul Variboba*, is regarded by many Albanians as the first genuine poet in all of Albanian literature.

Variboba was born in San Giorgio Albanese (Alb. *Mbuzati*) in the province of Cosenza to a family originally from the Mallakastra region of southern Albania. He studied at the Corsini Seminary in San Benedetto Ullano, a centre of learning and training for the Byzantine Greek priesthood. This seminary, founded in 1732 by Pope Clement XII, had an impact on the cultural advancement of the Arbëresh of Calabria in the eighteenth century similar to that of the Greek seminary of Palermo for the Arbëresh of Sicily. Variboba, one of its first students, was ordained as a priest in 1749 and returned to his native San Giorgio to assist his elderly father Giovanni, archpriest of the parish. Even

---

[57] cf. V. Librandi 1897; G. Schirò junior 1944; Sh. Demiraj 1953, 1956, 1958; M. Lambertz 1956b; T. Minisci 1959; G. Ferrari 1963; M. Cucci 1968, 1969; G. Gradilone 1974, p. 273-281; C. Laudone 1981; I. Fortino 1986; and M. Mandalà 1992.

during his studies at the Corsini Seminary, Variboba had shown a definite preference for the Latin (Catholic) rite over the traditional Byzantine Greek rite in the Arbëresh church. In later years, his polemic support for a transition to the Latin rite made him quite unpopular with both his parish and the local church hierarchy in Rossano, in particular after his direct appeal to the Pope. He was eventually forced into exile, initially to Campania and Naples, and in 1761 he settled in Rome where he spent the rest of his days.

Despite the turmoil of these years, Variboba must have known moments of tranquillity, too, for it was soon after his arrival in Rome that he published his long lyric poem *Ghiella e Shën Mëriis Virghiër*, Rome 1762 (The Life of the Virgin Mary), the only Arbëresh book printed in the eighteenth century. This loosely-structured poem of 4,717 lines, written entirely in the dialect of San Giorgio Albanese and loaded with much Calabrian Italian vocabulary, is devoted to the life of the Virgin Mary from her birth to the Assumption. Though from the poet's own life history and his uncompromising and polemic attitude to church rites, one might be led to expect verse of intense spiritual contemplation, the *Ghiella* evinces more of a light-hearted, earthy ballad tone, using Variboba's native Calabria as a background for the nativity, and transforming the devout characters of the New Testament into hearty eighteenth-century Calabrian peasants. Variboba is unique in early Albanian literature, both in his clear and simple poetic sensitivities and in the variety of his rhythmic expression, though the quality of his verse does vary considerably. The strength of 'The life of the Virgin Mary,' interspersed as it is with folk songs, lies indeed in its realistic and down-to-earth style, often pervaded with humour and naivety, and in the fresh local colour of its imagery.

One of the first and most illustrious students of the Greek seminary in Palermo was **Nicola Chetta**[58] (1740?-1803), Alb. *Nikollë Keta*. Chetta was born[59] in Contessa Entellina (Alb. *Kundisa*), the oldest Albanian settlement in Sicily, founded between 1450 and 1467. He was taught at the seminary by Giorgio Guzzetta and scholar Paolo Maria Parrino (1710-1765). In 1777, Chetta himself became rector of the seminary himself. As a poet, he wrote both religious and secular verse in Albanian and Greek, and has the honour of having composed the first Albanian sonnet (1777):

---

[58] cf. G. Schirò junior 1969, 1970; Dh. Shuteriqi 1976, p. 120, 130-132, 153-155, and 1977, p. 179-204; N. Chetta 1992, 1993; and M. Mandalà 2003.

[59] Giuseppe Gangale 1973, p. 57, states that he found indications in the manuscripts that Chetta was born in 1723 and insists that the usual 1740 derives from a mistake made by Gaetano Petrotta.

"Farie së ndeerme në Kuntisë u bii
Kolë Ketta, vllastar i t'arbrit dhee,
Shkoi në Palermë praa tek e Arbrit shpii,
Ç'e reshti, si zogu rep në folee.

E veshi e e ngjeshi me zakon, me urtësii,
Për në vapët e përtriijti ndënë hjee,
Si të veshkurin rremp stolis një dhrii,
E nani prift klisha kurorë e vee.

Si zok i sbjerrë praa t'di krahët çoi
Në Palermë e n'Kuntisë, po ktei e atei
Ndeern'e Arbreshet të gjithë gramët kërkoi.

Si krymp mundafshi gjith e svis vetëhei
E ktë vistaar tuar, kjëndisi e shkroi,
Se të kjosëj gjithë Arbrin ndjeer përtei."

(Of honourable lineage in Contessa was born
Nick Chetta, a scion of the Albanian soil.
He went to Palermo, to the Albanian home
Which received him like a featherless bird in a nest.

It clothed him, girded him with manners, with wisdom,
In the heat it refreshed him with its shade, like
The vine-stock readorning its withered branches,
And now a priest, the church took him for her spouse.

Like a lost bird he stretched his two wings
In Palermo and Contessa, both here and there
He sought honour for the Albanians in all his writings.

Like a silkworm he exhausted himself
And wove, embellished and wrote this treasure
To enrich Albania in every possible way.)

Chetta was an imaginative poet, though his verse, as far as can be
judged for the moment, is not distinguished by any sublime inspiration, or
unusually refined metric or linguistic skill. His significance, on the whole, lies
more in the variety and universality of his scholarly endeavours as a
lexicographer and linguist, as a 'creative' historian much influenced by Paolo

Maria Parrino and Giorgio Guzzetta, as a theologian of Neoplatonic proclivities, and as a public and religious figure in his capacity as rector of the Greek seminary. A definitive appreciation of Nicola Chetta and his work can only be made, however, when all his manuscripts have been published and properly evaluated.

3.3 Girolamo De Rada and the National Awakening

Girolamo De Rada[60] (1814-1903), known in Albanian as Jeronim De Rada, is not only the best known writer of Arbëresh literature but also the foremost figure of the Albanian nationalist movement in nineteenth-century Italy.

Born the son of a parish priest of Greek rite in Macchia Albanese (Alb. *Maqi*) in the mountains of Cosenza, De Rada attended the college of Saint Adrian in San Demetrio Corone. Already imbued with a passion for his Albanian lineage, he began collecting folklore material at an early age. In October of 1834, in accordance with his father's wishes, he registered at the Faculty of Law of the University of Naples, but the main focus of his interests remained folklore and literature. It was in Naples in 1836 that De Rada published the first edition of his best known Albanian-language poem, the 'Songs of Milosao,' under the Italian title *Poesie albanesi del secolo XV: canti di Milosao, figlio del despota di Scutari* (Albanian poetry from the 15th century: songs of Milosao, son of the despot of Shkodra). He was soon forced to abandon his studies due to a cholera epidemic in Naples and returned home to Calabria. His second work, *Canti storici albanesi di Serafina Thopia, moglie del principe Nicola Ducagino*, Naples 1839 (Albanian historical songs of Serafina Thopia, wife of Prince Nicholas Dukagjini), was seized by the Bourbon authorities because of De Rada's alleged affiliation with conspiratorial groups during the Italian Risorgimento. The work was

---

[60] There is a relatively substantial corpus of literature on Girolamo De Rada: cf. M. Marchianò 1902, 1903, 1906a, 1909; N. Douglas 1915; V. Gualtieri 1930; G. Gradilone 1960, p. 11-114, 1983, p. 13-38; J. Kastrati 1962; G. Valentini 1964; R. Ruberto 1966; E. Koliqi 1972, p. 81-116; and R. Qosja 1984-1986, vol. 2, p. 35-184. For specific studies on De Rada's poetic style, cf. M. Camaj 1969; A. Pipa 1969b, 1970c, 1973, 1977, 1978b, 1982, 1994; A. Desnickaja 1985a 1985b; K. Kodra 1988; J. Bulo, K. Kodra, K. Jorgo & L Smaqi (ed.) 2003; E. Kabashi 2003; and J. Kastrati 2003.

republished under the title *Canti di Serafina Thopia, principessa di Zadrina nel secolo XV*, Naples 1843 (Songs of Serafina Thopia, princess of Zadrina in the 15th century) and in later years in a third version as *Specchio di umano transito, vita di Serafina Thopia, Principessa di Ducagino*, Naples 1897 (Mirror of human transience, life of Serafina Thopia, princess of Dukagjini). His Italian-language historical tragedy *I Numidi*, Naples 1846 (The Numidians), elaborated half a century later as *Sofonisba, dramma storico*, Naples 1892 (Sofonisba, historical drama), enjoyed only modest public response. In the revolutionary year 1848, De Rada founded the newspaper *L'Albanese d'Italia* (The Albanian of Italy) which included articles in Albanian. This bilingual 'political, moral and literary journal' with a final circulation of 3,200 copies was the first Albanian-language periodical anywhere.

Girolamo De Rada's fame as a catalyst of Albanian national awareness spread in the mid-nineteenth century. He corresponded with leading figures of the Rilindja movement such as Thimi Mitko (1820-1890), Zef Jubani (1818-1880), Sami Frashëri (1850-1904) and Dora d'Istria (1828-1888), and with foreign scholars and writers interested in Albania such as French Albanologist Auguste Dozon (1822-1891), Baroness Josephine von Knorr (1827-1908) and Austrian linguist Gustav Meyer (1850-1900). He also received encouragement from French poet and statesman Alphonse de Lamartine (1790-1869) sojourning on Ischia. Provençal poet Frédéric Mistral (1830-1914), whose verse romance *Mirèio* (1859) was not without affinities to De Rada's work, expressed his admiration for the Songs of Milosao.

Discouraged by the events of 1848, Girolamo De Rada abandoned the publication of *L'Albanese d'Italia*, left Naples and returned to San Demetrio Corone to teach school. There he succeeded in having Albanian included in the curriculum but was fired in 1853 for his liberal political views. In 1850 he married Maddalena Melicchio of Cavallerizzo (Alb. *Kajverici*) with whom he had four children: Giuseppe, Michelangelo, Rodrigo and Ettore, all of whom died before their father. These were difficult years for De Rada, who was emotionally isolated even further by the loss of his wife and brothers, and lived in seclusion in his Calabrian mountain village without any substantial source of income as far as we know. In one moment of despair, he tragically destroyed the collection of folk songs he had so avidly gathered over the years. In 1868, he managed to get a position as director of the Garopoli secondary school in Corigliano Calabro, a job he was to hold for ten years. It was during these years that a number of further works appeared in print, mostly in Italian: *Principii di estetica*, Naples 1861 (Principles of aesthetics), *Antichità della nazione albanese e sua affinità con gli Elleni e i Latini*, Naples 1864 (Antiquity of the Albanian nation and its affinity with the Greeks and Latins), *Rapsodie d'un poema albanese raccolte nelle colonie del Napoletano*, Florence 1866 (Rhapsodies from an Albanian poem collected in the colonies of the Neapolitan region), *Scanderbeccu i pa-faan* (Misfortunate Scanderbeg) in four editions, Corigliano Calabro 1872, 1873, Naples 1877, 1884, and *Quanto di libertà ed ottimo vivere sia nello stato rappresentativo*, Naples 1882 (How much liberty and well-being is there in the representative state). In 1883, he founded the bilingual monthly journal *Fiàmuri Arbërit - La bandiera dell'Albania* (The Albanian flag). This periodical, published initially in Macchia Albanese and later in Cosenza 'by a committee of gentlemen from Albania and its colonies,' lasted until November 1887 and was also widely read by Albanians in the Balkans despite Turkish and Greek censorship.

In 1892, De Rada was reappointed to teach Albanian language and literature at the college of Saint Adrian in San Demetrio Corone and in 1895 organized the first Albanological congress in Corigliano Calabro. He also took an active part in the second Albanological congress in Lungro (Alb. *Ungra*) two years later in which he appealed for the setting up of a much-needed chair of Albanian studies at the Oriental Institute in Naples[61]. In these last years of his life, he published a *Caratteri e grammatica della lingua albanese*, Corigliano Calabro 1894 (Character and grammar of the Albanian language), based on his lectures at the college of Saint Adrian, an *Antologia albanese tradotta fedelmente in italiano*, Naples 1896 (Albanian anthology faithfully translated into Italian), including selections of the poetry of Variboba, Santori, etc. and a four-volume autobiography entitled *Autobiologia*, Cosenza 1898, Naples 1899. Shortly before his death, he also published a *Testamento politico*, a summary of his cultural and political views, which appeared in *La Nazione Albanese* on 30 September 1902. Alone and impoverished, half-blind and on the verge of starvation, Girolamo De Rada died in his native Calabrian mountains on 28 February 1903 - a tragic end to a great figure of Albanian culture.

Before Albania had become a political entity, it was already a poetic reality in the works of Girolamo De Rada. His vision of an independent Albania grew in the second half of the nineteenth century from a simple desire to a realistic political objective to which he was passionately committed.

De Rada was the harbinger and first audible voice of the Romantic movement in Albanian literature, a movement which, inspired by his unfailing energy on behalf of national awakening among Albanians in Italy and in the

---

[61] It was, however, not the elderly De Rada who was appointed to this chair in 1901, but the young Arbëresh poet and scholar Giuseppe Schirò senior (1865-1927) from Piana degli Albanesi.

Balkans, was to evolve into the romantic nationalism characteristic of the
Rilindja period in Albania. His journalistic, literary and political activities were
instrumental not only in fostering an awareness for the Arbëresh minority in
Italy but also in laying the foundations for an Albanian national literature.

The most popular of his literary works is the above-mentioned *Canti
di Milosao* (Songs of Milosao), known in Albanian as *Këngët e Milosaos*, a
long romantic ballad portraying the love of Milosao, a fictitious young
nobleman in fifteenth-century Shkodra (Scutari), who has returned home from
Thessalonika. Here, at the village fountain, he encounters and falls in love with
Rina, the daughter of the shepherd Kollogre. The difference in social standing
between the lovers long impedes their union until an earthquake destroys both
the city and all semblance of class distinction. After their marriage abroad, a
child is born. But the period of marital bliss does not last long. Milosao's son
and wife soon die, and he himself, wounded in battle, perishes on a riverbank
within sight of Shkodra.

The Songs of Milosao were published in three different versions in
1836, 1847 and 1873. De Rada was constantly altering, improving and
expanding this collection of lyric ballads of strong romantic inspiration from
an Ur-Milosao in twenty cantos to a much lengthier final version in thirty-nine
cantos.

Canto Four offers a poignant scene of discreet though unequivocal
erotic suspense which is quite uncharacteristic of Albanian verse:

> "*Ish e diella menat*
> *E i biri zonjës madhe*
> *Ngjitej tek e bukura*
> *Të m'i ljipën një pik uj,*
> *Se ish et' i djegurith.*
> *Vetëm e çoi ndë vatërët,*
> *Çë këshen më pjeksënej.*
> *Ata duhëshin e s'e thoshin.*
> *Vajza, me buzën mbë gaz:*
> *'Ç'ësht e ikën si ajri?'*
> *'Më presën ndë roljiet.'*
> *'Di moll t'ardhura*
> *Qëndro, u tij t'i ruata.'*
> *Me një dor ngrëjturith*
> *Mbanej mbi veshin e bardh*
> *Ljesht e saj të shpjeksurith;*
> *Kalli jetërën te gjiri*
> *E më goljq mollëzit,*

Më ja e vu ndë dorjet,
Ndë çerët e dhezurëz.
Thomnie ju, të dashurit,
Nd'ëmbëlj aqë të puthurit."

(It was Sunday morning
And the son of the noble matron
Went to visit the fair maid
To ask for a drop of water,
For he was dying of thirst.
He found her alone by the hearth
Braiding her hair.
They loved one another, but spoke not of their love,
The maiden with a smile on her lips:
'Why must you fly off like the wind?'
'They're awaiting me for discus throwing.'
'Wait a moment, I've kept
Two ripe apples for you.'
Holding her combed hair
With one raised hand
Over her pale ears,
She plunged the other into her bodice
And pulled out the apples,
Placing them in his hands,
Blushing with embarrassment.
Tell me, oh lovers,
Can a kiss be sweeter?)

The 'Songs of Serafina Thopia' also take us back to the nebulous romantic world of mid-fifteenth-century Albania. Serafina Thopia, daughter of the duke of Arta, and Bosdare Stresa are members of two rival mediaeval dynasties, an Albanian Romeo and Juliet, whose love is to remain forever unfulfilled. In this Gothic romance enhanced by much sorcery and Calabrian-Albanian folklore, Serafina sacrifices her own happiness to state interests, and marries Prince Nicholas Dukagjini so as to unite southern Albania with the north of the country on the eve of the Turkish invasion. The fate of all the characters in the poem seems marked by misfortune, suffering and untimely death, a mirror of the life of the poet himself. As with the 'Songs of Milosao,' De Rada altered and revised the 'Songs of Serafina Thopia' on several occasions, each new version reflecting his personal situation.

De Rada's third major literary work in Albanian is *Scanderbeccu i pa-faan* (Misfortunate Scanderbeg) which he considered to be his masterpiece. Again, this series of romantic ballads was published in a variety of editions reflecting the poet's state of mind at various ages. Broadly speaking, it covers the history of Scanderbeg's early exploits from 1418 to 1444 and is interspersed with many only vaguely related interludes. Scanderbeg, in actual fact, rarely appears in the work. Though 'Misfortunate Scanderbeg' contains many passages of moving verse, it is not the conventional epic about the Albanian national hero one might expect from an early torchbearer of the Albanian nationalist movement. It is distinctly meandering, particularly in later editions. Literary production of classical precision and conceptual unity was not De Rada's strength.

All in all, it is difficult to evaluate and even to delineate the corpus of Girolamo De Rada's Albanian-language poetry due to a ubiquitous lack of thematic unity in the three basic works and to his predilection for constant alterations and revised editions of his work, reflecting his mental states, emotional needs and literary penchants at the various stages of his long life. In most cases, the revised editions seem to diminish the literary value of the works in question. Though De Rada's verse is ostensibly about Albanian themes, it becomes evident on closer examination that, more than anything, it is about De Rada himself. It is not without reason that the veteran British Albanologist Stuart Mann (1905-1986) described De Rada's poetry as 'marred by weakness of plot and structure, obscurity of language, triteness of dialogue, and political irrelevance'[62]. Though De Rada was a writer of inestimable cultural significance he was by no means a poet's poet. There is no indication that he was fit for any poetic genre other than the romantic ballad. Some critics have gone so far as to deny him any merit at all as a poet and writer[63].

This said, Girolamo De Rada nonetheless remains a towering figure in the history of nineteenth-century Albanian literature. He was instrumental in waking the Arbëresh from their cultural obscurity and literary provinciality, and acted as a catalyst whose echo was clearly heard across the waters in Albania, as yet under the Ottoman yoke.

---

[62] cf. S. Mann 1955, p. 21.

[63] cf. G. Petrotta 1932, p. 219.

3.4 Romantic poets: Francesco Santori, Gabriele Dara and Giuseppe Serembe

The Romantic cultural awakening of the Arbëresh in the mid-nineteenth century brought forth another writer of original talent. **Francesco Antonio Santori**[64] (1819-1894) was born in Santa Caterina Albanese (Alb. *Picilia*) in the province of Cosenza. At the age of sixteen Santori began his training for the priesthood and in 1842 entered the Franciscan monastery of the Reformed Order in neighbouring San Marco Argentano. There he lived for eighteen years until 1860 when, after his failure to found a monastery in Lattarico about 1858, he abandoned monastic life altogether. Back in Santa Caterina Albanese he now eked out a modest living as a teacher and vendor of a spinning jenny of his own construction with three or four spindles. In 1885, he was assigned as a priest to the parish of San Giacomo di Cerzeto (Alb. *Shën Japku*) where he died on 7 September 1894.

Santori is the author of poetry, plays, short stories, novels, adaptions of 112 of Aesop's fables and an Albanian grammar written in verse. Much of his writing, in an original and rather difficult orthography, remained unpublished until recently. He was still in his twenties when he finished his first poetry bearing the Italian title *Canzoniere Albanese* (Albanian Songbook). This long lyric poem devoted to love and the beauties of nature appeared only three years after the first edition of De Rada's Songs of Milosao and in many respects bore the latter's mark. On the occasion of the enactment of the Neapolitan constitution of 1848, he also composed a hymn in Albanian entitled *Vale garees madhe* (Dance of great joy) which was printed in De Rada's journal *L'Albanese d'Italia* on 23 February of that year. His *Il prigionero politico*, Naples 1848 (The Political prisoner), is a poetic account in Italian, interpolated with Albanian, of the vicissitudes of a family persecuted during the Italian revolution in 1848. The spontaneity and ease with which Santori alternates between Italian and Albanian evince his creative talent for bilingual cultural expression. Santori is also the author of two religious works in Albanian published during his years at the monastery of San Marco Argentano:

---

[64] cf. A. Straticò 1896, p. 221-238; Z. Kodra 1954a; G. Gradilone 1974, p. 7-77: F. Altimari 1982; R. Qosja 1984-1986, vol. 2, p. 185-232; and K. Kodra 1987, 1991a, 1991b, 1996.

Rozhaari i S. Myriis Virgkiyry, Cosenza 1849 (Rosary of the Virgin Mary), religious verse, and the 230-page *Kryšten i šyityruory*, Naples 1855 (The Sanctified Christian), a collection of prayers, devotional texts in prose and poetry, and translations of religious songs. The latter also contains excerpts from Pjetër Bogdani's *Cuneus Prophetarum* (1685), which Santori included in his book as a token of the continuity of Albanian religious literature.

Of greater literary significance, historically speaking, are Santori's plays. His *Emira* (Emira) is considered to be the first original Albanian drama ever written. It was published rather erratically, some parts appearing in the journal *Fiàmuri Arbërit* in November 1887 and others in De Rada's Albanian anthology of 1896. Santori wrote a number of other melodramatic plays: both comedies and tragedies, some incomplete, which remained in manuscript form during his lifetime. Among these are the tragedy *Jeroboam* and the melodrama *Alessio Dukagino* written between 1855 and 1860.

In addition to the above-mentioned translation of Aesop's fables, Santori also composed 1,845 lines of satirical verse which have come to light only recently. It is here that his strong rural focus and his attachment to folk literature can best be seen, and indeed that his true poetic vocation comes to the fore.

That Santori was also a prose writer of significance to the history of Albanian literature has become increasingly evident through modern publications. With his two novels and six short stories he may now be considered the earliest Albanian writer to have produced a substantial corpus of literary prose, although none of these works, which remained unpublished during his lifetime, are of exceptional aesthetic value by modern standards. His unfinished novel, *Sofia Kominiate*, was written in two versions: a 282-page version in Albanian and a 714-page version in Italian, whereas *Il soldato albanese* (The Albanian soldier) was written in Italian only. His short stories, known by the names of their principal characters: *Panaini e Dellja, Kolluqi e Sorofina, Brisandi Lletixja e Ulladheni, Filaredo, Rosarja, Emilja, Miloshini, Virgjinia, Gnidhja e Kusari* and *Fëmija pushtjerote*, evince village motifs. Fused with rather awkward ethnographic and folkloric elements, they suffer from sentimental and naive happy endings, brought about in many cases by a deus ex machina.

Santori tried his hand at many genres: poetry, verse romances, prose, drama, translation and humorous verse, and it is this versatility that ensures him a place of honour in Arbëresh literature, right behind that of Girolamo De Rada. His literary works are in general more accessible to the reader than those of De Rada, in spite of the difficulty of his orthography (Santori's works are now invariably published in transliteration). They come no closer to artistic perfection or even hauteur, if such could be expected of mid-nineteenth century

Albanian writers. Despite its four centuries of written tradition, the Albanian language was still an unrefined tool for literature and was to remain so until the twentieth century.

The as yet sluggish current of Italo-Albanian literature in the early nineteenth century, which Girolamo De Rada had channelled so thoroughly into the Romantic movement, brought forth a work of truly Ossianic inspiration by **Gabriele Dara the Younger**[65] (1826-1885), also known *Gabrielo Dara* and in Albanian as *Gavril Dara i Ri*. Dara was born on 8 January 1826 in Palazzo Adriano in Sicily to an old Arbëresh family, reputed to have been one of the first to leave Albania after the death of Scanderbeg in 1468. He studied at the Greek seminary in Palermo and later received a degree in law, practising for a time in Agrigento. Dara became increasingly active in the turbulent political events of Garibaldi's overthrow of the Kingdom of the Two Sicilies and held a variety of offices. After an initial appointment as first councillor of the prefecture of Palermo, he served from 1867 to 1869 as prefect, or governor, of the city of Trapani. From 1871 to 1874 he was also director of the periodical *La Riforma* in Rome. Dara's literary and scholarly interests were wide-ranging, spanning poetry, folklore, philosophy, archaeology and jurisprudence. He wrote some Italian verse and one religious poem in Albanian dedicated to Saint Lazarus, but is remembered primarily for his romantic ballad *Kënka e sprasme e Balës*, Catanzaro 1906 (Engl. *The last lay of Bala,* Tirana 1967).

The enthusiasm generated by Scottish poet James Macpherson (1736-1796) with his ostensible discovery and publication in 1760 of 'Fragments of ancient poetry collected in the highlands of Scotland,' fired the romantic imagination of writers and scholars throughout Europe for over a century. Macpherson had claimed to have translated the Gaelic epic poems of the legendary warrior and bard Ossian but, when challenged, could not produce the 'ancient authentic manuscripts' in question. The Romantic movement, with its cult of the sublime and its 'noble savage' primitivism, awakened a passion for oral literature and folk traditions throughout Europe, and scholars of many languages began searching for the ancient epics of their peoples. Johann Wolfgang von Goethe (1749-1832), for one, was a great admirer of this 'Ossianic' verse. It was no doubt under the late effects of Ossianism that Gabriele Dara claimed to have recognized in his grandfather's collection of folk song, fragments an old Albanian epic by a mountain bard called Bala. The four-part poem, recounting the adventures of Nik Peta and Pal Golemi, Albanian heroes during the *moti i madh*, the 'great age' of Scanderbeg, was

---

[65] cf. G. Petrotta 1932, p. 228-232, 1950, p. 8-24; A. Varfi 1981; and R. Qosja 1984-1986, vol. 2, p. 349-374.

first published in installments in 1887 in the periodical *Arbri i ri* (Young Albania) by Giuseppe Schirò, and appeared in full in Italian and Albanian in the journal *La Nazione albanese* (The Albanian nation) from July 1900 on. Schirò described the alleged author of the verse epic in the following terms:

> "Bala was an ancient warrior among those who, after the fall of Albania, came to Sicily and founded the colony of Palazzo Adriano. The old people say that he was of ruddy complexion and churlish. He fled the company of men and spent days and months on end wandering over the mountain peaks to greet Albania. In the depths of the forests, on occasion, he would talk to himself and weep for the companions of his youth. Sometimes, when winter was harsh and the mountains and plains were white with snow, he would sit beside the fire and tell the children and young people of the deeds of the age he lamented. He was a warrior poet, like Ossian, who lived withdrawn in his memories."[66]

The 'Last Lay of Bala,' with its nine cantos, was soon recognized to be from Gabriele Dara's own pen. We may regard his allusion to the discovery of fragments of a non-existent old Albanian epic more as a romantic enhancement typical of the period than as a conscious forgery. Whatever the author's intentions may have been, the poem is not without literary merits in its own right and is in any case more unified and harmoniously balanced than the works of Dara's predecessor and guide, Girolamo De Rada. Its heroic treatment of the epic age of Albanian history, though presented in a romantic transfiguration which in modern literature would be regarded as excessive to say the least, is also more intelligible than De Rada's confused poetic meanderings in *Milosao* and *Serafina Thopia*. Indeed, the 'Last Lay of Bala' makes quite pleasant reading within the context of the nineteenth-century romantic literature of the Arbëresh and is still enjoyed by Albanians today.

Lyric poet **Giuseppe Serembe**[67] (1844-1901), known in Albanian as Zef Serembe, was a restless soul destined to bear the heavy burden of human suffering. The atmosphere of despair and tragedy that haunted him throughout his life surfaces time and time again in his verse. Serembe was born on 6 March 1844 in San Cosmo Albanese (Alb. *Strigari*) in the Calabrian province

---

[66] cf. *Arbri i ri* 3 (1 June 1887).

[67] cf. G. Gradilone 1960, p. 142-161, 1989; K. Kodra 1970, 1971, 1975; Dh. Shuteriqi 1961, 1974, p. 143-196, 1977, p. 251-309; R. Qosja 1968, 1984-1986, vol 3, p. 7-66; V. Belmonte (ed.) 1988; and V. Belmonte 1991.

of Cosenza and studied at the college of Saint Adrian. At an early age, he fell in love with a girl from his native village who emigrated to Brazil with her family and subsequently died. Obsessed by this loss and by the thought of finding at least her grave, Serembe set sail for Brazil in 1874 in search of a new life. He was received at the court of Emperor Dom Pedro II with the help of a letter of recommendation from Dora d'Istria, but he soon returned to Europe, disappointed and dejected. On his arrival in the Old World in September 1875 his fortunes took yet another turn for the worse. Robbed of all his money, apparently in the port of Marseille, he was forced to return to Italy on foot, and is said to have lost many of his manuscripts on the way. In Leghorn (Livorno), Demetrio Camarda provided him with train fare for the rest of his journey back to Cosenza. Despair, arising no doubt from chronic depression or some other form of psychiatric disorder, accompanied him wherever he went and rendered him solitary and insecure. He took refuge in the dream of the land of his forefathers, a vision marred by the reality of Turkish occupation in Albania and by the indifference of the Western powers to its sufferings. In his emotional isolation, Italy became more and more the *dheu i huaj*, a foreign land. In 1886, Serembe visited Arbëresh settlements in Sicily and in 1893 travelled to the United States where he lived for about two years. A volume of his Italian verse was published in New York in 1895. In 1897, he emigrated from his native Calabria to South America a second time and tried to start a new life in Buenos Aires. The following year he fell ill and died in 1901 in São Paolo.

Many of Serembe's works (poetry, drama and a translation of the Psalms of David), which he constantly altered and revised, were lost in the course of his unsettled existence. During his lifetime he published only: *Poesie italiane e canti originali tradotti dall'albanese*, Cosenza 1883 (Italian poetry and original songs translated from the Albanian) in Italian and Albanian, *Il reduce soldato: ballata lirica*, New York 1895 (The Returning soldier: lyric ballad), verse in Italian only, and *Sonetti vari*, (Naples 189?), an extremely rare collection of forty-two Italian sonnets with an introduction, all crammed onto four pages of tiny print. One poem also appeared in Giuseppe Schirò's journal *Arbri i ri* (Young Albania) on 31 March 1887. Thirty-nine of his Albanian poems were published posthumously in *Vjersha*, Milan 1926 (Verse), by his nephew Cosmo Serembe. Other works have been found in various archives and manuscripts in recent years and some of his poems indeed survived in oral transmission among the villagers of San Cosmo Albanese. This sign of his popularity at home is rather surprising in view of the fact that he spent much of his life away from his native village.

Serembe's verse, despondent and melancholic in character, and yet often patriotic and idealistic in inspiration, is considered by many to rank among the best lyric poetry ever produced in Albanian, at least before modern times. His themes range from melodious lyrics on love to eulogies on his native land (be it Italy, land of his birth, or Albania, land of his dreams), elegant poems on friendship and the beauties of nature, and verse of religious inspiration. Among his romantic poems of nostalgic nationalism, which cement the literary link with the rising generation of Rilindja poets in nineteenth-century Albania, are lyrics dedicated to his lost homeland, to Ali Pasha Tepelena, Dora d'Istria and Domenico Mauro. Patriot though he may have been, Serembe was not an intellectual poet who could provide us with a poetic chronicle of Albania's past. He was a poet of sentiment, primarily of solitude and disillusionment. One senses in his verse some of the more intimate facets of the Italian poets Francesco Petrarch, Dante Alighieri and Giacomo Leopardi, all of whom he had read and admired. His love lyrics, some about the childhood sweetheart he had lost so early in life, constitute a veritable diary of the heart, for example *Kënthimë tharosi*, also known as *Kënkë malli* (Song of longing):

> *"Rri e pikosur me mua, ku e di çë ke,*
> *O ti e të bjerrit Parrajs molla më e mirë!*
> *Thuomë çë të bëra u i shkret e kështu më le*
> *Sa gjellen bën - e rronj pa fare hirë.*
>
> *Oh! si të tharëta më shkuon kto dit, çë fare*
> *Nkë pe ninat e qeshur nd'ata si*
> *Çë shpirtin, dreq, m'e mbijin ndë gavnare*
> *Çë m'e pataksjin lart me mallëmadhi.*
>
> *Ballet terjorisur rrëmba dielli*
> *Ka jotja dritsorë u më nkë pe,*
> *Ne buzen me at çerë çë i qeshnej qielli,*
> *Se të vrëret m'i mbuluon paru shum re.*
>
> *Te gjiri, vash, mua zëmra mbështohon me zjarr,*
> *Gjith trutë më vruntullisnjin me noere,*
> *Pushimë u nkë mun çonj, paq nk' mun marr*
> *E gjellen kështu ti, vash, m'e vret njëhere!"*[68]

---

[68] Transcription by Giuseppe Gradilone from a manuscript of the Albanian Collection at the Royal Library of Copenhagen. cf. G. Gradilone 1989, p. 98-99.

(You are angry with me and I know not why,
Oh, fairest apple of paradise lost,
What have I done in my misery that you leave me thus,
How long shall I be deprived of all my joy?

Oh, how bitter were the days
When I saw joy vanish from your eyes
Which had filled this soul with such pride
And struck my breast with passion.

No longer did I see your forehead
At the window, embroidered with sunbeams,
Nor your fair lips, radiant heavens
Now thickly veiled in cloud.

Near your breast, my heart seethes with fire
And my mind with worry,
No respite do I encounter, no peace do I find,
Maid, you have ruined my life forever.)

3.5   Sicily's Scion: Giuseppe Schirò

Of major significance to Arbëresh literature are the works of **Giuseppe Schirò**[69] (1865-1927), who is known in Albanian as *Zef Skiroi*. Schirò was a neo-classical poet, prose writer and scholar whose literary works can be said to mark the transition to modern Albanian literature in Italy. He was born on 10 August 1865 in the Albanian-speaking village of Piana degli Albanesi near Palermo in Sicily. As a youth, he had already been encouraged to cherish his native language and culture by his cousin Cristina Gentile Mandalà (1856-1919) who later assisted him in collecting Albanian folktales and who was the author of an unpublished collection of folktales herself.

---

[69] cf. G. Petrotta 1950a, p. 25-36; G. Schirò jr. 1959, p. 205-226; E. Koliqi 1972b, p. 193-214; G. Gradilone 1974, p. 78-148, 1983, p. 39-85; R. Qosja 1986, vol. 3, p. 384-421; M. Mandalà 1990; and A. Berisha 1997a, 1997b. Schirò is often referred to as Giuseppe Schirò Senior to distinguish him from literary historian Giuseppe Schirò Junior (1905-1984).

Giuseppe Schirò began his literary career at the age of nine with a poem of nationalist inspiration dedicated to Scanderbeg. During his initial studies at the Italo-Albanian seminary in Palermo, he continued to show great interest in his native culture and, at the same time, in the classics of world literature which he read avidly: Homer, Dante, Ariosto, Cervantes, Klopstock, Goethe, Schiller and Tasso. In 1887, together with Francesco Petta, he founded the periodical *Arbri i ri* (Young Albania) in Palermo and published his first verse collection. He graduated with a law degree in 1890, but the focus of his interests remained folklore and literature, in particular classical and Italian, which he taught at the Garibaldi secondary school in Palermo from 1888 to 1894. It was a period of great literary productivity for Giuseppe Schirò, the years in which his major literary works began to appear. He was a friend of Italian novelist and playwright Luigi Pirandello (1867-1936) whom he had gotten to know at school and university in Palermo, though their literary activities show few similarities. Schirò also maintained correspondence with Albanologists and leading figures of Albanian culture of the period, among them Austrian philologist Gustav Meyer, Baroness Josephine von Knorr, French Albanologist Auguste Dozon, and Rilindja writers Kostandin Kristoforidhi (1827-1895), Pashko Vasa (1825-1892) and Vissar Dodani (ca. 1875-1939). In 1901 he was appointed to the newly-founded chair of Albanian studies at the Royal Oriental Institute in Naples, a post he held for the rest of his life, and in 1904 he published the short-lived fortnightly periodical *Flamuri i Shqiperîs / La Bandiera albanese* (The Albanian flag). Also in this period appeared his work on early Arbëresh literature and folk culture: *Canti popolari dell'Albania*, Palermo 1901 (Folk songs from Albania), a collection of Albanian folk verse, wedding songs, heroic verse and love songs with an Italian translation; *Canti sacri delle colonie albanesi di Sicilia*, Naples 1907 (Sacred songs of the Albanian colonies of Sicily); and *Canti tradizionali ed altri saggi delle colonie albanesi di Sicilia*, Naples 1923 (Traditional songs and other essays of the Albanian colonies of Sicily). Schirò worked in Albania as an inspector for Italian schools from 1912 to 1914, years which saw the final demise of the Ottoman Empire and the long-awaited birth of an independent Albania. He later pursued his Albanological activities at home in Naples, publishing, lecturing and attending congresses. The murder of his son Mino, a victim of political intrigue in July 1920, cast a heavy shadow over his final years. Giuseppe Schirò died in Naples on 17 February 1927, honoured and respected as the greatest figure of contemporary Sicilian Arbëresh literature.

Schirò's first literary publication, *Rapsodie albanesi*, Palermo 1887 (Albanian rhapsodies), appeared when he was twenty-two years old. He presented the work, in the Ossianic tradition of Gabriele Dara the Younger, as an anthology of traditional verse. The Albanian verse, accompanied by an

Italian translation, was so convincing that the experts and authorities of the age, including Giuseppe Pitrè (1841-1916) and Gustav Meyer, were quite taken in by it. His *Mili e Haidhia*, Palermo 1891 (Mili and Haidhia), is an imaginary love idyll in eighteen cantos in the tradition of Girolamo De Rada's *Milosao*. Scion of the first Albanians who had fled their battle-torn homeland for the eternal spring of Sicily, protagonist Mili is enraptured by a chance meeting with the fair Haidhia. In a subsequent dream, she encounters one of Scanderbeg's military companions who tells the tale of heroic resistance against the Turks. Mili, now engaged to Haidhia, sets off to fight for Albania. This sentimental poem, like De Rada's *Milosao*, concludes with the tragic death of the two lovers. With regard to its poetic diction and prosody, *Mili e Haidhia*, published in three editions, 1891, 1900 and 1907, can be considered a masterpiece of early twentieth-century Albanian verse and, from an aesthetic point of view, probably Schirò's best work, despite its exaggerated proportions and the sentimental delineation of the principal characters. The lack of conceptual unity, however, deriving in particular from alterations and supplements in the later editions, does tend to limit its overall artistic value and results in a confusing jumble, again not unlike the works of De Rada.

Kënkat e luftës, Palermo 1897 (The Battle songs), is a collection of poems dedicated to the goal of Albanian independence, and is in both form and content much in accord with the Rilindja verse of romantic nationalism being produced at the time in Albania. Though the zealous call to arms and patriotic fervour may be regarded from a modern standpoint as somewhat excessive, the nationalist ring is understandable in view of the immediacy of the struggle for independence at the turn of the century. Schirò sings of his people under the Turkish yoke, their struggles and the new day which was about to dawn for them. *Te dheu i huaj*, Palermo 1900 (To the foreign land), published with the financial assistance of Anselmo Lorecchio (1843-1924), is a long historical idyll, embellished with elements of folklore and mythology, which tells of the epic flight of the fifteenth-century Albanians from their homeland and of the colonization of Sicily. The final version of the work was published posthumously in 1940.

The eight-part elegy *Mino*, published in *Canti tradizionali ed altri saggi delle colonie albanesi di Sicilia*, introduces to Albanian literature a wide variety of new meters: hexameter, pentameter and Sapphic verse. It is the literary digestion of the tragic death of the poet's son Mino, aforementioned victim of a political murder in 1920. Though staunchly Albanian, Schirò held Italy's cultural potential among the nations in high esteem. In his concern for the fledgling Albanian state, he had often advocated the role that Italy, with its Arbëresh minority, might play in protecting the tiny country culturally and politically from the hostile designs of its Balkan neighbours. In *Kënkat e litorit*,

Palermo 1926 (The Songs of the littoral), he went further to glorify the rise of the early Italian fascist movement.

Këthimi, Florence 1965 (The Return), is a heroic poem of Albanian independence in forty-one cantos and 4,077 lines. It records the Arbëresh poet's return to Albania and his experiences there in the tumultuous years during which independence was finally declared. The protagonist Milo, a personification of the author, prostrates himself on arriving in the land of his ancestors. There he meets Essad Pasha Toptani (1863-1920), Dervish Hima (1873-1928) and Ismail Qemal bey Vlora (1844-1919), who proclaimed Albanian independence in Vlora in 1912. The heroic defence of Shkodra under Montenegrin siege is also evoked. In the second cycle, we encounter the contemplative world of the Bektashi in the figure of Baba Aliu, as seen through the eyes of the Christian Milo. The third cycle evokes Prenk Bibë Doda (1858-1920), prince of Mirdita, and the role of the Arbëresh and Italy in support of Albanian freedom. While individual parts of *Këthimi*, which is more biographical than historical in content, contain melodious verse that could be used for song lyrics, these parts do not succeed in forming a harmonious whole. The poem suffers from the same disunity as earlier works. Schirò's language is also worthy of comment. He employed a rich and varied lexicon with much phraseology derived from oral literature. He was also the first Arbëresh author to endeavour to avoid the many Italianisms which appear in most earlier works of Arbëresh literature. Where foreign words do occur, they are more likely to be of Greek origin, evincing Schirò's predilection for Byzantine civilization.

Despite his accomplishments, Schirò was less appreciated by literary historians in Stalinist Albania than earlier Arbëresh writers like Girolamo De Rada or Giuseppe Serembe. Schirò's unerring faith in Italy as a potential protector and custodian of the culture of the small Balkan state ran against the grain of subsequent aspirations of Albanian nationalism based on absolute independence from all other nations, including Italy. As was the case with many other writers of the prewar period, political criteria made an unfortunate intrusion into literary criticism of Schirò. The obvious fascination with the early fascist movement which seeps through in some of Schirò's later writings only contributed further to making an anathema of him in communist Albania.

It was, nonetheless, Schirò who first succeeded in blending the romantic elements of Arbëresh folk verse with the artistic precision of Italian classical and neo-classical poetry to form a harmonious and balanced poetic corpus. What Girolamo De Rada had done for Arbëresh literature in the nineteenth century, Giuseppe Schirò accomplished in the twentieth.

As we have seen, Italo-Albanian writing surged forth and flourished under the serene Italian sky, to form a body of literature which in its origins and development was quite independent of Albania itself. During the eighteenth and early nineteenth centuries, it was only in southern Italy that political, social and economic conditions, dire as they may have been from a modern perspective, were stable enough to allow Albanians to pursue the modest written culture which was to lay the foundations for modern Albanian literature.

But Albania, too, was at last awakening, politically and culturally, in the nineteenth century. In the collective memory of the Arbëresh, cast upon the shores of the *dheu i huaj,* 'the foreign land,' which they were always to regard with a certain degree of suspicion, Albania evolved from a vague recollection to become a concrete reality before their eyes, an ailing and struggling motherland which inspired them to preserve their own fragile culture. The indefatigable Girolamo De Rada had cemented the bonds between the Italo-Albanian colonies which were scattered throughout the isolated mountain ranges of southern Italy and their original Balkan homeland which was striving to maintain its identity. From then on and throughout the nineteenth century, political, cultural and literary ties were forged which proved fruitful and beneficial to both sides. Arbëresh literature had blossomed of its own accord and was certainly mature enough by this time to go its own way, but the ties of the *gjaku i shprishur*, 'the scattered blood,' enabled it to remain an integral part of Albanian culture. Deprived of its Arbëresh roots, Albanian literature itself would be inconceivable and barren.

4. Rilindja Literature of the Albanian National Awakening (19th cent.)

4.1 The Beginnings of the National Awakening

The gradual political and economic decay of the Ottoman Empire in the eighteenth century, accompanied by slow but certain territorial disintegration, created a power vacuum in Albania which resulted in the formation of two semi-autonomous pashaliks: that of Shkodra in the north ruled by the Bushati dynasty and that of Janina (Iôannina) in the south which in 1787 came under the formidable sway of Ali Pasha Tepelena, known as the Lion of Janina. Though the autonomy of the pashalik of Shkodra ceased with the death of Kara Mahmud Pasha in 1796, Ali Pasha, by using a skilful blend of diplomacy and terror, was able to extend his reign until 1822.

The restoration of power to the hands of the Sultan left Albania a backwater of poverty and provincial corruption. The centralist Tanzimat reforms which were decreed on 3 November 1839, and which were intended to modernize the whole of the Ottoman Empire, met with the firm opposition of local beys in Albania, intent on retaining their privileges. Nor were the wild tribes of the north, always sceptical of and recusant to anything the Turks might do, to be lured by promises of universal equality or of administrative and taxation reform. In this rugged mountainous region in particular, the Tanzimat reforms led directly to a series of uprisings against the Sublime Porte during which the seeds of Albanian nationalism were sown.

The European Romantic movement had stimulated an awareness for national identity among many smaller nations of northern Europe, but initially had no direct echo among the Albanians. Nonetheless, opposition to Turkish rule was now taking on a definite nationalist dimension, in particular in view of progress made by Albania's Christian neighbours. Serbia had attained a limited autonomy as a tributary state of the Ottoman Empire in 1817; Wallachia and Moldavia, in what is now Romania, formed self-governing principalities in 1829; and Greece won independence in 1830 after a long and bloody war begun in 1821. The battle for autonomy and cultural sovereignty in Albania was, however, to evolve at a much slower pace, due among other things to the higher degree of Islamisation and particularly to the lack of unity within the country itself. But the long-dormant seeds of an Albanian national awakening had begun to germinate, not only in Albania itself, but also in the thriving Albanian colonies abroad, in Constantinople, in Greece, Romania, Bulgaria and Egypt, and among the Arbëresh in southern Italy.

The struggle for political autonomy within the languishing Ottoman Empire and the will for cultural identity and survival among a backward and religiously divided people crystallized in the second half of the nineteenth century into the *Rilindja* (Alb: 'rebirth') movement of national awakening. This Rilindja period[70], which in its classical phase spans the years from the formation of the League of Prizren in 1878 to the declaration of Albanian independence in 1912, woke the Albanian people and united it into one linguistic identity, one culture and one nation. There was an intrinsic link between the goals of the nationalist movement in this period and the creative force of Albanian literature. Romantic nationalism accordingly became a dominant trait of expression in Rilindja literature[71].

The cultural awakening, which went hand in hand with the national and political consciousness raising, stimulated and presupposed of necessity the use of Albanian in all walks of life, in particular in writing and education, something which the Porte had banned.

Here lies the main reason for the sluggish evolution of Albanian literature throughout the Ottoman period. The Empire was divided not into national or ethnic groups, but into religious communities. The non-Muslim inhabitants of the Balkans enjoyed a certain degree of cultural autonomy, whereas the Muslim residents were considered by the authorities to be Turks and were thus forced to use Turkish. As such, the Greeks, Serbs, Romanians and Bulgarians of the Balkan peninsula, all Orthodox, were able to set up schools, to print books and newspapers in their native languages, to institutionalize their native cultures, and indeed to attain independence or at least a certain degree of political autonomy within the Empire. The Albanians, the majority of whom were now Muslims, did not have this right.

As nationalist resistance grew, the Porte regarded all Albanian-language education, school and publications as subversive and continually reinforced its ban on them, thus plunging the whole country into unremitting darkness and ignorance. Any Albanian-language schools which did manage to

---

[70] There is a substantial corpus of writing on the Rilindja period of Albanian history, both by Albanian and foreign authors. cf. for instance, K. Frashëri 1962; S. Skendi 1953a, 1953b, 1954, 1967; P. Bartl 1968; J. Faensen 1980; and G. Shpuza 1988.

[71] On Rilindja literature in general, cf. Dh. Fullani (ed.) 1973; J. Faensen 1980; K. Bihiku (ed.) 1981; R. Qosja 1984, 1986; Z. Xholi 1987; and M. Stavileci 2000.

open were soon shut down. Even into the twentieth century, the Ottoman authorities often went so far as to open people's handbags and correspondence, and search homes for anything written in Albanian. Publicist Eqrem bey Vlora (1885-1964) reports on a house search in April 1903: "The result was meagre. One postcard written in Albanian was found in a lady's dress. This earth-shattering discovery led to the banishment and incarceration of eighty notables in the Vlora region."[72] The prison in Vlora was said to be full of offenders having possessed writing in Albanian. "Some five hundred people are crammed into this narrow windowless room with no flooring. Most of them were supporters of the so-called national idea and were thus guilty of high treason. The judge, an Albanian himself, told me in the presence of several Turkish officials: 'Yes, we do have some murderers and thieves among them, but they are of less importance. Our attention is concentrated more on offenders found in possession of papers written in Albanian'."[73]

4.2   The Frashëri Brothers and the Literature of Romantic Nationalism

In a park above Tirana is a monument to the three Frashëri brothers who were the driving force behind the national Rilindja movement at the end of the nineteenth century. As diverse as their contributions were, politician Abdyl Frashëri, poet Naim Frashëri, and ideologist and scholar Sami Frashëri from the southern Albanian village of Frashër all had one thing in common: a profound desire to realize self-determination for their people suffering under the Turkish yoke.

After the death of their parents, Halid Bey (1797-1859) and Emine Imrahor (1814-1861), the aristocratic Frashëri family moved in 1865 from their mountain village in the district of Përmet to settle in Janina (Iôannina), now in northern Greece, where the younger sons attended the Greek-language Zosimaia secondary school.

Abdyl Frashëri[74] (1839-1892), the oldest of the eight children, worked as a merchant before entering the service of the Ottoman Empire. It was he who now bore the burden of raising the family. In 1877 he was appointed head of

---

[72] cf. E. Vlora 1911, p. 39.

[73] op. cit. p. 68.

[74] cf. P. Bartl 1968; J. Faensen 1980, p. 99-101; and K. Frashëri 1984a, 1984b.

the customs office in Janina and in the same year was elected as a Member of the Turkish Parliament. In December 1877, together with other Albanian intellectuals, among them his younger brother Sami, he founded the *Komitet qendror për mbrojtjen e të drejtave të kombësisë shqiptare* (Central committee for the defence of the rights of the Albanian people) in Constantinople (Istanbul) with a view to obtaining a certain autonomy for the Albanians within the Ottoman Empire. Following the Russian and Serbian victory over the Ottoman Empire on 31 January 1878 and the Treaty of San Stefano of March 1878, which provided for the annexation of much Albanian-speaking territory by the newly autonomous Bulgarian state and by the now independent kingdoms of Montenegro and Serbia, Abdyl turned his energy and talent increasingly and more urgently to the Albanian question. It was his articles in Turkish and Greek newspapers which first voiced the concerns and dismay of the Albanian population in the Balkans about the repercussions of the treaty. For although the subsequent Congress of Berlin on 13 June 1878 had confirmed the independence of Romania, Serbia and Montenegro and an autonomous government in Bulgaria, the interests of the Albanians had been entirely overlooked. As the majority of the Albanians by this time were Muslims and thus formed an integral part of the Ottoman Empire, which they had always been forced to defend in order to protect themselves from the expansionist aspirations of their Christian neighbours, they could not hope to find much understanding in Europe and had no great power at the congress to protect their interests. Their very existence as a people was not recognized. The impending division of the country galvanized the incipient nationalist movement into action: Muslim, Orthodox and Catholic Albanians alike.

On 10 June 1878, delegates from all over Albania assembled in Prizren to work out a common political platform in the *Lidhja e Prizrenit* (League of Prizren)[75], no doubt initially with the tacit support of the Ottoman government. Abdyl Frashëri, representing the central committee from Constantinople, gave the opening speech. The *Kararname*, resolutions of the League of Prizren, were passed and signed by forty-seven Albanian beys on 18 June 1878. They included:

1. a refusal to give up any territory to Serbia, Montenegro or Greece;
2. a demand for the return of all Albanian-speaking land annexed by Serbia and Montenegro;
3. Albanian autonomy within the Empire; and

---

[75] cf. C. Dako 1922; Mehdi Frashëri 1927; Xh. Belegu 1939; and K. Frashëri 1979.

4.　　　no more conscription for and taxation by the central government in Constantinople.

After this historic meeting which served to launch the national awakening, Abdyl Frashëri returned to southern Albania where he organized a League committee and began gathering troops to oppose the annexation of the south of the country by Greece. A key assembly of Muslim and Christian landowners at the Bektashi monastery of his native village of Frashër adopted a programme for autonomy which was accepted by the League in Prizren on 27 November 1878. The programme was later published by Sami Frashëri in the Constantinople daily newspaper *Tercümân-i-Şark*. In 1879, Abdyl Frashëri travelled to Berlin, Paris, Vienna and Rome with Mehmed Ali Vrioni to seek support for the Albanian cause and to submit a memorandum of Albanian demands to the Great Powers. In October 1879 he co-founded the Constantinople *Shoqëri e të shtypuri shkronja shqip* (Society for the publication of Albanian writing)[76]. In mid-1880, a programme for Albanian autonomy was passed with his assistance by delegates of the national movement in Gjirokastra. Although by this time his movements were under strict surveillance by the Constantinople authorities, he managed to get to Prizren in December 1880 and in the following month set up a Provisional Government (*Kuvernë e përdorme*) which extended its authority throughout Kosova down to Skopje. In Dibra, Abdyl Frashëri deposed the Turkish Mutasarrif and placed the town under the administration of the League, but at the end of April 1881, the Sublime Porte had had enough and sent in troops to quell the uprising. Following resistance in Gjakova and the suppression of the League, Abdyl Frashëri was obliged to flee westward towards the Adriatic where he hoped to escape to Italy. While crossing the Shkumbin river near Elbasan, he was captured by Turkish forces and sentenced to life in prison. After four years in a Turkish jail, Abdyl Frashëri was pardoned at the intercession of Gazi Osman Pasha at the end of 1885. He died on 23 October 1892 in Constantinople, not a figure of any direct significance to Albanian literature, but one who, through his political activities, acted as a torchbearer for his two younger brothers who were to stimulate Albanian literature and culture in the Rilindja period as no one had ever done before.

---

[76] cf. H. Myzyri 1979.

Naim Frashëri[77] (1846-1900) is nowadays widely considered to be the national poet of Albania. He spent his childhood in the village of Frashër where he no doubt began learning Turkish, Persian and Arabic and where, at the Bektashi monastery, he was imbued with the spiritual traditions of the Orient. In Janina (Iôannina), Naim bey Frashëri attended the Zosimaia secondary school which provided him with the basics of a classical education along Western lines. Here he was to study Ancient and Modern Greek, French and Italian and, in addition, was to be tutored privately in oriental languages. As he grew in knowledge, so did his affinity for his pantheistic Bektashi religion, for the poets of classical Persia and for the Age of Enlightenment. His education in Janina made of him a prime example of a late nineteenth-century Ottoman intellectual equally at home in both cultures, the Western and the Oriental. After finishing secondary school in 1870, he spent some time in Constantinople, where he published a *Kavâid-i fârisiyye dar tarz-i nevîn* Constantinople 1871 [1288 A.H.] (Grammar of the Persian language by a new method). For health reasons he soon returned to Albania, hoping to find relief in the mountain air from the tuberculosis he had contracted as a child. He worked as a civil servant initially in Berat and from 1874 to 1877 as a customs official in Saranda, across from Corfu. He is also known to have spent some time at the Austrian resort of Baden to recuperate from rheumatism and, during a visit to Vienna, had an opportunity to admire the sword and helmet of the Albanian national hero Scanderbeg, the very symbols of national resistance. In 1881 or 1882, he returned to Constantinople and, following the arrest of his brother Abdyl at the end of April 1881, began to play a serious role in the activities of Albanian nationalists there. He participated in the work of the aforementioned *Komitet qendror për mbrojtjen e të drejtave të kombësisë shqiptare* (Central committee for the defence of the rights of the Albanian people) and the *Shoqëri e të shtypuri shkronja shqip* (Society for the publication of Albanian writing) which had been founded in 1879. Although up to this time Naim Frashëri had published nothing of substance in Albanian itself, he and his younger brother Sami were soon to become the focal point of the Albanian nationalist movement on the Bosphorus.

Naim Frashëri is the author of a total of twenty-two works: four in Turkish, one in Persian, two in Greek and fifteen in Albanian. In view of his sensitive position as director of the board of censorship of the Ottoman Ministry of Education, Naim Frashëri deemed it wise not to use his full name

---

[77] cf. M. Kokojka 1901; Një grup studentësh 1925; Z, Xholi 1962, 1998; J. Faensen 1980, p. 101-105; Dh. Shuteriqi 1982; R. Qosja 1984-1986, vol. 3; and J. Bulo, E. Hysa & K. Jorgo (ed.) 2001.

in many of his own publications, and printed only a 'by N.H.', 'by N.H.F.' or 'by N.F.'

His foreign language publications, which predominated in the early period and which remained an integral part of his work throughout his life, include: *Ihtiraat ve kesfiyat,* Constantinople 1881-1882 [1298 A.H.] (Inventions and discoveries), an educative tract in Turkish; *Fusûli erbe'a* Constantinople 1883 (The Four seasons), a Turkish-language collection of prose-poems modelled on a work of French literature; *Tahayyulat* Constantinople 1884 (Reveries), a 200-page collection of Persian poetry; *Ilyada,* Constantinople 1886 (The Iliad), a Turkish translation of the first book of Homer's Iliad; *Ho alêthês pothos tôn skypetarôn,* Bucharest 1886 (The Genuine wish of the Albanians), a poem in Greek in which he set forth the goals of the nationalist movement to the Greeks and in particular to the southern Albanians, many of whom because of their educational background could only read Greek; and *Ho erôs,* Constantinople 1895 (Love), a lyric poem in eight cantos, also in Greek, in which he expressed his affinity for Greek culture.

Naim Frashëri's literary creativity in Albanian appears to have begun about 1880 when his patriotic poem *Shqipëria* (Albania) circulated in manuscript form among Albanian nationalists abroad, in Romania in particular. This 106-line work of rather bumpy octosyllabics, quick rhymes and, compared to subsequent works, superficial content was not published until much later in the poet's life (1897). Frashëri introduced here many of his favourite themes, ones he would repeat with substantially greater literary sophistication in later works: the ancient Pelasgian origins of the Albanians, the national heroes of the past, the need for schooling in Albanian to overcome backwardness, etc.

Since the Porte would not tolerate the publication of Albanian-language books in Constantinople, Naim Frashëri's best known works were published in Bucharest, where a substantial Albanian colony had settled and flourished, and where an Albanian printing press had been set up by the *Shoqëri e të shtypuri shkronja shqip* (Society for the publication of Albanian writing) in 1886. It was here that he published a series of manuals for Albanian elementary schools, such as the two-part *E këndimit çunavet këndonjëtoreja,* Bucharest 1886 (Readings for boys); *Vjersha për mësonjëtoret të para,* Bucharest 1886 (Poetry for elementary schools); *Istori e përgjithëshme për mësonjëtoret të para,* Bucharest 1886 (General history for elementary schools); and *Dituritë për mësonjëtoret të para,* Bucharest 1888 (Knowledge for elementary schools). He also brought his influence to bear to authorize the opening of the first Albanian elementary school in Korça in 1887.

The poetry collections for which Naim Frashëri is primarily remembered were also published in Bucharest. *Bagëti e bujqësija,* Bucharest

71

1886 (Bucolics and Georgics), is a 450-line pastoral poem reminiscent of Vergil (70-19 B.C.) and laden with the imagery of his mountain homeland. It proved extremely popular among Frashëri's compatriots and was smuggled into Albania on caravans. In it, the poet expresses his dissatisfaction with city life, no doubt from actual experience on the bustling banks of the Bosphorus, and idealizes the distant and longed-for Albanian countryside. It is a hymn to nature in the traditions of European romanticism and yet one of earthy substance in which, like Hesiod (8th cent. B.C.) in his 'Work and Days,' Vergil in his 'Georgics' or the great eighteenth-century Lithuanian poet Kristijonas Donelaitis (1714-1780) in his somewhat less idyllic 'Seasons,' Naim Frashëri sings of the herds and flocks, and of the joys and toil of agriculture and rural life. The pride of a people fighting for their freedom and the love of Albania which pervade this verse are succinctly expressed in the opening lines which every Albanian schoolchild knows, or is supposed to know by heart:

> "*O malet' e Shqipërisë e ju o lisat' e gjatë!*
> *Fushat e gjera me lule, q'u kam ndër mënt dit' e natë!*
> *Ju bregore bukuroshe e ju lumënjt' e kulluar!*
> *Çuka, kodra, brinja, gërxhe dhe pylle të gjelbëruar!*
> *Do të këndonj bagëtinë, që mbani ju e ushqeni,*
> *O vëndethit' e bekuar! ju mëndjenë ma dëfreni.*
> *Ti Shqipëri më ep nderrë, më ep emërin shqipëtar*
> *Zëmërnë ti ma gatove plot me dëshirë dhe me zjar.*
> *Shqipëri! o mëma ime! ndonëse jam i mërguar,*
> *Dashurinë tënde kurrë zëmëra s'e ka harruar.*"

(Oh mountains of Albania and you, oh trees so lofty,
Broad plains with all your flowers, day and night I contemplate you,
You highlands so exquisite, and you streams and rivers sparkling,
Oh peaks and promontories, and you slopes, cliffs, verdant forests,
Of the herds and flocks I'll sing out which you hold and which you
                                                                nourish.
Oh you blessed, sacred places, you inspire and delight me!
You, Albania, give me honour, and you name me as Albanian,
And my heart you have replenished both with ardour and desire.
Albania! Oh my mother! Though in exile I am longing,
My heart has ne'er forgotten all the love you've given to me.)

In the collection *Luletë e verësë*, Bucharest 1890 (The Flowers of spring), he also paid tribute to the beauties of the Albanian countryside in twenty-three poems of rich sonority. Here the pantheistic philosophy of his

Bektashi upbringing and the strong influence of the Persian classics are coupled harmoniously with patriotic idealism - literary creativity at the service of national identity. The verse collection *Parajsa dhe fjala fluturake*, Bucharest 1894 (Paradise and winged words), published together with the spiritual essays *Mësime*, Bucharest 1894 (Teachings), evinced his affinities for the heroes of the past and for the spiritual traditions of the Orient, in particular for the Persian mystics.

Istori' e Skenderbeut, Bucharest 1898 (History of Scanderbeg), is an historical epic of 11,500 verses which Frashëri must have written in about 1895 in his last creative years and one which the author himself regarded as his masterpiece. The figure of the Albanian national hero Scanderbeg, the symbol and quintessence of resistance to foreign domination, held a particular fascination for the intellectuals of the Rilindja period and for the common people. Frashëri could find no better theme for a national epic than the life of the virtuous prince who repulsed thirteen successive Ottoman invasions in the mid-fifteenth century and preserved his country's independence until his death. This chronologically ordered biography in twenty-two cantos of octosyllabic (*tetërrokësh*) verse, prevalent in oral literature, was the most widely read book of Albanian literature at the time. It also constituted the poet's political legacy. Though a fundamental work of Albanian romantic nationalism of the period, *Istori' e Skenderbeut* does not stand the test of time as a national epic. It suffers from the same artistic weaknesses to be found in Frashëri's other works and in many works of twentieth-century Albanian literature up to the present day: didactic and moralizing rhetoric and a black and white polarization of the protagonists into absolute saints and absolute demons huddling under a grey cloud of tear-jerking sentimentality.

Another work of similar proportions, published the same year as the 'History of Scanderbeg,' is *Qerbelaja*, Bucharest 1898 (Kerbela), a Shi'ite religious epic in twenty-five cantos, which deals with the Battle of Kerbela in Iraq in 680 A.D. in which Husein, grandson of the Prophet Mohammed, was killed. In contrast to the 'History of Scanderbeg,' *Qerbelaja* is a narrative epic devoid of a hero or principal character. It may have been modelled to some extent on the Albanian-language Islamic epics of his predecessors - *Myhtarnameja*, 1868, by Shahin Bey Frashëri and *Hadikaja*, 1842, by Dalip Frashëri, both of which remain unpublished, though Turkish and Persian religious literature would have provided the spiritually-minded poet with more than sufficient prototypes. Because of its exclusively religious theme, *Qerbelaja* has never really enjoyed the popularity of the 'History of Scanderbeg' among Albanian readers in the twentieth century.

Many elements of Naim Frashëri's religiosity are also present in Naim Frashëri's *Fletore e Bektashinjet*, Bucharest 1896 (Bektashi notebook), which is of major significance for our knowledge of the pantheistic but secretive Bektashi sect of dervishes.[78] Frashëri may have hoped that liberal Bektashi beliefs to which he had been attached since his childhood in Frashër would one day take hold as the new religion of all Albania. Since they had their roots both in the Muslim Koran and in the Christian Bible, they could promote unity among his religiously divided people. The Notebook contains an introductory profession of Bektashi faith and ten spiritual poems which provide a rare view into the beliefs of the sect[79] which in the nineteenth century played an important role in the survival of Albanian culture, in particular by the illegal distribution of Albanian books.

Despite pantheism and the universality of Bektashi beliefs, Naim Frashëri's faith had a decidedly nationalist flavour: "The Bektashi are brothers and one soul, not only among one another but to all mankind. They love other Muslims and Christians as their own soul and behave kindly and gently to all mankind. But most of all they love their motherland and their fellow countrymen, for this is the best of all things... May they strive day and night for that nation which calls them father and which swears by them. May they work together with the foremost citizens and with the elders for the salvation of Albania and the Albanians, for knowledge and culture for the nation and its fatherland, for their own language and for all progress and well-being." Naim Frashëri supported confessional independence from the central *pîr evi* in the village of Haci Bektaş Köy in Anatolia and proposed an Albanian *baba* or *dede* as leader of the Albanian Bektashi. He also introduced a number of Albanian terms to replace the Turkish ones traditionally used by the Albanian Bektashi: *atë* 'father or abbot' for Turkish *baba*, and *gjysh* for Turkish *dede* 'elder,' to give his Bektashi religion a national character and unite all Albanians.

The significance of Naim Frashëri as a Rilindja poet and indeed as a 'national poet' rests not so much upon his talents of literary expression nor

---

[78] On the Bektashi religion and community in Albania and the Balkans, cf. M. Hasluck 1925; M. Choublier 1927; F. Babinger 1928; F. W. Hasluck 1929; J. Birge 1937; K. Halimi 1957; H. Kissling 1962; Xh. Kallajxhi 1964; P. Bartl 1968, p. 98-111; B. Rexhebi 1970, 1984; G. Stadtmüller 1971; A. Popovic 1986; A. Popovic & G. Veinstein 1986, 1993, 1996; N. Clayer 1990, 1993, 2003; H. Norris 1993, p. 123-137; and F. Trix 1993.

[79] After the ban on all dervish orders in Turkey in the autumn of 1925, the Bektashi transferred their headquarters to Tirana and set up a recognized and independent religious community which existed there until the fifties. The community was dissolved in 1967 when a government edict banned all religious activity in Albania. After the lifting of the edict, a provisional committee for the revival of the Bektashi community was founded in Tirana on 27 January 1991.

upon the artistic quality of his verse, but rather upon the sociopolitical, philosophical and religious messages it transmitted, which were aimed above all at national awareness and, in the Bektashi tradition, at overcoming religious barriers within the country. His influence upon Albanian writers at the beginning of the twentieth century was enormous. Many of his poems were set to music during his lifetime and were sung as folk songs. If one compares the state of Albanian literature before and after the arrival of Naim Frashëri, one becomes aware of the major role he played in transforming Albanian into a literary language of substantial refinement.

The Frashëri brother with the most diverse and universal talent was certainly **Sami Frashëri**[80] (1850-1904), known in Turkish as *Şemseddin Sami*, who filled the roles of writer, publisher and ideologist of the nationalist movement. Like his brother Naim, he was first confronted with the currents of Western thought at the Zosimaia secondary school in Janina where he studied Greek, French and Italian. In addition, he was privately tutored in Arabic, Turkish and Persian. In 1871, Sami bey Frashëri was offered an initial position in the *vilayet* administration of Janina before moving to Constantinople in 1872 to work in the government press office.

It was in the bustling capital of the Ottoman Empire that he made friends with the Turkish writers Namik Kemal (1840-1888) and Ebüzziya Tevfik (1849-1913), and with the Albanian hodja Hasan Tahsini (1811-1881). In 1874, Sami Frashëri spent nine months in Tripolitania where he ran the Arabic and Turkish-language newspaper *Tarabulus*. It is not known whether he was sent into exile there (his friend Namik Kemal had been exiled to Famagusta on Cyprus for a publication which attracted the displeasure of the Porte in 1873) or was simply chosen as the right man for the job. Back in Constantinople at any rate, he became increasingly involved in publishing and ran the magazine called *Sabah* 1876 (The Morning). In 1877, he worked for five months as secretary to Sava Pasha, the Governor of Rhodes, and subsequently as secretary for the Janina military commission under Abedin Pasha. In the autumn of 1877, he returned to Constantinople once again and edited the Turkish-language daily *Tercümân-i-Şark* 1878 (Oriental Interpreter), in which his views and commentaries on the political events of the day were published. He also used this newspaper in particular as a platform for publicizing the demands and wishes of the Albanian minority in the Empire. An untiring editor, Sami Frashëri later published the magazines *Aile* 1879 (The

---

[80] cf. I. Hakki 1895; H. Daglioglu 1934; K. Frashëri 1955, 1966; E. Reso 1962; H. Kaleshi 1968, 1970, 1971; A. Levend 1969; Z. Xholi 1978; J. Faensen 1980, p. 105-112; Z. Bakiu 1982; and Sh. Çollaku 1985.

Family) and *Hafta* 1880/81 (The Week). Together with his brother Abdyl, then Member of Parliament, and with Koto Hoxhi (1824-1895), Zija Prishtina, Pandeli Sotiri (1843-1891), Hasan Tahsini (1811-1881), Pashko Vasa (1825-1892), Jani Vreto (1820-1900), etc., he also worked on the aforementioned *Komitet qendror për mbrojtjen e të drejtave të kombësisë shqiptare* (Central committee for the defence of the rights of the Albanian people) which supported Albanian demands for autonomy at the time of the League of Prizren.

One particular obstacle to the flourishing of Albanian culture in the Ottoman Empire, in addition to the generally hostile attitude of the Turkish authorities, was still the lack of an acceptable alphabet for the Albanian language. At the beginning of 1879, the central committee set up an alphabet commission under Sami Frashëri's direction to tackle the orthography problem once again. The alphabet Sami Frashëri devised, which was subsequently approved by the commission, was a phonetic system relying primarily on Latin letters, though with the addition of a number of Greek/Cyrillic characters. On 12 October 1879, leading members of the Albanian community in Constantinople set up the above-mentioned *Shoqëri e të shtypuri shkronja shqip* (Society for the publication of Albanian writing). It too was headed by Sami Frashëri. After its activities were banned, the Society transferred its headquarters to Bucharest where many Albanian-language books - among them the major works of Naim and Sami Frashëri - were printed in the so-called Istanbul alphabet. It was there for instance that Albanian-language school texts written by Sami Frashëri were published: *Abetare e gjuhësë shqip*, Bucharest 1886 (ABCs of the Albanian language), *Dheshkronjë*, Bucharest 1888 (Geography), and *Shkronjëtore e gjuhësë shqip*, Bucharest 1886 (Grammar of the Albanian language), the latter being the first Albanian school grammar.

The alphabet problem continued to preoccupy leading figures of the nationalist movement in the years to follow. On 14-22 November 1908, a congress was held in the Macedonian city of Monastir (Bitola) to decide upon a definitive alphabet. The congress was convoked on the initiative of the *Bashkimi* (Unity) Literary Society under Gjergj Fishta (1871-1940) and presided over by Mid'hat bey Frashëri (1880-1949), son of Abdyl Frashëri. The Congress of Monastir, as it is known, was attended by Catholic, Orthodox and Muslim delegates from Albania and abroad, among them Shahin Kolonja (1865-1919), Ndre Mjeda (1866-1937), Hilë Mosi (1885-1933) and Sotir Peci (1873-1932). The three main alphabets under discussion were the above-mentioned Istanbul alphabet devised by Sami Frashëri, the Bashkimi alphabet supported by Gjergj Fishta and his *Bashkimi* Literary Society of Shkodra, and the Agimi alphabet of the *Agimi* (Dawn) Literary Society represented by Ndre Mjeda. A committee of eleven delegates headed by Fishta was elected and after three days of deliberations they resolved to support two alphabets: a modified form of Sami Frashëri's Istanbul alphabet, which was most widely used at the time, and a new Latin alphabet almost identical to the Bashkimi in order to facilitate printing abroad.

Sami Frashëri is the author of about fifty works as well as numerous newspaper articles. His interests were on the whole more scholarly than literary. Between 1882 and 1902, he published six teaching manuals in Turkish and Arabic. His publications in Turkish are indeed of greater universal significance than his Albanian-language works. In 1872, Sami Frashëri published what is widely regarded as the first Turkish novel and, at the same time, the first novel written and published by an Albanian, the 180-page *Taaşşuk-u Tal'at ve Fitnat* (The Love of Tal'at and Fitnat)[81]. It is a period piece, a sentimental love story which was in full accord with the tastes of the time. While by no means realistic, the combination of oriental and occidental elements it contained did provide a good deal of social criticism, in particular of the status of women in Ottoman society. More than anything, Sami Frashëri was an educator.

Sami Frashëri's play, the 180-page *Besa yahud ahde vefa* ('Besa' or the fulfilment of the pledge), published in Constantinople in 1875, and translated into Albanian by Abdyl Ypi Kolonja in 1901 and into English by Nelo Drizari (1902-1978) as *Pledge of honor, an Albanian tragedy*, New York 1945, was premiered on 6 April 1874 at the 'Osmanli Tiyatrosu' (Ottoman Theatre). In this, for modern tastes somewhat melodramatic work on a very Albanian theme, we observe the tragic dilemma of an Albanian father who prefers to kill his own son rather than break his *besa*, his word of honour.

In 1884, with the help of the Armenian newspaperman Mihran, Sami Frashëri published a series of inexpensive books of general knowledge designed for the Turkish public at large and used this series, entitled *Cep Kütüphanesi* (Pocket library), to publish fifteen of his own works. He thus became a figure of note in Constantinople society.

As a Turkish lexicographer, Sami Frashëri published a 1,630-page *Kamûs-u fransevî, fransizcadan türkçeye lugat*, Constantinople 1882 [1299 A.H.] (French-Turkish dictionary); a *Kamûs-u fransevî, türkçeden fransizcaya lugat*, Constantinople 1885 [1301 A.H.] (Turkish-French dictionary); and a two-volume *Kamûs-u türkî*, Constantinople 1900/1901 [1317 A.H.], reprint Istanbul 1979 (Turkish dictionary), which is still regarded as useful and which was consulted by the Turkish Philological Society (Türk Dil Kurumu) in 1932 as a guideline for the creation of the modern Turkish literary language. Lack

---

[81] cf. A. Hetzer 1991.

of money caused him to abandon his vast project of a *Kamûs-u Arabî* (Arabic dictionary). After twelve years of preparation, he was however able to publish his monumental six-volume Turkish-language encyclopaedia of history and geography, *Kamûs al-a'lâm*, Constantinople 1889-1896 [1306-1313 A.H.] (Dictionary of the world). With a total of 4,830 pages, the *Kamûs al-a'lâm* was an exceptional work of reference for the period and also contained extensive information on the history and geography of Albania.

Sami Frashëri also seems to have compiled an Albanian dictionary. In a letter to Thimi Mitko written in Bucharest in 1885, Jani Vreto reports having seen a *fjalëtor* (dictionary) by Sami bey which contained over 6,000 main entries. In view of Sami Frashëri's assiduousness and experience as a lexicographer, it is quite possible that this Albanian dictionary was a major undertaking which he never finished. Nothing is known of the whereabouts of the manuscript now.

At the end of the nineties, despite the substantial financial difficulties he was encountering, Sami Frashëri designed and built a large house in the Constantinople suburb of Erenköy. He had not only his own family to take care of (wife Emine Velije and five children) but also the two children of his brother Abdyl who had died in 1892. It was in this mansion that he housed his large private library estimated at ten to twelve thousand volumes.

Of major significance to the Albanian national movement was Sami Frashëri's much-read political manifesto *Shqipëria - Ç'ka qënë, ç'është e ç'do të bëhetë? Mendime për shpëtimt të mëmëdheut nga reziket që e kanë rethuarë*, Bucharest 1899, reprint Sofia 1907 (Albania - what was it, what is it and what will become of it? Reflections on saving the motherland from the perils which beset it) which was translated into Turkish, Greek, French, Italian and German. After a brief and rather fanciful review of Albanian history, Sami Frashëri comes to the conclusion that the Ottoman Empire is in its last throes and that the time has come for Albania to break away (a demand which exceeded the usual appeal for autonomy at the time) and become the master of its own destiny. He compares the 'Sick Man of Europe' to a drowning man pulling down the lifeguard trying to save him. Sami Frashëri admits that the Albanians might have fared well under the Turks in the past, but protests that they have been treated like slaves ever since the Tanzimat legislation. Albania now served the Ottoman Empire only for conscripts and taxes. Nonetheless, the immediate goal of his manifesto was full autonomy within the Empire. Sami Frashëri proceeds to set forth his vision of a future Albania. He draws the borders of the country and expounds on a system of government with a *pleqësia*, council of elders, who will meet in a new centrally located capital city named Skander Begas. He writes of education (compulsory schooling from the age of seven to thirteen and the founding of two universities), public works (an

Albanian railway), an autocephalic church, agriculture and industry. Though somewhat utopian in the vision it offers, this historic monograph constitutes the first concrete political manifesto for an independent Albania. Indeed, the dream of total independence was new and particularly daring since, according to the reasoning of most Albanian intellectuals at the time, an autonomous Albania had more chance of survival within the Empire, protected as it would be from the hostile and aggressive designs of its Greek, Serbian and Montenegrin neighbours who would no doubt have swallowed the little state in the event of war. Sami Frashëri went further. This was the legacy he left to his people - that the great ideal of Albanian independence was indeed thinkable.

Throughout their history, Albanians had often made a name for themselves abroad, in particular as civil servants and statesmen in the service of the Sublime Porte. Abdyl, Naim and Sami Frashëri represented, for the first time, a new generation of Albanian intellectuals who, though educated in Greek schools and in the great cultural traditions of the Orient, devoted their talents and energies exclusively to their Albanian homeland.

In 1937 the remains of Abdyl and Naim Frashëri were transferred from Turkey to Tirana for burial on the outskirts of the new little capital. Sami Frashëri, the great Şemseddin Sami, in view of his contribution to Turkish culture, remains buried in Istanbul.

4.3   Rilindja Culture in Northern Albania

The Rilindja movement of national awakening was to take root more slowly in northern Albania than in the south. The harsh mountain terrain and the feudal tribal structure of the population inhabiting the barren and isolated valleys of the north had made the highland Ghegs a special breed: unbridled mountain tribesmen who were fiercely independent and who lived by their own traditional customs and laws. As there were no easy means of communication in the rugged northern Albanian Alps, which were snow-bound in the winter and scorching and arid in the summer, most of these tribes had little contact with the outside world. Their experience with Ottoman troops and tax collectors had, however, taught them to be on guard against everything and everyone from the outside. Traditional tribal laws, such as the *Kanun* or Code of Lekë Dukagjini[82], governed and regulated all facets of life in these mountains.

Only in the hybrid town of Shkodra with its merchant class and access to the sea, could traditional mountain wisdom be supplemented by the rudiments of formal education at the rare foreign schools. It was here that Albanian culture in the north began to flourish, initially under the aegis of the Catholic Church just as it had in the sixteenth and seventeenth centuries.

The Albanian Catholic Church, with its power base in the north of the country, i.e. Shkodra and the highlands, was traditionally Italian-oriented. In the mid-nineteenth century, Catholics in this region also came under the influence of Austria in the *Kultusprotektorat* (religious protectorate), a right Vienna had wrested from the Porte in a series of peace treaties with the Sultans beginning in 1616. The *Kultusprotektorat*, reconfirmed after the Austrian-Turkish war of 1683-1699, authorized Austria to serve as protectress to the Catholic population in the Balkans, among whom were the Catholics of northern Albania. Always more with political pragmatism than with altruistic evangelization in mind, Austria now began stepping up its activities under the protectorate as a means of wielding political influence in northern Albania to check the Ottoman Empire from within and to counter any political ambitions which the Orthodox southern Slavs might have. With Austrian assistance, schools and churches were built and repaired in northern Albania and the Catholic Church began to play a more active role in the fields of education and culture. The northern Albanian town of Shkodra, known abroad at the time as *Scutari*, was soon to develop into a literary and cultural capital not only for Albanian Catholics, who represented only about one-tenth of the population of Albania, but for all of the country.

One figure from northern Albania who played a key role in the Rilindja culture of the nineteenth century was **Pashko Vasa**[83] (1825-1892), also known as *Wassa Effendi*, *Vaso Pasha*, or *Vaso Pasha Shkodrani*. This statesman, poet, novelist and patriot was born on 17 September 1825 in Shkodra. From 1842 to 1847 he worked as a secretary for the British consulate in that northern Albanian city where he had an opportunity to perfect his knowledge of a number of foreign languages: Italian, French, Turkish and Greek. He also knew some English and Serbo-Croatian, and in later years learned Arabic. In 1847, full of ideals and courage, he set off for Italy on the eve of the turbulent events

---

[82] On traditional mountain law and the Code of Lekë Dukagjini, cf. Sh. Gjeçovi 1933, 1989; M. Hasluck 1954; G. Valentini 1968; and R. Elsie 2001e.

[83] cf. A. Khair 1973; J. Kastrati 1975; V. Bala 1979; R. Qosja 1984-1986, vol. 2, p. 306-348; P. Vasa 1987 and 1989.

that were to take place there and elsewhere in Europe in 1848. We have two letters from him written in Bologna in the summer of that revolutionary year in which he expresses openly republican and anti-clerical views. We later find him in Venice where he took part in fighting in Marghera on 4 May 1849, part of a Venetian uprising against the Austrians. After the arrival of Austrian troops on 28 August of that year, Pashko Vasa was obliged to flee to Ancona where, as an Ottoman citizen, he was deported to Constantinople. He published an account of his experience in Italy the following year in his Italian-language *La mia prigionia, episodio storico dell'assedio di Venezia*, Constantinople 1850 (My imprisonment, historical episode from the siege of Venice). It is no coincidence that this historical biography bears a title similar to that of the famous memoirs of Italian patriot and dramatist Silvio Pellico (1789-1845), *Le mie prigioni* (My prisons), published in 1832. In Constantinople, after an initial period of poverty and hardship, he obtained a position at the Ministry of Foreign Affairs, whence he was seconded to London for a time, to the Imperial Ottoman Embassy to the Court of St James's. He later served the Sublime Porte in various positions of authority. In 1863, thanks to his knowledge of Serbo-Croatian, as he tells us, he was appointed to serve as secretary and interpreter to Ahmed Jevdet Pasha, Ottoman statesman and historian, on a fact-finding mission to Bosnia and Hercegovina which lasted for twenty months, from the spring of 1863 to October 1864. The events of this mission were recorded in his *La Bosnie et l'Herzégovine pendant la mission de Djevdet Efendi*, Constantinople 1865 (Bosnia and Hercegovina during the mission of Jevdet Efendi). About 1867 he was in Aleppo. A few years later, he published another, now rare work of historical interest, *Esquisse historique sur le Monténégro d'après les traditions de l'Albanie*, Constantinople 1872 (Historical sketch of Montenegro according to Albanian traditions).

Despite his functions on behalf of the Porte, Pashko Vasa never forgot his Albanian homeland. In the autumn of 1877 he became a founding member of the *Komitet qendror për mbrojtjen e të drejtave të kombësisë shqiptare* (Central committee for the defence of the rights of the Albanian people) in Constantinople. Through his contacts there, he also participated in the organization of the League of Prizren in 1878. He was no doubt the author of the Memorandum on Albanian Autonomy submitted to the British Embassy in Constantinople. Together with other nationalist figures on the Bosphorus, such as hodja Hasan Tahsini, Jani Vreto and Sami Frashëri, he played his part in the creation of an alphabet for Albanian and, in this connection, published a 16-page brochure entitled *L'alphabet latin appliqué à la langue albanaise*, Constantinople 1878 (The Latin alphabet applied to the Albanian language), in support of an alphabet of purely Latin characters. He was also a member of the *Shoqëri e të shtypuri shkronja shqip* (Society for the publication of

Albanian writing), founded in Constantinople on 12 October 1879 to promote the printing and distribution of Albanian-language books. In 1879, Pashko Vasa worked in Varna on the Black Sea coast in the administration of the vilayet of Edirne with Ismail Qemal bey Vlora (1844-1919). He also acquired the title of Pasha and on 18 July 1883 became Governor General of the Lebanon, a post reserved by international treaty for a Catholic of Ottoman nationality. He is said to have held this position in an atmosphere of Levantine corruption and family intrigue, true to the traditions of the Lebanon then and now. There he spent the last years of his life and died in Beirut after a long illness on 29 June 1892. In 1978, the centenary of the League of Prizren, his remains were transferred from the Lebanon back to a modest grave in Shkodra.

Though a loyal civil servant of the Ottoman Empire, Pashko Vasa devoted his energies as a polyglot writer to the Albanian national movement. Aware of the importance of Europe in Albania's struggle for recognition, he published *La vérité sur l'Albanie et les Albanais: étude historique et critique*, Paris 1879, an historical and political monograph which appeared in an English translation as *The truth on Albania and the Albanians: historical and critical study*, London 1879, as well as in Albanian, German, Turkish and Greek that year, and later in Arabic (1884) and Italian (1916). The Albanian edition, *Shqypnija e shqyptart* (Albania and the Albanians), was published in *Allfabetare e gluhësë shqip*, Constantinople 1879 (Alphabet of the Albanian language), along with work by Sami Frashëri and Jani Vreto. In this treatise designed primarily to inform the European reader about his people, he gave an account of Albanian history from the ancient Pelasgians and Illyrians up to his time and expounded on ways and means of promoting the advancement of his nation. Far from an appeal for Albanian independence or even autonomy within the Empire, Pashko Vasa proposed simply the unification of all Albanian-speaking territory within one vilayet and a certain degree of local government. The possibility of a sovereign Albanian state was still inconceivable. He never lived to read Sami Frashëri's above-mentioned treatise 'Albania - what was it, what is it and what will become of it?', printed twenty years later, in which the concept of full independence had finally ripened.

To make the Albanian language better known and to give other Europeans an opportunity to learn it, he published a *Grammaire albanaise à l'usage de ceux qui désirent apprendre cette langue sans l'aide d'un maître*, Ludgate Hill 1887 (Albanian grammar for those wishing to learn this language without the aid of a teacher), one of the rare grammars of the period.

Pashko Vasa was also the author of a number of literary works. The first of these is a volume of Italian verse entitled *Rose e spine*, Constantinople 1873 (Roses and thorns), forty-one emotionally-charged poems (a total of ca. 1,600 lines) devoted to themes of love, suffering, solitude and death in the traditions of the romantic verse of his European predecessors Giacomo Leopardi, Alphonse de Lamartine and Alfred de Musset. Among the subjects treated in these meditative Italian poems, two of which are dedicated to the Italian poets Francesco Petrarch and Torquato Tasso, are life in exile and family tragedy, a reflection of Pashko Vasa's own personal life. His first wife, Drande, whom he had married in 1855, and four of their five children died before him, and in later years too, personal misfortune continued to haunt him. In 1884, shortly after his appointment as Governor General of the Lebanon, his second wife Catherine Bonatti died of tuberculosis, as did his surviving daughter Roza in 1887.

Bardha de Témal, scènes de la vie albanaise, Paris 1890 (Bardha of Temal, scenes from Albanian life), is a French-language novel which Pashko Vasa published in Paris under the pseudonym of Albanus Albano the same year as Naim Frashëri's noted verse collection *Luletë e verësë* (The Flowers of spring) appeared in Bucharest. 'Bardha of Temal,' though not written in Albanian, is - after Sami Frashëri's much shorter prose work 'Love of Tal'at and Fitnat' - the oldest novel written and published by an Albanian and is certainly the oldest such novel with an Albanian theme. Set in Shkodra in 1842, this classically-structured *roman-feuilleton*, rather excessively sentimental for modern tastes, follows the tribulations of the fair but married Bardha and her lover, the young Aradi. It was written not only as an entertaining love story but also with a view to informing the western reader of the customs and habits of the northern Albanians. Indeed the rather strained informative character of this prose fable is one of its major artistic weaknesses. Bardha is no doubt the personification of Albania itself, married off against her will to the powers that be. Above and beyond its didactic character and any possible literary pretensions the author might have had, 'Bardha of Temal' also has a more specific political background. It was interpreted by some Albanian intellectuals at the time as a vehicle for discrediting the Gjonmarkaj clan who, in cahoots with the powerful abbots of Mirdita, held sway in the Shkodra region. It is for this reason perhaps that Pashko Vasa published the novel under the pseudonym Albanus Albano. The work is not known to have had any particular echo in the French press of the period.

Though most of Pashko Vasa's publications were in French and Italian, there is one poem, the most influential and perhaps the most popular poem ever written in Albanian, which has ensured him his deserved place in Albanian literary history, the famous *O moj Shqypni* (Oh Albania, poor Albania). This stirring appeal for a national awakening is thought to have been written in the period between 1878, the dramatic year of the League of Prizren, and 1880. It was first published by Czech linguist Jan Urban Jarnik (1848-1923) in 1881[84]. Another copy of the 72-line poem, which begins *Mori Shqypni*, was found in the De Rada archives of the Biblioteca Civica in Cosenza in September 1975 and was thought for a time to have been in Pashko Vasa's handwriting. Upon closer inspection, however, this version, which was sent to Girolamo De Rada in 1881, turned out to be in the handwriting of Sami Frashëri. A third version of the poem has been found in the archives of Thimi Mitko in Alexandria[85]. It is the Jarnik version we quote here in its entirety:

> "*O moj Shqypni, e mjera Shqypni,*
> *Kush të ka qit me krye n'hi?*
> *Ti ke pas ken nji zoj e rand,*
> *Burrat e dheut të thirshin nan.*
> *Ke pas shum t'mira e shum begati,*
> *Me varza t'bukra e me djelm t'ri.*
> *Gja e vend shum, ara e bashtina,*
> *Me arm të bardha e me pushk ltina,*
> *Me burra trima e me gra t'dlira*
> *Ti ndër gjith shoqet ke ken ma e mira.*
>
> *Kur kriste pushka si me shkrep moti,*
> *Zogu i Shqyptarit gjithmonë i zoti*
> *Ka ken për luft e n'luft ka dekun*
> *E dhunë mprapa kurr s'i ka metun.*
> *Kur ka lidh besën burri i Shqypnis,*
> *I ka shti dridhën gjith Rumelis;*
> *Ndër lufta t'rrebta gjithkund ka ra,*
> *Me faqe t'bardh gjithmon asht da.*
>
> *Por sot, Shqypni, po m'thuej, si je?*
> *Por sikur lisi rrxuem për dhe!*
> *Shkon, bota sipri, me kamb e shklet,*
> *E nji fjal t'ambël kurrkush s'ia flet.*
> *Si mal me bor, si fush me lule,*
> *Ke pas ken veshun, sot je me crule*
> *E nuk t'ka metun as emn as bes,*
> *Vet e ke prishun për faqe t'zez.*

---

[84] cf. J. Jarnik 1881, p. 3-6.
[85] cf. J. Bulo 1986.

Shqyptar, me vllazën jeni t'u vra,
Ndër nji qind çeta jeni shpërnda;
Sa thon kam fe, sa thon kam din,
Njeni: jam turk, tjetri: latin
Do thom: jam grek, shkje disa tjerë,
Por jeni vllazën, t'gjith, more t'mjer!
Priftnit e hoxhët ju kan hutue,
Për me ju da e me ju vorfnue.
Vjen njeri i huej e ju rri n'votër,
Me ju turpnue me grue e me motër;
E për sa pare qi do t'fitoni,
Besën e t'parëve t'gjith e harroni,
Baheni robt e njerit t'huej,
Qi nuk ka gjuhën as gjakun tuej.

Kjani ju shpata e ju dyfeqe,
Shqyptari u zu si zok ndër leqe!
Kjani ju trima, bashk me ne,
Se ra Shqypnija me faqe n'dhe,
E s'i ka metun as buk as mish,
As zjarm në votër as drit as pish,
As gjak në faqe as nder ndër shok,
Por asht rrëxue e bamun trok!

Mblidhnju ju varza, mblidhnju ju gra,
Me ata sy t'bukur q'dini me kja,
Eni t'vajtojm Shqypnin e mjer
Qi met e shkret pa emn, pa nder,
Ka met e vej si grue pa burr,
Ka met si nan qi s'pat djal kurr!

Kujt i ban zemra me e lan me dek
Két far trimneshet qi sot asht mek?
Két nan të dashtun e do ta lam,
Qi njeri i huej ta shklas me kamb?

Jo! jo! Két marre askush s'e do,
Két faqe t'zez gjithkush e dro!
Para se t'hupet kështu Shqypnija,
Me pushk në dor le t'des trimnija.

Çonju, shqyptar, prej gjumit çonju,
Të gjith si vllazën n'nji bes shtrëngonju,
E mos shikjoni kish e xhamija,
Feja e shqyptarit asht shqyptarija!

Qysh prej Tivarit deri n'Prevezë,
Gjithkund lshon dielli vap edhe rrezë,
Asht tok e jona, t'part na e kan lan,
Kush mos na e preki, se desim t'tan!
Desim si burrat qi diqne motit
E mos turpnohna përpara Zotit!"

(Oh Albania, poor Albania,
Who has shoved your head in the ashes?
Once you were a great lady,
The men of the world called you mother.
Once you had such goodness and such wealth,
With fair maidens and youthful men,
Herds and land, fields and produce,
With flashing weapons, with Italian rifles,
With heroic men, with pure women,
You were the best of companions.

At the rifle's blast, at lightning's flash
The Albanian was always master
In battle, and in battle he died
Leaving never a misdeed behind him.
Whenever an Albanian swore an oath
The whole of the Balkans trembled before him,
Everywhere he charged into savage battle,
And always did he return a victor.

But today, Albania, tell me, how are you faring now?
Like an oak tree, felled to the ground!
The world walks over you, tramples you underfoot,
And no one has a kind word for you.
Like the snow-covered mountains, like blooming fields
You were clothed, today you are in rags.
Neither your reputation nor your oaths remain,
You have destroyed them in your own misfortune.

Albanians, you are killing your brothers,
Into a hundred factions you are divided,
Some say 'I believe in God,' others 'I in Allah,'
Some say 'I am Turk,' others 'I am Latin,'
Some 'I am Greek,' others 'I am Slav,'
But you are brothers, all of you, my hapless people!
The priests and the hodjas have deceived you
To divide you and keep you poor.
When the foreigner comes, you sit back at the hearth
As he puts you to shame with your wife and your sister,
And for how little money you are willing to serve him,
Forgetting the oaths of your ancestors,
Making yourselves serfs to the foreigners
Who have neither your language nor your blood!

Weep, oh swords and rifles,
The Albanian has been snared like a bird in a trap!
Weep with us, oh heroes,
For Albania has fallen with her face in the dirt.
Neither bread nor meat remain,
Neither fire in her hearth, nor light, nor pine torch,
Neither blood in her cheeks, nor honour among friends,
For she has fallen and is defiled!

Gather round, maidens, gather round, women
Who with your fair eyes know what weeping is,
Come, let us lament poor Albania,
Who is without honour and reputation,
She has become a widow, a woman with no husband,
She is like a mother who has never had a son!

Who has the heart to let her die,
Once such a heroine, and today so weak?
This beloved mother, are we to abandon her
To be trampled underfoot by the foreigners?

No, no! No one wishes such shame,
All dread such misfortune!
Before Albania is thus forlorn
Let all our heroes perish with rifle in hand.

Awaken, Albania, wake from your slumber,
Let us all, as brothers, swear a common oath
And not look to church or mosque,
The faith of the Albanian is Albanianism!

From Bar down to Preveza
Everywhere let the sun spend its warmth and rays,
This is our land, left to us by our forefathers,
Let no one touch us for we are all to die!
Let us die like men as our forefathers once did
And not bring shame upon ourselves before God!)

Pashko Vasa plays heavily on the sentiments of his Albanian reader here by comparing Albania to an 'oak tree, felled to the ground' or what is more, to a *zoj e rand* (great lady) now defiled and raped by the foreigners. He also stresses the divisive nature of religion among his people and proclaims: *Feja e shqyptarit asht shqyptarija* (The faith of the Albanian is Albanianism) which was to become a catchword of Albanian nationalists both in the Rilindja period and later.

Dom Ndoc Nikaj[86] (1864-1951), prose writer and publisher from northern Albania, has been called the father of the Albanian novel. Nikaj studied at the Jesuit *Kolegjia Papnore Shqyptare* (Albanian Pontifical Seminary) in Shkodra, was ordained in 1888 and subsequently worked as a parish priest in the Shkreli mountains. From an early age, he too devoted his energy to the nationalist movement to free his people from foreign occupation. Together with Preng Doçi (1846-1917), he founded the *Lidhja e mshehët* (The Secret League) which prepared the way for the uprising that began on 25 March 1910. He was also a member of the *Bashkimi* (Unity) Literary Society of Shkodra. Using the pseudonym *Nakdo Monici*, he also collaborated actively in Faik Konitza's noted periodical *Albania*, published in Brussels and later in London. As a publisher himself, Nikaj began his career by founding, in January 1910, the weekly newspaper *Koha* (The Time), the self-proclaimed mission of which was to 'deal with the affairs of the nation and of knowledge.' In the second edition, he changed the name of the newspaper to *Bashkimi* (Unity), no doubt to emphasize its affinities to the *Bashkimi* (Unity) Literary Society. This four-page journal in Albanian carried articles on politics, social affairs, culture, literature and the economy, and lasted until ca. 1912. In the spring of 1913, Ndoc Nikaj founded another newspaper, the *Besa Shqyptare*

---

[86] cf. H. Lacaj 1963; A. Plasari 1991d; and Gj. Kola 1997.

(The Albanian pledge), which was published two to four times a week until 1921. It also carried some articles in German and Italian. From 29 July 1915, for a short period, this same journal was called *Zani i Shkodërs* (The Voice of Shkodra). In addition to running newspapers, Ndoc Nikaj also had his own small publishing company, the *Shtypshkroja Nikaj* (Nikaj Press), founded in 1909, at which many of his own works and those of others were published. Here he printed Albanian-language readers, periodicals such as *Hylli i dritës* (The Day-star) and dozens of other works. Although the publishing company was not a financial success, businessman Nikaj was able to compensate for the loss with profits earned in other more lucrative fields such as lumber and gunrunning. After the First World War, Nikaj turned increasingly to writing, and published both educative works for schools, religious works for the church, and some literary prose. In 1921, he was arrested and spent forty-six days in Tirana prison for reasons unknown, and ceased writing about 1924. Little is known of his personal life in later years until the end of World War II. In 1946, during the persecution of the Catholic clergy in northern Albania at the end of the Second World War, Dom Ndoc Nikaj was arrested by the communists, at the age of eighty-two, on the absurd charge of 'planning to overthrow the government with violence,' and died in Shkodra prison in 1951 - a tragic end to a great figure of Albanian culture.

Among Nikaj's educational, religious and didactic publications of note are the 320-page *Vakinat e scêites kisc*, Rome 1888 (History of the holy church); *Bleta nner lule t'Parrizit*, Shkodra 1899 (The Bee amongst the flowers of paradise); the 416-page *Historia é Shcypniis*, Brussels 1902, Shkodra 1917 (History of Albania); the translation of an Italian-language history of Turkey, *Historia e Turkiis*, London 1902 (History of Turkey), which served as a school textbook, and other ecclesiastical works.

In the realm of creative literature, Nikaj is the author of numerous, now rare volumes of prose in the main, though some dramatic works, the best known of which are the novelettes: *Marzia e ksctenimi n'filles t'vet*, Shkodra 1892 (Marzia and the origins of Christianity); *Fejesa n'djep a se Ulqini i mârrun*, Shkodra 1913 (Marriage in the cradle or Ulcinj captured); and *Shkodra e rrethueme*, Shkodra 1913 (Shkodra under siege). The latter is a history, in the form of a short novel, of the siege of Shkodra during the 1912 Balkan war. Other works include the historical love tales *Bukurusha*, Shkodra 1918 (The Beautiful maiden), set in the years 1478-1479; *Lulet në thes*, Shkodra 1920 (The Flowers in a bag), set in the years 1830-1833; *Burbuqja*, Shkodra 1920 (The Little girl), set in the years 1815-1817; and the play for girls *Motra per vllàn*, Shkodra 1921 (The Sister for her brother). Though Nikaj was able to publish all his later works at his own printing press, he seems to have done so in extremely limited editions, with the result that his works are very difficult to come by nowadays. Only *Shkodra e rrethueme* (Shkodra under siege) and *Bukurusha* (The Beautiful maiden) were reprinted after his death. The reticence to publish more of the author often known as the 'father of the Albanian novel' was no doubt linked to embarrassment on the part of the communist authorities in Tirana about his tragic end.

It is certain that Ndoc Nikaj made a significant contribution to the development of Albanian prose, which was still in its infancy at the beginning of the twentieth century. As to the novel, which is usually rather vaguely defined as a prose work of over two hundred pages, Nikaj's books would not seem to qualify. Up until this period in literary history, there had been no novels published in Albanian at all. The only 'Albanian' novels to speak of had either been written in foreign languages, such as Sami Frashëri's Turkish-language *Taaşşuk-u Tal'at ve Fitnat* (The Love of Tal'at and Fitnat) published in 1872 and Pashko Vasa's French-language *Bardha de Témal, scènes de la vie albanaise*, Paris 1890 (Bardha of Temal, scenes from Albanian life), or remained unpublished, such as Francesco Antonio Santori's unfinished 282-page *Sofia Kominiate*. It is only when more of Nikaj's works are readily available that critics will be in a position to judge whether the epithet 'father of the Albanian novel' has any justification. A more precise term in the meantime would be 'father of twentieth-century Gheg prose.'

Also from Shkodra was **Luigj Gurakuqi**[87] (1879-1925), a writer and major political figure of the Rilindja movement in northern Albania. Born on 19 February 1879, Gurakuqi studied at the Saverian College run by the Jesuits in his native Shkodra, one of the best schools in the country at the time. Encouraged by his teachers Anton Xanoni (1862-1915) and Gaspër Jakova Merturi (1870-1941), he began writing poetry in Italian, Latin and Albanian, the latter published in the Jesuit periodical of religious culture, *Elçija i Zemers t'Jezu Krisctit* (The Messenger of the Sacred Heart). In 1897, he left for Italy to study at the Italo-Albanian college of San Demetrio Corone under Girolamo De Rada (1814-1903), who was to exercise a strong influence on him. He also studied medicine in Naples for three years, but his interests were focussed more on science and the humanities. In Naples he came into contact with Arbëresh literary and political figures such as poet and scholar Giuseppe Schirò (1865-1927), and collaborated in the Italo-Albanian periodicals *La Nazione albanese* (The Albanian nation), published by Anselmo Lorecchio and *La nuova Albania* (New Albania), published by Gennaro Lusi. It was also in Naples that Luigj Gurakuqi published Albanian school texts and a book on prosody.

---

[87] cf. H. Lacaj 1959; G. Gradilone 1974, p. 149-216; S. Pollo 1979; and P. Tako 1988.

In 1908, after the revolution of the Young Turks, Gurakuqi returned definitively to Albania and soon became a prominent figure in the nationalist movement which led to the country's independence in 1912. In November 1908, together with Gjergj Fishta, he represented the *Bashkimi* (Unity) Literary Society of Shkodra at the Congress of Monastir. Gurakuqi served as vice-chairman of this congress and was elected to the resulting committee which had the difficult task of deciding upon a definitive Albanian alphabet. In September 1909 he attended the Congress of Elbasan which was held to organize Albanian-language teaching and education. When Albania's first teacher-training college, the *Shkolla Normale* (Normal School), was set up in Elbasan on 1 December 1909, it was Luigj Gurakuqi who was appointed to be its director. Gurakuqi was also one of the leaders of the northern Albanian uprising around Shkodra in 1911 and, together with Ismail Qemal bey Vlora (1844-1919), who was later to become the first prime minister of Albania, he sent a twelve-point memorandum to the Turkish government in June 1911 demanding Albanian independence. He took part in the uprising in southern Albania in 1912, and travelled in March of that year to Skopje and Gjakova to stir up support for open resistance to Turkish rule and for the inclusion of Kosova in a new Albanian state. Gurakuqi was involved in the declaration of Albanian independence in Vlora on 28 November 1912 and served as minister of education in the first Albanian government, headed by Ismail Qemal bey Vlora. In 1915, when his native Shkodra was occupied by Montenegrin troops, Gurakuqi was taken prisoner and jailed in Montenegro until after the invasion of Austro-Hungarian forces. In 1916, he played a role in the Albanian Literary Commission (*Komisija Letrare Shqype*) on Albanian orthography which also served to encourage the publication of Albanian-language school texts. During the Austro-Hungarian occupation of Shkodra, he served as director-general of education and assisted in establishing about two hundred elementary schools. In 1918, Gurakuqi was again appointed minister of education in the newly-formed Durrës government. The following year, he travelled to Paris to attend the peace conference which confirmed the existence of the new Albanian state, though Albanian territory in Kosova and southern Yugoslavia had not been included. In 1921 he was appointed minister of the interior in the government of Hasan bey Prishtina (1873-1933), and in 1924 minister of finance in the short-lived government of Fan Noli (1882-1965). In August of 1924, Gurakuqi travelled to Geneva to defend Albanian interests at the League of Nations, but with the overthrow of Fan Noli's democratic administration by the more authoritarian forces of Ahmet Zogu (1895-1961), he was forced to flee to Italy and was murdered in Bari on 2 March 1925 by one Baltjon Stambolla, no doubt an agent of Zogu.

Luigj Gurakuqi served the national cause not only by playing an active role in public life but also by contributing informative articles to a good number of Albanian periodicals. He was, in addition, the author of both didactic and educational works and of poetry, much of which he published under the pseudonyms Lek Gruda and Jakin Shkodra. Gurakuqi also arranged with his Naples publishers, Tocco and Salvietti, for a third edition of Giuseppe Schirò's masterful love idyll *Mili e Haidhia*, Naples 1907 (Mili and Haidhia), for which he wrote an introduction and which he considered one of the finest works of Albanian literature.

Gurakuqi's own poetry is somewhat less inspiring. A collection of his verse, imbued with the strong patriotic emotion and sentimentality of romantic nationalism, was published posthumously in the 94-page *Vjersha*, Bari 1940 (Verse) by Gjikam, pseudonym of Gjon Kamsi. Though it contains much lively imagery, including moving descriptions of the seasons, of storms and of the cloud-hung mountain crags in his homeland, it often lacks melody and rhythm. Gurakuqi did have a talent for language, but he was not a sophisticated poet.

Gurakuqi is said to have had a good knowledge of many Albanian dialects and, had he devoted more of his time to literature, he would no doubt have enriched the literary language substantially. In view of the tempestuous course of Albanian history in the first two decades of the twentieth century, however, it is not surprising that he gave preference to political and patriotic activities over the abstract pleasures of creative writing. Shkodra has, at any rate, always been proud of Luigj Gurakuqi and, on 29 May 1991, it named the newly founded university there after this great figure.

4.4   The Significance of Rilindja Literature

It can be asserted without any hesitation that the Rilindja period was one of inestimable significance for Albania's political and cultural survival. In its political history, Albania evolved from an obscure and primitive backwater of the Ottoman Empire to take its place among the nation-states of Europe. Through its literature and cultural history, this age of 'rebirth' created an awareness for national identity and made the Albanian language the matter-of-course vehicle of literary and cultural expression for the Albanian people.

The Rilindja age of Albanian literature, primarily determined by the course of Albanian history, is in actual fact a period that is difficult to date precisely. The League of Prizren, held in 1878, is considered, by general consensus, to mark the beginning of the Rilindja period, although the preliminary stages of the national and cultural awakening can be traced back to the first half of the nineteenth century. The declaration of Albanian independence in November 1912 provides a convenient date for a conclusion, but as a literary movement the Rilindja period continued unabated well into the years of Albania's rather shaky and uncertain independence. We can indeed speak of Rilindja authors up to the 1930s.

It was the Rilindja period, more than any other, which moulded Albanian literature and determined many of its subsequent characteristics. What followed in the independence years up until the Second World War was, to a large extent, simply the growth and refinement of a sturdy and thriving plant rooted in the blood-stained soil of that troubled and decisive age. Rilindja literature thus laid the foundations for the development of modern Albanian literature, not only in journalism and poetry, the *élan vital* of the period, but also in prose, drama and essays, which for the first time evolved into solid if not overly sophisticated literary genres.

The influence of Rilindja poets, publicists and writers on the course of Albanian literature and culture was fundamental. Nonetheless, if we ask ourselves objectively whether there were any Rilindja writers of genuine literary quality equivalent to that of the more sophisticated *belles lettres* of late nineteenth-century England, France, Germany or Russia, we should probably answer no. Albanian literature in this period was characterized by vigorous and unprecedented development, but it was not one upon which the Muses had bestowed their kiss. No literary genre could attain refinement in an indigent and largely illiterate country devoid of urban culture. Albanian-language theatre, as yet in its infancy, consisted for the most part of tear-jerking melodramas not to be taken seriously, and, with some exceptions, literary prose was not much better. Nor did poetry itself, always the mainstay of Albanian letters, betray much lyrical or stylistic inspiration in this age, even though the themes of romantic nationalism when seen within the context of Albania's arduous political and social development, can be moving for any reader with a sense of comprehension and compassion for a nation treated so unfairly by history. Twentieth-century Albania cannot be comprehended without an understanding of the Rilindja period and its culture.

5. Writing in the Independence Period (early 20th cent. to 1944)

5.1 Poets of Transition: A. Z. Çajupi, Ndre Mjeda and Asdreni

What effect did Albanian independence have upon literature? Initially none at all. The first decade of independence from the proclamation in Vlora in 1912 to the rise of dictator Ahmet Zogu in the early twenties was marked by extreme political turmoil, bloodshed and starvation in Albania. The formal political goal of the nationalist movement, i.e. independence, had been achieved, and Albanian had become the official language of the country, but the continuing political chaos gave writers and intellectuals within the country little time to reflect on new dimensions for a national culture. The Rilindja culture of romantic nationalism, deeply ingrained in Albanian literature, continued to make its influence felt throughout the independence period.

The continuity of ideas and aspirations expressed in Albanian writing was, however, soon to achieve a much higher degree of sophistication than was ever attained in the Rilindja literature of the late nineteenth century. Writing in Albanian ceased to constitute simply a patriotic act of defiance against foreign cultural hegemony and Albanian intellectuals began, perhaps for the first time, to see that the possibilities for literary and cultural development were unlimited. The Catholic education facilities set up in the second half of the nineteenth century by the Franciscans and Jesuits in Shkodra, and, after independence, Albanian-language schooling throughout the country, had paved the way for the creation of an intellectual elite in Albania and bore fruit by the twenties. The literature produced by this slender stratum of intellectuals, educated in their own language and culture, expressed itself once again primarily in poetry, although virtually all literary genres made their appearance.

The independence period saw the rise of three poets who strongly reflected the continuity of Rilindja culture. They were Andon Zako Çajupi in Egypt, Ndre Mjeda in Shkodra and Asdreni in Romania.

Andon Zako Çajupi[88] (1866-1930) was born on 27 March 1866 in Sheper, a village in the Upper Zagoria region of southern Albania, as the son of a rich tobacco merchant, Harito Çako, who did business in Kavala, now in Greece, and Egypt. The young Andon Zako, who usually preferred this spelling of his surname and was later to adopt the pseudonym Çajupi, attended Greek-language schools in the region and in 1882 emigrated to Egypt where he studied for five years at the French lycée 'Sainte Catherine des Lazaristes' in Alexandria. In 1887, he went on to study law at the University of Geneva. Çajupi completed his law degree on 24 October 1892 and remained in Switzerland for two or three more years where he married a girl named Eugénie and where his son Stefan was born. Eugénie died in about 1892, a tragic loss for the poet, and Çajupi returned to Kavala to leave his small son in the charge of his mother Zoica. About 1894-1895, Çajupi returned to Egypt and articled for three years with a German law firm in Cairo. His legal career came to a swift conclusion, however, when he made the strategic mistake of defending a French company in a dispute against the interests of the khedive. Financially independent, however, Çajupi bore this professional calamity with ease. He withdrew to his villa in Heliopolis near Cairo and devoted himself subsequently to literature and to the consolidation of the thriving Albanian nationalist movement in Egypt. In the years following Albanian independence, Çajupi played an active role in the Albanian community on the Nile, organized as it was in various patriotic clubs and societies at odds with one another over political issues. The poet died at his home in Heliopolis on 11 July 1930. His remains were transferred to Albania in 1958.

The most significant phase of Çajupi's literary and nationalist activities was from 1898 to 1912. By 1902 he was an active member of the Albanian Fraternity of Egypt (*Vëllazëria e Egjiptit*) and that same year published the poetry volume for which he is best remembered: *Baba-Tomorri*, Cairo 1902 (Father Tomorr). This collection, named after Mount Tomorr in central Albania, the Parnassus of Albanian mythology, contains light verse on mostly nationalist themes and is divided into three sections: 1) Fatherland, 2) Love, and 3) True and False Tales. The work was an immediate success. Indeed no volume of Albanian poetry had proven so popular among Albanians at home and abroad since the collections of Naim Frashëri. Çajupi did not confine himself to the romantic nostalgia of earlier poets in exile. Nationalist he was, but he was also aware of the dreary realities of life in his homeland. One of the most memorable ballads in this collection, *Fshati im* (My village), focusses for instance on the inequalities of patriarchal society:

---

[88] cf. Gj. Zheji 1966; Dh. Shuteriqi 1977, p. 373-417; and F. Dado 1983.

"Maletë me gurë,
Fushat me bar shumë,
Aratë me grurë,
Më tutje një lumë.

Fshati për karshi
Me kish' e me varre,
Rrotull ca shtëpi
Të vogëla fare.

Ujëtë të ftohtë,
Era pun' e madhe,
Bilbili ia thotë,
Gratë si zorkadhe.

Burrat nënë hie,
Lozin, kuvendojnë,
Pika që s'u bie,
Se nga gratë rrojnë!..."

(The mountains rich in stone,
The meadows full of grass,
The fields replete with wheat,
Beyond them is a river.

Across from it the village
With church and rows of gravestones,
And standing all around it
Are humble, tiny houses.

Frigid is the water,
The wind blows, but no matter,
The nightingale proclaims it:
Gazelle-like are the women.

Lying in the shade, men
Playing, busy chatting,
Misfortune cannot strike them,
For they're living off their women...)

Though by far the most significant volume of verse in the early years of the twentieth century, *Baba-Tomorri* was not Çajupi's only publication. In 1921, he translated 113 fables of La Fontaine (1621-1695) in *Perralla*, Heliopolis 1920-1921 (Fables), and soon thereafter a selection of Sanskrit verse, *Lulé te Hindit*, Cairo 1922 (The Flowers of India), which he had adapted from a French anthology and dedicated to Faik bey Konitza (1875-1942). His other poetic works remained unpublished during his lifetime. Among these are the delightful 6,000-line satirical poem *Dhiat' é vjéter é chfacure* (Old Testament revealed), also known as *Baba Musa lakuriq* (Naked father Moses), which was written about 1903-1905 and is based on Old Testament history.

Though there are many technical imperfections in his poems, their straightforward octosyllabic rhythms reminiscent of southern Albanian folk songs, their unequivocal messages and their patriotic inspiration made them extremely popular both with adults and children, and proclaimed Çajupi the most important Albanian poet since Naim Frashëri.

Çajupi was also a playwright, author of a verse tragedy on Scanderbeg entitled *Burr' i dheut* (The Earthly hero) written in 1907. This was followed by a one-act original comedy *Pas vdekjes* (After death), written in 1910 and printed, like the former play, in 1937 by Sofokli Çapi. Another drama in verse, which remained unpublished during his lifetime, was the four-act situation comedy *Katërmbëdhjetë vjeç dhëndër* (A Bridegroom at fourteen). None of these dramatic works, written when Albanian theatre was in its infancy, is particularly inspiring by modern standards. Çajupi's play *Detyra* (Duty) has been lost, as has his poetry collection *Kenge dhé vomé* (Songs and laments), subtitled 'verse of the Great War of 1914.' Minor works by the author include two short stories written in French, an editorial on the 'Salonika Club' published in August 1909 in Jani Vruho's Cairo monthly *Rrufeja* (The Lightning), and some correspondence with Vissar Dodani (ca. 1857-1939), Jani Vruho (1863-1931) and Asdreni.

Çajupi was by no means a modern poet. His 'Weltanschauung' was too linked to the struggle of the nationalist movement and to Rilindja culture in general. At the same time, if one compares his verse to that of Naim Frashëri, one sees a definite evolution. This progression towards a sovereign culture for a sovereign nation becomes more apparent in the works of his northern Albanian contemporary Ndre Mjeda of Shkodra who was to have a far more extensive influence on early twentieth-century Albanian culture.

Like Çajupi, classical poet **Ndre Mjeda**[89] (1866-1937) bridges the gap between late nineteenth-century Rilindja culture and the dynamic literary creativity of the independence period. Mjeda was born on 20 November 1866 in Shkodra and, like so many other Gheg writers of the period, was educated by the Jesuits. Influential in his upbringing were Jesuit writer Anton Xanoni (1863-1915) and the Franciscan poet Leonardo De Martino (1830-1923). The Society of Jesus sent the young Mjeda abroad for studies and training. He spent an initial three months in the spring of 1880 in the village of Cossé-le-Vivien near Laval in the west of France and thereafter attended a college at the Carthusian monastery of Porta Coeli north of Valencia, Spain, where he studied literature. In 1883, we find him in Croatia studying rhetoric, Latin and Italian at a Jesuit institution in Kraljevica on the Dalmatian coast. From 1884 to the beginning of 1887, he trained at a college there which was run by the Gregorian University of Rome and in 1887 transferred to another Gregorian college in Chieri, southeast of Turin, where he remained until the end of that year.

It was during these years that Ndre Mjeda began writing verse in Albanian, including the melancholic and much read poem *Vaji i bylbylit* (The Nightingale's lament), published in 1887 in the booklet *Scahiri Elierz* (The Honorable poet), expressing his longing for his native Albania. Also of this period is the poem *Vorri i Skanderbegut* (Scanderbeg's grave). The theme of the exiled Albanian yearning nostalgically for his homeland under the Turkish yoke was nothing unusual in Rilindja literature, in particular in the decade following the defeat of the League of Prizren, and many of his other poems are devoted to such nationalist themes. In Mjeda's verse, however, we sense the influence not only of the Rilindja culture of the age, but also that of his mentor Leonardo De Martino, the Scutarine Catholic poet whose refined 442-page bilingual verse collection *L'Arpa di un italo-albanese* (The Harp of an Italo-Albanian) had appeared in Venice in 1881. An equally important component in Mjeda's verse were the contemporary poets of Italy: the patriotic Giosuè Carducci (1835-1907), the pensive Giovanni Pascoli (1855-1912) and the sensuous Gabriele D'Annunzio (1863-1938), as well as the Latin literature of classical antiquity.

From 1887 to 1891, Mjeda taught music at the College of Marco Girolamo Vida in Cremona on the River Po, the city of composer Claudio Monteverdi and of Antonio Stradivari. There and in Soresina he continued writing verse and at the same time devoted himself to the translation of religious literature. In 1888, the Propaganda Fide in Rome published his *Jeta*

---

[89] cf. G. Gradilone 1960, p. 162-206; Dh. Shuteriqi 1963; M. Gurakuqi 1967, 1980; R. Idrizi 1980; R. Qosja, 1884-1886, vol. 3, p. 427-510; and M. Quku 1990, 2004.

e sceitit sc' Gnon Berchmans (The Life of St John Berchmans) about a Jesuit saint from Brabant, and in 1892, *T' perghjamit e Zojs Bekume* (Imitation of the Holy Virgin) translated from Spanish. In later years he was to publish a translation of the *Katekizmi i madh* (The Great catechism) in three volumes, *Historia e shejtë* (Sacred history), and a life of St Aloysius of Gonzaga.

From 1891, Mjeda studied for several years at the theological faculty of a Gregorian college in Kraków in Catholic Poland. It was there that he became acquainted with the philological works of linguists Gustav Meyer (1850-1900) and Holger Pedersen (1867-1953). Mjeda's poem *Gjûha shqype* (The Albanian language), written in December 1892, was dedicated to the Austrian scholar Meyer, whose monumental *Etymologisches Wörterbuch der albanesischen Sprache* (Etymological Dictionary of the Albanian language) had been published earlier that year in Strasbourg. The works of Meyer and Pedersen awakened in Mjeda a fascination for the history and development of the Albanian language, an interest he was to pursue in later years with his contribution to the alphabet problem, with his school texts and with his studies on the early Catholic authors Pjetër Budi and Pjetër Bogdani. In 1893, we find the poet in Gorizia on the Italian-Slovene border and in the following year back in Kraljevica where he taught philosophy and philology and served as librarian at the Gregorian college. He was subsequently appointed professor of logic and metaphysics. It was in 1898 that a conflict is said to have broken out among the Jesuits of Kraljevica, apparently concerning their loyalties to Austria-Hungary and the Vatican. The exact details of the scandal are not known, but Ndre Mjeda was somehow involved and was promptly expelled or resigned that year from the Jesuit Order.

In 1899, with the assistance of his brother Lazër Mjeda, Bishop of Sappa since 1896 and later Archbishop of Prizren and Archbishop of Shkodra, and in particular of Preng Doçi, the influential Abbot of Mirdita and a nationalist poet himself, Ndre Mjeda was given a teaching position in Vig in the mountainous Mirdita region. He also participated initially in the activities of the *Bashkimi* (Unity) Literary Society which had been founded that year in Shkodra with Austro-Hungarian support by Preng Doçi, Ndoc Nikaj and Gjergj Fishta. In 1901, due to differing opinions on the alphabet question, Ndre and Lazër Mjeda founded an alternative organization, the *Agimi* (Dawn) Literary Society, which encouraged the use of Albanian in school texts and literature, and which supported a spelling system using Croatian as a model. It was in this alphabet that Ndre Mjeda and Anton Xanoni published a number of readers for Albanian schools, among them *Këndimet për shkollat e para të Shqypnisë* (Readings for the elementary schools of Albania) that contained a number of prose texts written by Mjeda. In early September 1902, Mjeda was invited to Hamburg to participate at the 13th International Congress of Orientalists and read a paper there entitled *De pronunciatione palatalium in diversis albanicae linguae dialectis* (On the pronunciation of palatals in various dialects of the Albanian language). Mjeda's passionate interest in the Albanian alphabet question led, in addition to problems with the Ottoman authorities, to his participation at the Congress of Monastir in 1908 at which his *Agimi* alphabet lost out to Gjergj Fishta's *Bashkimi* alphabet. Mjeda was a member of the Literary Commission set up in Shkodra on 1 September 1916 under the Austro-Hungarian administration, and from 1920 to 1924 he served as a deputy in the National Assembly. After the defeat of Fan Noli's June Revolution at the end of 1924 and the definitive rise of the Zogu dictatorship he withdrew from politics and served as a parish priest in Kukël, a village between Shkodra and Shëngjin. From 1930, he taught Albanian language and literature at the Jesuit college in Shkodra, where he died on 1 August 1937.

Mjeda's poetry, in particular his collection *Juvenilia*, Vienna 1917 (Juvenilia), is noted for its classical style and for its purity of language. It is probably no coincidence that the title of this work for which Mjeda is best remembered is the same as Giosuè Carducci's lyric volume *Iuvenilia* which was published almost half a century earlier. Mjeda's *Juvenilia* includes not only original poetry but also adaptations of foreign verse by Tommaso Grossi (1790-1853), Giuseppe Capparozzo (1802-1848), Charles Wolfe (1791-1823) and Johann Wolfgang von Goethe (1749-1832). A second cycle of poetry begun by Mjeda was to be devoted to the ancient cities of Illyria: *Lissus* (Lezha), *Scodra* (Shkodra), *Dyrrachium* (Durrës) and *Apollonia* (Pojan). However, only the first two parts of this cycle ever saw the light of day. *Lissus*, composed of twelve sonnets, appeared in May 1921 in the Franciscan monthly *Hylli i Dritës* (The Day-star), and *Scodra* was published posthumously in 1939.

Though not covering an especially wide range of themes, Mjeda's poetry evinces a particularly refined language under the influence of the nineteenth-century Italian classics and, in general, a high level of metric finesse. Like Andon Zako Çajupi, he builds a bridge of transition between Rilindja literature and that of the independence period, but, also like Çajupi, remains firmly entrenched on the first side of the bridge, i.e. at the beginning of this transition.

In the early decades of national independence, Naim Frashëri continued to be a major source of inspiration and a guiding light for most Albanian poets and intellectuals. His influence is particularly evident in the early works of his Tosk compatriot **Asdreni**[90] (1872-1947), pseudonym of *Aleks Stavre Drenova*, who is at the same time the first poet of transition we can plant, so to speak, on

---

[90] For an extensive study of Asdreni, cf. R. Qosja 1972.

the other side of the bridge. Like his influential Rilindja predecessor, Asdreni spent very little of his life in Albania itself and was equally obsessed with his national identity.

Asdreni was born on 11 April 1872 in the village of Drenova, about five kilometers from Korça in southeastern Albania. He attended a Greek-language elementary school in his native village and had just begun high school in Korça when his widowed father Stavri Thimiu died, leaving the thirteen-year-old Aleks an orphan.

Throughout the nineteenth century, the Korça region had been a prime source of Albanian emigration. The powerful earthquake which struck the city in 1879 only increased the despair and, thus, the steady flow of workers and peasants fleeing their native land in search of jobs and a better life. A good number of these Albanian emigrants settled in Egypt, some went to Bulgaria and many later sailed to the United States, but the main destination of emigration from southeastern Albania in the nineteenth century was Romania, where a thriving Albanian colony arose. In the autumn of 1885, the thirteen and a half-year-old Aleks arrived in Bucharest to join his two elder brothers.

It was here in the culturally active Albanian colony that he first came into contact with the ideas and ideals of the nationalist movement in exile. In the summer of 1881, Jani Vreto (1820-1900) had travelled from Constantinople to Bucharest to found the Bucharest section of the *Shoqëri e të shtypuri shkronja shqip* (Society for the publication of Albanian writing) and set up the first Albanian-language press which began publishing books in 1886. It was also in the Romanian capital that the torchbearer of the nationalist movement, Naim Frashëri, first published the literary works which were to set the pace for late nineteenth-century Albanian literature. On 15 May 1887, the first edition of a weekly periodical entitled *Drita* (The Light) appeared in the town of Brăila on the lower Danube, to be followed the next year by the four-page *Shqipëtari/Albanezul* (The Albanian) published in Bucharest by the *Drita* Society. Its editor, Nikolla Naço (1843-1913) of Korça, Asdreni's mentor so to speak, was later to found an Albanian-Romanian cultural institute to train Albanian teachers. All in all, Bucharest was the place to be for Albanian nationalists of the period and the young Asdreni, despite initial poverty and hardship, thrived in this most cosmopolitan city of the Balkans, the 'Paris of the East,' with which Albania itself had nothing to compare.

Asdreni worked initially as a coal-boy and an apprentice, and later continued his studies, both privately and for a short time at the Faculty of Political Science of the University of Bucharest. In January 1899, he was among the founders of the *Qarku i studentëvet shqiptarë* (Circle of Albanian students) which in March 1902 transformed itself into the *Shpresa* (Hope) Society, founded by Asdreni and fellow writer Christo Anastas Dako (1878-

1941). In the summer of 1899 at the age of twenty-seven, the poet returned to Korça via Constantinople to see his homeland for the first time as an adult. After five months there in the rural atmosphere of his childhood, he returned to Bucharest knowing that his home was now in Romania. In 1905, Asdreni taught at an Albanian school in the port city of Constanza and the following year became president of the new Bucharest chapter of the *Dija* (Knowledge) Society, originally founded in Vienna. Inspired by the creation of an independent Albanian state, he set off for Durrës on the Adriatic in the spring of 1914 to welcome the country's newly chosen head of state, Prince Wilhelm zu Wied (1876-1945), from whom he hoped to obtain an appointment as an archivist in the new royal administration. It soon became apparent, however, that there would be little to administer and no need for his services at all. After a short visit to Shkodra, Asdreni returned to Bucharest in July 1914, as Europe prepared for war. In the following years, Asdreni continued to take an active interest in the Albanian national movement. He chose, nonetheless, to remain in Romania, and served as secretary at the Albanian consulate in Romania which opened in March 1922. He made another visit to Albania in November 1937 on the twenty-fifth anniversary of independence, hoping after many years of service to the Albanian state to receive a government pension. He spent some time in Tirana before visiting Shkodra where he met Gjergj Fishta in February 1938. From there he carried on to his native Drenova in the Korça valley. The chaos caused by the Italian invasion of Albania on Easter 1939 made it bitterly obvious to him that his hopes for a pension were in vain and he returned to Bucharest again in July of that year, as Europe prepared once more for war. Asdreni died in poverty on 11 December 1947 at the age of seventy-five.

It was in the early years of the twentieth century that Asdreni had begun writing poetry and publishing articles in the local press. In 1904, he published his first collection of ninety-nine poems, *Rézé djélli*, Bucharest 1904 (Sunbeams), which he dedicated to the Albanian national hero Scanderbeg. This volume was well received by Albanian readers and critics at the time and established Asdreni's reputation as a leading Albanian poet four years after the death of Naim Frashëri and one year after the death of Girolamo De Rada. Its themes are typically Rilindjan: nostalgia for the distant homeland and exhortations to his people to unite and rise against the Turkish occupants, but there was also tender verse on the beauties of nature as well as some philosophical lyrics in the style of Naim Frashëri. It was Asdreni's firm belief that poetry must contribute to a strengthening of national awareness and to showing the world that the Albanian language existed. Despite the popularity of the nationalist pathos to which he gave voice, the artistic value of Asdreni's verse in this early period was limited with regard both to his form of expression and to the profundity of his thought. It remained fine stirring verse for school anthologies.

Asdreni's second volume *Endra e lote*, Bucharest 1912 (Dreams and tears), published eight years later, displayed much greater maturity. This collection of ninety-nine poems, like the previous one, was divided into the cycles: fatherland, nature, thought and beauty, and was dedicated to the English traveller and friend of Albania, Edith Durham (1863-1944). Possessing a wider range of themes and motifs, and a much firmer command of the language, Asdreni now proved that his verse was more than simple nationalist propaganda.

The improvement in form, style and technique and the broadening of the range of themes and ideas are even more evident in Asdreni's third volume of verse, *Psallme murgu*, Bucharest 1930 (Psalms of a monk), published eighteen years after *Endra e lote*. *Psallme murgu*, the last collection Asdreni was able to publish himself, marks the zenith of his poetic creativity. Together with the two exquisite collections by Lasgush Poradeci (1899-1987), published in Romania in 1933 and 1937, and the slender volume of 'Free Verse,' 1936, by the young Migjeni (1911-1938), *Psallme murgu* also marks a turning point in Albanian literature. The distant horizon of modernity had been sighted.

In his final years of bitterness and destitution, the septuagenarian Asdreni prepared a fourth collection of verse, *Kambana e Krujës* (The Bell of Kruja), but never lived to see its publication. In this volume, the universal element fades and nationalist pathos once again dominates as it had in his first work, to the detriment of both the range of themes and the general level of artistry. In the aging poet's defence, it must be noted that Asdreni may not have put the final touches on many of the poems in this collection, which was first published by Rexhep Qosja in 1971. The lack of freshness and spontaneity is also perhaps a reflection of age.

As has been suggested, Asdreni was strongly influenced by Naim Frashëri and Rilindja culture, in particular in his first collection *Rézé djélli* (Sunbeams). His period of maturity is, however, more deeply attuned to the works of his Romanian predecessors and contemporaries. Living for most of his life in Bucharest, Asdreni was deeply affected by the currents of Romanian literature, which throughout the nineteenth century and in the early decades of the twentieth showed a much higher level of development and sophistication than did Albanian writing. Lasgush Poradeci, too, found the road to modernity on Romanian soil[91]. Not unlike the element of romantic nationalism in

---

[91] On Albanian-Romanian literary ties, cf. V. Bala 1964-1965; R. Qosja 1972, p. 262-268; G. Maksutovici 1992, 1995, and C. Maksutovici 1995.

Asdreni's early verse are the patriotic lyrics of Romanian poet and playwright Vasile Alecsandri (1821-1890). *Kënga e bashkimit* (The Song of unity) in the volume *Endra e lote* is indeed a clear adaptation of Alecsandri's *Hora unirii*, 1857 (The Dance of unity). Romanian national poet Mihai Eminescu (1850-1889) of course played a major role in the works of Asdreni, as in those of Lasgush Poradeci, not only with his pantheistic idealism but also with concrete elements of poetic vocabulary. The expression of Asdreni's strong social and political commitment is mirrored in the verse of Gheorghe Coşbuc (1866-1918), poet of the Romanian peasantry, whose powerful *Noi vrem pămînt*, 1894 (We want land), finds its reflection in Asdreni's poem *Zëri i kryengritësvet* (The Voice of the rebels) of 1912. The influence of Alexandru Macedonski (1854-1920), the father of Romanian symbolism, and of the audacious Tudor Arghezi (1880-1967) are most apparent in Asdreni's third collection, *Psallme murgu* (Psalms of a monk). Three years before the appearance of this work, ex-monk Arghezi had published his masterful lyric *Psalmul de taină*, 1927 (The Psalm of secrecy) and was also at the centre of a literary controversy raging in Romania at the time. The Albanian writers of Bucharest, foremost among whom were Asdreni, Lasgush Poradeci and Mitrush Kuteli, could not help but be influenced by the more cosmopolitan Romanian culture of the period. Under the influence of these contemporary Romanian poets, the universal cult of beauty now began to replace the often shallow exhortations of romantic nationalism in nineteenth-century Albanian verse and helped raise Albanian literature to an artistic level more befitting the culture of a European nation.

All in all, Asdreni was not what one might call a modern poet like Lasgush Poradeci or Migjeni, nor was he a sublime and truly great figure like Gjergj Fishta, but he did play a decisive role in setting Albanian verse on the path towards modernity. His collection *Psallme murgu* with its classical refinement is still considered by many to be one of the best volumes of Albanian verse published in the 20th century.

5.2   Masters of Finesse: Faik bey Konitza and Fan Noli

The most influential of all Albanian writers and publishers of the turn of the century was **Faik bey Konitza**[92] (1875-1942), also spelt Faik Konica. He was born in April 1875 in the now Greek village of Konitza in the Pindus mountains, not far from the present Albanian border. After elementary schooling in Turkish in his native village, he studied, though from a Muslim family, at the Jesuit Saverian College in Shkodra which offered him not only some instruction in Albanian, but also an initial contact with central European culture and Western ideas. From there, he continued his schooling at the French-language Imperial Galata secondary school in Constantinople. In 1890, at the age of fifteen, he was sent to study in France where he spent the next seven years. After initial education at secondary schools in Lisieux (1890) and Carcassonne (1892), he registered at the University of Dijon, from which he graduated in 1895 in Romance philology. After graduation, he moved to Paris for two years where he studied mediaeval French, Latin and Greek at the Collège de France. He finished his studies at Harvard University in the United States, although little is known about this period of his life. As a result of his highly varied educational background, he was able to speak and write Albanian, Italian, French, German, English and Turkish. Konitza's stay in France, a country of long-standing liberal democratic traditions, was to have a profound effect on him and he was able to acquire and adopt the patterns of Western thinking as no Albanian intellectual had ever done before him. The young Konitza was particularly marked by the uninhibited freedom which the French press enjoyed in the years of open and caustic debate sparked by the Dreyfus affair. It was during this period that he began to take an interest in his native language and his country's history and literature, and to write articles on Albania for a French newspaper. In 1897 he moved to Brussels, where at the age of twenty-two he founded the periodical *Albania*, which was soon to become the most important organ of the Albanian press at the turn of the century. He moved to London in 1902 and continued to publish the journal there until 1909. In London he made friends with French poet and critic Guillaume Apollinaire (1880-1918) who stayed with him in 1903 and 1904.

---

[92] cf. G. Petrotta 1932, p. 302-309; E. Koliqi 1967; N. Ressuli 1987, p. 65-81; S. Hamiti 1991; A. Karjagdiu 1993; J. Kastrati 1995; M. Pirraku 1995; N. Jorgaqi 1996; Z. Rrahmani 1996; S. Fetiu, M. Halimi, and L. Lajçi (ed.) 1997; Sh. Galica 1997; and L. Starova 1998a.

In the autumn of 1909, Faik Konitza emigrated to the United States. His first stop was Boston where he became editor of the newspaper *Dielli* (The Sun), founded that year by Fan Noli. *Dielli* was the organ of the important Pan-Albanian *Vatra* (The Hearth) Federation of Boston, of which Konitza became general secretary in 1912. He also edited another short-lived periodical, the fortnightly *Trumbeta e Krujës* (The Trumpet of Croya) in St Louis, Missouri, which he ran for a short time (three editions) in 1911. In 1912 he travelled to London on behalf of the *Vatra* Federation to defend Albania's interests at the Conference of Ambassadors. This conference, held in the autumn of that year, was to consider recognition of the fledgling Albanian state which had declared its independence from the Ottoman Empire on 28 November. On 29 July 1913, the ambassadors agreed to recognize Albanian autonomy, though initially under the continued suzerainty of the Sultan. At the beginning of March 1913, Konitza, who had quarrelled with Ismail Qemal bey Vlora (1844-1919) and had initially given his support to the government of Essad Pasha Toptani (1863-1920), spoke before three hundred delegates at the Albanian Congress of Trieste who had gathered to discuss their country's fate during the political anarchy precipitated by the Balkan Wars. He became disillusioned with Austro-Hungarian policies, which he had earlier supported, when it became clear that Vienna was only interested in a fixed northern border for Albania and that his native town of Konitza was to be awarded to Greece. At the outbreak of the First World War, Faik Konitza was residing in Austria (Vienna, Feldkirch and Baden). There, in the political tension created, rumour spread that he was spying for Italy and he was obliged to leave the crumbling Austro-Hungarian Empire for neutral Switzerland. In Lausanne, he met up with Mehdi bey Frashëri (1874-1963) and Mid'hat bey Frashëri (1880-1949), and on 2 November 1915 published a treatise there entitled *L'Allemagne et l'Albanie* (Germany and Albania), in which he attacked German support for a proposal to partition Albania between the Greeks and Slavs. In March 1916 we find him in Sofia with Dervish Hima (1873-1928) and in July of that year back in Baden (Austria). He was subsequently obliged to leave Austria once again, this time for Italy, allegedly because of his criticism of Austrian and German policies in Albania and the consequent suspicion with which the Austrian authorities treated him. In 1921, back in the United States, he was elected president of the *Vatra* Federation in Boston and resumed editing the newspaper *Dielli* (The Sun) there, in which he now had his own column, *Shtylla e Konitzës* (Konitza's Column). In the summer of 1926, Faik Konitza was appointed Albanian ambassador to the United States by the dictator Ahmet Zogu (1895-1961), a post he held until the Italian invasion of his country over Easter 1939. He died in Washington on 15 December 1942 and was buried in Forest Hills cemetery in Boston. His remained were repatriated to Tirana after the fall of the communist dictatorship.

Faik Konitza unfortunately wrote little in the way of literature per se, but as a stylist, critic, publicist and political figure he had a tremendous impact on Albanian writing and culture at the turn of the century. His periodical *Albania*, published in French and Albanian under the pseudonym *Thrank Spirobeg*, not only helped make Albanian culture and the Albanian cause known in Europe, but also set the pace for literary prose in Tosk dialect. It is widely considered to be the most significant Albanian periodical to have existed up to the Second World War. Writers like Thimi Mitko, Kostandin Kristoforidhi, Andon Zako Çajupi and Gjergj Fishta first became known to a broader public through the pages of the periodical which Faik Konitza published faithfully over the course of twelve years. *Albania*, financed to some extent by the Austro-Hungarian authorities under the auspices of the *Kultusprotektorat* and accordingly betraying pro-Austrian proclivities, contained articles and information on a wide range of topics: history, language, literature, folklore, archaeology, politics, economics, religion and art, and as such, constitutes a mini-encyclopaedia of the Albanian culture of the period. Konitza valued a free exchange of ideas and he placed the columns of *Albania* at the disposal of his rivals whom he countered with caustic wit. In literature, he attacked the often banal nationalist outpourings on the lofty virtues of the Albanian people and called for a more realistic and critical stance towards his nation with all its failings. Steeped in Western culture, he found it difficult to appreciate the poets of early romantic nationalism like Naim Frashëri whose ideals were of a bygone age and whose verse he regarded as unsophisticated. How could they, with their sacrosanct expressions of patriotic fervour, compare with the high level of literary and artistic achievement he had encountered in France, to writers like Verlaine, Baudelaire and Apollinaire? The biting sarcasm with which he expressed his intransigence towards the naivity of his compatriots and towards the many sacred cows of Albanian culture and history let a breeze of fresh air into Albanian letters.

Konitza strove for a more refined Western culture in Albania, but he nonetheless valued his country's traditions. He was, for instance, one of the first to propagate the idea of editing the texts of older Albanian literature. In an article entitled *Për themelimin e një gjuhës letrarishte shqip* (On the foundation of a literary Albanian language), published in the first issue of *Albania*, Konitza also pointed to the necessity of creating a unified literary language. He suggested the most obvious solution, that the two main dialects, Tosk and Gheg, should be fused and blended gradually. His own fluid style, together with that of Fan Noli, was highly influential in the refinement of Tosk prose writing, which decades later was to form the basis of the modern literary language (*gjuha letrare*). Konitza's ties with the Zogu regime in later years created consternation among many Albanian intellectuals and it is this more than anything which caused his influence on Albanian literature and culture to be underestimated and ignored by post-war Marxist critics in Tirana. His sarcastic comments and polemics in *Albania* and elsewhere, and his irascibility and arrogance did not always make him a popular figure[93], but the spontaneity and refinement of his prose are universally recognized and admired.

Faik Konitza's writings were nonetheless fragmentary and his actual literary production was minimal, a fact lamented by many of his compatriots during his lifetime. Aside from his numerous editorials and articles on politics, language, literature and history which appeared for the most part in *Albania e vogël* (Little Albania), a fortnightly supplement to his periodical *Albania*, that was published alternatively in Tosk and Gheg dialect from 1899 to 1903, Konitza did write what could be regarded as a novel, although he never completed it. This is the satirical *Dr. Gjëlpëra zbulon rënjët e dramës së Mamurrasit* (Dr Needle discovers the roots of the Mamurras drama) in which he makes some delightfully pungent observations on the backwardness and the questionable hygienic standards of his compatriots. The origins of 'Dr Needle' lie in an historical event. In 1924, two American tourists were murdered near the village of Mamurras, allegedly by supporters of Ahmet Zogu. Faced with a protest from the American government, the Albanian administration, now under Fan Noli, brought the fugitives to trial and condemned them to death on 18 December 1924. Konitza nonetheless regarded the Noli administration as having been far too lenient on Zogu himself and began printing his 'Dr Needle' in serialized form in the Boston *Dielli* (The Sun) in 1924. When Konitza reconciled himself with Zogu's representatives the following year, publication of the serial ceased.

Konitza's only book publication in Albanian was a translation of Arabic tales from a Thousand and One Nights, entitled *Nën hien e hurmave*, Boston 1924 (In the shade of the date palms). In *Dielli* (The Sun) from 1929 on, he also edited the narrative of his travels to Albania, a series entitled *Shqiperia si m'u-duk* (How Albania appeared to me), in which he expressed much unflattering criticism of various character types he had encountered there: bureaucrats, social climbers, and pretentious aristocrats, etc. A selection of his work was posthumously edited in English by Qerim M. Panarity in the 175-page volume *Albania, the rock garden of southeastern Europe and other*

---

[93] Publicist Eqrem bey Vlora (1885-1964) noted for instance, "Faik Konitza as a person was intolerable: irritable, arrogant, self-conceited, sarcastic and sadly unproductive." cf. E. Vlora 1968-1973, vol. 1, p. 51.

essays, Boston 1957. His impulsive and sophisticated prose was unavailable in Albania until the fall of the dictatorship.

Fan Noli[94] (1882-1965), also known as *Theophan Stylian Noli*, was not only an outstanding leader of the Albanian-American community, but also a pre-eminent and multi-talented figure of Albanian literature, culture, religious life and politics. Noli was born in the village of Ibrik Tepe (Alb. *Qyteza*), south of Edirne (Adrianople) in European Turkey on 6 January 1882. His father Stylian Noli had been a noted cantor in the Orthodox church and had instilled in his son a love for Orthodox music and Byzantine tradition. Fan Noli attended the Greek secondary school in Edirne, and in 1900, after a short stay in Constantinople, settled in Athens where he managed to find occasional and badly-paying jobs as a copyist, prompter and actor. It was with one such itinerant theatre company touring Greek-speaking settlements in the eastern Mediterranean that Noli first arrived in Egypt. Abandoning the company in Alexandria, he found work from March 1903 to March 1905 as a Greek teacher and as a church cantor in Shibîn el Khôm and from March 1905 to April 1906 in El Faiyûm where a small Albanian colony had settled. Here he wrote a number of articles in Greek and translated Sami Frashëri's *Shqipëria - Ç'ka qënë, ç'është e ç'do të bëhetë?* (Albanian - what was it, what is it and what will become of it?) into Greek, works which were published at the Albanian press in Sofia. In Egypt, Noli learned more about the traditions of Byzantine music which so fascinated him, from his teacher, the monk Nilos, and resolved to become an Orthodox priest himself. He also came into contact with the nationalist leaders of the Albanian community such as Spiro Dine (1846?-1922), Jani Vruho (1863-1931) and Athanas Tashko (1863-1915) who encouraged him to emigrate to America where he could make better use of his talents. The young Noli agreed.

In April 1906, with a second-class steamer ticket which was paid for by Spiro Dine, Fan Noli set off via Naples for the New World and arrived in New York on May 10. After three months in Buffalo where he worked in a lumber mill, Noli arrived in Boston. There publisher Sotir Peci (1873-1932) gave him a job at a minimal salary as deputy editor of the Boston newspaper *Kombi* (The Nation), where he worked until May 1907 and in which he published articles and editorials under the pseudonym Ali Baba Qyteza. These were financially and personally difficult months for Noli, who did not feel at home in America at all and seriously considered emigrating to Bucharest.

---

[94] cf. M. Kuteli 1945; F. Noli 1960; V. Bala 1972; M. Raifi 1975, 1995; P. Tako 1975; F. Arapi 1980; E. Liço 1982; A. Pipa 1984; M. Kodra 1989; A. Puto 1990; E. Dodona 1996; B. Shtylla 1997; G. Ejntrej 1999; and N. Jorgaqi 2000, 2001.

Gradually, however, he found his roots in the Albanian community and on 6 January 1907 co-founded the *Besa-Besën* (Pledge) Society in Boston.

In this period, Orthodox Albanians in America were growing increasingly impatient with Greek control of the church. Tension reached its climax in 1907 when a Greek Orthodox priest refused to officiate at the burial of an Albanian in Hudson, Massachusetts, on the grounds that, as a nationalist, the deceased was automatically excommunicated. Noli saw his calling and convoked a meeting of Orthodox Albanians from throughout New England at which delegates resolved to set up an autocephalic, i.e. autonomous, Albanian Orthodox Church with Noli as its first clergyman. On 9 February 1908 at the age of twenty-six, Fan Noli was made a deacon in Brooklyn and on 8 March 1908, Platon, the Russian Orthodox Archbishop of New York, ordained him as an Orthodox priest. A mere two weeks later, on 22 March 1908, the young Noli proudly celebrated the liturgy in Albanian for the first time at the Knights of Honor Hall in Boston. This act constituted the first step towards the official organization and recognition of an Albanian Autocephalic Orthodox Church.

From February 1909 to July 1911, Noli edited the newspaper *Dielli* (The Sun), mouthpiece of the Albanian community in Boston. On 10 August 1911, he set off for Europe for four months where he held church services in Albanian for the colonies in Kishinev, Odessa, Bucharest and Sofia. Together with Faik bey Konitza who had arrived in the United States in 1909, he founded the Pan-Albanian *Vatra* Federation of America on 28 April 1912, which was soon destined to become the most powerful and significant Albanian organization in America. Fan Noli had now become the recognized leader of the Albanian Orthodox community and was an established writer and journalist of the nationalist movement. In November 1912, Albania was declared independent, and the thirty-year-old Noli, having graduated with a B.A. from Harvard University, hastend back to Europe. In March 1913, among other activities, he attended the Albanian Congress of Trieste which was organized by his friend and rival Faik bey Konitza.

In July 1913 Fan Noli visited Albania for the first time, and there, on 10 March 1914, he held the country's first Orthodox church service in Albanian in the presence of Prince Wilhelm zu Wied who had arrived in Durrës only three days earlier aboard an Austro-Hungarian vessel. In August of 1914, Noli was in Vienna for a time, but as the clouds of war darkened, he returned in May 1915 to the United States. From 21 December 1915 to 6 July 1916, he was again editor-in-chief of the Boston *Dielli* (The Sun), now a daily newspaper. In July 1917 he once more became president of the *Vatra* Federation which, in view of the chaotic situation and political vacuum in Albania, now regarded itself as a sort of Albanian government in exile. In September 1918, Noli founded the English-language monthly *Adriatic Review* which was financed by the federation to spread information about Albania and its cause. Noli edited the journal for the first six months and was succeeded in 1919 by Constantine Chekrezi (1892-1959). With *Vatra* funds collected under Noli's direction, Albanian-American delegates were sent to Paris, London and Washington to promote international recognition of Albanian independence. On 24 March 1918, Noli was appointed administrator of the Albanian Orthodox Church in the United States and in early July of that year attended a conference on oppressed peoples at Mount Vernon, Virginia, where he met President Woodrow Wilson (1856-1924), champion of minority rights in Europe. On 27 July 1919, Noli was appointed Bishop of the Albanian Orthodox Church in America, now finally an independent diocese.

In the following year, in view of his growing stature as a political and religious leader of the Albanian community and as a talented writer, orator and political commentator, it was only fitting that he be selected to head an Albanian delegation to the League of Nations in Geneva where he was successful in having Albania admitted on 17 December 1920. Noli rightly regarded Albania's admission to the League of Nations as his greatest political achievement. Membership in that body gave Albania worldwide recognition for the first time and was in retrospect no doubt more important than Ismail Qemal bey Vlora's declaration of independence in 1912. In a commentary on 23 July 1924, the Manchester Guardian described Fan Noli as a "man who would have been remarkable in any country. An accomplished diplomat, an expert in international politics, a skilful debater, from the outset he made a deep impression in Geneva. He knocked down his Balkan opponents in a masterly fashion, but always with a broad smile. He is a man of vast culture who has read everything worth reading in English and French." Noli's success at the League of Nations established him as the leading figure in Albanian political life. From Geneva, he returned to Albania and from 1921 to 1922 represented the *Vatra* Federation in the Albanian parliament there. In 1922, he was appointed foreign minister in the government of Xhafer bey Ypi (1880-1940) but resigned several months later. On 21 November 1923, Noli was consecrated Bishop of Korça and Metropolitan of Durrës. He was now both head of the Orthodox Church in Albania and leader of a liberal political party, the main opposition to the conservative forces of Ahmet Zogu (1895-1961), who were supported primarily by the feudal landowners. On 23 February 1924, an attempt was made in parliament on the life of Ahmet Zogu and two months later, on 22 April 1924, nationalist figure and deputy Avni Rustemi (1895-1924) was assassinated, allegedly by Zogist forces. At Rustemi's funeral, Fan Noli gave a fiery oration which provoked the liberal opposition into such a fury that Zogu was obliged to flee to Yugoslavia in the so-called June Revolution.

On 17 July 1924, Fan Noli was officially proclaimed prime minister and shortly afterwards Regent of Albania. For six months, he led a democratic government which tried desperately to cope with the catastrophic economic and political problems facing the young Albanian state. His twenty-point programme for the modernization and democratization of Albania, including agrarian reform, proved, however, to be too rash and too idealistic for a backward country with no parliamentary traditions. In a letter to an English friend, he was later to note the reasons for his failure: "By insisting on the agrarian reforms I aroused the wrath of the landed aristocracy; by failing to carry them out I lost the support of the peasant masses." With the overthrow of his government by Zogist forces on Christmas Eve 1924, Noli left Albania for good and spent several months in Italy at the invitation of Benito Mussolini (1883-1945). When the Duce finally reached agreement with Zogu on oil concessions in Albania, Noli and his followers were given to understand that their presence in Italy was no longer desired. Noli subsequently spent several years in northern Europe, primarily in Germany and Austria. In November 1927, he visited Russia as a Balkan delegate to a congress of 'Friends of the Soviet Union' marking the tenth anniversary of the October Revolution, and in 1930, having obtained a six-month visa, he returned to the United States.

Back in Boston, Noli founded the weekly periodical *Republika* (The Republic), the name of which alone was in open defiance of Ahmet Zogu who on 1 September 1928 had proclaimed himself Zog I, King of the Albanians. *Republika* was also published in opposition to *Dielli* (The Sun), now under the control of Faik bey Konitza who had come to terms with King Zog and become Albanian minister plenipotentiary in Washington. After six months, Noli was forced to return to Europe when his visa expired and his *Republika* was taken over by Anastas Tashko until it ceased publication in 1932. With the help of his followers, he was able to return from Germany to the United States in 1932 and was granted permanent resident status. He withdrew from political life and henceforth resumed his duties as head of the Albanian Autocephalic Orthodox Church. In December 1933, Noli fell seriously ill and was unable to pay for the medical treatment he so desperately needed until he received a gift of 3,000 gold franks from Albania, which was ironically enough from his archenemy Ahmet Zogu. This gesture, as intended, led to a certain reconciliation between Noli and Zogu and pacified Noli's now often tenuous relations with Konitza.

In 1935, Noli returned to one of his earlier passions - music - and, at the age of fifty-three, registered at the New England Conservatory of Music in Boston, from which he graduated in 1938 with a Bachelor of Music. On 12 April 1937, Noli's great dream of an Albanian national church was fulfilled when the Patriarch of Constantinople officially recognized the Albanian Autocephalic Orthodox Church. Not satisfied with ecclesiastical duties alone,

Noli turned to post-graduate studies at Boston University, finishing a doctorate there in 1945 with a dissertation on Scanderbeg. In the early years following the Second World War, Noli maintained reasonably good relations with the new communist regime in Tirana and used his influence to try to persuade the American government to recognize the latter. His reputation as the 'red bishop' indeed caused a good deal of enmity and polarization in emigré circles in America. In 1953, at the age of seventy-one, Fan Noli was presented with the sum of $20,000 from the *Vatra* Federation, with which he bought a house in Fort Lauderdale, Florida, where he died on 13 March 1965 at the age of eighty-three.

Politics and religion were not the only fields in which Fan Noli made a name for himself. He was also a dramatist, poet, historian, musicologist and in particular an excellent translator who made a significant contribution to the development of the Albanian literary language.

Noli's first literary work was a three-act drama entitled *Israilitë dhe Filistinë*, Boston 1907 (Israelites and Philistines). This forty-eight page tragedy written in 1902 is based on the Book of Judges 13-16 in the Old Testament, the famous story of Samson and Delilah. Published at a time when Albanian theatre was in its infancy, it is one of the rare Albanian plays of the period not gushing with sentimentality before reaching a superficial melodramatic conclusion. Such were the tastes of the period, however, and Noli's play found little favour with the public. Not only was the subject matter too distant and philosophical, but his language was too archaic or dialectal for the public to enjoy.

On his ordainment as an Orthodox priest and his celebration of the first Orthodox liturgy in Albanian in 1908, Noli recognized the need for liturgical texts in Albanian and set about translating Orthodox rituals and liturgies, which were published in two volumes: *Librë e shërbesave të shënta të kishës orthodoxe*, Boston 1909 (Book of holy services of the Orthodox Church), and the 315-page *Libre é te krémtevé te medha te kishes orthodoxe*, Boston 1911 (Book of great ceremonies of the Orthodox Church). Other religious translations followed, in an elegant and solemn language befitting such venerable Byzantine traditions. Noli indeed considered these translations to be his most rewarding achievement.

Fan Noli's most popular work today is a scholarly history of the life and times of the Albanian national hero Scanderbeg. A 285-page Albanian version was published as *Historia e Skënderbeut (Gjerq Kastriotit), mbretit të Shqipërisë 1412-1468*, Boston 1921 (The History of Scanderbeg, George Castrioti, king of Albania 1412-1468), and an English version, the fruits of his doctoral dissertation at Boston University in 1945, as *George Castrioti Scanderbeg (1405-1468)*, New York 1947. Another scholarly work in English which mirrors both his fascination with great figures of the past (Jesus, Julius Caesar, Scanderbeg and Napoleon) and his love of music is the 117-page *Beethoven and the French revolution*, New York 1947.

Noli has not been forgotten as a poet though his powerful declamatory verse is far from prolific. It was collected in a volume with the simple title *Albumi*, Boston 1948 (The Album), which he published on the occasion of his forty years of residence in the United States. *Albumi* contains primarily political verse reflecting his abiding nationalist aspirations and the social and political passions of the twenties and thirties. Typical of this genre is his poem *Anës lumenjve* (On river banks) which constitutes perhaps the most convincing verse ever written in Albanian on the theme of exile. During his stay in Germany, Noli was deeply troubled by the fate of his homeland, which he and many of his contemporaries compared to a defiled and abandoned maiden, as Pashko Vasa had done half a century earlier in his *O moj Shqypni* (Oh Albania, poor Albania). Noli's poem takes up this theme as follows:

> *"Arratisur, syrgjinosur,*
> *Rraskapitur dhe katosur,*
> *Po vajtonj pa funt pa shpresë,*
> *Anës Elbës, anës Spre-së.*
>
> *Ku e lam' e ku na mbeti*
> *Vaj vatani e mjer mileti,*
> *Anës detit i palarë,*
> *Anës dritës i paparë,*
> *Pranë sofrës i pangrënë,*
> *Pranë dijes e panxënë,*
> *Lakuriq dhe i dregosur,*
> *Trup e shpirt i sakatosur!..."*

(Taken flight and off in exile,
In restraints and held in bondage,
I despair with tears unending
On the banks of Spree and Elbe.

Where is it that we have left her,
Our poor homeland, wretched nation?
She lies unwashed at the seaside,
She stands unseen in the sunlight,
She sits starving at the table,
She is ignorant midst learning,

Naked, ailing does she languish,
Lame in body and in spirit...)

Fan Noli's main contribution to Albanian literature, however, was as a stylist, as seen especially in his translations. Together with Faik bey Konitza, Noli may indeed be regarded as one of the greatest stylists in the Tosk dialect of the Albanian language. His experience as an actor and orator, and his familiarity with other great languages of culture, Greek, English and French in particular, enabled him to develop Albanian into a language of refinement and flowing elegance.

Particularly impressive are Noli's translations of Shakespeare. His Othello (*Otello*) was printed in 1916 and his equally eloquent translations of Macbeth (*Makbethi*), Hamlet (*Hamleti*) and Julius Caesar (*Jul Qesari*) were all published in Brussels in 1926. In this same period he translated, no doubt from an English version, two plays by Norwegian dramatist Henrik Ibsen, another author in whom he had a passionate interest; part one of *Don Quixote* by Miguel de Cervantes; *La barraca*, 1898 (The Cabin), by Spanish novelist Vicente Blasco Ibañez (1867-1928); and in particular *The Rubáiyát of Omar Khayyám* by English poet Edward Fitzgerald. The translation of the Rubáiyát of the great Persian poet and mathematician 'Omar Khayyâm (d. 1122), which he published in Albanian under the pseudonym Rushit Bilbil Gramshi and dedicated to the Persian poets Nizâmî (1140-1209) and Hâfiz (1326-1390), is certainly among Noli's most exquisite works. It is as much a creative masterpiece as the English version by Edward Fitzgerald and is the only one of Noli's literary translations not to be motivated by ulterior didactic concerns. If we compare Noli's Albanian to Fitzgerald's English, we see that the Albanian text is in every way just as sublime as the (English) original. Here are the first three quatrains:

"*Natën kur flinja, më tha shpirti: 'Pi!*
Në gjumë dhe në Varr s'ka lumëri;
Ngrehu! Sa rron, zbras Kupa dhe puth Çupa;
Ke shekuj që të flesh në qetësi.'

Në ëndërr, kur agimi zbardhëllonte,
Një zë që nga Taverna po gjëmonte:
Çohuni, djem, e Verë sillnani,
Se Fati na e thau lëngun sonte.

Dhe posa në Tavernë këndoi gjeli,
Besnikët jashtë thirrë: 'Portat çeli!'

E shkurtër është Jeta, ja, u mplakmë
Dhe mbetmë si kofini pas të vjeli."

Awake! for Morning in the Bowl of Night
Has flung the Stone that puts the Stars to Flight:
And Lo! the Hunter of the East has caught
The Sultan's Turret in a Noose of Light.

Dreaming when Dawn's Left Hand was in the Sky
I heard a Voice within the Tavern cry,
"Awake, my little ones, and fill the Cup
Before Life's Liquor in its Cup be dry."

And, as the Cock crew, those who stood before
The Tavern shouted - "Open then the Door!
You know how little while we have to stay,
And once departed, may return no more."

Noli also translated poetry of various nineteenth-century European and American authors, and most often managed, with the ear of the musician he was, to reflect the style, taste and rhythmical nuances of the originals.

It is a pity that Fan Noli and Faik bey Konitza, these two greatest stylists of the modern Albanian language, who were both residents not of Albania but of the United States, should have devoted so little of their energies to creative literature. But such were the times. For historical and political reasons, the cult of nationalism has always had priority among the Albanians over the cult of the sublime. Though he wrote comparatively little in the way of literature per se, Fan Noli remains nonetheless a literary giant. He was instrumental in helping the Albanian language reach its full literary and creative potential. A modern literary language had been created, a language as yet in search of its literature.

5.3   The Voice of the Nation: Gjergj Fishta

By far the greatest and most influential figure of Albanian literature in the first half of the twentieth century was the Franciscan pater **Gjergj Fishta**[95] (1871-1940) who more than any other writer gave artistic expression to the searching soul of the now sovereign Albanian nation. Lauded and celebrated up until the Second World War as the 'national poet of Albania' and as the 'Albanian Homer,' Fishta was to fall into sudden oblivion when the communists took power in November 1944. The very mention of his name became taboo for forty-six years. Who was Gjergj Fishta and can he live up to his epithet as 'poet laureate' half a century later?

Fishta was born on 23 October 1871 in the Zadrima village of Fishta near Troshan in northern Albania where he was baptized by the Franciscan missionary and poet Leonardo De Martino (1830-1923). He attended Franciscan schools in Troshan and Shkodra where as a child he was deeply influenced both by the talented De Martino and by a Bosnian missionary, pater Lovro Mihačević, who instilled in the intelligent lad a love for literature and for his native language. In 1886, when he was fifteen, Fishta was sent by the Order of the Friars Minor to Bosnia, as were many young Albanians destined for the priesthood at the time. It was at Franciscan seminaries and institutions in Sutjeska, Livno and Kreševo that the young Fishta studied theology, philosophy and languages, in particular Latin, Italian and Serbo-Croatian, to prepare himself for his ecclesiastical and literary career. During his stay in Bosnia he came into contact with Bosnian writer Grga Martić (1822-1905) and with Croatian poet Silvije Strahimir Kranjčević (1865-1908) with whom he became friends and who aroused a literary calling in him. In 1894 Gjergj Fishta was ordained as a priest and admitted to the Franciscan Order. On his return to Albania in February of that year, he was given a teaching position at the Franciscan college in Troshan and subsequently a posting as parish priest in the village of Gomsiqja. In 1899, he collaborated with Preng Doçi, the influential abbot of Mirdita, with prose writer and priest Dom Ndoc Nikaj and with folklorist Pashko Bardhi (1870-1948) to found the *Bashkimi* (Unity) Literary

---

[95] cf. E. Çabej 1941; B. Dema 1941, 1942; B. Dema (ed.) 1940; F. Ercole 1941; E. Koliqi (ed.) 1941; G. Stadtmüller 1942a, 1942b; M. Lambertz 1949; G. Schirò 1959; E. Koliqi 1972a; Z. Nekaj 1981; G. Gradilone 1983: A. Berisha & B. Musliu (ed.) 1990; P. Duka-Gjini 1992; I. Zamputi 1993b; S. Çapaliku 1995; A. Plasari 1996b; A. Plasari (ed.) 1996; V. Bala 1998; T. Çobani 1999; Xh. Aliçkaj 2000; A. Hetzer 2000; P. Jaku 2000a, 2000b; A. Yzeiri 2001; K. Shala 2002a, 2004; A. Berisha 2003; K. Çefa 2003a, 2003b; and N. Krasniqi 2003.

117

Society of Shkodra which set out to tackle the thorny Albanian alphabet question. This society was subsequently instrumental in the publication of a number of Albanian-language school texts and of the *Bashkimi* Albanian-Italian dictionary of 1908, still the best dictionary of Gheg dialect. By this time, Fishta had become a leading figure of cultural and public life in northern Albania, especially in Shkodra.

In 1902, Fishta was appointed director of Franciscan schools in the district of Shkodra where he is remembered in particular for having replaced Italian with Albanian for the first time as the language of instruction. This effectively put an end to the Italian cultural domination of northern Albanian Catholics and gave young Albanians studying at these schools a sense of national identity. On 14-22 November 1908 he participated in the Congress of Monastir as a representative of the *Bashkimi* (Unity) Literary Society. This congress, attended by Catholic, Orthodox and Muslim delegates from Albania and abroad, was held to decide upon a definitive Albanian alphabet, a problem to which Fishta had given much thought. Indeed, the congress had elected Gjergj Fishta to preside over a committee of eleven delegates who were to make the choice. After three days of deliberations, Fishta and the committee resolved to support two alphabets: a modified form of Sami Frashëri's Istanbul alphabet which, though impractical for printing, was most widely used at the time, and a new Latin alphabet almost identical to Fishta's *Bashkimi* alphabet, in order to facilitate printing abroad.

In October 1913, almost a year after the declaration of Albanian independence in Vlora, Fishta founded and began editing the Franciscan monthly periodical *Hylli i Dritës* (The Day-star) which was devoted to literature, politics, folklore and history. With the exception of the turbulent years of the First World War and its aftermath, 1915-1920, and the early years of the dictatorship of Ahmet Zogu, 1925-1929, this influential journal of high literary standing was published regularly until July 1944 and became as instrumental for the development of northern Albanian Gheg culture as Faik bey Konitza's Brussels journal *Albania* had been for the Tosk culture of the south. From December 1916 to 1918, Fishta edited the Shkodra newspaper *Posta e Shqypniës* (The Albanian post), a political and cultural newspaper which was subsidized by Austria-Hungary under the auspices of the *Kultusprotektorat*, despite the fact that the occupying forces did not entirely trust Fishta because of his nationalist aspirations. Also in 1916, together with Luigj Gurakuqi, Ndre Mjeda and Mati Logoreci (1867-1941), Fishta played a leading role in the Albanian Literary Commission (*Komisija Letrare Shqype*) set up by the Austro-Hungarian authorities on the suggestion of consul general August Ritter von Kral (1869-1953) to decide on questions of orthography for official use and to encourage the publication of Albanian school texts. After some deliberation, the Commission sensibly decided to use the central dialect of Elbasan as a neutral compromise for a standard literary language. This was much against the wishes of Gjergj Fishta who regarded the dialect of Shkodra, in view of its strong contribution to Albanian culture at the time, as best suited. Fishta hoped that his northern Albanian *koine* would soon serve as a literary standard for the whole country, much as Dante's language had served as a guide for literary Italian. Throughout these years, Fishta continued teaching and running the Franciscan school in Shkodra, known from 1921 on as the *Collegium Illyricum* (Illyrian College), which had become the leading educational institution of northern Albania. He was now also an imposing figure of Albanian literature.

In August 1919, Gjergj Fishta served as secretary-general of the Albanian delegation attending the Paris Peace Conference and, in this capacity, was asked by the president of the delegation, Msgr. Luigj Bumçi (1872-1945), to take part in a special commission to be sent to the United States to attend to the interests of the young Albanian state. There he visited Boston, New York and Washington. In 1921, Fishta represented Shkodra in the Albanian parliament and was chosen in August of that year as vice-president of the assembly. His talent as an orator served him well in his functions both as a political figure and as a man of the cloth. In later years, he attended Balkan conferences in Athens (1930), Sofia (1931) and Bucharest (1932) before withdrawing from public life to devote his remaining years to the Franciscan order and to his writing. From 1935 to 1938, he held the office of provincial of the Albanian Franciscans. These most fruitful years of his life were now spent in the quiet seclusion of the Franciscan monastery of Gjuhadoll in Shkodra with its cloister, church and rose garden where Fishta would sit in the shade and reflect on his verse. As the poet laureate of his generation, Gjergj Fishta was honoured with various diplomas, awards and distinctions both at home and abroad. He was awarded the Austro-Hungarian *Ritterkreuz* in 1911, was decorated by Pope Pius XI with the *Al Merito* award in 1925, was given the prestigious *Phoenix* medal of the Greek government, was honoured with the title *Lector jubilatus honoris causae* by the Franciscan order, and was made a regular member of the Italian Academy of Arts and Sciences in 1939. He died in Shkodra on 30 December 1940.

Although Gjergj Fishta is the author of a total of thirty-seven literary publications, his name is indelibly linked to one great work, indeed to one of the most astounding creations in all the history of Albanian literature, *Lahuta e malcis*, Shkodra 1937 (The Highland Lute). The 'Highland Lute' is a 15,613-line historical verse epic focussing on the Albanian struggle for autonomy and independence. It constitutes a panorama of northern Albanian history from 1862 to 1913. This literary masterpiece was composed for the most part between 1902 and 1909, though it was refined and amended by its author over the following quarter of a century. It constitutes the first Albanian-language contribution to world literature.

In 1902, Fishta had been sent to a little village to replace the local parish priest for a time. There he met and befriended the aged tribesman Marash Uci (1810-1914) of Hoti, whom he was later to immortalize in verse. In their evenings together, Marash Uci told the young priest of the heroic battles between the Albanian highlanders and the Montenegrins, in particular of the famed battle at the Rrzhanica Bridge in which Marash Uci had taken part himself. The earliest parts of the 'Highland Lute,' subtitled 'At the Rrzhanica Bridge,' were printed in Zadar in 1905 and 1907, with subsequent and enlarged editions appearing in 1912, 1923, 1931 and 1933. The definitive edition of the whole work in thirty cantos was published in Shkodra in 1937 to mark the twenty-fifth anniversary of Albanian independence. Despite the success of the 'Highland Lute' and the preeminence of its author, this and all other works by Gjergj Fishta were banned after the Second World War when the communists came to power. The epic was, however, republished in Rome 1958 and Ljubljana 1990, and exists in German, Italian and English (forthcoming) translations.

The 'Highland Lute' is certainly the most powerful and effective epic to have been written in Albanian. It towers over other attempts at this genre: Dalip Frashëri's Persian-influenced *Hadikaja*, ca. 1842 (The Garden); Shahin bey Frashëri's Shi'ite epic *Myhtarnameja*, 1868 (The Tale of Myhtar); Girolamo De Rada's rather meandering *Scanderbeccu i pa-faan*, 1872-1884 (Misfortunate Scanderbeg); Naim Frashëri's nationalistic but not altogether successful *Istori i Skenderbeut*, 1898 (History of Scanderbeg), and his Shi'ite epic *Qerbelaja*, 1898 (Kerbela); Giuseppe Schirò's epic of exile *Te dheu i huaj*, 1900 (In a foreign land); and Francesco Crispi Glaviano's *Mbi Malin e Truntafilevet* (On the Mount of Roses).

The age of Bektashi and Shi'ite epics in the Turkish-Persian tradition was of course over and the classical theme for an Albanian epic, the tribulations of fifteenth-century national hero Scanderbeg, which had been approached with only limited success by the two most renowned Albanian writers of the nineteenth century, Girolamo De Rada and Naim Frashëri, was now too distant and nebulous to serve as the focal point for a twentieth-century epic. Gjergj Fishta chose as his subject matter what he knew best: the heroic culture of his native northern Albanian mountains. It was his intention with this epic, an unprecedented achievement in Albanian letters, to present the lives of the northern Albanian tribes and of his people in general in a heroic setting.

In its historical dimensions, the 'Highland Lute' begins with border skirmishes between the Hoti and Gruda tribes and their equally fierce

Montenegrin neighbours in 1862 when Prince Nikolla (Nicholas) I of Montenegro attacked Vranina in his war against the Turks (cantos 1-5). The core of the work (cantos 6-25) is devoted to the defence of Plava and Gucia during the events of 1878-1880 when the Congress of Berlin granted Albanian borderland to Montenegro, and to the resultant creation of the League of Prizren to defend Albanian interests. The third part (cantos 26-30) covers the Revolution of the Young Turks which initially gave Albanian nationalists some hope of autonomy, and the Balkan wars of 1912 and 1913 which led to the declaration of Albanian independence.

It was the author's fortune at the time to have been at the heart of the only intact heroic society in Europe. High Albania in the north differed radically from the more advanced and 'civilized' regions of the Tosk south. What so fascinated foreign ethnographers and visitors to northern Albania at the turn of the century was the tribal and staunchly patriarchal structure of society in the highlands, a social system based on customs handed down for centuries by tribal law, in particular by the Code of Lekë Dukagjini. All the distinguishing features of this society are present in the 'Highland Lute': funerary customs, beliefs, the generous hospitality of the tribes, their endemic blood feuding, an acute perception of male honour, and the *besa*, absolute fidelity to one's word, come what may.

The 'Highland Lute' is strongly inspired by northern Albanian oral verse, both by the cycles of heroic verse, i.e. the octosyllabic *Këngë kreshnikësh* (Songs of the frontier warriors), similar to the Serbo-Croatian *junačke pjesme*, and by the equally popular cycles of historical verse of the eighteenth century, similar to Greek klephtic verse and to the *haidutska pesen* of the Bulgarians. Fishta knew well this oral verse sung by the Gheg mountain tribes on their one-stringed *lahuta* and relished in its language and rhythm. The narrative of the epic is therefore replete with the rich, archaic vocabulary and colourful figures of speech used by the warring highland tribes of the north and does not make for easy reading nowadays, even for the northern Albanians themselves. The standard meter of the 'Highland Lute' is a trochaic octameter or heptameter which is more in tune with Albanian oral verse than is the classical hexameter of the Latin and Greek epics. The influence of the great epics of classical antiquity, Homer's Iliad and Odyssey and Vergil's Aeneid, is nonetheless ubiquitous in the 'Highland Lute' as has been pointed out by a number of scholars, in particular Maximilian Lambertz and Giuseppe Gradilone[96]. Many parallels in style and content have thus transcended the millennia. Fishta himself later translated book five of the Iliad into Albanian.

---

[96] cf. M. Lambertz 1949 and G. Gradilone 1983.

Among the major stylistic features which characterize the 'Highland Lute,' and no doubt most other epics, are metaphor, alliteration and assonance, as well as archaic figures of speech and hyperbole. The predominantly heroic character of the narrative with its extensive battle scenes is fortunately counterbalanced with lyric and idyllic passages which give the 'Highland Lute' a lightness and poetic grace it might otherwise lack.

The 'Highland Lute' relies heavily on Albanian mythology and legendry. The work is permeated with mythological figures of oral literature who, like the gods and goddesses of ancient Greece, observe and, where necessary, intervene in events. Among them are the *zanas*, dauntless mountain spirits who dwell near springs and torrents and who bestow their protection on Albanian warriors; the *oras*, female spirits whose very name is often taboo; the vampire-like *lugats*; the witch-like *shtrigas*; and the *drangues*, semi-human figures born with wings under their arms and with supernatural powers, whose prime objective in life is to combat and slay the seven-headed fire-spewing *kulshedras*.

The fusion of the heroic and the mythological is equally evident in a number of characters to whom Fishta attributes major roles in the 'Highland Lute': Oso Kuka (1810-1862), the fierce and valiant warrior who prefers death over surrender to his Slavic enemy; the old shepherd Marash Uci who admonishes the young fighters to preserve their freedom and not to forget the ancient ways and customs; and the valiant maiden Tringa, who takes care of her brother and is resolved to defend her land.

The heroic aspect of life in the mountains is one of the many characteristics which the northern Albanian tribes have in common with their southern Slavic, and in particular Montenegrin, neighbours. The two peoples, divided as they are by language and by the bitter course of history, have a largely common culture. Although the Montenegrins serve as 'bad guys' in the glorification of the author's native land, Fishta was not uninfluenced or unmoved by the literary achievements of the southern Slavs in the second half of the nineteenth century, in particular by verse of Slavic resistance to the Turks. We have referred to the role played by Franciscan pater Grga Martić whose works served the young Fishta as a model while the latter was studying in Bosnia. Fishta was also influenced by the writings of an earlier Franciscan writer, Andrija Kačić-Miošić (1704-1760), the Dalmatian poet and publicist of the Enlightenment who is remembered especially for his *Razgovor ugodni naroda slovinskoga*, 1756 (Pleasant talk of Slavic folk), a collection of prose and poetry on Serbo-Croatian history, and by the works of Croatian poet Ivan Mažuranić (1814-1890), author of the noted romantic epic *Smrt Smail-age Čengića*, 1846 (The Death of Smail Aga). A further source of literary inspiration for Fishta may have been the Montenegrin poet-prince Petar

Petrovič Njegoš (1813-1851). It is no coincidence that the title 'The highland (or mountain) lute' is similar to Njegoš's *Gorski vijenac*, 1847 (The Mountain wreath). This verse rendition of Montenegro's heroic resistance to the Turkish occupants is now generally regarded as the national epic of the Montenegrins and Serbs. Gjergj Fishta proved that the Albanian language was also capable of a refined literary epic of equally heroic proportions.

The narrative of the epic can be summarized as follows: The first five cantos, known as the cycle of Oso Kuka, are set in the year 1862. Canto 1(The Bandits) gives a historical survey of Albanian suffering under the Turkish yoke and of the plans of Prince Nikolla of Montenegro to attack Albania. In Canto 2 (Oso Kuka), Oso Kuka of Shkodra sets out with his forty men to counter the attack. Canto 3 (The Booty) is an interlude in which an Albanian shepherd, Avdi Hisa, is slain by the Montenegrins, thus giving Oso Kuka a pretext to take revenge. Avdi's sister bemoans the death of her brother with a traditional lament. The figure of Oso Kuka is further developed in Canto 4 (Vranina), in which the Montenegrin prince sends his finest men to seize the island of Vranina in Lake Shkodra. The poet appeals to the Albanian tribesmen to be as heroic as Oso Kuka. The cycle concludes with Canto 5 (Death), in which Oso Kuka is defeated, takes refuge in a powder tower, and blows himself and his foes up. The Montenegrin flag is raised over the island.

The second section of the epic, set in 1878-1880, begins with Canto 6 (Dervish Pasha), in which a mysterious traveller arrives in Istanbul and pleeds with the sultan to save Albania. The sultan seconds Dervish Pasha and fifty battalions of soldiers to repulse Montenegrin forces, but the Congress of Berlin prevents the Turks from advancing. Canto 7 (The Congress of Berlin) focusses on the historical Congress of Berlin of 1878, which gives Prince Nikolla free rein to occupy Hoti, Gruda, Plava and Gucia, indeed all of northern Albania down to the Drin river. In Canto 8 (Ali Pasha of Gucia), Ali Pasha happens upon a fairy-like *ora* in the high mountain pastures who appeals to him to summon all the Albanian Highlanders to war, and bestows on him magic powers. Canto 9 (The League of Prizren) describes the events of the historical meeting of Albanian nobles in 1878, who gather to counter the Treaty of San Stefano and the resolutions of the Congress of Berlin. They are observed from the high mountains by the *ora* of Albania and the *zana* of Sharri, who delight in listening to the fiery speeches of Abdul Frashëri, Shan Deda, Mar Lula, and Ali Pasha. The noblemen resolve to write a letter of protest to the Congress of Berlin. In Canto 10 (Mehmet Ali Pasha), a new Turkish pasha staying at the house of Abdullah Dreni, invites tribal leaders to Gjakova and deceitfully takes them prisoner. Friends besiege the house in order to free their leaders. Dreni is duty bound by the prerequisites of Albanian hospitality to defend his unwanted guest, and both he and the pasha perish in the fighting.

Canto 11 (The Vampire) provides some good comic relief. Prince Nikolla is at home drinking wine. He chides his wife Milena for believing in ghosts. When she retires, however, Nikolla is himself confronted with the ghost of the slain Mehmet Ali Pasha, who demands that he send forces against Albania. Nikolla discusses war plans with his general, Mark Milani. Canto 12 (Marash Uci), the first to have been written and still perhaps the best known, introduces another protagonist of the epic, the aged Marash Uci. Marash hastens to Çun Mula in Hoti and asks him to summon the tribal leaders of Hoti and Gruda to the Church of Saint John's without delay for a council meeting. Marash Uci speaks before the leaders in Canto 13 (At the Church of Saint John's). The men resolve to take to arms to defend their land, and make Çun Mula their commander. In Canto 14 (At the Rrzhanica Bridge), the Highlanders of Hoti and Gruda do battle with the forces of Mark Milani. The Montenegrins are defeated at Rrzhanica Bridge and Mark Milani is compelled to take flight. Prince Nikolla in Cetinje is informed of the defeat in Canto 15 (The Herald) and is told that Albanian forces are massing at the border.

Canto 16 (The Kulshedra) forms another interlude with a mythological analogy to the main conflict. The Albanian warriors are introduced as mythological beings called *drangues*, in battle with a dragon-like *kulshedra*. Also interwoven into this canto is the song of the maid Eufrozina of Janina. In Canto 17 (At the Grapevine Pass), two of the *drangue* heroes, on their way home through the mountains, are surprised by the advancing army of Mark Milani. They manage to hold the pass with the help of nearby shepherds, and Milani withdraws, sending his men to attack Sutjeska. The *zanas* take up residence over Sutjeska, wait and observe. The battle of Sutjeska is described in Canto 18 (At Sutjeska Bridge), in which Mark Milani's forces endeavour to take Gucia. The grim scenes of battle are interrupted by a lament on the death of Smajl Arifi. In a long and patriotic invective in Canto 19 (Father Gjon), the priest of Kelmendi, no doubt a personification of Fishta himself, bemoans Albanian sufferings at the hands of their Slav neighbours. He then sets off for Sutjeska with the men of Kelmendi behind him. Canto 20 (The Lekas) offers more grim scenes of battle at Sutjeska. In the midst of the fighting, Bec Patani recognizes his Slavic blood-brother Milo Spasi and brings him to safety. The story of their friendship is narrated as an interlude. Night falls over the bloodbath. Father Gjon re-appears in Canto 21 (Mediation). He visits Mark Milani to arrange for a truce in order to bury the dead.

In Canto 22 (Tringa), savage fighting continues in nearby Nokshiq, where the maiden Tringa is devotedly caring for her dying brother, Curr Ula. When the Slav warrior Gjur Kokoti approaches, she shoots him in the chest, only to be shot in the head herself. Canto 23 (At the Farmhouse of Curr Ula) continues with more scenes of bloody battle. Tringa's death is avenged. Mark Milani resolves to call in the army to assist his fighters.

Canto 24 (The *Zana* of Mount Vizitor) provides an idyllic interlude to the fighting. The Great *Zana* is outraged at witnessing the murder of her childhood companion Tringa. She brings the body back to the Alpine pastures where it is buried ceremoniously at the foot of a linden tree. In a spirit of vengeance, the Great *Zana* calls upon all good men to hasten to the battlefield of Nokshiq. Canto 25 (Blood-Vengeance Exacted), the longest of the cantos, is devoted once again to the savagery of battle, observed from on high by the Great *Zana* of Mount Vizitor and by the *Ora* of Montenegro. Other figures of Albanian mythology are introduced, as vengeance is exacted for the murder of Tringa.

In Canto 26 (The New Age), another interlude, the poet, spending the spring at the Franciscan convent in Lezha, invites the *zana*, his muse, to visit him. The long history of Lezha and Albania are portrayed. After much suffering, a new day has dawned. Freedom is at hand. In Canto 27 (The Committee), we find ourselves in the twentieth century. In 1908, a committee of Turkish pashas gathers in Istanbul to decide the fate of Albania. Hardliner Turgut Pasha resolves to lead a military expedition to Albania to stifle the independence movement. Canto 28 (Dedë Gjo' Luli), set in 1910-1911, focusses on the figure of Dedë Gjo' Luli, champion of the Albanian cause against the Turks. Another hero, Llesh Nik Daka, is betrayed, mortally wounded, and taken, according to his last wish, to the monastery of Rubik to be buried. Turkish forces win the day. In Canto 29 (The Balkan War), set in 1912, the Austrian Emperor Franz Josef warns the sultan to leave the Albanians alone. The King of England invites the Great Powers to London to settle the matter. The final Canto 30 (The Conference of London) provides a humourous description of the gathering of the Seven Kings in London. After much dispute, they agree to recognize Albania's independence. The red and black flag of Albania finally flutters in the breeze over the land of Scanderbeg "like the wings of all God's angels."

Although Gjergj Fishta is remembered primarily as an epic poet, his achievements are actually no less impressive in other genres, in particular as a lyric and satirical poet. Indeed, his lyric verse is regarded by many scholars as his best.

Fishta's first publication of lyric poetry, *Vierrsha i pershpirteshem t'kthyem shcyp*, Shkodra 1906 (Spiritual verse translated into Albanian), was of strong Catholic inspiration. Here we find translations of the great Italian poets such as the Arcadian Pietro Metastasio (1698-1782) of Rome, the romantic novelist and poet Alessandro Manzoni (1785-1873) of Milan whom

Fishta greatly admired, the patriotic Silvio Pellico (1789-1845) of Turin, and the lyricist and literary historian Giacomo Zanella (1820-1888) of Vicenza, etc.

Fishta's first collection of original lyric verse was published under the title *Pika voëset*, Zadar 1909 (Dewdrops), and dedicated to his contemporary Luigj Gurakuqi. It was followed in 1913, at the dawn of Albanian independence, by the first edition of *Mrizi i zânavet*, Shkodra 1913 (Noonday rest of the Zanas), which includes some of the religious verse of *Pika voëset*. The general tone of *Mrizi i zânavet* is, however, much more nationalist than spiritual, the patriotic character of the collection being substantially underlined in the subsequent expanded editions of 1924, 1925 and in the definitive posthumous edition of 1941. Poems such as *Shqypnija* (Albania), *Gjuha shqype* (The Albanian language), *Atdheut* (To the fatherland), *Shqypnija e lirë* (Free Albania) and *Hymni i flamurit kombtár* (Hymn to the national flag) express Fishta's satisfaction and pride in Albania's history and in its new-found independence. Also included in this volume are the allegorical melodrama *Shqyptari i gjytetnuem* (The Civilized Albanian man) and its sequel *Shqyptarja e gjytetnueme* (The Civilized Albanian woman).

With his nationalist verse concentrated in the above volume, Fishta collected his religious poetry in the 235-page edition *Vallja e Parrîzit*, Shkodra 1925 (The Dance of paradise). The verse in this collection, including poems such as *Të kryqzuemt* (The Crucifixion), *Të zânun e pafaj të Virgjërês Mri* (The Immaculate Conception of the Virgin Mary), *Nuntsiata* (The Annunciation) and *Shë Françesku i Asizit* (St Francis of Assisi), constitutes a zenith of Catholic literature in Albania.

Gjergj Fishta was also a consummate master of satirical verse, using his wit and sharpened quill to criticize the educational shortcomings and intellectual sloth of his Scutarine compatriots. His was not the benevolent, exhortative irony of Çajupi, but rather biting, pungent satire, often to the point of ruthlessness, the poetic equivalent of the blunt satirical prose of Faik bey Konitza. Fishta had printed many such poems in the periodical *Albania* using the telling pseudonym 'Castigat ridendo.' In 1907, he published, anonymously, the 67-page satirical collection *Anxat e Parnasit*, Sarajevo 1907 (The Wasps of Parnassus), which laid the foundations for satire as a poetic genre in Albanian literature and which is regarded by many critics as the best poetry he ever produced. In the first of the satires, *Nakdomonicipedija* (A Lesson for Nakdo Monici), he turns to his friend, Jesuit writer and publisher Dom Ndoc Nikaj, whom he affectionately calls by his pen name Nakdo Monici, to convey his sympathy that the latter's 416-page *Historia é Shcypniis* (History of Albania), published in Brussels in 1902, had not received due attention among their compatriots. The Albanians were quite indifferent to their own history and indeed to their present sorry state in general. The reason for this indifference,

Fishta tells us, was a contest between St Nicholas and the devil. St Nicholas had sailed the seas at the command of the Almighty to sell reason and taste. The devil, for his part, competed with a ship full of old boots which he offered for sale. When the two merchants arrived at the port of Shëngjin, the Albanians took counsel and decided to go for the boots on credit. With such uneducated masses, Fishta recommends that Nikaj take solace in the aloof and cynical attitude of Molière's Tartuffe. *Anxat e Parnasit*, later spelled *Anzat e Parnasit* (The Wasps of Parnassus), which contains many a delightfully spicy expression normally unbecoming to a mild Franciscan priest, was republished in 1927, 1928, 1942 and 1990, and made Fishta many friends and enemies.

Gomari i Babatasit, Shkodra 1923 (Babatasi's ass), is another volume of amusing satire, published under the pseudonym Gegë Toska while Fishta was a member of the Albanian parliament. In this work, which enjoyed great popularity at the time, he rants at false patriots and idlers.

Aside from the above-mentioned melodramas, Fishta was the author of several other works of theatre, including adaptations of a number of foreign classics, e.g., the three-act *I ligu per mend*, Shkodra 1931 (Le malade imaginaire), of Molière, and *Ifigenija n'Aullí*, Shkodra 1931 (Iphigenia in Aulis), of Euripides. Among other dramatic works he composed and/or adapted at a time when Albanian theatre was in its infancy are short plays of primarily religious inspiration, among them the three-act Christmas play *Barìt e Betlêmit* (The Shepherds of Bethlehem); *Sh' Françesku i Asisit*, Shkodra 1912 (St Francis of Assisi); the tragedy *Juda Makabé*, Shkodra 1923 (Judas Maccabaeus); *Sh. Luigji Gonzaga*, Shkodra 1927 (St Aloysius of Gonzaga); and *Jerina, ase mbretnesha e luleve*, Shkodra 1941 (Jerina or the queen of the flowers), the last of his works to be published during his lifetime.

The national literature of Albania had been something of a Tosk prerogative until the arrival of Gjergj Fishta on the literary scene. He proved that northern Albania could be an equal partner with the more advanced south in the creation of a national culture. The acclaim of the 'Highland Lute' has not been universal, though, in particular among Tosk critics. Some authors regarded his blending of oral and written literature as disastrous and others simply regarded such a literary epic with a virtually contemporary theme as an anachronism in the twentieth century. Only time will tell whether Fishta can regain his position as 'national poet' after half a century of politically motivated oblivion.

The Scutarine Catholic school of letters which Gjergj Fishta dominated entered a golden age in the first decades of the twentieth century and much credit for this blossoming of Gheg culture goes to him. Franciscan poets and scholars like Pashko Bardhi (1870-1948), Shtjefën Gjeçovi (1874-1929), Pal Dodaj (1880-1948), Vinçenc Prennushi (1885-1949), Marin Sirdani (1885-

1962), Anton Harapi (1888-1946), Justin Rrota (1889-1964), Bernardin Palaj (1894-1947), Donat Kurti (1903-1969), Benedikt Dema (1904-1960) and Gjon Shllaku (1907-1946), and indeed virtually all other Albanian intellectuals who spent their productive years in Shkodra at some time during the first four decades of the century were influenced in one way or another by the imposing figure of Father Gjergj Fishta. Scholar Eqrem Çabej in his 1941 obituary of the poet, wrote:

> "Rooted profoundly in the soil of his native land, which he rarely abandoned and always returned to, he derived the best of his human and poetic talents from this soil. He spent his life in an annex of the monastery of his order, situated far from the city of Shkodra, in the courtyard of which ancient trees provided soothing shade, and there he listened devoutly to the silent inspiration of the Muses. He was not one of those intellectual writers, not uncommon in the Balkans, who spend most of their lives in large cities abroad. He was one of those types who grow slowly and organically from their roots. He was a true son of his people and in his symbiosis with the soil, in a manner quite different from Naim Frashëri, has become the national poet of Albania[97]."

At the outbreak of the Second World War, Gjergj Fishta was indeed universally recognized as the 'national poet.' Austrian scholar Maximilian Lambertz (1882-1963) described him as "the most ingenious poet Albania has ever produced"[98] and Gabriele D'Annunzio called him "the great poet of the glorious people of Albania." For others, he was the "Albanian Homer."

After the war, Fishta was nonetheless attacked and denigrated perhaps more than any other prewar writer, and fell into prompt oblivion. The national poet became an anathema. The official Tirana 'History of Albanian Literature' of 1983, which carried the blessing of the Albanian Party of Labour, restricted its treatment of the country's 'national poet' to an absolute minimum:

> "The main representative of this clergy, Gjergj Fishta (1871-1940), poet, publicist, teacher and politician, ran the press of the Franciscan order and directed the cultural and educational activities of this order for a long time. For him, the interests of the church and of religion rose above those of the nation and the people, something he openly

---

[97] cf. E. Çabej 1941.

[98] cf. M. Lambertz 1948, p. 368.

declared and defended with all his demagogy and cynicism, [a principle] upon which he based his literary work. His main work, the epic poem, *Lahuta e Malcis* (The Highland Lute), while attacking the chauvinism of our northern neighbours, propagates anti-Slavic feelings and makes the struggle against the Ottoman occupants secondary. He raised a hymn to patriarchalism and feudalism, to religious obscurantism and clericalism, and played with patriotic sentiments wherever it was a question of highlighting the events and figures of the national history of our Rilindja period. His other works, such as the satirical poem *Gomari i Babatasit* (Babatasi's ass), in which public schooling and democratic ideas were bitterly attacked, were characteristic of the savage struggle undertaken by the Catholic church to maintain and increase its influence in the intellectual life of the country. With his art, he endeavoured to pay service to a form close to folklore. This was often accompanied by prolixity, far-fetched effects, rhetoric, brutality of expression and style to the point of banality, false arguments which he intentionally endeavours to impose, and an exceptionally conservative attitude in the field of language. Fishta ended his days as a member of the academy of fascist Italy[99]."

The real reason for Fishta's fall from grace after the 'liberation' in 1944 is to be sought, however, not in his alleged pro-Italian or clerical proclivities, but in the origins of the Albanian Communist Party itself. The ACP, later to be called the Albanian Party of Labour, had been founded during the Second World War under the auspices of the Yugoslav envoys Dušan Mugoša (1914-1973) and Miladin Popović (1910-1945). In July 1946, Albania and Yugoslavia signed a Treaty of Friendship, Co-operation and Mutual Assistance and a number of other agreements which gave Yugoslavia effective control over all Albanian affairs, including the field of culture. Serbo-Croatian was introduced as a compulsory subject in all Albanian high schools, and by the spring of 1948, plans were even under way for a merger of the two countries. It is no doubt the alleged anti-Slavic sentiments expressed in the 'Highland Lute' which caused the work and its author to be proscribed by the Yugoslav authorities, even though Fishta was educated in Bosnia and inspired by Serbian and Croatian literature. In actual fact, it is as ridiculous to describe

---

[99] cf. Dh. Shuteriqi (ed.) 1983, p. 470-471. In all fairness it must be noted, according to Shuteriqi, that Vehbi Bala (1923-1990) had prepared 40 pages on Fishta for the Academy's literary history, coverage equal to that given to Naim Frashëri, but he was not allowed to publish it.

the 'Highland Lute' as being anti-Slavic as it would be to describe *El Cid* and the *Chanson de Roland* as being anti-Arab. They are all historical epics with national heroes and foreign foes. In fact, Fishta does not view the Montenegrin Slavs as eternal enemies, rather he sees the hostilities as being a result of interference from the Great Powers, in particular from Russia. It is nonetheless the so-called anti-Slavic element in Fishta's work which was, however, also stressed in the first post-war edition of the Great Soviet Encyclopaedia of Moscow. It reads as follows (March 1950):

> "The literary activities of the Catholic priest Gjergj Fishta reflect the role played by the Catholic clergy in preparing for Italian aggression against Albania. As a former agent of Austro-Hungarian imperialism, Fishta, in the early years of his literary activity, took a position against the Slavic peoples who opposed the rapacious plans of Austro-Hungarian imperialism in Albania. In his chauvinistic, anti-Slavic poem the 'Highland Lute,' this spy extolled the hostility of the Albanians towards the Slavic peoples, calling for an open fight against the Slavs[100]."

After relations with Yugoslavia were broken off in 1948, it is quite likely that expressions of anti-Montenegrin or anti-Serb sentiment would no longer have been considered a major sin in Party thinking. However, an official position had been taken with regard to Fishta and, possibly with deference to the new Slav allies in Moscow, it could not be renounced without a scandal. Gjergj Fishta, who but a few years earlier had been lauded as the national poet of Albania, disappeared from the literary scene, seemingly without a trace. Such was the fear of him that his home was razed to the ground and, in later years, his bones were dug up and secretly thrown into the river.

Yet despite four decades of unrelenting Party harping and propaganda endeavouring to reduce Fishta to the rank of a minor 'clerical poet,' the people of northern Albania, and in particular the inhabitants of his native Shkodra, did not forget him. After almost half a century of silence, Gjergj Fishta was commemorated openly on 5 January 1991 in Shkodra. During this first public recital of Fishta's works in Albania in forty-five years, the actor at one point hesitated in his lines, and was immediately and spontaneously assisted by members of the audience - who still knew many parts of the 'Highland Lute' by heart.

---

[100] cf. *Bol'šaya Sovetskaya Entsiklopediya*, vol. 2, Moscow, 18 March 1950, p. 49.

5.4   Harbingers of Modernity: Migjeni and Lasgush Poradeci

Gjergj Fishta and the Scutarine school represented the mainstream of Albanian literature up until the Second World War - creative, innovative and yet traditionalist. Fishta had raised the little Balkan country to the level of literary sophistication which the more advanced nations of Europe had known in the second half of the nineteenth and early years of the twentieth century. This in itself was quite a significant step forward in view of Albania's tardy consolidation as a nation and its sluggish political and cultural development. This period of Albanian literature was to some extent, however, now losing touch with the realities of the independent Albanian state of the 1930s.

The road to modernity, and thus to Europe, was to be taken by two poets of a new generation, two outsiders who broke with the traditions of mainstream literature and gave Albanian culture its place in a contemporary Europe: the messianic Migjeni and the pantheistic Lasgush Poradeci.

Migjeni[101] was born in Shkodra on 13 October 1911. His father, Gjergj Nikolla (1872-1924), came from an Orthodox family of Dibran origin and owned a bar there. In 1900, Gjergj Nikolla married Sofia Anastas Kokoshi (1881-1916) who bore him four daughters, Jelena (Lenka), Jovanka, Cvetka and Ollga, and two sons, Nikolla (1901-1925) and Millosh (Mirko).

The young Mirko attended a Serbian Orthodox elementary school in Shkodra and from 1923 to 1925 began studying at a secondary school in Bar (Tivar) on the Montenegrin coast, where his eldest sister, Lenka, was living. In the autumn of 1925, when he was fourteen, he obtained a scholarship to attend a secondary school in Monastir (Bitola) in southern Macedonia. This ethnically diverse town, not far from the Greek border, must have held a certain fascination for the young lad from distant Shkodra, since he came into contact there not only with Albanians from different parts of the Balkans, but also with Macedonian, Serb, Aromunian, Turkish and Greek students. Being of Slavic origin himself, he was not confined by narrow-minded nationalist perspectives and was to become one of the very few Albanian authors to bridge the cultural chasm separating the Albanians and Serbs. In Monastir he studied Old Church Slavonic, Russian, Greek, Latin and French. Graduating from school in 1927, he entered the Orthodox Seminary of St John the Theologian, also in Monastir,

---

[101] cf. A. Pipa 1945, 1971; G. Ejntrej 1973; M. Kraja 1973; V. Bala 1974; M. Raifi 1975, 1986; P. Janura 1982; S. Fetiu 1984; A. Llunji 1990; I. Kadare 1991; R. Idrizi 1992; and L. Radi 1998.

where, despite incipient health problems, he continued his training and studies until June 1932. Mirko read as many books as he could get his hands on: Russian, Serbian and French literature in particular, which were more to his tastes than theology. His years in Monastir confronted him with the dichotomy of East and West; with the Slavic soul of Holy Mother Russia and of the southern Slavs, which he encountered in the works of Fyodor Dostoyevsky, Ivan Turgenev, Lev Tolstoy, Nikolay Gogol and Maksim Gorky; and with socially critical authors of the West from Jean-Jacques Rousseau, Friedrich Schiller, Stendhal and Emile Zola to Upton Sinclair, Jack London and Ben Traven.

On his return to Shkodra in 1932, after failing to win a scholarship to study in the 'wonderful West,' Mirko decided to take up a teaching career rather than join the priesthood for which he had been trained. On 23 April 1933, he was appointed teacher of Albanian at a school in the Serb village of Vraka, seven kilometers north of Shkodra. It was during this period that he also began writing prose sketches and verse which reflect the life and anguish of an intellectual in what certainly was and has remained the most backward region of Europe. In May 1934, his first short prose piece, *Sokrat i vuejtun a po derr i kënaqun* (Suffering Socrates or the satisfied pig), was published in the periodical *Illyria*, under his new pen-name Migjeni, an acronym of *Millosh Gjergj Nikolla*. Soon though, in the summer of 1935, the twenty-three-year-old Migjeni fell seriously ill with tuberculosis, which he had contracted earlier. He journeyed to Athens in July of that year in hope of obtaining treatment for the disease which was endemic on the marshy coastal plains of Albania at the time, but returned to Shkodra a month later with no improvement in his condition. In the autumn of 1935, he transferred for a year to a school in Shkodra itself and, again in the periodical *Illyria*, began publishing his first epoch-making poems.

In a letter of 12 January 1936 written to translator Skënder Luarasi (1900-1982) in Tirana, Migjeni announced, "I am about to send my songs to press. Since, while you were here, you promised that you would take charge of speaking to some publisher, 'Gutemberg' for instance, I would now like to remind you of this promise, informing you that I am ready." Two days later, Migjeni received the transfer he had earlier requested to the mountain town of Puka and on 18 April 1936 began his activities as the headmaster of a rundown school there.

The clear mountain air did him some good, but the poverty and misery of the mountain tribes in and around Puka were even more overwhelming than that which he had experienced among the inhabitants of the coastal plain. Many of the children came to school barefoot and hungry, and teaching was interrupted for long periods of time because of outbreaks of contagious diseases, such as measles and mumps. After eighteen hard months in the mountains, the consumptive poet was obliged to put an end to his career as a teacher and as a writer, and to seek medical treatment in Turin in northern Italy where his sister Ollga was studying mathematics. He set out from Shkodra on 20 December 1937 and arrived in Turin before Christmas day. There he had hoped, after recovery, to register and study at the Faculty of Arts. The breakthrough in the treatment of tuberculosis, however, was to come a decade too late for Migjeni. After five months at the San Luigi sanatorium near Turin, he was transferred to a Waldensian hospital at Torre Pellice and died there on 26 August 1938. His demise at the age of twenty-six was a tragic loss for modern Albanian letters.

Migjeni made a promising start as a prose writer. He is the author of about twenty-four short prose sketches which he published in periodicals, for the most part between the spring of 1934 and the spring of 1938. Ranging from one to five pages in length, these pieces are too short to constitute tales or short stories. Although he approached new themes with unprecedented cynicism and force, his sketches cannot all be considered great works of art from a literary point of view.

It is far more as a poet that Migjeni made his mark on Albanian literature and culture, though he did so posthumously. He possessed all the prerequisites for being a great poet. He had an inquisitive mind, a depressive pessimistic nature and a repressed sexuality. Though his verse production was no more voluminous than his prose, his success in the field of poetry was no less than spectacular in Albania at the time.

Migjeni's only volume of verse, *Vargjet e lira*, Tirana 1944 (Free verse), was composed over a three-year period from 1933 to 1935. A first edition of this slender and yet revolutionary collection, a total of thirty-five poems, was printed by the Gutemberg Press in Tirana in 1936 but was immediately banned by the authorities and never circulated. The second edition of 1944, undertaken by scholar Kostaç Cipo (1892-1952) and the poet's sister Ollga, was more successful. It nonetheless omitted two poems, *Parathanja e parathanjeve* (Preface of prefaces) and *Blasfemi* (Blasphemy), which the publisher, Ismail Mal'Osmani, felt might offend the Church. The 1944 edition did, however, include eight other poems composed after the first edition had already gone to press.

The main theme of 'Free verse,' as with Migjeni's prose, is misery and suffering. It is poetry of acute social awareness and despair. Previous generations of poets had sung the beauties of the Albanian mountains and the sacred traditions of the nation, whereas Migjeni now opened his eyes to the harsh realities of life, to the appalling level of misery, disease and poverty which he discovered all around him. He was a poet of despair who saw no way out, who cherished no hope that anything but death could put an end to suffering. "I suffer with the child whose father cannot buy him a toy. I suffer with the young man who burns with unslaked sexual desire. I suffer with the middle-aged man drowning in the apathy of life. I suffer with the old man who trembles at the prospect of death. I suffer with the peasant struggling with the soil. I suffer with the worker crushed by iron. I suffer with the sick suffering from all the diseases of the world... I suffer with man."[102] The poet paints a grim portrait of our earthly existence: sombre nights, tears, smoke, thorns and mud. Rarely does a breath of fresh air or a vision of nature seep through the gloom. When nature does occur in the verse of Migjeni, then of course it is autumn, as in *Vjeshta në parakalim* (Autumn on parade):

"Vjeshtë në natyrë dhe vjeshtë ndër ftyra t'ona,
Afshon erë e mekun, lëngon i zymtë dielli,
Lëngon shpirt' i smum ndër krahnore t'ona,
Dridhet jet' e vyshkun ndër gemba të një plepi.

Ngjyrët e verdha losin në vallen e fundme -
(dëshirë e mârrë e gjethve që një nga një vdesin!)
Gëzimet, andjet t'ona, dëshirat e fundme
Nepër balta të vjeshtës një nga një po shkelin.

Një lis pasqyrohet në lotin e qiellit,
Tundet dhe përgjaket në pasjon të vigânit:
"Jetë! Jetë unë due!" - e frymë merr prej fellit,
Si stuhi shkynë ajrin... por në fund i a nis vajit.

Dhe m'at vaj bashkohet horizont' i mbytun
Në mjegullë përpîse. Pemët, degët e lagun
Me vaj i mshtjellin në lutje - por kotë! E dinë të fikun,
Se nesër do vdesin... Vall! A ka shpëtim ndokund?!

Mallëngjehet syni, mallëngjehet zêmra
N'orën e vorreses, kur heshtin damaret,
E vorri naltohet nën qiella mâ t'epra
Me klithëm dëshprimi që në dhimbë të madhe xvarret.

---

[102] cf. A. Pipa 1978, p. 148.

Vjeshtë në natyrë dhe vjeshtë ndër ftyra tona,
Rrënkoni dëshirat fëmitë e jetës së varfun,
Rrënkoni në zije, qani mbi kufoma,
Që stolisin vjeshtën nepër gemba të thamun. "

(Autumn in nature and autumn in our faces.
The sultry breeze enfeebles, the glowering sun
Oppresses the ailing spirit in our breasts,
Shrivels the life trembling among the twigs of a poplar.

The yellow colours twirl in the final dance,
(A frantic desire of leaves dying one by one).
Our joys, passions, our ultimate desires
Fall and are trampled in the autumn mud.

An oak-tree, reflected in the tears of heaven,
Tosses and bleeds in gigantic passion.
"To live! I want to live!" - it fights for breath,
Piercing the storm with cries of grief.

The horizon, drowned in fog, joins in
The lamentation. In prayer dejected fruit trees
Fold imploring branches - but in vain, they know.
Tomorrow they will die... Is there nowhere hope?

The eye is saddened. Saddened, too, the heart
At the hour of death, when silent fall the veins
And from the grave to the highest heavens soar
Despairing cries of long-unheeded pain.

Autumn in nature and autumn in our faces.
Moan, desires, off-spring of poverty,
Groan in lamentation, bewail the corpses,
That adorn this autumn among the withered branches.)

If there is no hope, there are at least suffocated desires and wishes.
Some poems, such as *Të birtë e shekullit të ri* (The Sons of the new age),
Zgjimi (Awakening), *Kanga e rinis* (Song of youth) and *Kanga e të burgosunit*
(The Prisoner's song), are assertively declamatory in a left-wing revolutionary
manner. Here we discover Migjeni as a precursor of socialist verse or rather,
in fact, the zenith of genuine socialist verse in Albanian letters, long before the

so-called liberation and socialist period from 1944 to 1990. Migjeni was, nonetheless, not a socialist or revolutionary poet in the political sense, despite the indignation and the occasional clenched fist he shows us. For this, he lacked the optimism as well as any adherence to political commitment and activity. He was a product of the thirties, an age in which Albanian intellectuals, including Migjeni, were particularly fascinated by the West and in which, in Western Europe itself, the rival ideologies of communism and fascism were colliding for the first time in the Spanish Civil War. Migjeni was not entirely uninfluenced by the nascent philosophy of the right either. In *Të lindet njeriu* (May the man be born) and particularly, in the Nietzschean dithyramb *Trajtat e Mbinjeriut* (The Shapes of the Superman), a strangled, crushed will transforms itself into an "ardent desire for a new genius," for the Superman to come. To a Trotskyite friend, Andrea Stefi (1911-1963), who had warned him that the communists would not forgive for such poems, Migjeni replied, "My work has a combative character, but for practical reasons, and taking into account our particular conditions, I must manoeuvre in disguise. I cannot explain these things to the [communist] groups, they must understand them for themselves. The publication of my works is dictated by the necessities of the social situation through which we are passing. As for myself, I consider my work to be a contribution to the union of the groups. André, my work will be achieved if I manage to live a little longer."[103]

Part of the 'establishment' which he felt was oblivious to and indeed responsible for the sufferings of humanity was the Church. Migjeni's religious education and his training for the Orthodox priesthood seem to have been entirely counterproductive, for he cherished neither an attachment to religion nor any particularly fond sentiments for the organized Church. God for Migjeni was a giant with granite fists crushing the will of man. Evidence of the repulsion he felt towards god and the Church are to be found in the two poems missing from the 1944 edition, *Parathania e parathanieve* (Preface of prefaces) with its cry of desperation "God! Where are you?," and *Blasfemi* (Blasphemy).

In *Kanga skandaloze* (Scandalous song), Migjeni expresses a morbid attraction to a pale nun and at the same time his defiance and rejection of her world. This poem is one which helps throw some light not only on Migjeni's attitude to religion but also on one of the more fascinating and least studied aspects in the life of the poet, his repressed heterosexuality.

Eroticism has certainly never been a prominent feature of Albanian literature at any period and one would be hard pressed to name any Albanian author who has expressed his intimate impulses and desires in verse or prose.

---

[103] cf. A. Pipa 1978, p. 150n.

Migjeni comes closest, though in an unwitting manner. It is generally assumed that the poet remained a virgin until his untimely death at the age of twenty-six. His verse and his prose abound with the figures of women, many of them unhappy prostitutes, for whom Migjeni betrays both pity and an open sexual interest. It is the tearful eyes and the red lips which catch his attention; the rest of the body is rarely described. For Migjeni, sex too means suffering. Passion and rapturous desire are ubiquitous in his verse, but equally present is the spectre of physical intimacy portrayed in terms of disgust and sorrow. It is but one of the many bestial faces of misery described in the 105-line *Poema e mjerimit* (Poem of poverty).

> *"Mjerimi tërbohet në dashuni epshore.*
> *Nepër skâje t'errta, bashkë me qejë, mijë, mica,*
> *Mbi pecat e mbykta, të qelbta, të ndyta, të lagta*
> *Lakuriqen mishnat, si zhangë, të verdhë e pisa,*
> *Kapërthehen ndjenjat me fuqí shtazore,*
> *Kafshojnë, përpijnë, thithen, puthen buzët e ndragta*
> *Edhe shuhet ûja, dhe fashitet etja*
> *N'epshin kapërthyes, kur mbytet vetvetja.*
> *Dhe aty zajnë fillin të mârrët, shërbtorët dhe lypsat*
> *Që nesër do linden me na i mbushë rrugat..."*

(Poverty wallows in debauchery.
In dark corners, together with dogs, rats, cats,
On mouldy, stinking, filthy mattresses,
Naked breasts exposed, sallow dirty bodies,
With feelings overwhelmed by bestial desire,
They bite, devour, suck, kiss the sullied lips,
And in unbridled lust the thirst is quenched,
The craving stilled, and self-consciousness lost.
Here is the source of the imbeciles, servants and beggars
Who will tomorrow be born to fill the streets...)

How far Albanian literature has suddenly progressed from the quaint folklore and remote artificialities of Çajupi and Fishta! Though he did not publish a single book during his lifetime, Migjeni's works, which circulated privately and in the press of the period, were an immediate success. Migjeni paved the way for modern literature in Albania.

This literature was, however, soon to be cut down before it flowered. Indeed the very year of the publication of 'Free Verse' saw the victory of Stalinism in Albania and the proclamation of the People's Republic.

Many have speculated as to what contribution Migjeni might have made to Albanian letters had he managed to live longer. The question remains highly hypothetical, for this individualist voice of genuine social protest would no doubt have suffered the same fate as most Albanian writers of talent in the late forties, i.e. internment, imprisonment or execution. His early demise has at least preserved the writer for us undefiled.

The fact that Migjeni did perish so young makes it difficult to provide a critical assessment of his work. Though generally admired, Migjeni is not without critics. Some have been disappointed by his prose, nor is the range of his verse sufficient to allow us to acclaim him as a universal poet. Albanian-American scholar Arshi Pipa (1920-1997) has questioned his very mastery of the Albanian language, asserting: "Born Albanian to a family of Slavic origin, then educated in a Slavic cultural milieu, he made contact again with Albania and the Albanian language and culture as an adult. The language he spoke at home was Serbo-Croatian, and at the seminary he learned Russian. He did not know Albanian well. His texts swarm with spelling mistakes, even elementary ones, and his syntax is far from being typically Albanian. What is true of Italo Svevo's Italian is even truer of Migjeni's Albanian."[104]

Post-war Stalinist critics in Albania rather superficially proclaimed Migjeni as the precursor of socialist realism though they were unable to deal with many aspects of his life and work, in particular his Schopenhauerian pessimism, his sympathies with the West, his repressed sexuality, and the Nietzschean element in *Trajtat e Mbinjeriut* (The Shapes of the Superman), a poem conveniently left out of some post-war editions of his verse. While such critics have delighted in viewing Migjeni as a product of 'pre-liberation' Zogist Albania, it has become painfully evident that the poet's 'songs unsung,' after half a century of communist dictatorship in Albania, are now more compelling than ever.

The road to modernity in Albanian literature was also taken by a poet of a very different nature, another outsider who, half a century later, is now regarded by many as the greatest Albanian poet of the twentieth century: **Lasgush Poradeci**[105] (1899-1987). This last classic writer of our times died at the age of eighty-seven. He had lived the final years of his life in his beloved town of Pogradec on Lake Ohrid, not far from the Macedonian border, tending

---

[104] cf. A. Pipa 1978, p. 134.

[105] cf. E. Çabej 1929, reprinted 1986-1989, vol. 5, p. 87-89; M. Kuteli 1938b; K. Maloku 1938; R. Qosja 1968, p. 135-177; S. Hamiti 1983, p. 257-274; M. Raifi 1986, p. 13-31 et passim; P. Kolevica 1988, 1992; M. Lalaj 1995; E. Kabashi 1997; S. Hamiti 1999; T. Mato 2000; and H. Matoshi 2000.

his garden and studying the ever-changing moods of the lake. The rhythmic and gentle lapping of the waves had always been among the fundamental sources of his pantheistic verse.

Lasgush Poradeci, pseudonym of Llazar Gusho, was born in Pogradec on 27 December 1899 - being only three or four days older than the twentieth century, as he once remarked. He attended a Romanian-language school in Monastir (Bitola), Macedonia, from 1909 to 1916. In the middle of the First World War, his father, despite the tenuous relations between Albanians and Greeks in southeastern Albania at the time, sent the adolescent Llazar to Greece to continue his schooling, on the condition that he not study at a Greek-language institution. Llazar therefore enrolled at the French-language Lycée des Frères Maristes in Athens where he remained until 1920. For health reasons, however, the last two years of his stay in the Greek capital were spent not at school but in a sanatorium to which, despite his desperate financial situation, he was referred with the assistance of Sophia Schliemann, widow of the famed German archaeologist, Heinrich Schliemann (1822-1890). Although not completely recovered, the twenty-year-old Llazar was expelled from the sanatorium prematurely in 1920 after having been caught *in flagranti* with a nurse. The following year we find the budding poet in Bucharest, where he joined his brother. Llazar wanted to study at the Academy of Fine Arts, but registering proved to be difficult, since the Romanian government, in a wave of anti-semitism, had imposed restrictions on study by all non-Romanian nationals. After much tribulation, however, he succeeded in enrolling. The poet's stay in Bucharest was to have a decisive influence on his literary development. It was here that he met and befriended the romantic poet Asdreni, whom he replaced as secretary of the Albanian colony in 1922, short-story writer Mitrush Kuteli (1907-1967), and numerous Romanian writers and poets. He also began publishing verse in various Albanian-language periodicals: *Shqipëri' e re* (New Albania), an illustrated national weekly published in Constanza, and *Dielli* (The Sun) of Boston, among others. His verse of this period was already revealing a certain theosophical affinity to the Romanian lyric poet Mihai Eminescu (1850-1889).

A scholarship provided by the Fan Noli government in 1924 enabled him to continue his studies abroad. Poradeci immediately left for Berlin, where he hoped to study under Austrian Albanologist Norbert Jokl (1877-1942). The chair appears to have been vacant at the time and Poradeci continued on to the University of Graz in southeastern Austria where he registered at the Faculty of Romance and Germanic philology. The poet spent a total of ten years in Graz which he counted as the most enjoyable of his life. In May 1933, he finished his doctorate there with a dissertation on *Der verkannte Eminescu und seine volkstümlich-heimatliche Ideologie* (The Unappreciated Eminescu and his native folk ideology). The following year, Poradeci returned to Albania and taught art at a secondary school in Tirana, where he remained during the war. From 1944 until 1947, the first turbulent years of communist rule, he was unemployed, and lived with his wife in Tirana on the latter's meagre salary as a teacher. After brief employment at the Institute of Science, forerunner of the University of Tirana, he got a job translating literature for the state-owned Naim Frashëri publishing company where he worked, keeping a low profile, until his retirement in 1974. He died in absolute poverty at his home in Tirana on 12 November 1987.

Lasgush Poradeci is the author of two much-enjoyed collections of poetry. *Vallja e yjve* (The Dance of the stars) and *Ylli i zemrës* (The Star of the heart), published in Romania in 1933 and 1937 respectively, are indeed just as much a revolution in Albanian verse as was Migjeni's *Vargjet e lira* (Free verse). *Vallja e yjve* was published at the Albania Press in Constanza from funds collected in 1932 with the help of Asdreni and a group of Albanian students in Bucharest. It contains verse first written and published in the years 1921-1924. The second volume, published with the assistance of Poradeci's friend, prose writer Mitrush Kuteli, contains not only later work but also many of the poems of the 1933 edition in amended versions. It is a synthesis of the best of his lyric production and offers some of the most melodious and metrically refined poetry ever written in Albanian.

Poradeci's position in Albanian literature has never been satisfactorily defined. He had little in common with his contemporaries: the romantic Asdreni, the political Fan Noli or the messianic Migjeni. He imbued Albanian letters with a quite exotic element of pantheistic mysticism, introducing what he called the metaphysics of creative harmony. What other Albanian poet of his period would have devoted his energy to the study of Sanskrit in order to comprehend the Veda? Poradeci's verse creates a metaphysical bridge from the psychic states and trying moods of earthly existence to the lofty spheres of the sublime, to the source of all creative energy.

Primordial to the work of Lasgush Poradeci are the waters of Lake Ohrid on the Albanian-Macedonian border. It was in the town of Pogradec that he spent his youth, not far from where, at the foot of the 'Mal i Thatë' (Dry Mountain), the River Drin takes its source, and but a few kilometers from the famed mediaeval monastery of St Naum's just over the border. And there in retirement, he also spent his last summers in a run-down little house, tending his garden and strolling along the lake with his dog. Lake Ohrid never ceased to fascinate and enchant him. He studied its hues, the reflection of light both upon its waves and in the depths of its sparkling waters, and observed the surrounding mountains cast their shadows over it. There, in a simple grave overlooking the lake to which he dedicated his incomparable *Mëngjes* (Morning), the poet lies buried.

> "*Si shpirt' i zi në kraharuar,*
> *U mbyll liqeri nënë male.*
> *Ndaj fund' i ti e pasqyruar,*
> *Po shuhet nata me-nga-dale.*
>
> *E shoh ku vdes e ku po vuan,*
> *E syt' e saj dyke pulitur;*
> *E syt' e saj q'u mavijuan,*
> *Jan' yjt' e qjellit të venitur.*
>
> *Tashi dh' agimi llambaritës*
> *Po svagullon në fund liqeri,*
> *Po tretet tinës yll' i dritës*
> *Posi një sumbull prej sheqeri.*
>
> *Pra ja! pra ja! se dita ndezi,*
> *Se fund' i ujit vetëtiti,*
> *Se posi lajmëtar - mëngjezi,*
> *Del zogu-i bardh' i një nositi...*"

(Like a spirit sombre within the breast
Lies the lake encased in hills.
Mirrored in its depths,
Night expires breath by breath.

I watch how she suffers, how she dies,
Her eyes blinking,
Azure-circled pools,
Like the stars of a fading sky.

But now the light of dawn
Shimmers deep within the lake.
The daystar steals away, melting
Like a piece of sugar candy.

Behold, day has dawned,
And lightning flashes from the depths.

Like a harbinger of morn
Appears, bird-white, a pelican.)

An eclectic child of his age, Poradeci was and remains one of the many paradoxes of southeastern European literature. Kosova critic Rexhep Qosja has aptly noted that "he felt like a Romantic, thought like a Classicist, was as solitary and spiritually hermetic as a Symbolist and as precise as a Parnassist in the form of his verse. He was eclectic and original from every point of view."[106]

Apart from the two main poetry collections of the thirties, Poradeci published some verse in literary journals of the late thirties and forties, in particular in Branko Merxhani's cultural monthly *Përpjekja shqiptare* (The Albanian endeavour). With the rise of Stalinism, however, the venerable quill of Lasgushi, as he was to be affectionately known to posterity, began to run dry. Though secretly lauded by many a critic and connoisseur, this romantic aesthete, devoid of any redeeming ideological values, never enjoyed the approbation of post-war Marxist dogmatists. They were not able to understand his works and the poet himself is reported to have preferred to break his pencil in two rather than write the kind of poetry 'they' wanted. A few works did appear from time to time in the Tirana literary periodicals *Drita* (The Light) and *Nëntori* (November), carefully perused beforehand by party censors, but Poradeci's main field of activity in the socialist period was, nolens volens, translation, a safer haven for literary heretics.

Aside from verse on nature and that in a metaphysical vein, reworked and republished in numerous versions, Poradeci was also the author of much love poetry as well as of some verse on national themes, all in all about one hundred poems. He loved archaic words and expressions but also delighted in neologisms and a novel juxtaposing of substantives to create unusual effects. The result was startling, breathtaking at the time, and he was immediately acclaimed. The age of romantic nationalism, which had been fostered by a myriad of Rilindja poets of varying quality, had now drawn to a definitive close.

Poradeci's subjects, his structures and language were very much attuned to southern Albanian oral literature, in particular to Tosk folk verse from which he drew a good deal of his inspiration. Mitrush Kuteli, who edited his *Ylli i zemrës*, called him "the only Albanian poet to think, speak and write only in Albanian." Lasgush Poradeci is, at the same time, an artist of truly European stature. He combined the verbal sensuousness of Charles Baudelaire,

---

[106] R. Qosja 1979, p. 144.

142

the aesthetic philosophy of form and the discerning elegance of Stefan George, the humanity and philosophy of Naim Frashëri, and the cosmic immortality of his master, Mihai Eminescu. Scholar Eqrem Çabej said of him that he was the "poet whom Albania would one day bequeath to the world," and although Poradeci's verse does not lend itself particularly to translation, time may prove Çabej right.

5.5   The Prose of the Independence Period: Ernest Koliqi and Mitrush Kuteli

Poetry has always been the mainstay of Albanian letters. Indeed, one of the most conspicuous discrepancies in the historical development of Albanian writing has been the one between the vigorous growth of poetry and the exceptionally sluggish evolution of prose. This phenomenon is apparent from the early literature of the sixteenth and seventeenth centuries right up to the second half of the twentieth century. Although the classic authors of the seventeenth century, Pjetër Budi and Pjetër Bogdani in particular, did lay foundations for Albanian prose with their religious translations and original prose texts of artistic quality and style, original literary prose remained a marginal phenomenon well into the twentieth century. The first 'Albanian' novels, products of the second half of the nineteenth century, were either written in foreign languages, as we have seen, or remained unpublished. Late-nineteenth-century journalism provided a solid foundation for modern prose writing, though the first substantial corpus of literary prose appeared only at the beginning of the twentieth century with the works of Dom Ndoc Nikaj of Shkodra. Many other Rilindja authors, such as Mihal Grameno (1872-1931) and Mid'hat bey Frashëri, had dabbled in prose writing, but it was actually only after Albanian independence, with the essays of Faik bey Konitza and works of Fan Noli, that a satisfactory stylistic level was achieved. Unfortunately, however, though Konitza and Noli were writers of great talent and potential, neither of them devoted much energy to the production of original literary prose.

The independence period saw a dramatic increase in the volume and range of prose being written and published in Albanian, in both the northern Gheg and the southern Tosk dialects. The zenith of this period of Albanian literature was reached in the nineteen thirties and early forties when intellectuals in Shkodra, Tirana and elsewhere in the country, having accessed many of the ideas and models of the outside world, began producing prose, some drama and of course verse more worthy of Albania as a rising European nation.

Of all the prose writers of the period, none was more imposing and influential than **Ernest Koliqi**[107] (1903-1975). Koliqi was born in Shkodra on 20 May 1903 and was educated at the Jesuit college of Arice in the Lombardian town of Brescia, where he became acquainted with Italian literature and culture and first began writing verse, short stories and comedies in Italian. In Bergamo, he and some fellow pupils founded a weekly student newspaper called *Noi, giovanni* (We, the young) in which his first poems appeared.

With the formation of a new regency government in Albania under Sulejman Pasha Delvina (1884-1932) and the return of a semblance of stability in the country with the Congress of Lushnja (28-31 January 1920), the young Ernest arrived back in Shkodra to rediscover and indeed to relearn his mother tongue and the culture of his childhood in a newly independent country. His mentor, Msgr. Luigj Bumçi (1872-1945), who had served as president of the Albanian delegation to the Paris Peace Conference in 1919, introduced Ernest to some of the leading proponents of a new generation of Scutarine culture: Kolë Thaçi (1886-1941), Kolë Kamsi (1886-1960), Lazër Shantoja (1892-1945) and Karl Gurakuqi (1895-1971).

What Albania needed most after the ravages of the First World War was knowledge and to this end Koliqi resolved to set up a newspaper. Together with Anton Harapi (1888-1946) and Nush Topalli, he thus founded the opposition weekly *Ora e maleve* (The Mountain fairy), the first issue of which appeared in Shkodra on 15 April 1923. *Ora e maleve*, widely distributed during the course of its ephemeral existence, was the organ of the Catholic Democratic Party which, with the support of the Catholic clergy, had won the elections in Shkodra. The following year, having gained acceptance as a rising poet among the more established literary and political figures of the age, Gjergj Fishta, Luigj Gurakuqi, Mid'hat bey Frashëri and Fan Noli, Ernest Koliqi published a so-called dramatic poem entitled *Kushtrimi i Skanderbeut*, Tirana 1924 (Scanderbeg's war cry), a series of odes on the Albanian national hero and other great figures of the past, composed very much in the traditions of Rilindja literature.

Political and economic life in Albania continued to be chaotic in the early twenties. When conservative landowner Ahmet Zogu (1895-1961) took power in a coup d'état in December 1924, Koliqi escaped to Yugoslavia where

---

[107] cf. A. Guzzetta 1968; P. Bartl 1973; G. Gradilone 1969, 1974, p. 230-272; Shêjzat commemorative issue 1976; A. Plasari 1996b; S. Schwartz 1992; A. Berisha 1995a; and P. Vuçani 1995.

he was interned in Tuzla in northeastern Bosnia. He lived for five years in Yugoslav exile, three of them in Tuzla, where he spent much of his time with the leaders in exile of the northern Albanian mountain tribes. From them he learned of the ancient customs, oral literature and heroic lifestyle of the mountain peoples. These years were to have a profound impact on his academic and literary career. From 1930 to 1933, Koliqi taught at a commercial school in Vlora and at the state secondary school in Shkodra until he was obliged, once again by political circumstances, to depart for Italy.

Ernest Koliqi's solid Jesuit education enabled him from the start to serve as a cultural intermediary between Italy and Albania. In later decades, he was to play a key role in transmitting Albanian culture to the Italian public by publishing, in addition to numerous scholarly articles on literary and historical subjects, the monographs: *Poesia popolare albanese*, Florence 1957 (Albanian folk verse), *Antologia della lirica albanese*, Milan 1963 (Anthology of Albanian poetry), and *Saggi di letteratura albanese*, Florence 1972 (Essays on Albanian literature). In the mid-thirties he was concerned with cultural transmission in the other direction. Koliqi published a large two-volume Albanian-language anthology of Italian verse entitled *Poetët e mëdhej t'Italis*, Tirana 1932, 1936 (The Great poets of Italy), to introduce Italian literature to the new generation of Albanian intellectuals eager to discover the world around them.

Now thirty years of age, Koliqi registered at the University of Padua in 1933. After five years of study under linguist Carlo Tagliavini (1903-1982), and of teaching Albanian there, he graduated in 1937 with a thesis on the *Epica popolare albanese* (Albanian folk epic). Though working in Padua, he had not lost contact with Albania and collaborated on the editorial board of the noted cultural weekly *Illyria* (Illyria) which began publication in Tirana on 4 March 1934. Koliqi was now a recognized Albanologist, perhaps the leading specialist in Albanian studies in Italy. In 1939, as the clouds of war gathered over Europe, he was appointed to the chair of Albanian language and literature at the University of Rome, at the heart of Mussolini's new Mediterranean empire.

Koliqi's strong affinity for Italy and Italian culture, in particular for poets such as Giosuè Carducci, Giovanni Pascoli, and Gabriele D'Annunzio, may have contributed to his acceptance of fascist Italy's expansionist designs. Though few minor Albanian writers, such as Vangjel Koça (1900-1943) and Vasil Alarupi (1908-1977), were genuine proponents of fascism, some did see a certain advantage to Italian tutelage despite their general opposition to foreign interference in Albanian affairs. Ernest Koliqi and all other intellectuals of the period were forced, at any rate, to come to terms in one way or another with the political and cultural dilemma of Italy's growing influence in Albania and, on Good Friday 1939, with its military conquest and consequent

145

absorption of the little Balkan country. As much of an Albanian nationalist as any other, Koliqi, now the country's *éminence grise*, chose to make the best of the reality with which he was faced and do what he could to further Albanian culture under Italian rule. Accepting the post of Albanian minister of education from 1939 to 1941, much to the consternation of large sections of the population, he assisted, for instance, in the historic publication of a major two-volume anthology of Albanian literature, *Shkrimtarët shqiptarë*, Tirana 1941 (Albanian writers), edited by Namik Ressuli and Karl Gurakuqi, an edition to which the best scholars of the period contributed. In July 1940, he founded and subsequently ran the literary and artistic monthly *Shkëndija* (The Spark) in Tirana. Under Koliqi's ministerial direction, Albanian-language schools, which had been outlawed under Serbian rule, were first opened in Kosova, which was reunited with Albania during the war years. Koliqi also assisted in the opening of a secondary school in Prishtina and arranged for scholarships to be distributed to Kosova students for training abroad in Italy and Austria. He also made an attempt to save Norbert Jokl (1877-1942), the renowned Austrian Albanologist of Jewish origin, from the hands of the Nazis by offering him a teaching position in Albania. From 1942 to 1943, Koliqi was president of the newly formed Institute of Albanian Studies (*Istituti i Studimevet Shqiptare*) in Tirana, a forerunner of the Academy of Sciences. In 1943, on the eve of the collapse of Mussolini's empire, he succeeded Terenzio Tocci (1880-1945) as president of the Fascist Grand Council in Tirana, a post which did not endear him to the victorious communist forces which 'liberated' Tirana in November 1944. With the defeat of fascism, Koliqi fled to Italy again, where he lived, no less active in the field of literature and culture, until his death on 15 January 1975.

It was in Rome that he published the noted literary periodical *Shêjzat / Le Plèiadi* (The Pleiades) from 1957 to 1973. *Shêjzat* was the leading Albanian-language cultural periodical of its time. Not only did it keep abreast of contemporary literary trends in the Albanian-speaking world, it also gave voice to Arbëresh literature and continued to uphold the literary heritage of prewar authors, many dead and some in exile, who were so severely denigrated by communist critics in Tirana. Ernest Koliqi thus served as a distant voice of opposition to the cultural destruction of Albania under Stalinist rule. Because of his activities and at least passive support of fascist rule and Italian occupation, Koliqi was virulently attacked by the post-war Albanian authorities - even more so than Gjergj Fishta, who had the good fortune of being dead - as the main proponent of bourgeois, reactionary and fascist literature. The 1983 party history of Albanian literature refers to him in passing only as "Koliqi the traitor."[108]

Ernest Koliqi first made a name for himself as a prose writer with the short story collection *Hija e maleve*, Zadar 1929 (The Spirit of the mountains), twelve tales of contemporary life in Shkodra and in the northern Albanian mountains. His comparatively realistic approach and his psychological analysis of human behaviour patterns did not find favour with all the established writers of the period, many of whom were still languishing in the sentimentality of romantic nationalism. The book nonetheless sold well and was much appreciated by the reading public at large. *Hija e maleve* contains short stories revolving around the basic theme of 'east meets west,' of the confrontation of traditional mountain customs, such as arranged marriages and tribal vendetta, with modern Western ideas and values. Though less autobiographical than Migjeni's short story *Studenti në shtëpi* (The Student at home), the tales are a direct reflection of the quandary in which Koliqi, like most other Scutarine intellectuals who had studied abroad in the twenties and thirties, found himself upon his return to the wilds of northern Albania. At the beginning of the tragic story *Gjaku* (The Blood feud), the young and idealistic teacher Doda asks, "Is there anything on earth more wonderful than bringing civilization to a people suffocating in darkness and ignorance?", but he himself is soon constrained by loyalty to his family to cleanse his honour and avenge the murder of his brother. Other tales tell, for instance, of a folk musician using his talents to woo a Shkodra maiden; of murder and vendetta among the mountain tribes; of an 'ugly duckling' transformed by the spirits of the mountains into a fair maiden and of the subsequent disillusionment of her boyfriend; of a manhunt by the gendarmes which is confounded by loyalties and obligations under tribal law; of the spell of the supernatural cast upon an outlaw; and of Scanderbeg. The spirits of the mountains are ever present in the mind of the writer and add an aura of the supernatural to many of the tales.

Tregtar flamujsh, Tirana 1935 (Flag merchant), Koliqi's second collection of tales, offered themes similar to those in the first collection. The narrative in this volume of sixteen short stories is more robust and the psychological insight reminiscent at times of Sicilian author Luigi Pirandello (1876-1936) with whom Koliqi was no doubt acquainted. The stories in *Tregtar flamujsh* are considered by many to rank among the best Albanian prose of the prewar period. A quarter of a century later, Koliqi also published a short novel, *Shija e bukës së mbrûme*, Rome 1960 (The Taste of sourdough bread). This 173-page work revives the theme of nostalgia for the homeland

---

[108] cf. Dh. Shuteriqi (ed.) 1983, p. 460.

felt by Albanian immigrants in the United States. Not devoid of political overtones, the novel was little known in Albania during the dictatorship.

The literary production of Ernest Koliqi was by no means restricted to prose. Rare is the Albanian writer not tempted by the poetic muse. *Gjurmat e stinve*, Tirana 1933 (The Traces of the seasons), is a verse collection composed for the most part during Koliqi's years of exile in Yugoslavia. It is the philosophical return to the poet's native Shkodra set forth in different emotional seasons, an entwinement of Albanian folk verse and Western European symbolism. *Symfonija e shqipevet*, Tirana 1941 (The Symphony of eagles), is prose poetry on historical and nationalist themes reminiscent of Koliqi's earlier *Kushtrimi i Skanderbeut* (Scanderbeg's war cry)[109]. Koliqi's final volume of verse, entitled *Kangjelet e Rilindjes*, Rome 1959 (Songs of rebirth), was composed again in his refined Gheg dialect and published with an Italian translation.

During the Stalinist period, Ernest Koliqi was judged in Albania much more for his political activities than for his literary and cultural achievements. Modern critics in Albania, having themselves survived half a century of Stalinism, should tend now to be more understanding of and sensitive to the compromises writers and intellectuals have often been forced to make under extremist regimes. As a literary and cultural figure, Ernest Koliqi was and remains a giant, in particular for his role in the development of northern Albanian prose. Literary production in Gheg dialect reached a zenith in the early forties from every point of view - style, range, content, volume - and much credit for this development goes to publisher, prose writer and scholar Ernest Koliqi. The northern Albanian dialect as a refined literary medium and indeed Scutarine culture in general had achieved a modest golden age, only to be brought to a swift demise at the end of the Second World War.

The name which immediately comes to mind in the search for a Tosk counterpart to Ernest Koliqi in the prose of the late thirties and early forties is that of **Mitrush Kuteli**[110] (1907-1967), pseudonym of *Dhimitër Pasko*, known in Romanian as *Dimitrie Pascu*. Kuteli, like Lasgush Poradeci, was born in Pogradec on the banks of Lake Ohrid on 13 September 1907 and, like Lasgush, attended a foreign-language school in Greece (a Romanian commercial college in Thessalonika) and later moved to Bucharest, where he studied economics and graduated in 1934 with a dissertation on the banking systems of the

---

[109] There is a now rare English translation with the title *The Symphony of eagles*, Rome 1972.

[110] cf. A. Jasiqi 1968; A. Vinca 1977, p. 7-104, 1996; N. Jorgaqi 1987, p. 89-112; S. Bashota 1988, 1998, 1999; and A. Plasari 1995.

Balkans. He collaborated for a time as a journalist at the Albanian weekly newspaper *Shqipëri' e re* (New Albania), edited in Constanza from 1919 to 1936. For his journalistic activities, he employed the pseudonym Janus, after the two-headed Roman god able to see into the past and into the future at the same time. It was also in Bucharest that Kuteli began publishing the collections of short stories for which he is best known. His first book, *Nete shqipëtare*, Bucharest 1938 (Albanian nights), was a compilation of eight tales on village life in and around his native Pogradec. Of the 1,200 copies of the first edition, about 1,000 were destroyed in a fire in Constanza before they could be sold, and the book only became widely known after the second edition of 1944. It was in Bucharest, too, that Kuteli arranged for the publication of Lasgush Poradeci's breathtaking verse collection *Ylli i zemrës* (The Star of the heart) in 1937. Romanian culture, still under the spell of national poet Mihai Eminescu, had left its impact on Mitrush Kuteli, as it had on Asdreni, Lasgush Poradeci and the many Albanian writers and intellectuals living there in the early decades of the twentieth century.

In the autumn of 1942, as the destruction and horror caused by the Second World War was gradually approaching its peak in the Balkans and the Soviet Union, Kuteli returned to Albania, which was itself on the verge of disintegrating into open civil war. It was during these war years that Kuteli, at his own expense, was able to publish most of his major works: *Ago Jakupi e të tjera rrëfime*, Tirana 1943 (Ago Jakupi and other tales), a collection of seven tales of peasant life; *Kapllan Aga i Shaban Shpatës. Rrëfime - Rrëfenja*, Tirana 1944 (Kapllan Aga of Shaban Shpata. Tales - Stories), five short stories written between 1938 and 1944; *Këngë e brithma nga qyteti i djegur*, Tirana 1944 (Songs and cries from a charred city), a collection of folk songs; *Shënime letrare*, Tirana 1944 (Literary notes); and *Sulm e lotë*, Tirana 1944 (Assault and tears), a collection of modest nationalist verse written by Kuteli and a fictitious friend named Izedin Jashar Kutrulija whom Kuteli claimed to have met in Prizren in May 1943. Also in this period, he edited a collection of the verse of Fan Noli (1882-1965) entitled *Mall e brengë*, Tirana 1943 (Longing and grief), and published a number of works on the finance and monetary system.

Mitrush Kuteli set the pace for the short story in southern Albania and managed to attain a higher level of literary sophistication than most other sentimental prose writers of the period: Milto Sotir Gurra (1884-1972), Foqion Postoli (1889-1927), Haki Stërmilli (1895-1953) or Kolë Mirdita (1900-1936). He derived many elements for his tales from the Tosk oral literature he had heard as a child, using them to create crystalline motifs of village life and a lively narrative style. Kuteli's syntax and lexicon are elaborate and his diction is often compelling. The peasant themes and the mixture of folksy humour and old-fashioned adventure made his tales popular with broad sections of the reading public during the war and thereafter. In some of his short stories one senses the atmosphere of nineteenth-century Russian prose, of Nikolay Gogol and Ivan Turgenev, whom the author had read and particularly enjoyed in his earlier years, and of Romanian prose writer Mihail Sadoveanu (1880-1961).

At the end of the Second World War Mitrush Kuteli, now an executive at the Albanian State Bank, was a leading figure of Albanian letters. On 15 February 1944, together with Vedat Kokona (1913-1998), Nexhat Hakiu (1917-1978) and Sterjo Spasse (1914-1989), he founded the fortnightly literary periodical *Revista letrare* (Literary review), which had a significant impact on Albanian culture during its short life. He was also a founding member of the Albanian Writers' Union, which was set up under the direction of Sejfulla Malëshova (1901-1971) on 7 October 1945, and a member of the editorial board of Albania's first post-war literary journal *Bota e re* (New world).

Kuteli managed to survive the transition of political power in Albania until the real terror began in 1947. During a purge which ensued after the Albanian Communist Party had come under Yugoslav domination, he unwisely disapproved of the proposed customs and monetary union between Albania and Yugoslavia. As a member of an official delegation to Yugoslavia, received among others by writer Ivo Andrić (1892-1975), he is also said to have expressed a critical attitude to the Serb re-occupation of Kosova, a stance reflected earlier in his *Poem kosovar* (Kosovar poem), published in 1944. Upon his return to Albania, he was arrested and sentenced to fifteen years in prison.

For Kuteli, as for most writers of the late forties, life had become a nightmare. He survived the first two years of his prison sentence (April 1947 to April 1949) in a labour camp near Korça where inmates were put to work draining the infamous mosquito-infested swamp of Maliq. Working and living conditions for the prisoners were unimaginably harsh, and Kuteli, amidst such horror, attempted suicide. But with the elimination of Yugoslav influence in Albanian party politics, the open persecution of Kuteli subsided and he was released. He returned to Tirana and was allowed, like Lasgush Poradeci and a number of other suspicious intellectuals, to work as a literary translator for the state-owned Naim Frashëri publishing company.

Zhdanovism, which had penetrated and taken thorough control of what was left of Albanian literature in the fifties, made it expedient at the time to translate Russian literature to serve as a model for the introduction of socialist realism in Albania. Kuteli willingly acquiesced by producing noted translations of recognized Soviet authors such as Maksim Gorky, Aleksey Tolstoy, Konstantin Paustovsky, Aleksandr Aleksandrovich Fadeyev and Nikolay Ostrovsky. Aside from these writers recommended by Soviet cultural and political advisors, Kuteli also managed to publish some translations of his favourite Russian authors of the nineteenth century: Nikolay Gogol, Ivan Turgenev, Ivan Krylov, and Mikhail Saltykov-Shchedrin.

In addition to these many translations from Russian, and others from Romanian (Mihai Eminescu, Mihail Sadoveanu), Spanish (Pablo Neruda), and French (André Maurois, Paul Eluard), etc., Kuteli is remembered in particular for his prose adaptation of a collection of Albanian oral verse, including the heroic cycle of Mujo and Halili, in *Tregime të moçme shqiptare*, Tirana 1965 (Early Albanian tales). He was also able to publish some verse and tales for children, the safest pastime for Eastern European writers in the Stalinist period. A novel on an Illyrian theme remained unfinished. Mitrush Kuteli died of a heart attack in Tirana on 4 May 1967, bereft of the honour and recognition due to the man who had made the short story a popular genre in Albania and who, had politics not interfered, might otherwise have been the leading prose writer of the fifties.

5.6   Other Authors Before the Communist Takeover

There were many other authors who contributed to the awakening of an independent Albanian culture, both in the more advanced south of the country and in the wild and traditional north. The educational foundations laid by the Catholic Church in Shkodra in the second half of the nineteenth century had visibly borne fruit in the independence period. Northern Albania, and in particular the isolated regions of the northern Albanian Alps with their unique tribal culture, had always lagged behind the more advanced south from an educational point of view, and indeed still do today. In the first third of the twentieth century, however, Shkodra itself overshadowed the country's new capital city Tirana by far, both educationally and culturally.

One Catholic writer from Shkodra, more than any other, would now seem to symbolize the final decades of Scutarine Catholic culture and its demise during the communist takeover, poet, folklorist and translator **Vinçenc Prennushi**[111] (1885-1949). In his ecclesiastical career, Prennushi served as a provincial from 1929 to 1936. On 19 March 1936, he was made Bishop of Sapa and in 1940 was appointed Archbishop of Durrës, thus becoming one of the two highest dignitaries of the Catholic Church in Albania. In 1924 Prennushi

---

[111] cf. A. Çapaliku 1996. For an account of Prennushi's last final years and death, cf. Arshi Pipa in Gj. Sinishta 1976, p. 79-90.

published a volume of elegant lyric verse in Gheg dialect entitled *Gjeth e lule*, Shkodra 1924 (Leaves and flowers), which was reprinted in 1931. This collection of sixty-five poems contains verse of both nationalist and religious inspiration. His patriotic poems are reminiscent of the standard motifs of Rilindja verse: Scanderbeg, the flag and self-sacrifice to the homeland in bondage, and often have a martial, indeed rather un-Franciscan ring to them. Such poems were popular at the time and many were recited by the public, such as *Grueja shqiptare* 1918 (The Albanian woman), in which a maiden spends her days embroidering a red and black Albanian flag, but in her concern for the nation she dies of grief and is buried in the flag herself. His spiritual poems, of mood rather than of ideas, are pensive. Many take up typically Catholic themes: the saviour on the cross, the Virgin Mary, St Francis of Assisi and Duns Scotus. The general tone of these poems, some of which offer poignant reflections on the futility of life, is sombre and melancholic rather than serene and confident. He is also remembered for his folklore collection *Kângë popullore gegnishte*, Sarajevo 1911 (Gheg folk songs), which made a major contribution to the study of Albanian oral literature, and for his translations.

Prennushi was arrested by the communist authorities after the war, and was tortured and sentenced by a military court in Durrës to twenty years of prison and hard labour as an enemy of the people. Weakened by prison conditions and suffering from asthma and heart disease, the sixty-three year old archbishop died in the prison hospital on 19 March 1949.

Another Franciscan poet with a passionate interest in folklore was **Bernardin Palaj**[112] (1894-1947), author of classical lyric and elegiac verse, much of which was published in the thirties in the Franciscan periodical *Hylli i Dritës* (The Day-star). This poetry of harmonious musicality and technical perfection, like that of Italian poet Giosuè Carducci, evinces a patriotic vision of the historic past and of the rich native culture of his people. His first poem *Prej burgut të jetës* (From life's prison), published in 1933 under the pseudonym Kukel Lapaj, is a 248-line religious hymn on the fall of man and his redemption. In deference to his master Gjergj Fishta, Palaj did not compose epic verse, although his affinity for the magical rhapsodic world of frontier heroes Mujo and Halili gave him both a talent and an inclination to do so. Fishta died on 30 December 1940 and Palaj was moved by the occasion to compose the 1,180-line elegy *Kah nata e vetme* (Towards the solitary night) in his honour. Here again it is the *zana*, the awesome muse of Fishta and that of the Albanian nation, who laments cruel fate and the solitude of the tomb in the tradition of the *gjamë*, the dirge of Gheg oral literature. Palaj was arrested in

---

[112] cf. A. Çapaliku 1999.

Shkodra, severely mishandled and then sentenced to death for treason. He died on 8 December 1947 in a Shkodra prison.

These Catholic poets stand for a host of scholars and secondary writers from among the Catholic clergy who were active in the field of culture and education up until 1944 and who made a significant contribution to Albanian letters. The death of these men, concomitant with the death of the Gheg dialect as a literary language, is also symbolic of the demise of Scutarine Catholic writing as a current of Albanian literature and indeed of the golden age of Scutarine Catholic culture in Albania.

In southern Albania, the quarter of a century before the communist takeover was also one of solid evolution in poetry, prose and, indeed, drama. Of the many Tosk authors of the period, mention may be made of the following.

Satirical poet and diplomat **Ali Asllani** (1884-1966) from Vlora is the author of one of the most delightful poetic works of pre-communist Albanian literature: the folksy narrative poem *Hanko Halla*, Tirana 1942 (The Lady aunt). Asllani was educated in Janina (Iôannina) and Constantinople before working as a public servant in the Ottoman administration. In 1912, he collaborated in the first independent Albanian government of Ismail Qemal bey Vlora (1844-1919) and subsequently held numerous government posts. In the thirties, he represented Albania at its diplomatic missions abroad as consul in Trieste and as ambassador in Sofia and Athens. Although Asllani wrote some love lyrics of note, it is *Hanko Halla* with its bouncy hendecasyllabic rhythm and colourful folk vocabulary for which he is best remembered. This humorous verse narrative depicts the struggles and apprehensions of a high-spirited lady of good breeding who is constantly at odds with the newfangled ways of the world. Raised in a traditional patriarchal society, she is flabbergasted by the innovations of youth, yet at the same time, she manages to laugh at her own conservatism. *Hanko Halla* ranks among the best verse of this genre in Albanian literature.

In the burgeoning field of literary prose, mention may be made of journalist and short story writer **Milto Sotir Gurra** (1884-1972) from the Korça region of southeastern Albania, who spent most of his productive life abroad: first in Odessa on the Black Sea, and later in America, Constantinople, Sofia and Constanza. As an emigrant, he well understood the loneliness and isolation of those in exile. Many of his short stories, written in an unpretentious narrative style, therefore reflect the nostalgia and bitterness of southern Albanians forced to emigrate from their homeland in search of work and a better life. A collection of twenty-two of these tales was published under the title *Plagët e kurbetit*, Tirana 1938 (The Torments of exile).

Also from Korça was sentimental novelist and playwright **Foqion Postoli** (1889-1927). The two novels and one play for which he is remembered were all written in America within the years 1910-1919 and first published in the pages of *Dielli* (The Sun). His first novel *Për mprojtjen e atdheut*, 1921 (In Defence of the homeland), is a typical product of the romantic nationalism of the late Rilindja period, a sentimental love story full of patriotic ideals and virtue. The novel *Lulja e kujtimit*, Korça 1924 (The Flower of remembrance), though suffering from the same artificiality and triteness of plot, is, artistically speaking, a slight improvement for those who can stomach so much sentimentality. This two-part tale of romance and patriotism proved, at any rate, more popular and has been reprinted several times. It was in fact one of the best known Albanian novels of the twenties and thirties.

Haki Stërmilli[113] (1895-1953) from Dibra was another very sentimental prose writer and dramatist. He is the author of three novels, over thirty short stories, five plays, two diaries and several dozen newspaper articles. Foremost among his works is the novel *Sikur t'isha djalë*, Tirana 1936 (If I were a boy), which recounts in diary form the struggles of a young girl named Dije Kërthiza for emancipation in an oppressive society. Dije (meaning 'knowledge') has been deprived of school education by her patriarchal father Sulë and been shut indoors for almost all her childhood. She wishes to marry her Shpend Rrëfe but is instead married off at the will of her domineering father to a rich elderly merchant whom she does not love. Her anguish, compounded by physical illness (tuberculosis), leads her to reflect in her diary on the necessity of social change for Albanian women in general. Her only hope is that a leader, a Migjenian superman, will one day arrive and liberate women from their sorry lot. As one of the most popular Albanian novels of the thirties, *Sikur t'isha djalë* was the first substantial work of Albanian literature to deal with the theme of women's emancipation. Many Albanian girls of the time are said to have learned to read and write for the sole purpose of being able to read this book. It was one of the first Albanian novels in diary form, which gave its author much opportunity to develop the character of its protagonists in a forceful dramatic monologue. Though on the whole persuasive in its ideas and rich in the lexical elements of the author's Dibran dialect, the novel has nonetheless many stylistic weaknesses which preclude it from being considered as great literature. It is written in a very down-to-earth narrative style enhanced by little more than romantic sighs, interjections and curses. Despite his good intention of provoking the reading public into reflecting on an important social issue, Stërmilli was not able to transcend the

---

[113] cf. F. Hoxha 1998.

tear-jerking sentimentality of the period which he indeed helped to cement in Albanian letters. Consequently, *Sikur t'isha djalë*, a modest revolution for the mid-thirties, was soon outdated as a work of literature.

Another writer who survived the bloody transition of power in 1944-1945 more or less unscathed and who was able to pursue his writing career during the Stalinist period was **Sterjo Spasse** (1914-1989), a novelist and short story writer of (Slav) Macedonian origin from Lake Prespa. It was while teaching in the little village of Derviçan south of Gjirokastra that the eighteen-year-old Spasse began writing his first novel, and his masterpiece, *Nga jeta në jetë - Pse!?*, Korça 1935 (From life to life - Why!?), usually referred to for short as *Pse!?* (Why!?). Like Haki Stërmilli's *Sikur t'isha djalë* (If I were a boy), *Pse!?* is written in the form of a diary and focusses on the tragic dilemma of a young intellectual in a backward rural society. Gjon Zaveri is an intelligent young man who, after his studies, returns to his native village. His parents, intent on adhering to custom and upholding tradition, insist that he marry the girl they have chosen for him, the village maiden Afërdita. Gjon knows that such a marriage would be a disastrous mistake, but after much soul-searching and anguish, he reluctantly concedes to the alliance, thus submitting to tradition and patriarchal society, and bringing about his own downfall. *Pse!?* is a nihilistic work, a *roman i mohimit* (novel of denial). Its pessimistic hero Gjon Zaveri suffers from all the *Weltschmerz* of Goethe's young Werther, a hero with whom he feels great affinity. In the end, resigned to his fate, Gjon commits suicide by throwing himself into the lake. Two weeks later, a letter of farewell is found, with which the novel concludes:

"'It is better to be ruled by an inanimate yet visible object than by philosophy which is invisible! It is better to become a murderer with a rifle than by thoughts. Only a few people are killed with a rifle whereas thousands are killed by thoughts. I know that books have alienated me from life and that philosophy has caused me to lose my feelings as a human being. Love was not born for me, nothing was created for me! I was born superfluous in this world, I sat down to the dinner table by mistake. Having wished so desperately to right some of the wrongs of man, I find myself with no one close to me in this world, I am not even close to myself. I am like a reed floating in the middle of the ocean and shall soon sink to the very bottom of the sea. And I must drown, for though alive, I am as if dead. It is all the same to me... No one should pardon me for that which the world calls sin, for I pardon no one, especially not the philosophers. As for my body after death, I am a Diogenes. Let it rot where it collapses, let it be devoured by the first wild beasts that find it. But if mankind cannot

155

endure such a thing and insists on burying me, then I have one wish. Let them bury me in a lonely spot, surrounded by thorns and thistles, without a tear or a lament, without offerings or mourning clothes, because for me: *A world of nothing, from nothing for nothing, revolves around the essence of nothing!'*

The villagers buried their only intellectual with due respect, but in a lonely spot - at the top of a hill overlooking the village where the gentle breezes blow in all directions. In the shade of a wild rose lies that young man's simple grave. On it there is no name, no date or sign, all that is inscribed are his last words: *A world of nothing, from nothing for nothing, revolves around the essence of nothing!* A young man on the path of the philosophers."

Post-war Marxist critics were unable to deal with *Pse*, though it may be considered one of the major Albanian novels of the early twentieth century. The Schopenhauerian pessimism and the *Weltschmerz* conflicted too sharply with the positive hero demanded by socialist realism and they dismissed the work simply as the product of the suffering and oppression of the working masses in pre-liberation feudal-bourgeois society. It was referred to publicly only in order to show what progress Spasse had made with his subsequent novels of socialist realism. From a purely aesthetic point of view, exactly the opposite is true. Although *Pse?!* is the work of youthful inspiration by a writer as yet unskilled in his métier, this first novel contrasts favourably with all the later 'classics of socialist realism' he produced.

With what ease Spasse passed from a prewar writer of Nietzschean inspiration to a leading proponent of socialist letters is quite intriguing when one considers the extreme level of persecution of virtually all Albanian writers and intellectuals during and after the communist takeover. On 15 February 1944, under German occupation, Spasse co-founded the cultural periodical *Revista letrare* (Literary review), later to be decried as fascist, in which, up to 15 August of that year, he published no less than fifteen short stories and prose fragments. By the end of 1944, shortly after the communist victory, he had already published his first work of socialist realism in the party newspaper *Përpara* (Forwards) of Korça, at a time when many other progressive writers of the left, such as Petro Marko (1913-1991), found themselves silenced or imprisoned after the war.

Probably the most interesting figure among the prose writers of the pre-communist period, both as an individual and as an author, was **Musine Kokalari** (1917-1983) of Gjirokastra. Kokalari is the first female writer of Albania, and was the only one up until the 1960s. Born on 10 February 1917 in Adana in southern Turkey to a patriotic and politically active family of

Gjirokastrite origin, Kokalari returned to Albania with her family in 1920. She early acquired a taste for books and learning because her brother Vejsim operated a bookstore in Tirana in the mid-thirties. In January of 1938, she left for Rome to study literature at the university there and graduated in 1941 with a study on Naim Frashëri. Her stay in the eternal city gave her an ephemeral glimpse into a fascinating world of intellectual creativity and her sole aim in life upon her return to Albania was to become a writer. In 1943 she declared to a friend, "I want to write, to write, only to write literature, and to have nothing to do with politics." At the age of twenty-four, she already published an initial 80-page collection of ten youthful prose tales in her native Gjirokastrite dialect: *Siç më thotë nënua plakë*, Tirana 1941 (As my old mother tells me). This historic collection, strongly inspired by Tosk folklore and by the day-to-day struggles of women in Gjirokastra, is thought to be the first work of literature ever written and published by a woman in Albania. Kokolari called the book, "the mirror of a world gone by, the path of transition from girlhood with its melodies and the first years of marriage to the world of a grown woman, once again bound by the heavy chains of slavery to patriarchal fanaticism." Three years later, despite the vicissitudes of the civil war, Kokalari, now twenty-seven, published a longer collection of short stories and sketches entitled ...*sa u-tunt jeta*, Tirana 1944 (...how life swayed), a total of 348-pages which established her - ever so briefly - as a writer of substance. A third volume of her folksy tales was entitled *Rreth vatrës*, Tirana 1944 (Around the hearth).

As the Second World War came to an end, Kokalari opened a bookstore herself and was invited to become a member of the Writers' Union, created on 7 October 1945 under the chairmanship of Sejfulla Malëshova. All the time, she was haunted by the execution without trial of her two brothers, Mumtaz and Vejsim, on 12 November 1944 by the communists and candidly demanded justice and retribution. Having herself been closely associated in 1944 with the fledgling Albanian Social-Democratic party and its press organ *Zëri i lirisë* (The Voice of freedom), she was arrested on 17 January 1946 in an age of terror concomitant with the fall of Malëshova, and on 2 July 1946 was sentenced by the military court of Tirana to twenty years in prison as a 'saboteur and enemy of the people.' The next eighteen years of her life she spent in the infamous prison of Burrel in the Mati region, isolated and under constant surveillance, persecuted and provoked by boorish and uneducated prison officers. A broken woman, she was released around 1964 and given a job as a street sweeper in the provincial town of Rrëshen. Musine Kokalari, once a gifted young teller of tales, was persecuted to the end of her days. Terminally ill with cancer, she was even refused a hospital bed before her death on 14 August 1983.

Professional theatre is the prerogative of an urban society. In Albania, which has always had a strong rural population and lacked large urban centres until recently, theatre never developed to the extent that literary poetry and prose did, nor did it ever capture the attention of the Albanian public to any substantial degree. There is little in the way of Albanian theatre on which to report before the second half of the nineteenth century and, in fact, little professional theatre at all before the second half of the twentieth century. By the beginning of the twentieth century, nonetheless, drama in Albania had at least come into existence as an independent literary genre.

Kristo Floqi (1873-1951) of Korça was certainly the most popular of all Albanian dramatists in the first half of the twentieth century. He was a prolific writer, whose popularity is due on the whole not so much to the literary quality of his works, but to the whole-hearted pleasure his plays gave to audiences and to the reading public. He is the author of four tragedies on nationalist and historical themes, seventeen comedies and sketches, as well as several volumes of poetry, legal, political and educational texts and translations of Sophocles, Euripides and Molière. After the Second World War, Floqi was arrested by the communists, as were most prewar intellectuals who had not fled the country, and died in or around 1951 after several years in prison.

Dramatist and poet **Etëhem Haxhiademi** (1902-1965), from Elbasan, is remembered as the best playwright of the independence period. During the Second World War, he was director of municipal government in Albania and a member of the new Institute of Albanian Studies in Tirana. In 1945, immediately after the war, he was made an executive member of the newly formed Writers' Union and became head of its Elbasan chapter. He also taught Albanian at the *Shkolla Normale* in Elbasan in 1946. In the witch hunts of 1946-1947, Haxhiademi was arrested and sentenced to death. His library and manuscripts were confiscated. At the intercession of the influential Aleksandër Xhuvani (1880-1961) and Omer Nishani (1887-1954), his sentence was converted to life in prison. He died on 17 March 1965, having worked in Burrel prison for many years as a translator.

Haxhiademi was the author of a remarkable hexameter translation of Vergil's Bucolics (1932) and of a 73-page volume of wistful poetry entitled *Lyra*, Tirana 1939 (The Lyre). His solid western European education nonetheless found its optimal expression in his classical tragedies based on Greek and Latin models. Haxhiademi's first three five-act tragedies were published as a trilogy: *Ulisi*, Tirana 1931 (Ulysses), written in Berlin in 1924; *Akili*, Tirana 1931 (Achilles), written in Vienna in 1926; and *Aleksandri*, Tirana 1931 (Alexander), written in Lushnja in 1928. Next came *Pirrua* (Pyrrhus), written in Gjirokastra in 1934, a tragedy on a theme already treated by Mihal Grameno in 1906 and Kristo Floqi in 1923. The five-act *Skënderbeu*,

Tirana 1935 (Scanderbeg), completed in Gjirokastra on 1 May 1935, was followed by two elegant masterpieces, *Diomedi*, Tirana 1936 (Diomedes); and *Abeli*, 1939 (Abel) in hendecasyllabic verse. Though treating figures of ancient history and mythology, Haxhiademi regarded them as somehow part of Albania's own heritage. With the tragedies of Haxhiademi, Albanian actors for the first time had material which transcended the trite nationalist dramas and sentimental outpourings of the late Rilindja period. Though the general public may have preferred the light-hearted farces of middle-class mores offered to them by Kristo Floqi, the hollow nationalism of Mihal Grameno and the pathetic sentimentality of Foqion Postoli, Etëhem Haxhiademi's tragedies were not unappreciated. They were much performed throughout the thirties and early forties, initially by amateur groups stemming from the *Shkolla Normale* in Elbasan but later also in Tirana and elsewhere. The qualitative step forward in the mid-thirties in Albanian letters may not have been as great in theatre as it had been in poetry and prose, but it had been taken, and it is thus to the classical dramas of the now forgotten Etëhem Haxhiademi that we must return for the best of prewar Albanian drama.

5.7   The Cultural Zenith of the Mid-Thirties

For almost a quarter of a century after the declaration of political independence on 28 November 1912, Albanian writers and intellectuals continued to draw their inspiration from the ideas and ideals of the nineteenth-century Rilindja movement. By the thirties, however, Albanian culture had entered a new phase. An influx of new ideas from abroad and a higher level of formal education among intellectuals flung open the gates to cultural advancement. For a decade, Albanian literature and culture flourished as never before, initially in Shkodra and later in Tirana and throughout the country.

Within the space of five years in the mid-thirties, an advance in quality was made in literature. In poetry, Lasgush Poradeci published his breathtaking lyric collections *Vallja e yjve* 1933 (The Dance of the stars) and *Ylli i zemrës* 1937 (The Star of the heart); the consumptive Migjeni managed to send his slender *Vargjet e lira* 1936 (Free verse) to press before it was banned and before death put an end to his brief literary career; and Gjergj Fishta came out with the definitive version of his incomparable epic *Lahuta e malcis* 1937 (The Highland Lute), in thirty cantos. Albanian prose witnessed the publication of the nihilist novel *Nga jeta në jetë - Pse!?* 1935 (From life to life - Why!?), by Sterjo Spasse; of Ernest Koliqi's second collection of short stories, *Tregtar flamujsh* 1935 (Flag merchant); of the much-read novel of social criticism *Sikur t'isha djalë* 1936 (If I were a boy) by Haki Stërmilli; and of Mitrush Kuteli's first volume of tales *Nete shqipëtare* 1938 (Albanian nights). Migjeni, too, published twenty-four of his trenchant prose sketches in periodicals within the five years from 1933 to 1938 and completed the manuscript of his unpublished *Novelat e qytetit të veriut* 1936 (Tales of a northern city). In drama, Etëhem Haxhiademi captivated the discerning public with his classical tragedies which, though not revolutionary in conception or content, evinced a linguistic refinement previously unknown to the Albanian stage.

Journalism, which had continued to play a fundamental role in the affirmation of national culture in Albania since the Rilindja age, advanced just as rapidly as literature per se. Out of the myriad of short-lived nationalist weeklies and second-rate monthly magazines issued in various Balkan cities arose a newspaper and publishing industry of quality which served to diffuse information, be it political, cultural or literary. Despite the primitive political structures which still prevailed in the country under the despotic Ahmet Zogu (1895-1961), who now called himself King Zog I of the Albanians, the press developed in a surprisingly liberal manner. As long as publishers did not attack the royal family and the monarch's foreign policy, they could print more or less whatever they wanted. There was censorship, as in any dictatorship, and some periodicals were shut down, but it never reached the awesome level of control attained in the period after the 'liberation.'

Compared to other European countries in the thirties and forties, relatively few books were published in Albania. This was due primarily to the lack of general economic development, Albania being by far the poorest country in Europe, and to the high degree of illiteracy in the country. Reading remained the prerogative of a small, male minority. The dramatic increase in serious literary production, indeed the flourishing of a solid written culture in Albania, was therefore very much dependent upon the literary periodicals of the age which not only offered a forum for many new writers and ideas but also made these original works and ideas available throughout the country.

With time, the culture of the late independence period had come to reflect the increasing polarization between East and West. Albania had been little affected by the ideas and ideals of the October Revolution in Russia, although a small number of literary figures had visited the Soviet Union under Stalin: Fan Noli, known subsequently as the 'red bishop,' novelist Haki Stërmilli, rebel poet Sejfulla Malëshova and Tajar Zavalani (1903-1966). The blatant social inequities existing in the impoverished Balkan country, exacerbated by a backward and uncaring dictatorship, and the growing power of fascist Italy now caused many intellectuals of the thirties to look with interest to Soviet communism, or at least to some form of socialism, as a prospective means of overcoming class differences and the harsh exploitation of the vast majority of the population. The brief hour of constitutional democracy under Fan Noli in 1924 had failed and all attempts at land reform, so urgently needed, had been stifled by the country's landowning rulers. The polarity of ideologies became more apparent in 1936 with the outbreak of the Spanish Civil War. Young poet and novelist Petro Marko departed with translator Skënder Luarasi and a group of forty Albanians for the battlefields of Catalonia to take part in the International Brigades, and marvelled there at meeting Ernest Hemingway and other socially committed writers. Socialist ideas were growing in Albania. But, at the same time, so was fascism.

Albanian writers of the thirties were fascinated by the West and were preoccupied with discovering Albania's role in a rapidly evolving Europe. It was one of the major topics of literary discussion in periodicals at the time. A good number of intellectuals had now been abroad and seen Western industrialized society. Coming as they did from a country which, to quote the saying, 'God loves so much because it has changed so little since Creation,' they were enticed but disoriented, and were frustrated at Albania's oriental languishings under a virtually Byzantine monarch. But the West was an ambiguous concept. It was represented in Albania, ironically enough, by Mussolini's Italy, the country's closest Western neighbour which was vying with Yugoslavia at the time to extend its influence in the mountainous little kingdom. However, the intellectual debate about Albania's relations with and role in the West soon became superfluous and irrelevant when Italian troops crossed the Straits of Otranto and landed in Durrës, Vlora and Shëngjin on 7 April, Good Friday, 1939 with the firm intention of staying, welcome or not.

It will remain for historians to decide whether or not Italy's cultural embrace and subsequently outright political absorption of Albania was, at the time, a cultural gain for the Balkan country or not. A world war soon intervened. The polarization of ideas in Europe between the new East and the new West, between the doctrines of communism and fascism, led to the ultimate confrontation in Albania, as elsewhere, leaving the country at the mercy of political and military extremists and, in the end, bringing its writers and intellectuals of all political stripes to their knees.

Intellectual life in the mid-thirties and early forties had reached unprecedented heights, a zenith in Albanian written culture. A modern literature had been created in Albania and the nation had finally come of age. It was a brief blossoming in the shadow of the apocalypse to come, which would snuff out all genuine literary production for about twenty years. The tender flower of Albanian literature was to be plucked... and the roots of the plant severed once again.

6. Albanian Socialist Realism and Beyond (late 20th cent.)

6.1   The Onslaught of Socialist Realism

Enver Hoxha (1908-1985) and the new partisan leaders who took power at the end of November 1944 were suspicious of Albanian writers and intellectuals of all political hues, regarding the vast majority of them as representatives of the 'ancien régime.' A very few writers such as Vangjel Koça (1900-1943) and Vasil Alarupi (1908-1977) had been genuine proponents of fascism, and a number of intellectuals, while not fascists themselves, had collaborated with the Italian and German occupants in one way or another. Most wanted simply to survive in an age of turmoil.

Many figures of note in Albanian intellectual life fled the country before or during the communist takeover: Ernest Koliqi (1903-1975), Mehdi bey Frashëri (1874-1963), Mid'hat bey Frashëri (1880-1949) and Karl Gurakuqi (1895-1972) to Italy, Branko Merxhani (1894-1981) to Turkey, and left-wing writer Tajar Zavalani (1903-1966) to Britain.

Others cherished the illusion that, having survived the war, they could come to some sort of arrangement with the new communist leaders and work actively with them on the building of a new Albania, a new socialist society. Soon, however, the demagogy of Enver Hoxha, the Stalinist show trials under General Mehmet Shehu (1913-1981) and the witch hunts under Koçi Xoxe (1917-1949) made it apparent that liberation and the ideals of socialism were a façade for brutal dictatorship and terror. Neither indoctrination nor education were the primary means of persuasion but naked fear. The immediate post-war period had become an apocalypse for Albanian writers and intellectuals.

Writers of the Scutarine Catholic school suffered particularly. General Mehmet Shehu, in a public address in Shkodra on 28 January 1945, had called the Catholic stronghold a 'nest of reaction' and warned that church leaders would receive their 'just' rewards before the people's court. Playwright Ndre Zadeja (1891-1945), poet Lazër Shantoja (1892-1945), poet Bernardin Palaj (1894-1947), novelist Anton Harapi (1888-1946) and publicist Gjon Shllaku (1907-1946) were executed. Poet Vinçenc Prennushi (1885-1949) died in prison after gruesome torture, as did prose writer and publisher Dom Ndoc

Nikaj (1864-1951), the father of twentieth-century Gheg prose. Other intellectuals of note to be executed included Arbëresh publisher Terenzio Tocci (1880-1945), editor Nebil Çika (1893-1944), Bektashi writer Baba Ali Tomori (Ali Tyrabiu) (1900-1947) and poet Manush Peshkëpia (1910-1951).

Among the many other writers and intellectuals who were arrested and imprisoned during the witch hunts after the Second World War were noted playwrights Kristo Floqi (1873-1951) and Etëhem Haxhiademi (1902-1965), Muslim writer and publisher Hafiz Ibrahim Dalliu (1878-1952), minister of education Mirash Ivanaj (1891-1953) and poet Gjergj Bubani (1899-1954), all of whom died in prison; short story writer Mitrush Kuteli (1907-1967), novelist Petro Marko (1913-1991), poet Sejfulla Malëshova (1901-1971), short story writer Musine Kokalari (1917-1983), poet and scholar Arshi Pipa (1920-1997), Bektashi poet Ibrahim Hasnaj (1912-1995), poet Nexhat Hakiu (1917-1978), poet Andrea Varfi (1914-1992), translators Jusuf Vrioni (1916-2001) and Pashko Gjeci (b. 1918), novelist Mustafa Greblleshi (1922-1986), poet Kudret Kokoshi (1907-1991), novelist and editor Andon S. Frashëri (1892-1965), humorist Mid'hat Araniti (1912-1992), linguist Selman Riza (1909-1988), critic Filip Fishta (1904-1973), folklorists Father Donat Kurti (1903-1969) and Stavro Frashëri (1900-1965) of Kavaja, and writer Lazër Radi (1916-1998) who was released in 1991 after an incredible forty-six years of prison and internment.

The persecution of intellectuals, in particular of all those who had been abroad before 1944, and the break with virtually all cultural traditions, created a literary and cultural vacuum in Albania which lasted until the sixties, the results of which can still be felt today. No one will ever know how many intellectuals and budding writers of talent were dispatched over the following years to labour in dangerous branches of industry, or banished to the provinces forever, to internment in some isolated mountain village with no hope of return.

The forced marriage between Albanian literature and Marxism-Leninism was firmly cemented from the start with the founding in October 1945 of the Writers' Union. Initially, responsibility for cultural policies in post-war Albania was conferred upon poet **Sejfulla Malëshova** (1901-1971). Originally from the Përmet region of southern Albania, Malëshova spent a good deal of his life abroad. Most of the verse of this self-styled rebel poet was written in exile under the pseudonym Lame Kodra and was published in the now rare volume *Vjersha*, Tirana 1945 (Verse). He had studied medicine in Italy and in 1924, at the age of twenty-three, became Fan Noli's personal secretary in the latter's democratic government. With the overthrow of Noli, Malëshova fled to Paris and from there, inspired by the October Revolution, he continued on to Moscow where he studied and later taught Marxism. In the Soviet Union he joined the Communist Party (1930-1932) but was subsequently expelled as a Bukharinist. As minister of culture in the communist-controlled provisional government, Malëshova followed a relatively liberal and conciliatory course in order to encourage the reintegration of non-communist forces into the new structures of power. He was not one to condemn all prewar writers such as Gjergj Fishta as reactionaries, nor was he in favour of a total break with the West. Malëshova soon became the spokesperson of one of the two factions vying for power within the party. With the backing of the Yugoslav communists, however, the faction of his adversary Koçi Xoxe (1917-1949) gained the upper hand by early 1946 and Malëshova fell into disgrace. At a meeting of the Central Committee on 21 February 1946, Malëshova was accused of opportunism and right-wing deviationism and was expelled both from the Politburo and from the Central Committee. Strangely enough, Malëshova survived his fall. This left-wing idealist who had once been a member of the Comintern was interned in Ballsh for two or three years and spent all his later life in internal exile as a humble stock clerk in Fier where, for years, no inhabitant of the town dared speak to him. His only social contact was to play soccer with the children. Whenever anyone approached he would pinch his lips with his fingers, signifying the vow of eternal silence which ensured his survival. Malëshova died on 9 June 1971 of appendicitis in unimaginable isolation. Although everyone in town knew his poems by heart, no one dared to attend his funeral. He was buried in the presence of his sister, the gravedigger and two *Sigurimi* agents.

The witch hunts that followed the purge of Malëshova numbed all creative writing and thinking in Albania. Most intellectuals who had not been executed by now were in prison or permanently silenced. The third conference of the Writers' Union took place in October 1949, five months after the elimination of minister of the interior, Koçi Xoxe. This conference set the course for socialist realism in Albanian literature, a course which was to remain unchanged throughout the fifties. The intellectual freedom which had existed, ironically enough, under the prewar Zogu dictatorship and during the Italian occupation, had now been snuffed out completely. The party demanded nothing less than absolute obedience and all writers came under its surveillance and critical guidance.

Albanian cultural politics in the early years of the Soviet-Albanian alliance were very much influenced by Zhdanovism, the literary doctrine formulated by Andrey Aleksandrovich Zhdanov (1896-1948) which wreaked such havoc in Russian literature and culture. Albanian writers were encouraged to concentrate their creative energies on specific themes such as the partisan struggle of the so-called 'national liberation war' and the building of socialism, and to avoid the cosmopolitan influences of the West. The political message was the essential element for those who wished to survive. Subjects devoid of any educational value in Marxist terms were considered alien and taboo. Albanian literature, which had evolved so rapidly in the mid-thirties, had virtually disappeared. The country had become a literary wasteland.

With Albania's increasing integration into the Soviet bloc during the fifties, Soviet literary models were introduced and slavishly imitated in order to lay the foundations for a new literature. With time, a fresh generation of proletarian writers arrived on the scene, most of whom had little formal education. Inspired by a surrealist mixture of fear and revolutionary pathos, they showed themselves willing to take part in the radical political and social transformation which the little Balkan country was going through. The verse, short stories and novels produced by this new generation of Albanian writers, whose works, later republished in large editions, were soon elevated to the position of classics of socialist realism, were for the most part not literary works at all. Of the few publications which can stand the test of time mention can be made here of *Lumi i vdekur*, Tirana 1965 (The Dead river) by **Jakov Xoxa** (1923-1979) from Fier. In this novel, modelled on the Russian *Tikhiy Don*, Moscow 1928 (And quiet flows the Don), by Mikhail Aleksandrovich Sholokhov, Xoxa decried the exploitation of the impoverished peasantry by ruthless beys on the once marshy and mosquito-infested plain of Myzeqe.

Despite the extremely unfavourable conditions under which it had evolved, Albanian literature managed to recover somewhat by the mid-sixties and, although it continued to make very sluggish progress, there was no more danger of it disappearing completely as had, for instance, the literature of the Scutarine Catholic school before the Second World War. As an organism, it was now strong enough to survive the political turmoil that the country would continue to undergo.

It was the second generation of post-war Albanian writers who came more and more to realize that political convictions, though important within the context of the Albanian political system and society of the period, were not enough as a criterion of literary merit and that Albanian literature was in need of renewal. The road to rejuvenation was facilitated by a certain degree of political stability and self-confidence within the Albanian Party of Labour in spite of worsening relations between Enver Hoxha and the Soviet leader Nikita Khrushchev.

The first turning point in the evolution of Albanian prose and verse, after a quarter century of stagnation, came in the stormy year of 1961 which, on the one hand, marked the definitive political break with the Soviet Union and thus with Soviet literary models and, on the other hand, witnessed the publication of a number of trend-setting volumes, in particular of poetry: *Shekulli im* (My century) by Ismail Kadare, *Hapat e mija në asfalt* (My steps on the pavement) by Dritëro Agolli, and in the following year *Shtigje poetike*

(Poetic paths) by Fatos Arapi. It is ironic to note that while Albania had broken with the Soviet Union ostensibly to save socialism, leading Albanian writers, educated in the Eastern bloc, took advantage of the rupture to try to part not only with Soviet models but also with socialist realism itself. The attempt made here to broaden the literary horizon "in search of something new" inevitably led to a literary and of course political controversy at a meeting of the Albanian Union of Writers and Artists on 11 July 1961. The debate, conducted not only by writers but also by leading party and government figures, was published in the literary journal *Drita* (The Light) and received wide public attention in the wake of the Fourth Party Congress of that year. It pitted writers of the older generation such as Andrea Varfi (1914-1992), Luan Qafëzezi (1922-1995) and Mark Gurakuqi (1922-1970), who voiced their support for fixed poetic standards and the traditions of Albanian literature and who opposed new elements such as free verse as un-Albanian, against a new generation led by Ismail Kadare, Dritëro Agolli and Fatos Arapi, who were in favour of a literary renewal and a broadening of the stylistic and thematic horizon. This road to renewal was given the green light by Enver Hoxha himself who saw that the situation was untenable and declared that the young writers of renewal seemed to have the better arguments.

Though it constituted no radical change of course, no liberalization or political 'thaw' in the Soviet sense, 1961 set the stage for a few years of serenity and, in the longer perspective, for a quarter of a century of trial and error, which led to greater sophistication in Albanian literature. Themes and styles were diversified and somewhat more attention was paid to formal literary criteria and to the question of individuality. Though one would certainly not characterize Albanian literature of the period by its surfeit of non-conformists and eccentrics, it evolved to such an extent as to provide requisite scope within the framework of socialist realism for some individual creativity and originality.

The three decades of Stalinist dictatorship which were to follow the breaking off of relations with the Soviet Union in 1961 established a clear and fixed path for the evolution of modern Albanian letters. What Stalinist rule also did, however, was to impede Albanian writing from evolving into a literature comparable to that of the more developed countries of Europe. A high degree of conformity continued due to the extreme level of pressure exerted upon writers and intellectuals throughout the rule of Enver Hoxha. Successful writers learned how to lie low and present what they wished to express in thick layers of political wrapping, so that only the trained eye of an experienced reader could comprehend the analogies being drawn. As such, Albanian literature remained political, but in a sense radically different from that intended by party dogmatists. In the rare moments when political pressure abated somewhat, some interesting works were produced and published. Due to the particular political circumstances in the country, it is, therefore, impossible for us to speak of good writers in modern Albanian literature but only of good books which managed to squeeze past the censors at the right moment. In other words, the quality of a novel or volume of poetry depended just as much on the year of publication as upon the talent of its author.

6.2 Innovation and Dissent: the Works of Ismail Kadare

Despite the constraints of socialist realism and Stalinist dictatorship, Albanian literature made much progress in the seventies and eighties. The best example of creativity and originality in contemporary Albanian letters is that of **Ismail Kadare**[114] (b. 1936), still the only Albanian writer to enjoy a broad international reputation. Kadare's talents both in poetry and in prose have lost none of their innovative power over the last four decades. His courage in attacking literary mediocrity within the system, and later - though subtly - in attacking the political system itself, brought a breath of fresh air to Albanian culture.

Born on 28 January 1936 in the museum-city of Gjirokastra, Kadare studied at the Faculty of History and Philology of the University of Tirana and subsequently at the Gorky Institute of World Literature in Moscow until 1960 when relations between Albania and the Soviet Union became tense. He began his literary career in Albania with poetry, but turned increasingly to prose, of which he soon became the undisputed master and by far the most popular writer of the whole of Albanian literature. Ismail Kadare lived the next thirty years of his life in Tirana, constantly under the Damocles Sword of the Party. He was privileged by the authorities, in particular once his works became known internationally. Indeed, he was able to pursue literary and personal objectives for which other writers would certainly have been sent into internal exile or to prison. But Kadare knew well that liberties in Albania could be withdrawn easily, by an impulsive stroke of the tyrant's quill.

---

[114] cf. J. Byron 1979a, 1984; A. Pipa 1983-1984, 1987, 1991, p. 49-123; A. Mitchell 1990; Sh. Beqiri 1991; E. Faye 1991a, 1991b; A. Klosi 1991; F. Terpan 1992; T. Çaushi 1993, 1995, 2001, 2002; M. Druon 1993; E. Nauni 1993; I. Zamputi 1993a; A. Zotos 1997; P. De Moor 1998; E. Kabashi 1998; S. Schwartz 2000, p. 119-125; R. Hoti 2002; P. Kolevica 2002; M. Schmidt-Neke 2002; T. Çaushi & Gj. Shkurtaj 2004; M. M'Raihi 2004; and Sh. Sinani 2005.

At the end of October 1990, a mere two months before the final collapse of the dictatorship, Ismail Kadare left Tirana and applied for political asylum in France. His departure caused a flurry of interest and consternation in the Albanian and international press at a politically explosive moment in the country's history. Kadare explained his motives in an article in the Parisian daily *Le Monde* shortly after his arrival. Whatever rationale may have lain behind this late departure, it did enable Kadare, for the first time, to exercise his profession with complete freedom.

His years of Parisian exile were productive and accorded him further success and recognition, as a writer both in Albanian and in French. He published his collected works in twelve thick volumes, each in an Albanian-language and a French-language edition, and was honoured with membership in the prestigious Académie Française (28 October 1996) and in the French Legion of Honour. He has also been nominated on several occasions for the Nobel Prize for literature.

Though Kadare is not unadmired as a poet in Albania, his reputation and, in particular, his international reputation now rests entirely upon his prose. A brief, but by no means exhaustive survey of his principal works of literary prose, here in chronological order, is thus called for.

Ismail Kadare's first major prose work was *Gjenerali i ushtrisë së vdekur*, Tirana 1963 (Engl. trans. *The General of the dead army,* London 1971). In view of the early publication date - the author was a mere twenty-seven years old at the time - *The General* could almost be viewed as a work of youth, and yet, it is still one of Kadare's most effective novels, and one of his best known.

"Like a proud and solitary bird, you will fly over those silent and tragic mountains in order to wrest our poor young men from their jagged, rocky grip." Such was the vision of the Italian general in the company of a laconic priest on his mission to Albania to recover the remains of his soldiers who had perished some twenty years earlier. He began his duties with a sense of grandeur befitting his rank: "In the task he was now undertaking there was something of the majesty of the Greeks and the Trojans, of the solemnity of Homeric funeral rites." But the general found himself in a sombre, rainy country with a sullen and resentful population as he set about his noble task of exhuming the bones of a dispersed, fallen army from Albania's muddy soil. Gradually, and inevitably, the general is confronted with the grim realities of the past and is haunted by the futility of his mission. His grand intentions have long since become a personal nightmare when suddenly the bones of the infamous Colonel Z are thrown at his feet by a deranged old woman.

The rain, which streamed down the windshield of the military vehicle which was put at the general's disposal, is a common metaphor in Ismail Kadare's prose. At the time of original publication, this constant downpour and many other features of the novel made it a clear step forward in Albanian letters. Grey storm clouds, mud and the humdrum reality of everyday life contrasted sharply with the otherwise obligatory sunshine and blithe victories of socialist realism. So did the Italian general. Here, too, we find a favourite device of the writer who, more than any other, was to bring his country's literature out of its stylistic and thematic lethargy: that of a remote and haunted Albania as seen through the eyes of the innocent or uncomprehending foreigner. This perspective not only gave shape to a European country which at the time was more isolated from the Western world than Tibet, but also helped Albanians themselves to see their homeland as others might. After the initial Albanian edition of 1963, and a revised Albanian edition in 1967, it was the French-language edition *Le général de l'armée morte*, Paris 1970, which laid the foundations for Kadare's deserved renown abroad. The English-language edition first appeared shortly thereafter, in 1971, and has been republished at least five times.

What gave Ismail Kadare, living in the most severe Stalinist regime imaginable, the courage to publish a novel whose main characters were a Fascist general and an Italian priest? Courage was definitely needed to publish anything in communist Albania beyond party panegyrics and the standard fare of communist partisan heroism. Albania had broken off ties with the Soviet Union and the Eastern bloc countries in 1961 and had embarked upon a new alliance with Red China. Certain of economic assistance from China, the communist regime in Albania was enjoying a certain degree of political and economic stability in the early 1960s. In 1962, the Democratic Front won 99.99 percent of votes in parliamentary elections, with 99.99 percent participation. A world record! Although there was obviously no semblance of choice or real democracy here, the Communist Party felt sufficiently confident that all open opposition had been stifled, and permitted a modicum of liberality in cultural affairs for a brief period before the Cultural Revolution swept into the country from China in 1966. Kadare took full advantage of this period of political stability.

Shortly after the success of *The General of the Dead Army*, Kadare published a short novel entitled *Përbindëshi* (The Monster) in volume 12 (1965) of the official Tirana literary journal *Nëntori* (November). 'The monster,' however, soon fell victim to Stalinist censorship. The writer later explained that an article vilifying 'The monster' had sufficed to exclude this tale from Albanian literature. "It was so barbarically flogged, forbidden and buried so deeply that it would take me over a quarter of a century to exhume it[115]." The monster in question was none other than the Trojan horse poised before the gates of sacred Ilium, though here, a monster in a time warp. The fall of ancient Troy takes place both in the future and in the past of its characters. This time warp was quite enough to unnerve Stalinist censors who were petrified at the very thought of possible political allusions, and the novel was conveniently suppressed. Who could blame the authorities for suspecting that the tale of the insidious conquest of Troy might, in the final analysis, be more about Albania than anything else? The book was first republished a quarter of a century later.

Kadare's works have always been a strict reflection of the vicissitudes of Albanian political life. His second published novel, *Dasma*, Tirana 1968 (Engl. trans. *The Wedding*, Tirana 1968), took up the theme of women's liberation in Albania at a time when Enver Hoxha's two major social campaigns were in full swing: the abolition of religion and the emancipation of women among a population of predominantly Muslim origin. As a product of the 1966-1969 Albanian Cultural Revolution, *The Wedding* is a novel of limited artistic value, though it is interesting as a period piece. It was translated into English, primarily for propaganda purposes.

In the seventies, Kadare turned increasingly to historical prose, a safer haven after the Cultural Revolution, and became an unrivalled master of the genre. The 244-page *Kështjella*, Tirana 1970 (Engl. transl. *The Castle*, Tirana 1974), a novel reminiscent of Dino Buzzati's *Il deserto dei Tatari*, Milan 1940 (The Tatar steppe), takes us back to the fifteenth century, the age of the Albanian national hero Scanderbeg, and in carefully composed, minute detail, depicts the siege of a mediaeval Albanian fortress, symbolic of Albania itself, by the Turks during one of their numerous punitive expeditions to subdue the country. As in *The General of the dead army*, Albania is seen through the eyes of a foreigner, the Turkish pasha. Scanderbeg himself does not even appear in person. The allusion to political events of the sixties as seen by many critics was not unintentional. In 1961, ties had been broken off with the mighty Soviet Union, and after the 1968 invasion of Czechoslovakia, the Albanian leaders felt the very real possibility that the Soviets might try to use military force to bring the country back into the fold.

It was in the period of relative calm between the end of the Cultural Revolution in 1969 and the Purge of the Liberals in 1973 that Ismail Kadare published one of his most impressive works, *Kronikë në gur*, Tirana 1971 (Engl. transl. *Chronicle in stone*, New York 1987). This novel in eighteen chapters and an epilogue is the chronicle of the beautiful city of Gjirokastra in

---

[115] cf. I. Kadare, *Pesha e kryqit*, Paris 1991, p. 27.

southern Albania under occupation during the Second World War. Fabled Gjirokastra with its lofty fortress manors of stone looming from the mountainside over narrow cobblestone alleys was successively occupied, like much of Albania at the time, by the Greeks, the Italians and the Germans. *Kronikë në gur*, which was based on an earlier version entitled *Qyteti i jugut*, Tirana 1967 (The Southern city), is a novel of linguistic finesse and subtle political references. It offers not so much a portrait of the grim historical events of a city under occupation, but a compelling mixture of childhood observations, impressions and fantasies by a young Albanian lad. Kadare, as has been noted, was himself born in Gjirokastra in 1936, as was the inscrutable dictator, Enver Hoxha, a generation before him. Autobiographical in inspiration at least, the novel follows the young boy through the streets of his occupied city and through the realms of his own imaginary world as he views events and as he overhears and interprets bits of gossip, conversations and local superstitions. A neighbour is seen as Lady Macbeth, whereas a cabbage in the market takes the form of a severed head. Passing troops become Crusaders until the lad and his friends grow up to join a band of partisans, and the world of childhood fantasy finally gives way to that of our often savage maturity.

The Purge of the Liberals during the Fourth Plenary Session of the Central Committee on 26-28 June 1973 and the fall of their would-be leaders, Fadil Paçrami (b. 1922) and Todi Lubonja (b. 1923), caused shockwaves in intellectual circles, as had been intended. Ismail Kadare, being as a leading literary dissident, had to tread lightly to ensure his survival. In *Nëntori i një kryeqyteti*, Tirana 1975 (November of a capital city), he duly returned to a politically more acceptable theme, the partisan struggle against the German occupation of Tirana in 1944. Like *Dasma* (The Wedding) before it, this 223-page novel was a work of propaganda, written initially for the 'ideological struggle against foreign manifestations and liberal attitudes,' though it is not devoid of artistic merit.

Dimri i madh, Tirana 1977 (The Great winter), is a literary digestion of the traumatic rupture of relations with the Soviet Union. Published originally in a shorter version entitled *Dimri i vetmisë së madhe*, Tirana 1973 (The Winter of great solitude), 'The Great winter' is a novel of monumental historical and political dimensions. The harsh winter of 1960-1961 was indeed a momentous one in post-war Albanian history. It was that year which marked the break between Nikita Khrushchev and Enver Hoxha and saw the definitive withdrawal of Albania from the Soviet sphere. When Khrushchev stopped grain deliveries in 1961 to show his displeasure at the Sino-Albanian alliance, Enver Hoxha countered haughtily, "We will eat grass rather than give in!" The humiliation for the proud but impoverished Albanians was particularly acute in view of a now famous remark Khrushchev had earlier made on a visit to

171

Albania that mice in the grain silos of the Soviet Union consumed more grain than Albania was able to produce. Once again the Albanians were forced to fend for themselves, this time fully aware that they had no direct allies but the distant Chinese. Tension climaxed as Hoxha openly accused the Soviet Union of colonial politics. 'The Great winter' portrays these moving events on two levels: the political and the personal, from the negotiating table in the Kremlin to the homes of the simple people of Tirana. The principal character of the novel is Besnik Struga, a Tirana journalist, who finds himself assigned to the Albanian delegation as an interpreter and who departs for Moscow as the first snows of the great winter descend over Eastern Europe. There, he takes part in negotiations, receptions and secret high-level talks, experiencing political intrigue and power politics at first hand. Kadare also evokes a host of secondary characters from street-sweepers to aging members of the bourgeoisie caught unawares by the events of the great winter. Albanian students pursuing advanced education at the universities of Moscow and Leningrad are forced to interrupt their studies in mid-term and return home. The Soviet Union recalls all its advisors and, after tense negotiations, concedes to abandon its strategically vital submarine base at Pashaliman ("Pasha's Harbour") near Vlora. Economic and political relations are definitively ruptured. Kadare reconstructed much of the dialogue in this novel from minutes of actual negotiations and from the memoirs of Enver Hoxha, offering a unique glimpse into the dealings of Albania's communist leadership. His portrait of Enver Hoxha, as one might expect, is somewhat flattering, and strengthened his position as the party's 'writer in residence.' Kadare later alleged that it was 'The Great winter' which had ensured his physical survival. Enver Hoxha appreciated the portrait made of him in the book and did not wish to jeopardize it. Kadare's liquidation would have been incompatible with the survival of the novel[116].

Muzgu i perëndive të stepës, 1978 (The Twilight of the gods of the steppes) is an autobiographical novel like *Kronikë në gur* (Chronicle in stone). It is a portrayal of Kadare's years as a student in Moscow at the Gorky Institute of World Literature shortly before the rupture of the Soviet-Albanian alliance. The novel includes the tale of Kadare's romance with a Russian girl and a chapter on dissident writer Boris Pasternak who was awarded the Nobel Prize in 1958 for his novel 'Doctor Zhivago,' much to the displeasure of the Soviet authorities. *Muzgu i perëndive të stepës* shows some intriguing similarities to the noted Russian novel *Master i Margarita* (The Master and Margarita) by Mikhail Afanas'evich Bulgakov, published a decade earlier.

---

[116] cf. I. Kadare, *Pesha e kryqit*, Paris 1991, p. 140.

With *Ura me tri harqe*, Tirana 1978 (Engl. transl. *The Three-arched bridge*, New York 1997), Kadare returns to the mythical fountainhead of Albania's haunted history to bring to life one of the most awesome motifs of Balkan legendry - that of immurement. The legend of a human being being walled in during the construction of a bridge or castle is widespread in Albanian oral literature (cf. the tale of Rozafa Castle) and is based no doubt on a reality. Even at the beginning of the twentieth century, animals (sheep, goats, chickens) were still being sacrificed on such occasions in Albania, and their remains immured to 'stabilize' the foundations of bridges - indeed the practice can still be encountered today. The novel takes us back to early March in the year of our Lord 1377 in the company of the Monk Gjon. As the first chapter of the book makes evident, crime is involved in the construction of the new bridge over the Ujana e Keqe (Wicked Waters) river and there is more to the immurement than meets the eye. A fierce dispute has broken out between the constructors and their interest group on the one hand, and the district ferry company on the other. This local altercation is woven into a conflict of a much greater dimension, that soon to be brought about by the invasion of Christian Albania by the invincible hordes of the Ottoman Empire. "The shadows of its minarets are slowly falling over us." The novel has been interpreted as an Albanian response to Bosnian Serb Nobel Prize winner Ivo Andrić's *Na Drini ćuprija*, Sarajevo 1948 (Bridge on the Drina). Kadare is at his spellbinding best with Balkan themes.

More of Kadare's tales and shorter novels were published in this period of increasing literary maturity in three collections: *Emblema e dikurshme*, Tirana 1977 (Signs of the past), *Gjakftohtësia*, Tirana 1980 (Cold-bloodedness), and *Koha e shkrimeve*, Tirana 1986 (Epoch of writings). The latter two volumes were decidedly non-conformist by Albanian standards at the time, and added new dimensions to the Albanian short story with respect to both style and subject matter. The shorter novels appeared in the form of short stories for the simple reason that the short story editor at the state publishing house was less severe in his political vigilance than was the editor of novels.

In *Kush e solli Doruntinën?*, 1979 (Engl. transl. *Doruntine*, New York 1988), Kadare plunges once again into Albania's legendary past - legendary in the purest sense. The story of Constantine and his sister Doruntine is one of the best-known in Albanian folklore - simple and yet, as we see, with many possibilities:

> An old woman has nine sons and one daughter. Eight of the sons have already died by the time the daughter is to marry a distant suitor. Because the aging mother is apprehensive about giving her consent to the marriage and thereby losing her daughter too, perhaps forever, the

only surviving son, young Constantine, makes a solemn pledge (*besa* in Albanian) to his mother to bring back his sister whenever the mother should express the desire to see her. Time passes, but of the surviving members of the family, it is Constantine who dies first. The old woman, now alone, regrets her decision, longs for her daughter, and curses the dead Constantine for having broken his *besa*. Thereupon, Constantine, faithful beyond the grave to his pledge, rises from the tomb, mounts his steed and sets off in the night to find his sister, whom he returns to the arms of their dying mother.

Such is the Balkan legend which Kadare skilfully transforms into the period thriller. The action revolves around Captain Stres, a minor official in Albania during the Middle Ages who is responsible for sorting out the facts of the case and preparing a report: the daughter's unexpected arrival from distant Bohemia on a misty October night, the sudden death of mother and daughter, persistent rumours of an incestuous relationship - a desire so strong as to overcome death itself - the gravestone ajar, devious attempts to hush up the growing scandal and preserve the interests of church and state, and finally, a suspect. The atmosphere of mediaeval intrigue offered by Kadare is reminiscent of that in Italian writer Umberto Eco's highly successful novel *Il nome della rosa* (The Name of the rose).

Prilli i thyer, 1978 (Engl. transl. *Broken April*, New York 1990), published in the volume *Gjakftohtësia*, is not dissimilar to the mediaeval *Doruntine*, though its plot, which begins with a murder, is set in the 1930s. Gjorg Berisha has accomplished what all his family and relatives insisted he must do: cleanse his honour by slaying his brother's murderer who belongs to the rival Kryeqyqe clan. There was no way out of the bloody rituals of vendetta, anchored in the ancient Code of Lekë Dukagjini. Whole families had been wiped out in the 'taking of blood' and now he, too, would be obliged to follow suit, only to set himself up as the next victim. Everything was regulated by tribal law, including a thirty-day truce during which he would be allowed to spend his last days out in the sunlight, and during which he would have to journey through the mountains to submit 'blood money' to the feudal *qeheja e gjakut* (blood steward), keeper of the records. When the protagonist of the novel, writer Besian Vorpsi announces at a dinner party in Tirana that he intends to spend his honeymoon in the tribal highlands, he is met by stunned silence. His young bride Diana, too, is taken aback at the thought of spending a holiday on a desolate plateau in the northern Albanian Alps. Some friends can appreciate that Besian, as a writer, is fascinated by the prospects of a journey by car into the past, among the feudal and feuding mountain tribes of the north, a primitive society as yet untouched by modern civilisation. But what of his poor bride Diana? The more adventuresome envy her: "You will leave this world for the world of legends, ancient epics which are rarely encountered anywhere on the face of the earth today." Later, on Gjorg's journey to the bleak fortress of Orosh, he is startled to see one of the rare horseless carriages of which he had heard, a vehicle carrying a beautiful young lady from the city. Diana, too, has not failed to notice the young tribesman on his way to the 'Inn of the Two Roberts.' Inevitably, Besian's morbid fascination with the custom of vendetta and Diana's erotic attraction to Gjorg Berisha, a growing obsession which draws her into the other world, lead to the couple's estrangement.

Broken April is a popular novel because it provides the Western reader with much 'local colour.' Vendetta which, since the fall of the communist dictatorship, has come back to the mountains of northern Albania with a vengeance, if one will excuse the play on words, is the cultural particularity of the Albanians which perhaps most fascinates the outside world. Kadare has managed here to give it the epic proportions of an Aeschylean or Shakespearian tragedy.

Nëpunësi i pallatit të ëndrrave, 1981 (Engl. transl. *The Palace of dreams,* New York & London 1993) is considered one of Kadare's masterpieces. It is the world of Franz Kafka and of George Orwell's *1984* set in the sybaritic if somewhat torpid atmosphere of the Ottoman Empire. Mark-Alemi, scion of a noted family of public servants, is appointed to work at the Tabir Sarai, the awesome government office responsible for the study of sleep and dreams. It is his duty to analyse and categorize the dreams and nightmares of the Sultan's subjects and to interpret them in order to enable the authorities to stifle any incipient rebellion and to prevent criminal acts. *The Palace of dreams* is a surprisingly humorous novel, though certainly not so for those who have lived in a totalitarian state. The analogy for the Albanians was more than evident. The novel was conceived in the years 1972-1973 and was finished and published in 1981. In early 1982, an emergency meeting of the Albanian Writers Union was convened in the presence several members of the Politburo, including Ramiz Alia, who was to take power in 1985 after the death of Enver Hoxha. Terrified by the obvious allusions, writers and party members criticized *The Palace of dreams* severely. At the end of the meeting, Ramiz Alia warned Kadare: "The people and the Party have raised you to Olympus, but if you are not faithful to them, they will cast you into an abyss." But the Albanian Communist Party was weary by this time. After the rupture of its alliance with and aid from China, Albania was in rapid economic decline and had other concerns. Ismail Kadare was already an important and internationally recognized literary figure and could no longer be imprisoned or purged without a scandal. As a result, *The Palace of dreams* passed, and its author surprisingly survived the turmoil to continue his literary career. In doing so, he put Albanian literature on the map for the first time.

Krushqit janë të ngrirë (Engl. transl. *The Wedding procession turned to ice*, Boulder 1997), published in *Koha e shkrimeve* in 1986, evokes the explosive events of the Albanian uprising in the then autonomous region of Kosova in March-April 1981. The Albanian demand for republic status within the Yugoslav federation met with severe reprisals as well as the imposition of martial law by the Serb authorities in Belgrade. Tension between the Albanians and Serbs who had shared the plains of Kosova for centuries reached yet another tragic zenith that year - two peoples pitted against one another instead of united in a marriage of harmonious co-existence. It is to such a union rendered impossible by circumstance that the title of the novel alludes. According to legend, the 'oras,' spirits of Albanian mythology, would turn a wedding procession into ice before it reached home in order to prevent what was simply not permitted to be. Kadare's allegory touches on an unpleasant reality. We follow two days in the life of Teuta Shkreli, a surgeon at a Prishtina hospital during the bloody events, who finds herself caught up in a web of intrigue and incrimination. Who was responsible for the extra beds being set up in the ward the night *before* the uprising? Who removed the list of patients' names from the hospital files? Who was providing medical care to enemies of the state? And were Serbs being sterilized by Albanian doctors, or vice versa? Teuta, aware of impending repression, senses that her loyalty to her people and to her profession outweighs her passive allegiance to the state. Kadare is unsparing in his portrayal of political realities in Kosova, in particular in his description of drunken Serb ruffians longing for the good old days of Aleksandar Ranković, the head of the Yugoslav security police who was responsible for the systematic persecution of the Albanian population until his dismissal in July 1966.

Viti i mbrapshtë (The Year of misfortune), also published in *Koha e shkrimeve*, takes us back to 1914, not only a dark page in the annals of European history, but also a chaotic and decisive year in the struggle of the fledgling Albanian state for survival. What evils did the comet crossing the Albanian skies portend? It was anarchy that reigned and not German Prince Wilhelm zu Wied, the choice of the European powers, who, after much delay, disembarked at the port of Durrës in March 1914 to accept the crown of his unknown little kingdom. However, his government under Turhan Pasha, which was composed for the most part of rival feudal landowners, controlled only a small part of the country, and the proposed International Control Commission was unable to cope with the multitude of conflicting interests, not simply among the Albanians themselves, but also among the French, British and Dutch 'military advisors' and the ever-expanding neighbouring states. In the midst of such chaos, rumours spread like wildfire. Is Prince Wilhelm to have himself circumcised as a gesture of goodwill towards the majority Muslim community, or has he been circumcised in secret already? Who knows but his wife, and perhaps the lovely Sara Stringa, whose parties and receptions are the focus of social life for the rather skimmed crème de la crème of Albania's newly improvised capital? As the warlords continue their struggle for power in the mountains, and Montenegrin, Serb and Greek forces descend upon the country, the resident diplomatic corps is busy trying to interpret the possible significance of a plate of baklava presented to the British mission by the Turkish consul. After six months of inglorious rule, the well-meaning Prince sets sail from Durrës, leaving a regency council to cope with the country's affairs, and the mysterious comet gradually sinks below the horizon. *Viti i mbrapshtë* also contains many a cautious allusion to communist Albania.

In contrast to his many shorter novels of the period, Kadare's *Koncert në fund të dimrit*, Tirana 1988 (Engl. transl. *The Concert,* New York & London 1994), returns to the epic proportions of 'The Great winter' with which it has many parallels. This 700-page chronicle has a candidly symbolic title which in itself leads us to assume a continuity with 'The Great winter.' Here Kadare offers the reader a new panorama of recent Albanian history - a monumental review of Albania's dramatic break with post-Maoist China in 1978. The writer actually began writing the novel at the time of rupture of the Sino-Albanian alliance and only completed it in 1988. Relations between China and Albania had begun to sour with China's gradual opening to the West in the seventies, and the historic invitation to President Nixon to visit the Middle Kingdom was more or less the last straw. Enver Hoxha and the Albanian Party of Labour ceased viewing their only ally as a bastion of Marxism-Leninism. The political scenario was virtually the same as it had been for the severance with the Soviet Union: an ideological divergence of views, power politics, a strong-willed Enver Hoxha and the final departure of the foreign specialists from their only stronghold in the Mediterranean. The basic fabric of *The Concert* and the narrative techniques employed therein also reveals obvious parallels to 'The Great winter.' Kadare loves symbols and employs them to advantageous effect, in this novel as elsewhere.

In the novel *Dosja H*, Tirana 1990 (Engl. transl. *The File on H,* London & New York 1997), two fictive Irish-American scholars, Max Roth and Willy Norton, set off for the isolated mountains of pre-war northern Albania, tape recorder in hand, in search of the homeland of the epic. The two folklorists, based on the figures of Milman Parry and Albert Lord of Harvard University, are intent on investigating the possibility of a direct link between Homeric verse and the heroic songs sung by the Albanian mountain dwellers on their one-stringed 'lahutas.' Is this heroic and epic poetry, still sung by the

Albanians and southern Slavs, indeed the last outpost of the Homeric epic? It is a hypothesis which has particularly fascinated Ismail Kadare. The field trip is somewhat of a puzzle to the Albanian authorities, in particular to the sub-prefect of the region who, just to be on the safe side, sends out the bumbling secret agent Dullë Baxhaja to observe and report on their activities and movements. The sub-prefect's wife Daisy, reminiscent of the figure of Diana Vorpsi in *Broken April*, is equally fascinated by the presence of the two male scholars. Suspicion soon arises among the native population that the intruders from abroad are indeed spies. Their quarters at the Buffalo Bone Inn are eventually ransacked and the recording equipment which had captured the peasants' voices, is destroyed. End of mission to Albania. *The File on H* is a delightful satire on two innocent foreigners endeavouring to fathom the Albanian soul and, in particular, on the foibles of Albanian life at which foreign visitors often marvel: the Balkan love of rumours and gossip, administrative incompetence, and a childish fear or suspicion on the part of the authorities of anything foreign. By placing his tale in the 1930s once again, Kadare was able to take a safe sideswipe at his country's isolationist proclivities and at the bungling interference of the security apparatus in all spheres of contemporary life.

The novel *Piramida*, 1993 (Engl. transl. *The Pyramid*, London & New York 1996), is an historical and political allegory which was originally published in the form of a short story serialized in the initial issues of the first opposition newspaper in Tirana, *Rilindja Demokratike* (Democratic Renascence), in January 1991. In Parisian exile, Kadare expanded the tale to create a seventeen-chapter political allegory set in ancient Egypt. The pyramid was of course the 'Enver Hoxha Museum' erected on the main boulevard of Tirana, the last representative monument erected to the memory of the tyrant before the collapse of the system he perfected. It was a prestigious construction of shining white marble, crowned with a huge blood-red star made of plastic, a symbol which was discreetly removed together with all the relics after the fall of the regime. A direct and imaginative reflection of Ismail Kadare's fascination with that once much-lauded and secretly reviled museum is to be found in this intriguing historical novel. Like so many of his works, it can only be understood properly if read as a political allegory.

The Pyramid is the mind-boggling tale of the conception and construction of the Cheops pyramid in ancient Egypt, but also of absolute political power and indeed of human folly. Cheops, the Egyptian pharaoh, realized that he had dismayed his courtiers when he vowed one autumn morning to break with tradition by not constructing a pyramid as his predecessors had done. The pharaonic establishment and the power of custom and conformity were, however, to prove all too strong. Cheops was soon convinced by the high priest Hemiunu that a pyramid was more than simply a tomb. "It is power, Your Majesty. It is repression, might and money. It will also blind the masses, suffocate their spirit and break their will. It is monotony and detrition. It will be your best bodyguard, my pharaoh, it is the secret police, the army, the navy, the harem. The loftier it rises, the more minute you will seem in its shadow, and the more minute you are, Sire, the better you can act in all your glory." And so, the Egyptian masses set to work on an absurd construction in the desert, just as four and a half millennia after them, the Albanian people set to work on the building of literally hundreds of thousands of cement bunkers throughout the country to defend themselves against a supposedly imminent imperialist invasion, and on the construction of a marble mausoleum for their own 'pharaoh.'

Shkaba, Tirana 1996 (The Eagle), is a short novel written by Kadare in the summer of 1995. The twenty-two-year-old Max goes out one evening to buy a packet of cigarettes. On his way down the street, he passes under some scaffolding, slips on a board, and falls... into another world. There he finds himself in a community not dissimilar to his own, a small town in the provinces with a bar, a bank and a zoo. Max discovers that he is not the only stranger to have made the abrupt descent from the world he knew; even some of his acquaintances are there. He also learns that there is no going back. Like everyone else, he comes to realize he will have to make due. For the Albanian reader, the immediate analogy to Max's plight is the infamous institution of political internment practised widely under the communist regime. For political motives, or for no apparent reason at all, one could suddenly find oneself despatched to a remote mountain village with no hope of return. Only recently have statistics been made available as to the real number of people who suffered internment during the long years of Stalinist rule. The unspeakable concentration camps which the regime set up in Spaç and Burrel meant almost certain death for genuine and supposed adversaries of the regime, but political internment conveyed horrors of its own. At times, it was practised almost at random and could strike anyone. For intellectuals of the period, it was like being buried alive. Max learned to come to terms with his new underground environment and, with time, began to hear rumours of a possible method of flight, in both senses of the word. Escape was said to be possible with the help of the one remaining eagle in the zoo. An ancient legend had it that the eagle would take you wherever you wished, on the condition that you fed it meat. Should the supply of meat run out while you straddled the bird and overflew the chasms, it would demand your flesh: an arm, a leg, your liver or your heart, and then finally, your soul. Max knew what he was in for with the bird, the symbol that drapes the Albanian flag.

Spiritus, Elbasan 1996 (Spiritus), is another solidly constructed work of fiction which enlivens the sombre and sobering realities of recent Albanian history, i.e. the Hoxha dictatorship, with the brilliant hues of legend and fantasy. A group of foreigners, touring post-communist eastern Europe in search of the grotesque, hears exciting rumours during its stay in Albania about the capture of a spirit from the dead. The spirit, as we subsequently learn, is in actual fact a listening-device, affectionately known to the notorious secret service as a 'hornet,' which the murdered actor Shpend Guraziu took to the grave with him. The country's aging Leader - certainly an evocation of Enver Hoxha - was going blind and, perhaps as compensation, had asked the Chinese comrades for technical assistance in the form of a cargo of bugging equipment. On its arrival, a horde of secret agents, personified by Arian Vogli, gears into action to install the hornets and listen in on everything from clandestine baptisms to otherworldly seances and worldly sex, "Let's place a hornet in the apartment of the engineer Gjikondi, yes, right under his bed. They say that, when having sex, his wife divulges secrets of great importance..." Kadare takes up many of the elements which characterized his novels in the past: Albania as seen through the eyes of the innocent foreigner, the bumbling secret agent doting nefariously over his equipment as if it were his offspring, and the fantastical realms of Albanian and Balkan legendry.

Nothing has been more central to the historical and emotional identity of the southern Balkans than the Battle of Kosova in 1389. It was on June 28, St. Vitus Day, of that year that a coalition of Balkan forces made up of Serbs, Bosnians, Albanians and Romanians confronted an invading Ottoman army led by Sultan Murad. Their defeat at the hands of the Turks led to five centuries of Ottoman rule and changed the face of the Balkans forever. The ghosts of Kosova, where Europe meets the Third World, where the east-west axis of Islam meets the north-south axis of Eastern Orthodoxy, and where Slav meets non-Slav, have haunted the Balkans ever since. In the slender volume, *Tri këngë zie për Kosovën,* Tirana 1998 (Engl. transl. *Elegy for Kosovo,* New York 2000 / *Three Elegies for Kosovo,* London 2000), Ismail Kadare has assembled three of his tales about the Battle of Kosova and its aftermath. The first, 'The Ancient battle,' is a literary narrative in the author's mature style, of the circumstances of the battle. Though the Turks were the obvious victors over the uneasy coalition of Christian forces, the Ottoman sultan himself perished during or shortly after the battle. "The bizarre decision that the monarch's body be taken to the Ottoman capital, but that his blood and intestines should be buried in the Christian soil of Kosova, had a clear significance... By pouring the monarch's blood on the Plains of Kosova, they wanted to give those plains, just as they had done with their invasion, a direction, a fatality, both a curse and blessing at the same time, in other words, a 'programme,' as one would call it today." The second tale, 'The Great lady,' views the defeat on the plains of Kosova from the perspective of a group of minstrels: a Serb, an Albanian, a Walachian and a Bosnian, who had been summoned to the battlefield to play near the tent of Prince Lazar and who, caught up in the fighting, escape with the masses of Christian refugees fleeing from the victorious forces of Islam. The eternal message of the battle rings true when the Serb and Albanian minstrel friends attempt to explain their roles to a group of Hungarians whom they meet on their way: "It is a tangled matter. A Serb or Albanian can understand, but for you it would be too hard... For hundreds of years the evil persisted, what I mean is that Serbian and Albanian songs said the exact opposite from each other, particularly when it came to Kosova, as each side claimed Kosova was theirs. And each side cursed the other. And this lasted right up to the eve of the battle. Which was why the princes in the big tent laughed at the songs, for the princes had come together to fight the Turks while the minstrels were still singing songs against each other, the Serbs cursing the Albanians, and the Albanians the Serbs. And all the while, across the plain, the Turks were gathering to destroy them both the following day!" The volume concludes with the short tale, 'The Royal prayer,' in which the weary ghost of Sultan Murad, apprehensive that his blood may be the origin of six hundred years of horror, prays to Allah for release. "Make them remove my blood from these cold plains. And not just the leaden vessel, but make them dig up the earth around where my tent stood, where drops of my blood spattered the ground." Although the 'Three elegies for Kosovo' have nothing directly to do with recent political events: the 1998-1999 Kosova war and the final liberation of the long-suffering population, the very title of the book, and perhaps its modest size, made it one of the most widely read and already one of the most widely translated books which Ismail Kadare has written.

The novel *Lulet e ftohta të marsit,* Tirana 2000 (Engl. transl. *Spring flowers, spring frost,* New York 2002), literally 'The Cold flowers of March,' which his French translator preferred to entitle 'The Cold flowers of April,' reminds one immediately of *Broken April.* This time it is the painter Mark Gurabardhi who is confronted with the constraints and legendry of northern Albanian society in a small provincial town in the mountains. Though the plot has much in common with *Broken April*, the novel is set not in the 1930s, but in the 1990s when the bloody rites of vendetta had returned to the country after fifty years of suppression under the communist dictatorship. The backdrop to *Spring flowers, spring frost* is thus one of blood and the rites of feuding as codified in the famed *Kanun* of Lekë Dukagjini. Feuding was and is practised as a means of exercising tribal justice in wide regions of northern Albania and Kosova. Behind the blood feud is the principle of 'male honour,' i.e. that a man cannot cleanse his honour until he has given satisfaction in blood for a crime or infringement upon that honour. The *Kanun* originally sanctioned the slaying of the murderer himself, but the practice was later extended so that male honour or blood could also be 'cleansed' by the slaying of any male relative of the murderer. It is in this framework that a simple love story between the painter and a young woman evolves until the customs of the north offer a dramatic turn of events. Albanian legendry, too, plays its part. Interwoven into the book is Kadare's literary adaptation of the folk tale of the maiden who was forced to marry a snake. *Spring flowers, spring frost* is very much a novel in the traditional style of Kadare. It is a complex work with many levels of interpretation and intertwining themes.

The novel *Hija*, 2001 (The Shadow), was written in 1984-1986 and was deposited in a French bank for safekeeping during the final years of the dictatorship. Like a number of Kadare's earlier works, 'The Shadow' focusses on the fate of the intellectual in an age of political turmoil. An Albanian movie director is invited to Paris within the framework of a cultural exchange agreement, and travels, not merely from one European city to another, but from one cosmos to another, from death to life. The fictive director uses his modest freedom to the full in days of intensive professional activity and in nights of emotionally charged intimacy until he is forced to return home. Travelling abroad was an extremely rare privilege, a schizophrenic experience under the Hoxha dictatorship. Kadare himself was one of the very few creative individuals allowed to leave the country during the long decades of unbridled terror. In a sense, therefore, 'The Shadow' can be interpreted as an extended work of autobiography, a voyage from silence, from the cold and grey of the Stalinist East to the creative freedom and bustle of the *ville lumière*, where Kadare ultimately chose to reside.

Ismail Kadare has lost none of his elan in recent years. In addition to reprints and numerous works of a journalistic and political nature, he has published the short story collection *Përballë pasqyrës së një gruaje*, Tirana 2001 (In a lady's looking-glass); the novel *Jeta, loja dhe vdekja e Lul Mazrekut*, Tirana 2002 (Life, game and death of Lul Mazreku); a play, the Promethean tragedy *Stinë e mërzitshme në Olymp*, Tirana 2002 (Boring season on Olympus); the poetry collection *Ca pika shiu ranë mbi qelq*, Tirana 2003 (Some Raindrops fell on the window-pane); and the novels *Pasardhësi*, Tirana 2003 (The Successor) and *Vajza e Agamemnonit*, Tirana 2003 (Agamemnon's daughter).

As we have seen, there can be no doubt that, during the dictatorship, Ismail Kadare was a profoundly dissident writer although he led a conformist, if you will, collaborationist life. Dissent is, of course, a relative term and varies largely from one country to another and from one political system to another. The communist regime which ruled Albania during Kadare's most productive years cannot be compared with the communist regimes in other Eastern European countries where a certain amount of public dissent was tolerated or at least left unstifled. Communism in Albania, a small, isolated and tightly-knit society in which everyone was spying on everyone else, must best be compared with Russian Stalinism in the 1930s, or to isolationist dictatorships like North Korea with an extremely high level of political control over the individual and society. Expectations of finding political dissent in the works of Kadare to the extent found in the works of other Eastern European writers such as Boris Pasternak, Vaclav Havel or Aleksandr Solzhenitzin have led to disappointment on the part of Western critics who do not appreciate the political distinctions which must be made. As such, there has been a misrepresentation as to the true level of dissent, or lack thereof, in Ismail Kadare's works.

Dissent in Kadare's prose up to the fall of the dictatorship was very discreet but ubiquitous. Notwithstanding its subtle nature, it was sufficiently evident at all times to the educated Albanian reader, and this is one of the major factors that contributed to his popularity at home. Ismail Kadare left no opportunity untouched to attack the follies, weaknesses and excesses of the Albanian communist system, yet many of his subtle barbs are difficult to grasp for those who did not grow up in or live through that system. The very treatment in a conformist manner of a taboo subject, i.e. of virtually anything beyond the very narrow scope of socialist realism and communist partisan heroism, constituted in itself an act of extreme dissent, amounting to treason in Albania.

Though some observers in Albania silently viewed him as a political opportunist, and many Albanians in exile later criticized him vociferously for the compromises he made, it is Ismail Kadare more than anyone else who, from within the system, dealt the death blow to the literature of socialist realism. There can be no doubt that he made use of his relative freedom and his talent under the dictatorship to launch many a subtle but effective fusillade against the regime in the form of political allegories which occur throughout his works. Ismail Kadare was thus the most prominent representative of Albanian literature under the dictatorship of Enver Hoxha and, at the same time, the regime's most talented adversary. His works were extremely influential and, for many readers, he was the only ray of hope in the chilly, dismal prison that was communist Albania.

6.3   Other Prose Writers of the Socialist Period and Thereafter

Prose in Albania remained weak throughout the communist dictatorship. Ismail Kadare's talent and overriding position in Albanian literature, compounded by his international reputation, cast a shadow over all other contemporary prose writers, and not without reason. Many writers tried their hand at novels and short stories throughout the long decades of the communist dictatorship, but the awesome level of social and political control over individual thought and the cultural isolation under which the Albanians were forced to live for so long prevented most of them from producing works which can stand the test of time. It was not talent and potential that Albanian writers lacked, but rather a positive, creative and stable environment in which to develop this potential. Political fluctuations meant that a work of quality could be accepted one year for publication and then banned the very next. For several decades writing in Albania was a potentially lethal pastime.

Petro Marko (1913-1991) from Dhërmi on the coast of Himara, is an author who paved the road to modernity before Kadare and influenced his early development. Marko began writing when he was twenty. His first short stories appeared in journals of the period with the assistance of his mentor Ernest Koliqi. From 1 March 1936, Marko edited the short-lived periodical *ABC* in Tirana, a fortnightly literary journal soon to be shut down by the Zogist authorities. Always something of a revolutionary and an anarchist in spirit, Marko set off in 1936 for the Spanish Civil War with a group of forty Albanians to join the Garibaldi Unit of the International Brigades. The consumptive poet Migjeni, soon to die in a sanatorium in northern Italy, bid him farewell with these words: "Your departure for Spain is your most beautiful poem." In Madrid, the twenty-three year old Marko and Skënder Luarasi started up a twenty-page Albanian-language periodical called *Vullnetari i lirisë* (The Volunteer of freedom), of which, however, only two numbers appeared. Marko met Ernest Hemingway at a congress of writers held in Valencia in 1937, which was also attended by Aleksey Tolstoy, Ludwig Renn, Anna Seghers, André Malraux and Pablo Neruda.

It was Petro Marko's experience in the Spanish Civil War that formed the basis of his best-known novel *Hasta la vista*, Tirana 1958 (Hasta la vista). In 1940, Marko was forced to return home from exile in France. Arrested by the Italian occupants the following year, he was interned with six hundred other Balkan prisoners on the isolated island of Ustica in the Tyrrhenian Sea north of Sicily. The 380-page novel *Nata e Ustikës*, Tirana 1989 (Ustica night), is the literary digestion of this period of internment. In October 1944, Marko returned to Albania as a partisan. After a couple of years as editor-in-chief of the periodical *Bashkimi* (Unity), he was arrested in 1947, by the communists this time, and imprisoned. After the fall of Koçi Xoxe, he was released and allowed to teach in Tirana. It was in the late fifties and early sixties that several volumes of prose and a collection of Marko's verse first appeared. The surrealist novel *Qyteti i fundit*, Tirana 1960 (The Last city), portrays the bitter end of the Italian army of occupation in Albania. It is regarded by some observers as the first modern novel of Albanian literature. The 204-page *Rrugë pa rrugë*, Tirana 1964 (Road by road), is a collection of sixty tales and sketches that Marko wrote in his early years, from 1933 to 1937. The novel *Një emër në katër rrugë*, Tirana 1973 (A Name at the crossroads), was set in the Zogu era. Published in the politically volatile year of the so-called Purge of the Liberals, it was banned and burned, as was a volume of Marko's poetry. In the wake of the purge, the writer lost his right to publish anything until 1982.

As the author of eight novels, Petro Marko is considered by many critics to be one of the founding fathers of modern Albanian prose. Though some writers have criticized his telegraphic style, the passion of his search for new descriptive techniques and his treatment of original subjects met with wide approval, and many of this works are still read today.

Martin Camaj[117] (1925-1992) is an emigrant writer of major significance to modern Albanian prose and poetry. He was born in Temal in the Dukagjini region of the northern Albanian Alps, and benefited from a classical education at the Jesuit Saverian College in Shkodra. Camaj studied at the University of Belgrade and from there he went on to do postgraduate research in Italy, where he taught Albanian and finished his education in linguistics at the University of Rome in 1960. From 1970 to 1990 he was professor of Albanian studies at the University of Munich and lived in the mountain village of Lenggries in Upper Bavaria until his death on 12 March 1992. Camaj's academic research focussed on the Albanian language and its dialects, in particular those of southern Italy. He was also active in the field of folklore.

Camaj's literary activities over a period of forty-five years cover several phases of development. His first major prose work was *Djella*, Rome 1958 (Djella), a novel interspersed with verse about the love of a teacher for a young girl of the lowlands. This was followed, twenty years later, by the novel *Rrathë*, Munich 1978 (Circles), which has been described as the first psychological novel in Albanian. It is the author's most extensive prose work, one which he took fifteen years to write. Agron, a writer and agronomist in post-revolutionary 'Arbenia,' is sent to the village of Middle Ripa to report on the arrival of some new tractors. There he becomes enthralled with the haunted

---

[117] cf. A. Berisha 1994, 1995b; Y. Çiraku 2003.

history of the mountains after saving the life of the wild and beautiful shepherdess Sose, the personification of the mountain nymphs. The 'circles' of water, fire and blood into which the novel is divided symbolize not only metaphysical and social constraints but also the writer's progress through the mythical heritage of Albania's past towards a new and personal future. After *Shkundullima*, Munich 1981 (Quaking), a collection of five short stories and one play, came the novel *Karpa*, Rome 1987 (Karpa), which is set on the banks of the river Drin in the year 2338, a long prose work which Camaj preferred to call a parable. General themes which occur in Martin Camaj's work are the loss of tradition, loneliness in a changing world, and the search for one's roots. Needless to say, his works only became known to the Albanian public after the fall of the dictatorship. Up until then, only a handful of people in Albania had ever heard of Martin Camaj.

One writer who has had a far from negligible influence on the course of contemporary literature is **Dritëro Agolli** (b. 1931), who was head of the Albanian Union of Writers and Artists from the purge of Fadil Paçrami and Todi Lubonja at the Fourth Plenary Session in 1973 until 1992. Agolli was born to a peasant family in Menkulas in the Devoll region near Korça and finished secondary school in Gjirokastra in 1952. He later continued his studies at the Faculty of Arts of the University of Leningrad and took up journalism upon his return to Albania, working for the daily newspaper *Zëri i Popullit* (The People's Voice) for fifteen years. Agolli not only served as president of the Writers' Union from 1973 to his retirement on 31 January 1992, but was also a deputy in the People's Assembly.

Like Kadare, Dritëro Agolli turned increasingly to prose in the seventies after attaining success as a poet of the soil. He first made a name for himself with the novel *Komisari Memo*, Tirana 1970 (Commissar Memo), originally conceived as a short story. This didactic novel with a clear social and political message was translated into English as *The Bronze bust*, Tirana 1975. Memo Kovaçi is the prototype of the enlightened partisan hero with a double role: waging war in the mountains against the German occupants and educating the population in his capacity as a political commissar.

Agolli's second novel, *Njeriu me top*, Tirana 1975 (The Man with a cannon), translated into English as *The Man with the gun*, Tirana 1983, takes up the partisan theme from a different angle and with a somewhat more subtle approach. Mato Gruda is a simple peasant who is 'at blood' with the clan of the Fizis, i.e., caught up in a sanguinary vendetta passed on from one generation to the next. In the forest one day, he discovers a cannon abandoned by the retreating Italian army and hides it in his shed, obsessed by the idea of revenge. His personal conflict with the Fizis and their patriarch, old Mere, blinds him to the increasing political dissension in the village caused by the presence of rival resistance movements and to the urgent needs of the partisans in their struggle against the invading Germans. Disillusioned by his own ignorance and his failure to blow up the house of old Mere, and saddened by the murder of his friend Murat Shtaga, Mato Gruda comes to realize the overriding interests at stake and hauls his lonely cannon out to come to the aid of his partisan allies.

After these two rather conformist novels of partisan heroism, the standard theme encouraged by the party, Agolli produced a far more interesting work, his satirical *Shkëlqimi dhe rënja e shokut Zylo*, Tirana 1973 (The Splendour and fall of comrade Zylo), which has proved to be his claim to fame. Comrade Zylo is the epitome of the well-meaning but incompetent *apparatchik*, director of an obscure government cultural affairs department. His pathetic vanity, his quixotic fervour, his grotesque public behaviour, in short his splendour and fall, are all recorded in ironic detail by his hard-working and more astute subordinate and friend Demkë who serves as a neutral observer. The turning point in comrade Zylo's career finally comes when he is required to express his views on a play:

> "The drama is ideologically faulty. First of all, the negative hero inspires strength. Did you notice him climbing a hill? What does this mean, my friends? It means he has mounted a pedestal, i.e. the hill. He should get off the hill and be tossed into a well. It is for the positive hero to climb the hill."

These words which, according to Agolli, were actually spoken in Tirana by some astute proponent of socialist realism, precipitate Zylo's fall when the play in question is later deemed a success by others higher up on the ladder. Comrade Zylo is a universal figure, a character to be found in any society or age, and critics have been quick to draw parallels ranging from Daniel Defoe and Nikolay Gogol's *Revizor* to Franz Kafka and Milan Kundera's *Zert*. But it is doubtless the Eastern European reader who will best appreciate all the subtleties of the novel. *Shkëlqimi dhe rënja e shokut Zylo* first appeared in 1972 in the Tirana satirical journal *Hosteni* (The Goad) and was published the following year in book form. That it was published at all in Stalinist Albania is linked to the fact that the character of Zylo was modelled on a well-known liberal journalist and writer of the time and thus served to discredit the so-called liberal movement in general.

All in all, Agolli's strength in prose lies in the short story rather than in the novel. Sixteen of his short stories have been published in English in the volume: *Short stories*, Tirana 1985. One early collection of tales, the 213-page *Zhurma e erërave të dikurshme*, Tirana 1964 (The Noise of winds of the past), had the distinction of being banned and 'turned into cardboard.' The author was accused of Soviet revisionism at a time when the party had called for more (Maoist) revolutionary concepts in literature and greater devotion to the working masses.

Though Agolli was a leading figure in the communist nomenclature, he remained a highly respected figure of public and literary life after the fall of the dictatorship, and is still one the most widely read authors in Albania. In the early 1990s, he was active for several years as a member of parliament for the Socialist Party of Albania. He also founded his own *Dritëro* Publishing Company by means of which he has been able to publish many new volumes of prose and poetry, and make an impact on literary and intellectual life in the country. Among recent volumes of prose are: the short story collection *Njerëz të krisur,* Tirana 1995 (Insane people); the novels *Kalorësi lakuriq,* Tirana 1996 (The Naked horseman); and in particular the volume *Arka e djallit,* Tirana 1997 (The Devil's box). Dritëro Agolli was a prolific writer throughout the nineties, a rare voice of humanity and sincerity in Albanian letters.

Prose author **Fatos Kongoli** (b. 1944) has recently become one of the most forceful and convincing representatives of contemporary Albanian literature. He was born and raised in Elbasan and studied mathematics in China during the tense years of the Sino-Albanian alliance. Kongoli chose not to publish any major works during the dictatorship. Rather than this, he devoted his creative energies at the time to an obscure and apolitical career as a mathematician, and waited for the storm to pass. His narrative talent and individual style only really emerged, at any rate, in the nineties, since the fall of the communist dictatorship.

His first major novel, *I humburi,* Tirana 1992 (The Loser), is set in March 1991, when over 10,000 refugees scrambled onto a decrepit and heavily rusting freighter to escape the past and to reach the marvellous West. There they washed up, unwanted, on the shores of southern Italy. At the last moment before setting sail, protagonist Thesar Lumi, the 'loser' for whom all hope is too late, abandons his companions, disembarks and walks home. "I returned to my neighbourhood at the fall of night. No one had seen me leave and no one saw me come back." The narrative of the novel returns at this point to the long and numbing years of the Hoxha dictatorship to revive the climate of terror and universal despair which characterized day-to-day life in Albania in the sixties and seventies. Thesar Lumi was born on the banks of a river (Alb. *lumi*) in the looming shadow of the people's own cement factory, which produced more dust than it ever did cement. Despite a skeleton in the family closet, an uncle who had earlier fled the country, Thesar manages to get himself registered at the university, and penetrates briefly into a milieu which is not his own and never will be, that of the ruling families of Albania's red aristocracy. "At a tender age I learned that I belonged to an inferior race or, as I saw things at the time, to a category of mangy dogs to be kicked about and chased away." Thesar, whose fate in Albania's hermetic and suffocating society has been sealed once and for all, returns to live a life of futility and despair in a universe with no heroes. Far from the active protagonist struggling to control of his own destiny or even from the staid positive hero of socialist realism, Thesar Lumi is incapable of action and incapable of living. He is the voice of all the 'losers' who glimpse the silver clouds on the horizon and know full well that they will never reach them. "My existence is that of the mediocre, setting out from nothing and going nowhere." When first published in 1992, in what was a comparatively large edition of 10,000 copies, the novel found immediate success among the reading public. Who could not identify with the confessional monologue and the unending tribulations and torment of Thesar Lumi?

Kongoli's second novel, *Kufoma,* Tirana 1994 (The Corpse), has clear affinities with its predecessor, both with respect to Kongoli's now crystallized and somewhat more elaborate narrative style, and to his innate preoccupations. Protagonist Festim Gurabardhi is another loser, caught up in the inhumane machinery of the last decade of the Stalinist dictatorship in Albania. As an orphan in the fifties he could never understand why his parents, killed in a car crash eight months after his birth, had given him the name Festim, meaning 'feast, celebration.' What was there to celebrate? "My childhood was endless solitude in boarding-schools, refectories and dormitories which made the solitary souls in them even lonelier." He observes his playmates slit the throats of cats in the street, observes his brother Abel being arrested and taken away in a sinister black limousine, and then, as an adult employed at the state-run publishing company, he observes himself ... being observed. The communist dictatorship in Albania was the perfection of insanity. What the country produced more than anything was paranoia and schizophrenia. Intellectual life in Albania, or what remained of it after the countless arrests, purges and suicides, was concentrated in the Tirana publishing companies. There, under the thumb of boorish directors and under the constant observation of spies and submissive apparatchiks, the nation's traumatized writers and translators were assembled to edit the sage works of the supreme leader and other members of the politburo. Like the characters of an ancient tragedy, they had resigned themselves to their fates and capitulated, emotionally and intellectually. In the macabre and Kafkaesque game of cats and mice which Kongoli portrays, Festim and his colleagues are destined to play both roles, that of the victim and that of the perpetrator. The metaphorical background is grey and realistic, depressing even for those who knew Albania at the time: the sombre and filthy hallways, the furtive drunkenness, sordid copulation in the director's office, and the eternal stench of the rat-infested toilets. Fatos Kongoli is at his best in portraying this very atmosphere, in providing a detailed autopsy of an unending nightmare.

Kongoli's *Dragoi i fildishtë*, Tirana 1999 (The Ivory dragon), focusses primarily on the life of an Albanian student in China in the 1960s. For Genc Skampa and the other fictive Albanian students highlighted in the novel, studies in China provided an opportunity to discover the world. Having contact not only with their Chinese comrades but also with foreign students from all over the globe. they were able to pursue their goals of intellectual and personal development. Among these pursuits were discreet sexual freedoms which would have been unthinkable in puritanical Albania itself, where everyone was watching everyone with a malevolent eye. Interwoven into the novel is the life of the protagonist in post-communist Albania thirty years later when, as a journalist, he is invited to Paris with a group of Balkan colleagues. Now divorced and suffering from personal isolation and the ravages of alcohol, he looks back in a haze to the decisive years of his life in China and ponders over the emotional consequences of his turbulent love affair with Sui Lin. 'The Ivory dragon' is the tragic parable of one man's life, of adventure, alienation and self-destruction. Although the backdrop to this novel is quite different from the earlier works, the underlying themes of despair and isolation are the same.

Among the other prose authors of the period, mention may be made of **Sabri Godo** (b. 1929) from Delvina, an author of historical novels such as *Ali Pashë Tepelena*, Tirana 1970 (Ali Pasha of Tepelena), and *Skënderbeu*, Tirana 1975 (Scanderbeg), who, after the dictatorship, embarked upon a political career; **Kasëm Trebeshina** (b. 1926), a committed dissident who for many years was denied the right to publish; **Naum Prifti** (b. 1932), short story writer from the Korça district; the prolific **Dhimitër Xhuvani** (b. 1934); **Bilal Xhaferi** (1935-1986) from Çamëria who in 1969 escaped to Greece and the United States; **Vath Koreshi** (b. 1936), a prolific writer from Lushnja; **Teodor Laço** (b. 1936) of Korça; **Elena Kadare** (b. 1943), the first woman in Albania to publish a full novel; **Zija Çela** (b. 1946) of Shkodra; **Ylljet Aliçka** (b. 1951) from Tirana; **Diana Çuli** (b. 1951) from Tirana; **Bashkim Shehu** (b. 1955), who, as son of the purged communist leader Mehmet Shehu, spent many years in prison; **Preç Zogaj** (b. 1957) from the region of Lezha who in June 1991 became the first non-communist minister of culture; **Teodor Keko** (1958-2002); **Besnik Mustafaj** (b. 1958) from Bajram Curri who served as Albanian ambassador in Paris; **Ridvan Dibra** (b. 1959) of Shkodra; and **Lazër Stani** (b. 1959) from Pult near Shkodra.

Among more recent prose authors of note, including an increasing number of women, one may mention: **Mira Meksi** (b. 1960) from Tirana; **Elvira Dones** (b. 1960) now living in Switzerland, who is author of the successful and exceptionally frank novel *Yjet nuk vishen kështu*, Elbasan 2000

(Stars don't dress up like that) on the subject of Albanian prostitution abroad; **Mimoza Ahmeti** (b. 1963) from Kruja; **Flutura Açka** (b. 1966) from Elbasan; **Arian Leka** (b. 1966) from Durrës; **Agron Tufa** (b. 1967), author of the novel *Dueli*, Tirana 2002 (The Duel); **Virion Graçi** (b. 1968) of Gjirokastra; and **Ardian-Christian Kyçyku** (b. 1969) of Pogradec, now living in Bucharest.

6.4   The People's Poets

The gradual refinement of style and the diversification of themes seen in the Albanian prose of the seventies and eighties were apparent in modern poetry, too. The aesthetic appeal of poetic language, the relative freedom of expression offered by verse, plus the opportunity to pursue one's fantasies in a society seemingly obsessed with industrial output, manufacturing statistics and the construction of dams continued to attract a good many Albanian writers to poetry rather than to prose. Publishing statistics reflected this penchant: in Tirana about 40% of literary publications in the 1980s were poetry volumes, in Prishtina up to 70%, something quite unimaginable in the rational West.

Nonetheless, the social and political message, couched at times in more subtle terms, was no less present in poetry publications in Tirana than in prose. The framework set by socialist realism provided of necessity the foundation for all publications in the country until the fall of the dictatorship. By its very nature, however, poetry remains an individualistic matter and is difficult to reconcile with a planned society. The position of the poet in such a society, no less than that of the prose writer, had, as a matter of course, to conform to the functions assigned to him or her by the powers that be. Fortunately, from the mid-sixties onwards, these functions were combined with enough individuality on the part of the poets to save Albanian verse from the sterile panegyrics of the early years which party dogmatists continued to long for.

This being said, the story of modern verse from Albania begins with an exception, a poet who managed to flee from Stalinist Albania in 1949 and thus escaped the all-pervasive influence of socialist realism. **Martin Camaj** (1925-1992) began his literary career with poetry, a genre to which he remained faithful throughout his life, though in later years he devoted himself increasingly to prose, as we have seen. His first volumes of classical verse, *Nji fyell ndër male*, Prishtina 1953 (A Flute in the mountains), and *Kânga e vërrinit*, Prishtina 1954 (Song of the lowland pastures), were inspired by his native northern Albanian mountains to which he never lost his attachment, despite long years of exile and the impossibility of return. His collections

Legjenda, Rome 1964 (Legends), and *Lirika mes dy moteve*, Munich 1967 (Lyrics between two ages), which contained revised versions of a number of poems from *Kânga e vërrinit*, were reprinted in *Poezi 1953-1967*, Munich 1981 (Poetry 1953-1967). Two volumes have appeared in English: *Selected Poetry*, New York 1990, and *Palimpsest*, Munich & New York 1991.

Camaj's mature verse shows the influence of the hermetic movement of Italian poet Giuseppe Ungaretti. The metaphoric and symbolic character of his language increased with time as did the range of his poetic themes. Camaj's language is discreet, reserved and trying at times, although the author himself regarded the term hermetic as coincidental. He relied on the traditional and colourful linguistic fountainhead of his native Gheg dialect in order to convey a poetic vision of his pastoral mountain birthplace near the Drin with its sparkling streams and shining forests. It is no coincidence that Camaj chose as his place of residence in exile, the splendid if somewhat orderly and domesticated setting of the Bavarian Alps, a daily reminder of the rugged mountain homeland to which he was never to return.

Fatos Arapi (b. 1930) from Zvërnec near the port city of Vlora, is the author of philosophical verse, love lyrics and poignant elegies on death. He studied economics in Sofia from 1948 to 1953 and worked in Tirana as a journalist and lecturer in modern Albanian literature. In his first two collections, *Shtigje poetike*, Tirana 1962 (Poetic paths), and *Poema dhe vjersha*, Tirana 1966 (Poems and verse), he made use of more modern verse forms than his contemporaries and set the course for a renewal of Albanian poetry after years of stagnation. Criticized in the 1973 purge for the volume *Më jepni një emër*, Tirana 1973 (Give me a name), which was 'turned into cardboard' along with many other works of literature, he fell silent and published little of significance until 1989.

Child of the Ionian coast, Arapi has never lost his fascination with the sparkling waters of the sea, the tang of the salt air and the intensity of Mediterranean light, all of which flood his verse. Indeed, beyond the echoing pathos of much of his revolutionary verse production on industrial and political themes in numerous publications during the dictatorship, his true poetic vocation can be seen in the creation of an equilibrium between the harmony of the waves and the rhythmic impulses of his being.

Dritëro Agolli (b. 1931) made his name originally as a poet before turning to prose in later years. He is still widely admired in both genres. His first verse collections *Në rrugë dolla*, Tirana 1958 (I went out on the street), *Hapat e mija në asfalt*, Tirana 1961 (My steps on the pavement), and *Shtigje malesh dhe trotuare*, Tirana 1965 (Mountain paths and sidewalks), introduced him to the reading public as a sincere and gifted lyric poet of the soil and demonstrated masterful verse technique. One senses in this early verse the influence of his training in the Soviet Union, and in particular the spirit of Russian authors Eduard Bagritsky and Dmitri Kedrin. An attachment to his roots came to form the basis of his poetic credo, in particular in *Devoll, Devoll*, Tirana 1964 (Devoll, Devoll), which begins as follows:

> "*Po, Devoll,*
> > *i tillë qenkam unë,*
> *Paskam marrë baltën tënde arave,*
> *Në një trastë leshi*
> > *ndënë gunë,*
> *Për t'ia sjellë*
> > *Lidhjës së Shkrimtarëve.*"

> (Yes, Devoll,
> > I'm one of them,
> I gathered the mud from your fields
> In a woollen sack
> > under my coat,
> To carry it
> > to the Writers' Union.)

Agolli delights in earthy rhyme and unusual figures of speech. His fresh, clear and direct verse, coloured with the warm foaming milk of brown cows in the agricultural co-operatives, with ears of ripening corn in the Devoll valley and with the dark furrows of tilled soil, has lost none of the bucolic focus which remained the poet's strength, and one which he cultivates consciously.

With the cycle *Baballarët*, Tirana 1969 (The Fathers), Agolli's verse began losing some of its spontaneity and tilted towards 'official' poetry in the service of ideology. A prime example of such party panegyrics enjoying much publicity and official acclaim was the nationalistic *Nënë Shqipëri*, Tirana 1974 (Engl. transl. *Mother Albania*, Tirana 1985), which was widely disseminated at the time. Agolli had replaced Dhimitër Shuteriqi (1915-2003) as president of the Albanian Writers' Union in 1973 after the Purge of the Liberals and, as the nation's new poet laureate, something grandiose was expected of him for the thirtieth anniversary of the 'liberation,' something which school children could learn by heart. The ten cantos of *Mother Albania*, which time will show to be very much a period piece, were the result.

Nonetheless, Agolli advanced and managed to remain true to himself and to his readers despite the vicissitudes of public life. In the volume *Pelegrini i vonuar*, Tirana 1993 (The Belated pilgrim), his first book ever written without an eye to the invisible censor, we encounter a new chapter, not only in the life of the poet, but also in the struggle of his people for survival. Agolli confesses in a postscript: "For poets of my generation, an age of disappointments and dilemmas has dawned, an age in which to re-evaluate what we produced, without forgetting or denying those fair and humane values we brought forth. But the fortress of ideas and ideals which we believed in, some of us completely, others partially, has all but collapsed, and in its walls burn the fires of our dreams. Those fires have awakened a different type of verse..." Dritëro Agolli has been exceptionally productive in recent years, with numerous well-received verse collections: *Lypësi i kohës,* Tirana 1995 (The Contemporary beggar), *Shpirti i gjyshërve,* Tirana 1996 (The Spirit of our forefathers), *Vjen njeriu i çuditshëm,* Tirana 1996 (The Strange man approaches), *Baladë për tim atë dhe për vete,* Tirana 1997 (Ballad for my father and myself), *Fletorka e mesnatës,* Tirana 1998 (Midnight notebook), and *Kambana e largët,* Tirana 1998 (The Distant bell).

Prose writer **Ismail Kadare** (b. 1936), it must be noted, began his literary career with verse and, although he has been much less active in this genre in recent years, he is still recognized and admired as one of his country's leading poets. The young Albanian writer who was so firmly to set his mark on Albanian literature for decades to come, was dispatched in the late fifties to study abroad at the Gorky Institute of World Literature in Moscow where the sentimental Slavic soul of Holy Mother Russia lived on amidst the sobering realities of Soviet communism under Nikita Khrushchev. Here he had intimate contact with Russian intellectuals, writers and poets, and it comes as no surprise that their influence is felt in his verse, the confidence of Yevgeny Yevtushenko (b. 1933) and the sensitivity of Andrey Voznesensky (b. 1933). In 1959, on a visit to Yalta, Kadare wrote of poetry:

> "*Poezi,*
> *Udhën gjer tek unë si e gjete?*
> *Mamaja ime shqipen mirë s'e di,*
> *Letrat si Aragoni i shkruan, pa pikë dhe presje.*
> *Babaj u end në rini në të tjera dete;*
> *Po ti erdhe*
> *Duke ecur nëpër kalldrëmin e qytetit tim të gurtë të qetë,*
> *Trokite drojtur në shtëpinë trekatëshe*
> *Nr. 16.*
>
> *Shumë gjëra kam dashur dhe çdhashur në jetë,*
> *Për shumë dëshira kam qenë 'Çita aperta,'*
> *Por prapë*

Si ai djali që kthehet vonë në shtëpi,
I lodhur dhe i shqyer nga bredhjet e natës;
Ashtu dhe unë, i lodhur përsëri
Pas çdo amatorije, jam kthyer tek ti.

Dhe ti,
Pa më mbajtur mëri për tradhëtitë,
Më ke përkëdhelur flokët me ëmbëlsi,
Stacioni im i fundit,
Poezi."

(Poetry,
How did you find your way to me?
My mother does not know Albanian well,
She writes like Aragon, without periods and commas,
My father roamed other seas in his youth,
But you have come,
Walking down the pavement of my quiet city of stone,
And knocked timidly at my three-storey house,
At Number 16.

There are many things I have loved and hated in life,
For many a problem I have been an 'open city,'
But anyway...
Like a young man returning home late at night,
Exhausted and broken by his nocturnal wanderings,
Here too am I, returning to you,
Worn out after another escapade.

And you,
Not holding my infidelity against me,
Stroke my hair tenderly,
My last stop,
Poetry.)

It was Kadare's collection *Shekulli im*, Tirana 1961 (My century), which, together with contemporary works of Agolli and Arapi, helped set the pace for renewal in Albanian verse. Kadare's poetry was less bombastic than previous verse and gained direct access to the hearts of the readers who saw in him the spirit of the times and who appreciated the diversity of his themes. He soon became widely admired among the youth of Albania for his verse. With candidness and sincerity, Kadare contributed in particular to the evolution of love lyrics, a genre traditionally neglected in Albanian literature. He was courageous in form, but perhaps less so in content. Much of his verse production in the sixties was politically motivated. *Përse mendohen këto male*, Tirana 1964 (What are these mountains thinking about), is a hymn to the party in twenty-four devout cantos and came to be one of the clearest expressions of Albanian self-image under the rule of Enver Hoxha. Other longer poems during his most productive poetic years, such as *Ëndërr industriale,* 1960 (Industrial dream), *Poema e blinduar,* 1962 (The Armoured poem), and *Shqiponjat fluturojnë lart,* 1966 (Eagles fly high), provided the party's favourite mixture of nationalist pathos and revolutionary fervour. Though more formally innovative than his contemporaries, Ismail Kadare was on the whole not as consistent a poet as Dritëro Agolli in the latter's early years or as Fatos Arapi throughout his poetic career. What he did accomplish, however, was to bridge the gulf between poetry and prose and to transpose many elements of the former into his short stories and novels. A collection of forty of his best poems has recently appeared in the edition *Ca pika shiu ranë mbi qelq,* Tirana 2003 (Some raindrops fell on the window-pane).

Visar Zhiti (b. 1952) is the Albanian writer whose life and works perhaps best mirror the history of his nation. He was one of the many to have suffered appalling persecution for no apparent reason. But he survived - physically, intellectually and emotionally, and is now among the most popular poets of present-day Albania. Born in the Adriatic seaport of Durrës as the son of the stage actor and poet Hekuran Zhiti (1911-1989), Visar Zhiti grew up in Lushnja where he finished school in 1970. After studies at a teacher training college in Shkodra, he embarked upon a teaching career in the northern mountain town of Kukës. Zhiti showed an early interest in verse and had published some poems in literary periodicals. In 1973, he was preparing the collection *Rapsodia e jetës së trëndafilave* (Rhapsody of the life of roses) for publication when the Purge of the Liberals broke out in Tirana at the Fourth Plenary Session of the Communist Party. Zhiti, whose father had earlier come into conflict with the authorities, was to become one of the many scapegoats selected as a means of terrifying the intellectual community. He was arrested in November 1979 in Kukës where he was teaching, and spent the following months in solitary confinement. To keep his sanity, he composed and memorized over one hundred poems. Sentenced at a mock trial in April 1980 to thirteen years in prison, he was taken to Tirana jail and, from there, transferred up to the isolated northern mountains to do the rounds in the infamous concentration camps similar to the Soviet gulags, among them, the living hell of the copper mines at Spaç and the icy mountain prison of Qafë-Bari. Many of his fellow prisoners died of mistreatment and malnutrition, or went mad. Visar Zhiti was released on 28 January 1987 and was then 'permitted' by the Party to work in a brick factory in his native Lushnja, where he kept a low profile until the end of the dictatorship. He later embarked upon a political and diplomatic career.

Visar Zhiti's first volume of verse *Kujtesa e ajrit,* Tirana 1993 (The Memory of the air), contains some of the so-called prison poems as well as verse inspired by his first journeys outside the 'big prison' that was Albania. The second collection, *Hedh një kafkë te këmbët tuaja,* Tirana 1994 (I cast a skull at your feet), contains the full cycle of 110 prison poems composed between 1979 and 1987, verse which survived miraculously in the recesses of the poet's memory. Both volumes were well received. Someone had finally given voice to the hundreds of silenced and broken intellectuals.

Zhiti is the author of four other verse collections, including most recently *Si shkohet në Kosovë,* Tirana 2000 (Where is the road to Kosova), a volume which mirrors, among other things, the poet's horror at the sufferings of Kosova and its people during the ten years of oppression and the two years of war leading to NATO intervention and to the final liberation in 1999. A collection of Zhiti's verse has also appeared in English in *The Condemned apple,* Los Angeles 2005.

Emotion and ideas were always an integral part of Albanian poetry, but there has been a conspicuous lack of sensuality and lust for life in literature, both in Albania and in Kosova. The watchful eye of the Albanian Party of Labour curtailed any would-be expressions of intimacy and certainly succeeded in eliminating sincerity in creative writing until it was overwhelmed by the tide of frustration which swept Eastern Europe in the late eighties. **Mimoza Ahmeti** (b. 1963) from Kruja is one of the 'enfants terribles' of the nineties, who set about to expand the horizons and explore the possibilities offered to her by her own senses. Dragging the nation, in her idiosyncratic manner, along the bumpy road to Europe, she managed to provoke Albania's impoverished and weary society into much needed reflection. After two volumes of verse in the late eighties, it was the fifty-three poems in the collection *Delirium,* Tirana 1994 (Delirium), that took their departure, for the first time, essentially from the senses. Her candid expressions of wide-eyed feminine desire and indulgence in sensual pleasures, and the crystalline fluidity of her language have already made of her a modern classic.

Other fine poets whom Albania gave rise to over the last two decades of the twentieth century are: **Jorgo Bllaci** (1938-2001), who spent ten years in prison; **Koçi Petriti** (b. 1941) from Korça; **Frederik Rreshpja** (b. 1941) of Shkodra; **Sadik Bejko** (b. 1944) from Komar in Tepelena; **Ndoc Gjetja** (b. 1944) from the Shkodra region; **Anton Papleka** (b. 1945) from Tropoja; **Xhevahir Spahiu** (b. 1945) from the Skrapar region, **Natasha Lako** (b. 1948) from Korça; **Bardhyl Londo** (b. 1948) from the Përmet region; **Rudolf Marku** (b. 1950) from Lezha, now living in London; **Agim Spahiu** (1952-1993) from the Kukës region; and **Preç Zogaj** (b. 1957) from Lezha.

Among contemporary poets of note, mention may be made in particular of: **Gëzim Hajdari** (b. 1957) living in Italy, who publishes in Albanian and Italian; **Gazmend Krasniqi** (b. 1963) from Shkodra; **Flutura Açka** (b. 1966) from Elbasan; **Arian Leka** (b. 1966); **Agron Tufa** (b. 1967) from Sohodoll in Dibra; **Luljeta Lleshanaku** (b. 1968) from Elbasan, whose verse has appeared in English in the volume *Fresco*, New York 2002; **Ilir Belliu** (1970-2002) from Korça; **Rudian Zekthi** (b. 1970) from Elbasan; **Rudi Erebara** (b. 1971) from Tirana, who lives in the United States; **Lindita Arapi** (b. 1972) from Lushnja; **Gentian Çoçoli** (b. 1972) from Gjirokastra; **Romeo Çollaku** (b. 1973) from Saranda; **Ervin Hatibi** (b. 1974) from Tirana; **Ledia Dushi** (b. 1978); **Ensard Telegrafi** (b. 1980) from Tirana; and **Parid Teferiçi.**

7. Modern Albanian Literature in Kosova, Macedonia and the Diaspora

7.1   The Albanians in the Former Yugoslavia

Albanian is spoken by between two and three million people in what used to be Yugoslavia (as compared to three million people in Albania itself). The centre of the Albanian population is Kosova (Kosovo) with its capital Prishtina, which was once an autonomous region of the Yugoslavia federation, was then incorporated against its will into Serbia, and since the 1999 war, has been a United Nations protectorate on the road to independence. In addition to Kosova, there are about half a million Albanians in the Republic of Macedonia, where they make up about one-quarter of the total population (Skopje, Tetova, Gostivar, Dibra, Struga). There are also substantial Albanian communities in southern Serbia (Presheva valley) and in Montenegro (Ulqin/Ulcinj and virtually all of the region south of the capital Podgorica).

Written literature in Kosova was late to develop because of widespread illiteracy and Serb cultural hegemony. It was only with the improvement of Yugoslav-Albanian relations in the wake of the Soviet invasion of Czechoslovakia in 1968 and the establishment of full diplomatic ties between the two countries in February 1971 that a political thaw gave the Albanians of Kosova a semblance of cultural freedom. In 1968, they won the right to fly their national flag and in November 1969 the University of Prishtina was opened, facilitating higher education in Albanian for the first time. Full cultural autonomy was first achieved after much delay under the Yugoslav constitution of 1974, though only in Kosova itself, and not for the large Albanian community in Macedonia.

With access to Albanian-language education and cultural facilities having been granted, Albanian literature and culture in Kosova flourished in the mid-seventies. It was a brief blossoming in which tremendous progress was made within a short period of time, in education, culture and literature. This semblance of autonomy and freedom which the Albanians enjoyed was, alas, brought to an abrupt end in 1981 when the popular demand for republic status and equality with the other peoples of the Yugoslav federation was met by

Belgrade with tanks and automatic rifles. From there, it was a downhill slide until the Kosova War of the spring of 1999.

Literature in Kosova evolved without the severe ideological constraints imposed upon writers in Albania itself. Emigration also brought about contacts with the outside world, which enabled the written word to develop in a more cosmopolitan manner from the start. Literature here, as such, was more experimental and offered the reader a much wider range of styles, subject matter and ideas. Though the level of formal training for prose writers in Kosova was not to reach Tirana standards, young Kosova writers were eager to assimilate foreign influence and the currents of contemporary European thought that were rejected out of hand in Tirana. At the same time, this much more eclectic literature lost surprisingly little of its traditional Albanian flavour. Its strength and dynamism were a direct result of the need perceived by Kosova Albanians to defend their cultural values in a region plagued by political turmoil and ethnic conflict.

7.2   The Rise of Albanian Prose in Kosova

It was the founding in 1949 of the literary periodical *Jeta e re* (New life) which gave voice to the young generation of Albanian writers in Yugoslavia and which served as an initial forum for literary publications. While some monographs were published in the fifties, it was not until the mid-sixties that Albanian and Kosova Albanian literature began to appear in print in Yugoslavia on a significant scale. The beginnings of serious prose in Kosova date from the period 1956 to 1960. Conditions at this time were not much easier in Kosova for the handful of Albanian intellectuals than they were in Albania. The Belgrade authorities were ever reluctant to promote educational and cultural progress for the Albanian population as intellectuals constituted the greatest threat to their power. Equally nefarious was the role played by the local Albanian leaders, who did their utmost to ensure communist discipline in the field of literature and culture.

Tragically, therefore, the first generation of writers, who might have laid the foundations for Kosova prose, was annihilated politically before it could give birth to a real written culture. Kosova prose did not reach a satisfactory level for many years to come, and the loss to Albanian literature can be felt even today.

A start to serious prose in the 1950s was made by **Hivzi Sulejmani** (1912-1975) of Mitrovica who helped bring early Kosova literature out of its regional focus and provinciality. His short story collections, such as *Era dhe kolona,* Prishtina 1959 (The Wind and the column), and his novels, among which *Fëmijët e lumit tim,* Prishtina 1969 (The Children of my river), were widely read in the early years.

Writer and longtime political prisoner **Adem Demaçi** (b. 1936) was born in Prishtina. Demaçi's early short stories, many of them with socially critical overtones, were published in *Jeta e re* in the fifties. It was, however, his controversial novel *Gjarpijt e gjakut,* Prishtina 1958 (The Snakes of blood), that established his literary reputation. This novel, of more ethnographic than literary interest, focusses on the bloody institution of vendetta which plagued and continues to plague northern Albania and Kosova. Demaçi spent twenty-eight years of his life in Serb jails as a political prisoner. He was released in 1990 and has been an active figure of public life ever since.

Anton Pashku[118] (1938-1995) is a writer who does not appeal to the broad masses of the public, but rather to the educated reader who relishes the hermetic observations and details of character analysis of the psychological novel. It was the harsh political suppression of the first generation of prose writers in the late fifties which caused him to withdraw from the mainstream of literary production and create a reclusive world of his own. Pashku was born in Grazhdanik near Prizren of a peasant family from the Has mountains. He worked as a journalist in Prishtina for some time and thereafter edited prose and drama for the Rilindja publishing company there. His experimental short stories, novels and plays, showing affinities with the works of George Orwell, Franz Kafka and Robert Musil, are in themselves subtle and masterful studies of the psyche, though they can be taxing to the innocent and down-to-earth reader. Among his publications are: the short story collections *Tregime,* Prishtina 1961 (Short stories); *Kjasina,* Prishtina 1973 (The Oozing); *Lutjet e mbrëmjes,* Prishtina 1978 (Evening prayers); and the novel *Oh,* Prishtina 1971 (Oh), which is an exercise in style, a product of the grotesque, and something quite unique in Albanian literature. He is also the author of dramas such as *Sinkopa,* Prishtina 1969 (Syncope), and *Gof,* Prishtina 1976 (Explosion). Anton Pashku ranks among the best stylists in Albanian literature, though he will certainly never be widely read.

Rexhep Qosja (b. 1936) is one of the most eminent and prolific literary critics in the Balkans, academician, former director of the Albanological Institute in Prishtina and author of anthologies and numerous scholarly monographs, including a three-volume history of Albanian literature in the romantic period. He is also the author of a widely translated novel,

---

[118] cf. A. Berisha 2002; and K. Shala 2002b.

Vdekja më vjen prej syve të tillë, Prishtina 1974 (Death comes from such eyes). It is a work of original narrative technique and composition, 'thirteen tales which might constitute a novel.' The protagonist of the novel, Xhezairi i Gjikës, is a professional writer caught up in a frightening web of political intrigue, secret police, interrogation and torture, a world full of very definite political allusions to the difficult situation faced by Albanian intellectuals in Kosova under Serb rule. Qosja remained active as a writer in the struggle for freedom in Kosova.

Among other prose writers of the last three decades of the twentieth century are **Murat Isaku** (b. 1928) of Tetova; **Ramiz Kelmendi** (b. 1930) of Peja, whose works, such as *Ahmet Koshutani,* Prishtina 1973 (Ahmet Koshutani), were widely published and enjoyed in the seventies; **Azem Shkreli** (1938-1997) of Rugova; **Nazmi Rrahmani** (b. 1941) from the Podujeva region, a prolific and popular novelist of Kosova village life; **Luan Starova** (b. 1941) of Skopje, whose novels have been translated into French and German; **Teki Dërvishi** (b. 1943) of Gjakova whose novels and short stories have penetrated the psyche of modern man; **Musa Ramadani** (b. 1944) from Gjilan; **Beqir Musliu** (1945-1996) from Gjilan; **Jusuf Buxhovi** (b. 1946) of Peja, noted for his three-part novel *Prapë vdekja,* Prishtina 1991-1995 (Death again); **Eqrem Basha** (b. 1948) from Dibra whose short story collection *Marshi i kërmillit,* Peja 1994 (The Snail's march), and the recent novel *Dyert e heshtjes,* Peja 2001 (The Gates of silence), have been well received; **Sabri Hamiti** (b. 1950) of Podujeva, a leading and innovative literary critic, poet and playwright; **Mehmet Kraja** (b. 1952) from Ulqin; **Zejnullah Rrahmani** (b. 1952) of Podujeva, an elegant stylist of modern Kosova literature; **Kim Mehmeti** (b. 1955) of Skopje who has added new dimensions to short story writing in the nineties; and **Migjen Kelmendi** (b. 1959) of Prishtina.

7.3   Poetry on the Plain of the Blackbirds

Poetry has always been the vanguard of literature in Kosova and has enjoyed more popularity among writers and the reading public there than prose. This poetic imagination has solid roots in the soil, in the land and in its people with their aspirations, sufferings and dreams.

The writer widely considered to be the father of modern Albanian poetry in Yugoslavia, **Esad Mekuli** (1916-1993), was not born in Kosova itself but in the mountain village of Plava on the Montenegrin-Albanian border where national traditions are still revered. Mekuli went to school in Peja on the

Kosova side of the wild Rugova canyon and studied veterinary medicine at the University of Belgrade. There he came into contact with Marxist teachings and subsequently took part in the partisan movement of World War II. In 1949, he founded the above-mentioned literary periodical *Jeta e re* (New life), whose editor-in-chief he remained until 1971. Mekuli was a committed poet of social awareness whose outrage at injustice, violence, genocide and suffering mirrors that of the pre-revolutionary verse of the messianic Migjeni of Shkodra. His first collection, *Për ty*, Prishtina 1955 (For you), was dedicated to the people of Kosova. His final collection, *Drita që nuk shuhet*, Prishtina 1989 (The Light that does not go out), appeared over thirty years later. Mekuli also published translations of much Yugoslav literature, including the works of the Montenegrin poet-prince Petar Njegoš (1813-1851), as well as Serbian translations of many volumes of Albanian literature.

Din Mehmeti (b. 1929) is among the best-known and consistent representatives of modern verse in Kosova. He was born in the village of Gjocaj i Junikut near Gjakova and, after schooling in Gjakova, studied Albanian language and literature at the University of Belgrade. Mehmeti also lectured at the teacher training college in Gjakova. Although he has published some prose, literary criticism and a play, he is known primarily for his figurative poetry which appeared from 1961 to 2004 in eighteen volumes. Mehmeti's verse is characterized by indigenous sensitivity. He relies on many of the figures, metaphors and symbols of northern Albanian popular verse to imbue and stabilize his restless lyrics with the stoic vision of the mountain tribes. Despite the slight breeze of romanticism which wafts through his verse, as critic Rexhep Qosja once put it, this creative assimilation of folklore remains strongly fused with a realist current, at times ironic, which takes its roots in part from the ethics of revolt in the tradition of Migjeni and Esad Mekuli. Mehmeti's poetic restlessness is, nonetheless, not focussed on messianic protest or social criticism but on artistic creativity and individual perfection.

Kosova's leading poetry critic Agim Vinca, himself a poet of note, has described **Azem Shkreli** (1938-1997) as a poet of profound ideas and critical judgments. Azem Shkreli was born in the Rugova mountains near Peja and became head of Kosova Film Studios in Prishtina. He is an intellectual poet who, though highly expressive, is by no means verbose. His urban perception of things has given new significance to his experience of rural customs among the rugged tribes of the Rugova highlands with their traditional wisdom and way of life. His early volumes of verse offered masterful portraits of these legendary mountain inhabitants. The idyllic though specifically organized landscape which Azem Shkreli paints does not blind him to problems of ethics. Some of his verse, a moral catharsis in words, expresses a poetic solidarity with the victims of exploitation and suffering. Shkreli is also the author of the short story collection *Sytë e Evës*, Prishtina 1965 (Eve's eyes), and the novel *Karvani i bardhë*, Prishtina 1960 (The White caravan).

Ali Podrimja (b. 1942) was born in Gjakova at the foot of the so-called 'Accursed Mountains.' After a difficult childhood, he studied Albanian language and literature in Prishtina. Author of over a dozen volumes of cogent and assertive verse since 1961, he is recognized both in Kosova and in Albania itself as a leading and innovative poet. Indeed, he is considered by many to be the most typical representative of modern Albanian verse in Kosova and is certainly the Kosova poet with the widest international reputation. Podrimja's first collection of elegiac verse, *Thirrje*, Prishtina 1961 (The Calls), was published while he was still at secondary school in Gjakova. Subsequent volumes introduced new elements of the poet's repertoire, a proclivity for symbols and allegory, revealing him as a mature symbolist at ease in a wide variety of rhymes and meters. In the early eighties, he published the masterful collection *Lum Lumi*, Prishtina 1982 (Lum Lumi), which marked a turning point not only in his own work but also in contemporary Kosova verse as a whole. This immortal tribute to the poet's young son Lumi, who died of cancer, introduced an existentialist preoccupation with the dilemma of being, with elements of solitude, fear, death and fate. Ali Podrimja is nonetheless a laconic poet. His verse is compact in structure, and his imagery is direct, terse and devoid of any artificial verbosity. Every word counts. What fascinates the Albanian reader is his compelling ability to adorn this elliptical rocky landscape, reminiscent of Albanian folk verse, with unusual metaphors, unexpected syntactic structures and subtle rhymes.

Among the most respected contemporary writers in Kosova in recent years is **Eqrem Basha** (b. 1948). He was born in 1948 in Dibra in the western Albanian-speaking region of what is now the Republic of Macedonia, but his life and literary production are intimately linked to Kosova and its capital Prishtina, where he has lived and worked for the past three decades. It was in the early 1970s, during the only real years of freedom in Kosova, that Eqrem Basha moved to Prishtina to study language and literature at the newly created Albanian-language university there. He later worked for Prishtina television as editor of the drama section, but was fired for political reasons during the Serb takeover of the media in 1989-1990. Basha is the author of eight volumes of innovative verse spanning the years from 1971 to 1995, three volumes of short stories, a novel and numerous translations (in particular French literature and drama). He is currently in the publishing industry in Prishtina. Eqrem Basha is an enigmatic poet. Perplexing, fascinating and difficult to classify in a literary sense, he succeeds in transmitting a certain mystique to the inquisitive reader. At one moment he seems coolly logical and shows an admirable ability to reason deductively, and the next moment he is overcome by absurd flights of fancy into a surrealistic world where apparently nothing makes any sense. Basha has an urbane view of things and delights in the daily absurdities of life. Nothing could be more foreign to him than the inspiration many of his fellow poets derive from the rich folklore traditions of the northern mountain tribes or verse of social commitment. His verse is light, colloquial and much less declamatory than that of many of his predecessors.

One critic recently described modern Albanian writing in Kosova and western Macedonia as a literature with more poets than readers. There is, at any rate, no lack of poetry collections on the book market, and they range, as one might expect, from the abominable to the sublime. Of the many poets who have made a notable contribution to contemporary verse in this region of the world, mention may be made of: **Enver Gjerqeku** (b. 1928) of Gjakova, a pensive elegiac poet of classical forms; **Murat Isaku** (b. 1928) of Tetova; **Besim Bokshi** (b. 1932) of Gjakova, author of two slender but exquisite volumes; **Adem Gajtani** (1935-1982) of Podujeva; **Fahredin Gunga** (1936-1997) of Mitrovica; **Rrahman Dedaj** (b. 1939) of Podujeva, now living in London, a neo-symbolist of rich, emotive expression; **Mirko Gashi** (1939-1995); **Resul Shabani** (b. 1944) of Struga, author of a dozen volumes of verse; **Ymer Shkreli** (b. 1945) from the Rugova highlands, now living in Switzerland; **Agim Vinca** (b. 1947) of Struga, noted also as a leading poetry critic; **Flora Brovina** (b. 1949) of Skënderaj, poet, pediatrician, women's rights activist; **Sabri Hamiti** (b. 1950) of Podujeva, author of well-structured, intellectual texts; **Edi Shukriu** (b. 1950) of Prizren; **Shaip Beqiri** (b. 1954) of the Podujeva region, now living in Switzerland; **Nehas Sopi** (b. 1954) of Sllupçan in Macedonia who teaches literature in Skopje; **Mustafë Xhemaili** (b. 1954) of Ferizaj, now living in Switzerland; **Milazim Krasniqi** (b. 1955) of Prishtina; **Abdullah Konushevci** (b. 1958) of Prishtina; **Valdet Berisha** (b. 1959) from Peja, now living in Switzerland; **Basri Çapriqi** (b. 1960) of Ulqin; journalist **Beqë Cufaj** (b. 1970) of Gramaqel; and **Lindita Ahmeti** (b. 1973) of Skopje.

7.4   Contemporary Italo-Albanian Letters

It was not until the 1950s that the Italo-Albanians began to sense the need for an awakening or revival of cultural activity. The idyllic and sentimental lyrics of village life and the romantic nationalism which had inspired past generations were now out of place. An initial forum for literary creativity in this period was provided by the journal *Shêjzat / Le Pleiadi, Revista culturale, sociale ed artistica* (The Pleiades, cultural, social and artistic review), founded in Rome in 1957 by Ernest Koliqi. This literary periodical, which lasted seventeen years until Koliqi's death, encouraged not only a re-examination of the specific characteristics of Arbëresh culture, oral literature in particular, but also an awareness for Albanian literature as a whole. In addition, it served to make known a whole new 'pleiad' of young and talented poets and writers.

With modest publishing facilities at their disposal, a new generation of writers, poets for the most part, has arisen who are demonstrating how definitively modern Italo-Albanian letters have abandoned the narrow if solid literary traditions of the past. Contemporary Arbëresh literature has grown up and entered the mainstream of modern Western culture. It has overcome a good deal of the provinciality which characterizes many small and primarily rural literatures, but at the same time has lost much of its specificity, to take up residence in one of the uniform condominiums of the global village.

The most popular and respected of the Arbëresh poets is no doubt **Domenico Bellizzi** (1918-1989), better known by his pseudonym *Vorea Ujko*. He was a modest priest from Frascineto (Alb. *Frasnita*) in Calabria who taught modern literature in Firmo (Alb. *Firma*), where his memory has been much cherished since his death in a car accident in January 1989. Ujko's verse, a refined lyric expression of Arbëresh being, appeared in many periodicals and anthologies as well as in seven collections, four of them published in Italy, two in Albania and one in Kosova. Vorea Ujko is a poet of rich tradition. He is the worthy heir of Girolamo De Rada and Giuseppe Serembe, both of whom he greatly admired. His verse is intimately linked to the Arbëresh experience and bathed in the *gjaku i shprishur* (the scattered blood). At the same time it surpasses by far the lingering sentiments of romantic nationalism in Albanian verse and the standard motifs of exile lyrics. In the depth of emotion expressed in his verse, Ujko does not, however, fail to evince the strength of Arbëresh attachment to the culture of his Balkan ancestors despite five hundred years in the *dheu i huaj* 'foreign land.'

Other major authors who have made or are making a noted contribution to contemporary Arbëresh literature include: **Francesco Solano** (1914-1999), poet and scholar from Frascineto, also known by his pen name of *Dushko Vetmo*; **Enza Scutari** (b. 1926) of Farneta in Cozenza; **Carmelo Candreva** (1931-1982), poet from San Giacomo di Cerzeto (Alb. *Shën Japku*) in Cosenza; **Giuseppe Del Gaudio** (b. 1921), poet from San Nicola dell'Alto (Alb. *Shën Kolli*); **Giuseppe Schirò Di Maggio** (b. 1944), poet and playwright from Piana degli Albanesi (Alb. *Hora e Arbëreshëvet*); **Matilda Ferraro** (b. 1950), poet from San Nicola dell'Alto; **Agostino Giordano junior** (b. 1950) from Eianina (Alb. *Ejanina*), who uses the pen name *Buzëdhelpri*; **Kate Zuccaro** (b. 1955), poet from Civita (Alb. *Çifti*) in the province of Cosenza; and **Mario Bellizzi** (b. 1957), an eccentric poet from San Basile (Alb. *Shën Vasili*).

8.   Freedom and Chaos: Contemporary Albanian Letters

> *"It is hard to be hurled from somewhere about the fourth century,*
> *at latest, into the twentieth, without one breathing-space."*
> (Edith Durham, *High Albania*, London 1909)

The Stalinist dictatorship imploded in 1991 and the Albanians, after forty-five years of total isolation from the rest of the world, as if they had been living on a different planet, found themselves robbed of any chance they might have had at keeping up with the rest of Europe. In material terms, they had been deprived of all but the barest essentials needed to stay alive.

It is difficult for the foreign observer to appreciate what the people of Albania went through when the only world they knew, i.e. the awesome political system set up by the communist aristocracy, and the economy and social order which arose with it, collapsed and was initially replaced by... nothing. For writers and intellectuals it was a period of relief, of joy and of apprehension. Freedom had finally dawned, but no one really knew what freedom was. Rumours spread in the early nineties that ships laden with gold and riches would appear on the horizon and that little Albania would be transformed overnight into a 'second Switzerland,' the country it would allegedly have been from the start, had Enver Hoxha not refused so stubbornly to shake hands with the West. Others literally took to the ships themselves, believing that they would be welcomed in Italy with open arms after having suffered so many years of oppression and horror. The little prisons in that big prison which was Albania were opened, and political prisoners resurfaced in the cities. Among them were many talented writers, old before their time and broken after fifteen to forty years in the concentration camps of Spaç, Qafë-Bari and Burrel, or in the dreary internment villages on the mosquito-infested plains of Myzeqe. But their tales were of a bygone age. Everyone was too busy merely surviving.

As the country's socialist economy collapsed like a little matchstick house, so too did the modest institutions of Albanian culture: the state publishing companies, the Writers' Union and the national theatres. Funding for libraries, concert halls, theatres and higher education vanished overnight.

By the mid-nineties, new private structures, at least for printing, had been put in place and Albanian literature was once again being published and marketed, though still under very primitive and chaotic conditions. Books in Albania were sold in the same manner as soap and other commodities. Young men, otherwise unemployed, arrived in Tirana by bus in the morning and returned to their provincial hometowns in the late afternoon with sacks of books, which were hawked on the muddy sidewalks. Such were the distribution structures of the publishing industry in Albania until quite recently. Even in the nation's capital, more books were sold on overturned cardboard boxes in the streets and in improvised kiosks than in the bookstores themselves.

Publishers were understandably interested in a quick profit and demanded cash in advance for the publication of a book, any book. There were no more editors and no more revisions of texts before publication. After decades of total regulation in the publishing industry, there were no controls on books in the nineties at all. Anyone who had money or a sponsor could publish and market whatever he or she wished. The result for the reading public was mistrust and disorientation, and a growing suspicion that Albanian writers could produce nothing of sustainable value.

Most foreign literature, and virtually all contemporary foreign works devoid of a Marxist message, had been banned, or at least were not available under the dictatorship. It is understandable, therefore, that Albanian readers in the nineties were much more interested in translations of foreign literature than they were in books originally written in Albanian. The truth of the matter is that, with the exception of the works of Ismail Kadare, few Albanian novels published in Tirana in recent years have sold more than 100 copies.

Surprisingly enough, though quality control has been nonexistent and interest in new works of Albanian literature has fallen dramatically, the quantity of books published in Albanian over the last five years has risen substantially. Bookstores are better stocked than ever before, at least in Tirana.

One phenomenon which has had an extremely negative impact on Albanian society and culture in recent years has been mass emigration. After the collapse of the Albanian State in March 1997 following the implosion of the pyramid investment schemes and the plundering of military installations and arms depots, many young people came to believe that they had no future in their country. Hardship and deprivation have always been part of life in Albania, but patience by then had come to an end. By the close of the century, the vast majority of writers and intellectuals, young and old, had indeed left Albania in search of a better life abroad. Few will ever return.

The early nineties also marked a turning point for the Albanians of Kosova and Macedonia. The communist system in Yugoslavia had collapsed, and so had Yugoslavia. The Albanians in Kosova, now under harsh Serb rule, were faced with an appalling form of discrimination, that of ethnic persecution, which led ultimately to ethnic cleansing. Politically, the country found itself in a downward spiral which led inevitably to the 1999 war, but also to final liberation after so many years of torment.

Writers in Kosova, as opposed to their counterparts in Albania itself, had no desire or intention to leave their country. They were solidly committed to building a new nation. By the second half of the nineties, the political and economic situation in Kosova had, however, become so untenable that many writers had no choice but to flee the country or suffer imprisonment... or indeed be murdered by the State in which they lived.

Literature, nonetheless, continued to be published in Prishtina, even in the darkest hours of Yugoslav rule. For the Albanians, books were an act of resistance to Serbian cultural hegemony. The Serbs themselves, who had been taught to despise the Albanians as an 'inferior race,' regarded the very thought of creative literature in Albanian as ridiculous. As such, once Belgrade had lost its political authority over the Kosova Albanians, it had no more opportunity, and probably no particular interest, in banning or censoring Albanian books. With Belgrade's illegal takeover and liquidation of the state-owned Rilindja Publishing Company, quality controls in publishing, however, disappeared, as they had in Albania. But books in fact did continue to circulate. Draped over the hoods of cars on street corners, they were hawked throughout Kosova in an impromptu manner. All traces of them could be removed instantly if the Serb police did decide to intervene. The Kosova Albanians were proud of every one of the books, although few of the latter were actually read.

In addition to the consequences of political developments up to the summer of 1997, there are two other factors which had a negative influence on the development of creative literature in Kosova. Firstly, the standard literary language, *gjuha letrare*, more akin to the southern Albanian Tosk dialect, is quite different from the language spoken in Kosova. Having been deprived by the Belgrade authorities of an Albanian-language public education system for a whole generation, many young Kosova authors now have trouble expressing themselves in standard Albanian with requisite literary refinement. Secondly, after years of ethnic strife and oppression, many works of Kosova literature are understandably pervaded in one form or another by a strong sense of Albanian identity. Although a nationalist perspective does not necessarily preclude good literature, it is an ideological framework which, at the end of the day, proves to be just as constrictive of free creative thought as any other political or religious ideology. Many readers from Albania, at any rate, seem to have difficulties appreciating literature from Kosova.

210

If one were to ask what the main achievement of Albanian written culture has been over the last few decades, the reply would certainly be, "Poetry, here, there and everywhere!" Verse collections still account for over fifty per cent of literary output in all the major centres of Albanian-language publishing: Tirana, Prishtina, Skopje, Shkodra and Tetova. Even under the harsh conditions of a free market economy in an underdeveloped region, Albanian poetry has managed to survive and maintain its dynamism.

When impoverished and ill-educated Albanian emigrants and refugees gather in Western Europe or in North America in their often dingy and always smoke-filled clubs, it is more often than not that they come together for a poetry reading. It is here that the soul of the Albanian nation finds its expression. Readable Albanian prose is admittedly a recent phenomenon and drama is still a very much neglected genre, but the Albanians have always opened their hearts spontaneously to lyrics.

Modern Albanian literature, both in Albania and in Kosova, is now, for the first time, at liberty to evolve and go its own way. Closer contacts with the works of other literatures, albeit in often shabby translations, have given rise to some initial copying of styles and themes, but in the long run, such influence can only serve to enrich creative writing in Albanian itself.

Throughout the decades of the Hoxha dictatorship, and indeed up to the final months of Serb rule in Kosova, the border between the two halves of the Albanian nation was kept sealed by their respective rulers. Rare were those who crossed it without suffering political repercussions. The Berlin Wall between the two halves of Germany was, in comparison, a sieve. The result of this imposed separation was the rise of two very different Albanian cultures and two different Albanian literatures.

Since 1999, the two countries have been getting to know one another, and getting used to one another. Their citizens are now able to meet and mingle. It has not been easy for the population at large, and many misunderstandings have arisen, but the exchange of experience has proven particularly broadening and fruitful for Albanian writers on both sides of the border. For the first time, they have become members of one common literary culture, a culture which is now twice as large as and much more diverse than the smaller ones they had known.

The tender plant of Albanian literature, whose stalks and roots have been torn out of the sparse soil so often over the course of history, is set to blossom anew. The once barren and rocky landscape of Albanian culture is now unfettered and fertile.

9. Glossary

Aljamiado literature
>   Spanish term denoting literature written in Arabic script but in a vernacular language, in this case Albanian, and strongly influenced by Islamic culture.

Arbëresh
>   Term for the Italo-Albanians, i.e. the Albanian minority in Italy, the descendants of refugees who fled Albania after the death of Scanderbeg and settled in southern Italy. As an ethnic minority, the Arbëresh now consist of about 100,000 individuals, a mere 20,000 actual speakers, most of whom live in the mountain villages of Cosenza in Calabria and in the vicinity of Palermo in Sicily.

Ashik
>   Lit. 'lover.' Alternative term for the popular poets of Muslim literature. In Bektashi theology, it refers to those faithful to the order but not yet initiated.

Baba
>   Lit. 'father,' a Bektashi abbot.

Bejtexhinj
>   Alb. *bejtexhi*, plur. *bejtexhinj*. Term for popular poets in the Muslim tradition, literally 'couplet makers,' from the Turkish *beyit* 'couplet.'

Bektashi
>   Religious order of dervishes founded in Asia Minor in the thirteenth century by Haci Bektaş Veli (Alb. *Haxhi Bektash Veli*). In the fifteenth century, the Bektashi exercised considerable political power in the Ottoman Empire due to their influence among the janissaries. It was no doubt via these elite troops that the sect spread to Albania where it flourished, especially in the nineteenth century. Though the Bektashi and all other dervish orders were banned in Turkey in the autumn of 1925, they survived in Albania as an independent religious community up to the 1950s. In some areas, in particular extensive regions of southern Albania and Kruja, the Bektashi formed the majority of the population. The Bektashi community has revived since the fall of the dictatorship.

Besa   Alb. *besë, besa* 'word of honour, sworn oath, pledge, cease-fire.' In Albanian culture, the *besa* was regarded as something sacred and its violation was quite unthinkable.

Bey

Alb. *bej*, plur. *bejlerë*, Turk. *beg*. Title given in the Ottoman Empire to the governor of a *sandjak* or a *vilayet*. Later, broadly equivalent to the traditional English 'squire.'

Çamian

Or *Çamerian*. Pertaining to Çameria, the region in the extreme southern tip of Albania and in adjacent northern Greece.

Dervish

Member of a Muslim order or sect.

Divan

An oriental poetry collection with a specific sequence. It usually begins with prayers to Allah, continues with verse celebrating love and earthly pleasures or dealing with religion and philosophy, and concludes with panegyric odes on the Sultan or local potentates and patrons.

Efendi

Engl. *effendi*, Turk. *efendi*. Title of respect in the Ottoman Empire for men of social standing. Modern Turkish equivalent of 'Mr.'

Firman

Turkish *ferman*, Persian *fermân*. Decree or grant of permission in the Ottoman Empire.

Ghazal

Shorter poem in the Muslim tradition, especially love lyrics.

Gheg

Also spelled *Geg*. Term for the northern Albanians and their dialect group, as opposed to the Tosks of the south. Speakers of Gheg dialects are to be found throughout northern Albania, including Kosova, down to the Shkumbin river south of Elbasan, which marks the traditional dialect border between Gheg and Tosk.

Gjaku i shprishur

Alb. 'the scattered blood.' Arbëresh term symbolizing the ethnic blood-ties between the Arbëresh in Italy and the Albanians in the motherland.

Gjysh

Lit. 'grandfather,' term denoting a Bektashi dervish of a higher degree than a *baba*.

Hodja

Alb. *hoxhë* or *hoxha*. A Muslim priest.

Ilâhî

Religious hymn in the Muslim tradition.

Kultusprotektorat

German: 'religious protectorate.' A right which Catholic Austria had wrested from the Turks in a series of peace treaties with the Sultans beginning in 1616 to protect the Christians of the Turkish-occupied Balkans. Under the *Kultusprotektorat*, Austria and later Austria-Hungary served as protectress of the northern Albanian Catholics in religious, educational and cultural affairs.

Lahuta

One-stringed, lute-like musical instrument which is played with a bow to accompany oral verse, in particular the heroic and epic verse of the northern Albanian tribes. Much like the Serbian *gusle*.

Medresa

Muslim college or school for the study of theology and Islamic law.

Mesnevî

Long oriental poem, often a narrative romance, in rhymed couplets.

Mevlud

Religious poem on the birth of the prophet Mohammed.

Mexhmua

Verse collection in the Muslim tradition.

Mezzogiorno

Italian term denoting the southern part of Italy from Rome to Sicily.

Moti i madh

Alb. term, lit. 'the great age,' referring to the age of Scanderbeg and Albanian resistance to the Turks in the fifteenth century.

Mufti

Interpreter of Islamic law, head of a legal school in a region, head of a religious community.

Mullah

Alb. *mulla*. Muslim scholar, teacher or religious leader. Turkish *molla*, Persian *mulla*.

Murabba'

Quatrain in Muslim poetry.

Mutasarrif

Governor of a province of the Ottoman Empire.

Pashalik

The province of a pasha.

Pîr evi

> Turkish term (literally 'saint's house') for the religious headquarters of a dervish sect.

Porte

> cf. Sublime Porte.

Propaganda Fide

> From Lat. *Congregatio de Propaganda Fide* 'Congregation for the Propagation of the Faith.' Term for the Catholic congregation established in 1622 by Pope Gregory XV to defend and spread Catholicism.

Qasîde

> Longer panegyric odes in the Muslim tradition.

Rayah

> Alb. *raja*. Non-Muslim inhabitants of the Ottoman Empire.

Rilindja

> Albanian term signifying 'rebirth' and denoting the period of the so-called Albanian national renaissance in the nineteenth century or, more specifically, of the political and literary activity of the ideologists of the nationalist movement from 1878 or earlier, up to independence in 1912.

Sanjak

> Alb. *sanxhak*. Subdivision of a *vilayet*, geopolitical division of the Ottoman Empire.

Scanderbeg

> Also Skanderbeg, Alb. *Skënderbeu*. Pseudonym of George Castrioti, Alb. *Gjergj Kastrioti*, Albanian prince and national hero (1405-1468).

Scutarine

> Of or pertaining to the northern Albanian city of Shkodra, formerly Scutari.

Sigurimi

> Alb. 'security.' Albanian secret service under the communist regime.

Sublime Porte

> Government or court of the Ottoman Empire. This originally French term for 'high gate' derived from the Turkish title *Babi Ali*, the imperial gate or seat of government in Constantinople.

Teke

> Also spelled *tekke*. Alb. *teqe*. Bektashi monastery.

Tosk

> Term for the southern Albanians and their dialect group, as opposed to the Ghegs of the north. Speakers of Tosk dialects are to be found in Albania south of the Shkumbin river which marks the traditional

dialect border between Gheg and Tosk, in Greece and in most Arbëresh settlements in Italy.

Turbeh

Alb. *tyrbe*. Muslim mausoleum.

Vilayet

Alb. *vilajet*. Province of the Ottoman Empire.

10. Bibliography

AÇKA, Flutura

(2003), *Poezi, 1993-2003.* Tirana: Skanderbeg Books, 312 pp.

- (2004), *Kryqi i harresës. Roman.* Tirana: Skanderbeg Books, 200 pp.

AGOLLI, Dritëro

(1958), *Në rrugë dolla.* Tirana: Ndërm. Shtetërore e Botimeve. 100 pp.

- (1961), *Hapat e mija në asfalt. Vjersha dhe poema.* Tirana: Naim Frashëri. 98 pp.
- (1964), *Devoll, Devoll.* Tirana: Naim Frashëri.
- (1964), *Zhurma e erërave të dikurshme.* Tirana: Naim Frashëri. 213 pp.
- (1965), *Shtigje malesh dhe trotuare. Vjersha dhe poema.* Tirana: Naim Frashëri. reprint 1998. 87 pp.
- (1970), *Komisari Memo. Roman.* Tirana: Naim Frashëri. 302 pp.
- (1973), *Shkëlqimi dhe rënja e shokut Zylo. Roman.* Tirana: Naim Frashëri. reprint Prishtina: Rilindja, Tirana: Dritëro 1999. 263 pp.
- (1974), *Nënë Shqipëri. Poemë.* Tirana: Naim Frashëri.
- (1975), *The bronze bust. A novel.* Tirana: 8 Nëntori. 300 pp.
- (1975), *Nënë Shqipëri. Poemë.* Tirana: Naim Frashëri. 144 pp.
- (1975), *Njeriu me top. Roman.* Tirana: Naim Frashëri. 247 pp.
- (1979), *Poezi.* Tirana: Naim Frashëri. 660 pp.
- (1981-1987), *Vepra letrare 1-11.* Tirana: Naim Frashëri.
- (1983), *The man with the gun. A novel.* Tirana: 8 Nëntori. 272 pp.
- (1985), *Mother Albania. A poem.* Tirana: 8 Nëntori. 181 pp.
- (1985), *Short stories.* Tirana: 8 Nëntori. 211 pp.
- (1985), *Udhëtoj i menduar. Poezi.* Tirana: Naim Frashëri. 365 pp.
- (1990), *Splendeur et décadence du camarade Zulo.'* Roman traduit de l'albanais par Christian Gut. Paris: Gallimard. 286 pp.
- (1993), *Pelegrini i vonuar. Poezi.* Tirana: Progresi. reprint 1998. 270 pp.
- (1995), *Lypësi i kohës. Poezi.* Tirana: Enciklopedike. reprint 1998. 209 pp.
- (1995), *Njerëz të krisur. Novela, tregime.* Tirana: Apollonia. 163 pp.
- (1996), *Kalorësi lakuriq. Roman.* Tirana: Çabej. 102 pp.
- (1996), *Shpirti i gjyshërve. 101 këngë.* Tirana: Dritëro. 150 pp.
- (1996), *Vjen njeriu i çuditshëm. Poezi.* Tirana: Dritëro. 249 pp.
- (1997), *Arka e djallit. Roman.* Tirana: Dritëro. 466 pp.
- (1997), *Baladë për tim atë dhe për vete.* Tirana: Dritëro. 151 pp.
- (1998), *Fletorka e mesnatës. Poezi.* Tirana: Dritëro. 244 pp.
- (1998), *Kambana e largët. Poezi.* Tirana: Dritëro. 208 pp.
- (1998), *Këngët e buzëqeshjes. Poezi.* Tirana: Dritëro. 216 pp
- (1999), *Shekulli i argjendtë.* Tirana: Dritëro. 554 pp.

- (2000), *Dialog me artistët.* Tirana: Toena. 275 pp.
- (2000), *Gdhihet e ngryset. Poezi.* Tirana: Dritëro. 330 pp.
- (2004), *Poezi të zgjedhura.* Tirana: Naim Frashëri. 96 pp.

AHMETI, Lindita
  (1993), *Mjedra dhe bluz.* Skopje: Flaka e vëllazërimit, 74 pp.
- (1996), *Ishulli aduluar.* Skopje: Shkupi, 160 pp.

AHMETI, Mimoza
  (1988), *Sidomos nesër. Poezi.* Tirana: Naim Frashëri. 80 pp.
- (1993), *Arkitrau. Një histori të bukurish. Roman.* Tirana: Marin Barleti. 64 pp.
- (1994), *Delirium.* Tirana: Martin Barleti. 78 pp.
- (1996), *Absurdi koordinativ.* Tirana: Marin Barleti. 72 pp.
- (2002), *L'absurde coordinatif.* Paris: Agnès Pareyre, 151 pp.
- (2002), *Delirium.* Versión en español de Ramón Sánchez Lizarralde. Malaga: Diputación Provincial de Málaga, 112 pp.
- (2002), *Palmimi i luleve. Poezi.* Tirana: Ora, 95 pp.

ALIÇKA, Xhavit
  (2000), *Lahuta e malcis e Gjergj Fishtës. Studim monografik.* Prishtina: Faik Konica. 287 pp.

ALIÇKA, Ylljet
  (1999), *Les slogans de pierres. Nouvelles traduites de l'albanais.* Castelnau-Le-Lez: Climats. 155 pp.
- (2000), *Kompromisi. Tregime.* Elbasan: Onufri, 137 pp.
- (2003), *Parullat me gurë. Tregime.* Tirana: Albimazh, 160 pp.

ALIU, Ali
  (2002), *Antologji e poezisë shqipe. Gjysmështekulli i artë.* Tirana: Albin, 449 pp.
- (2003), *Kronikë letrare.* Skopje: Logos-A, 244 pp.
- (2003), *Magjia e fjalës.* Peja: Dukagjini, 263 pp.

ALIU, A., SINANI, Sh., ÇAPALIKU, S., ÇOBANI, T. (ed.)
  (2001), *Letërsia bashkëkohore shqiptare. Pas luftës së Dytë Botërore.* Tirana & Tetova: Alb-Ass. 252 pp.

ALTIMARI, Francesco
  (1982), *Un saggio inedito di F. A. Santori sulla lingua albanese e i suoi alfabeti.* Cosenza: Quaderni di Zjarri. 63 pp.
- (1984), *Studi sulla letteratura albanese della 'Rilindja'.* Cosenza: Quaderni di Zjarri. 94 pp.

ARAPI, Fatos
  (1962), *Shtigje poetike. Vjersha dhe poema.* Tirana: Naim Frashëri. 67 pp.
- (2003), *Ah, sikur të isha një përrallë. Poezi.* Tirana: Toena, 72 pp.
- (2003), *Në Tiranë kur s'ke ç'të bësh. Tregime.* Tirana: Toena, 120 pp.

ARNOLD, T. W.
  (1896), *The preaching of Islam. A history of the propagation of the Muslim faith.* London: Luzac. reprint 1913, 1935, 1961, 1979.

Bibliography

ASDRENI (= DRENOVA, Aleks Stavre)

   (1904), *Rézé djélli. Vjersha liriké.* Bucharest: Shtypeshrim e Perghitheshme. 224 pp.
-   (1912), *Endra e lote. Vjersha.* Bucharest: Gutenberg. 248 pp.
-   (1930), *Psallme murgu. Vjersha.* Bucharest: Bucharest. 223 pp.
-   (1976-1980), *Vepra 1-2.* Tirana: Akademia e Shkencave, 592 + 758 pp.

ASHTA, Kolë

   (1957), Shënime e vërejtje rreth gjuhës dhe leksikut të Lekë Matrëngës. in: *Buletin për Shkencat Shoqërore,* Tirana 1, p. 83-107.
-   (1962), Vezhgim historik në fjalorin e parë të shqipes. Bardhi 1635. in: *Shkodra,* Shkodra, p. 33-64.
-   (1964-1966), Leksiku i plotë i veprës së Gjon Buzukut (1555). in: *Buletini Shkencor i Institutit të Lartë Pedagogjik,* Shkodra, 1964, 1, p. 97-130; 1964, 2, p. 19-184; 1965, 3, p. 59-66; 1966, 4, p. 27-66.
-   (1965), Në kërkim të anës letrare të Matrëngës. in: *Shkodra,* Shkodra, 5, p. 188-202.
-   (1966), Rreth disa çeshtjeve të leksikut të Pjetër Budit. in: *Studime Filologijike,* Tirana, 4, p. 159-165.
-   (1971-1974), Leksiku i shqipes nxjerrë nga Dictionarium Latino-Epiroticum i F. Bardhit. in: *Buletini Shkencor i Institutit të Lartë Pedagogjik,* Shkodra, 1971, 1; 1972, 1; 1973, 2; 1974, 1.
-   (1996), *Leksiku historik e gjuhës shqipe I.* Shkodra: Universiteti i Shkodrës, Sektori Shkencor i Albanologjisë. 496 pp.
-   (1998), *Leksiku historik i gjuhës shqipe, II.* Tirana: Toena 311 pp.
-   (2000). *Leksiku historik i gjuhës shqipe, III.* Shkodra: Universiteti i Shkodrës, Sektori Shkencor i Albanologjisë. 303 pp.
-   (2002), *Leksiku historik i gjuhës shqipe, IV.* Shkodra: Camaj-Pipa, 457 pp.

ASLLANI, Ali

   (1942), *Hanko Halla.* Tirana: Shtëpija Botonjëse Kristo Luarasi. 55 pp.
-   (1984), *Vepra, 1-2.* Prishtina: Rilindja. 184 + 219 pp.

AUTISSIER, Anne-Marie, MONTECOT, Christiane, ZOTOS, Alexandre (ed.)

   (1999), *Kosovo dans la nuit.* Textes réunis, traduits, présentés par Anne-Marie Autissier, Christiane Montécot et Alexandre Zotos. Préface de Jean-Yves Potel. Paris: Editions de l'Aube. 121 pp.

BABINGER, Franz

   (1928), Bei den Derwischen von Kruja. in: *Mitteilungen der Deutsch-Türkischen Vereinigung,* IX (1928), 8-9, p. 148-149, 10, p. 164-165, reprint in: *Münchner Neueste Nachrichten,* Munich, 7. Januar 1929, p. 3-4.

BAKIU, Zyber Hasan

   (1982), *Bibliografi e zgjeruar e veprave të Sami Frashërit. Veprat, përmbajtja e tyre me shënime dhe veprat e artikujt mbi të në gjuhën shqipe e turqishte.* Tirana: 8 Nëntori. 292 pp.

BAJRAJ, Xhevdet

   (2003), *Blues nën qiellin e indianëve [Në hijen e kaktusit].* Tetova: Brezi 9, 200 pp.

Bibliography

BAJRAMI, Vehbi

(2003), *Shqiptarët e Amerikës.* Me parathënie të Ismail Kadares. New York: Albanian Publishing, 1,008 pp.

BALA, Vehbi

(1964-1965), Lidhjet kulturore shqiptare-rumune. in: *Buletin Shkencor i Institutit Pedagogjik Dyvjeçar të Shkodrës.* Shkodra, 1964. p. 53-88; 1965, p. 3-57.

- (1972), *Jeta e Fan Nolit. Portret monografi.* Tirana: 8 Nëntori. 191 pp.
- (1974), *Migjeni. Portret monografi.* Tirana: Naim Frashëri. 137 pp.
- (1979), *Pashko Vasa, portret monografi.* Tirana: Naim Frashëri. 264 pp.
- (1998), *Gjergj Fishta. Jeta dhe vepra.* Shkodra 1961. Tirana: Ombra GVG. 165 pp.

BARDHI, Frang (= BLANCHUS, Franciscus)

(1635), *Dictionarivm latino-epiroticvm, vna cum nonnullis vsitatioribus loquendi formulis.* Per R. D. Franciscvm Blanchvm, Epirotam Coll. de Propag. Fide alumnum. Rome: Sac. Congr. de Propag. Fide. 238 pp.

- (1636), *Georgius Castriottus Epirensis vulgo Scanderbegh, Epirotarum Princeps fortissimus ac invictissimus suis et Patriae restitutus.* Per Franciscum Blancum de Alumnis, Collegij de Propaganda Fide Episcopum Sappatensem & Sardanensem, necnon Pulatensium, aliorumque Albaniae Populorum Administratorem. Serenissimi, Amplissimique Senatus Veneti Liberalitate. Venice: Typ. Marci Ginammi. 76 pp.
- (1957), *Skënderbeu. Apologji.* Përktheu nga latinishtja Stefan I. Prifti. Tirana: Ndërm. Shtetërore e Botimeve, reprint 1967, 1999. 95 pp. / 183 pp.
- (1983), *Fjalor latinisht-shqip 1635.* Përgatiti Engjëll Sedaj. Prishtina: Rilindja. 385 pp.

BARTL, Peter

(1968), *Die albanischen Muslime zur Zeit des nationalen Unabhängigkeitsbewegung 1878-1912.* Albanische Forschungen 8. Wiesbaden: Harrassowitz. 207 pp.

- (1973), Ernest Koliqi zum 70. Geburtstag. in: *Südost-Forschungen,* Munich, 32, p. 321-322.
- (1981), Fasi e modi dell'immigrazione albanese in Italia. in: *Congresso sulle relazioni tra le due sponde adriatiche. N. 2. I rapporti demografici e popolativi.* Rome, p. 199-212.

BASHA, Eqrem

(1982), *Atleti i ëndrrave të bardha.* Prishtina: Rilindja. 93 pp.
- (1986), *Udha qumështore.* Prishtina: Rilindja. 90 pp.
- (1989), *Brymë ne zemër.* Prishtina: Rilindja. 218 pp.
- (1994), *Marshi i kërmillit.* Peja: Dukagjini. 207 pp.
- (1995), *Zogu i zi.* Skopje: Flaka e Vëllazërimit. 137 pp.
- (1999), *Les ombres de la nuit et autres récits du Kosovo.* Traduit de l'albanais par Christiane Montécot et Alexandre Zotos. Paris: Fayard. 203 pp.
- (2001), *Dyert e heshtjes.* Peja: Dukagjini. 182 pp.

- (2003), *Neither a Wound nor a Song: poetry from Kosova in a bilingual Albanian-English edition.* With a foreword by Janice Mathie-Heck. Selected, translated from the Albanian and edited by Robert Elsie. New York: Gjonlekaj. xviii + 171 pp.
- (2004) *Alpinisti.* Peja: Dukagjini. 160 pp.

BASHOTA, Sali

(1988), Vepra letrare e Mitrush Kutelit dhe studimi i saj. in: *Gjurmime albanologjike, Seria e shkencave filologjike,* Prishtina, 18, p. 175-188.

- (1998), 'Netët shqiptare' të Mitrush Kutelit. in: *Filologji,* Universiteti i Prishtinës, Fakulteti i Filologjisë, Prishtina, 5, p. 217-229.
- (1999), *Kuteli. Prozator, poet, kritik.* Prishtina: Rilindja. 251 pp.

BASHOTA, Sali (ed.)

(2002), *Shtatë shkrimtarë. A. Podrimja, D. Mehmeti, E. Gjerqeku, M. Kraja, S. Hamiti, R. Qosja, E. Basha).* Prishtina: Rozafa, Prishtinë 2002) 446 pp.

BELEGU, Xhafer

(1939), *Lidhja e Prizrenit e veprimet e sajë, 1878-1881.* Tirana: Kristo Luarasi. 199 pp.

BELLINI, Giuseppe

(1938), *Storia della tipografia del Seminario di Padova 1684-1938.* Padua: Gregoriana editrice. 453 pp.

BELLIZZI, Mario

(1997), *Who are we now?* Në shqipen e sotme i ktheu dhe pasthënien e shkroi Rexhep Ismajli. Peja: Dukagjini. 150 pp.

- (2003), *Last exit to Bukura Morea. Gjeo-poezi arbëreshe mërgimesh të pandalshme. Nga Historia në eterotopi. Hyrje dhe shënime të hartuesit, përkthime në gjuhën italiane përballë. Ultima uscita per la bella Morea. Geopoesia arbëreshe di migrazioni multiple. Dalla Storia all'eterotopia.* Introduzione e note dell'autore, testo albanese contraduzione in italiano a fronte. Castrovillari: Il Coscile, 158 pp.

BELMONTE, Vincenzo

(1991), *Alla ricerca del Serembe autentico.* Cosenza: Benvenuto. 176 pp.

BELMONTE, Vincenzo (ed.)

(1988), *Omaggio a Giuseppe Serembe.* Cosenza: Vatra. 368 pp.

BEQIRI, Shaip

(1991), *Sfida e gjeniut. Kadare, Ekzili, Kosova.* Prishtina: Buzuku. 491 pp.

BERISHA, Anton Nikë

(1994), *Vepra letrare e Martin Camajt.* Radhonjtë e Zjarrit 18. Cosenza: Zjarri. reprint Tirana: Lajmtari 2000. 97 pp.

- (1995a), *Ernest Koliqi. Poet e prozator.* Radhonjtë e Zjarrit 21. Rende: Diadia, reprint Tirana 1997. 107 pp.
- (1995b), Das literarische Werk Martin Camajs. in: *Dardania. Zeitschrift für Geschichte, Kultur und Information,* Vienna, 4, p. 165-178.
- (1997a), *Mbi tri vepra poetike të Zef Skiroit.* Prishtina: Rilindja. 99 pp.
- (1997b), *Tri saggi sull'opera di Giuseppe Schirò.* Palermo. 64 pp.

-       (1999a), *Antologjia e poezisë bashkëkohore arbëreshe. Antologia della poesia contemporanea italo-albanese.* Cosenza: Centro Editoriale e Librario della Università degli Studi della Calabria. 431 pp.

-       (1999b), *Burim drite e dashurie. Antologji e poezisë së përshpirtshme shqipe 1618-1998.* Prishtina: Shpresa. 368 pp.

-       (2000), *Mbi letërsinë e arbëreshëve të Italisë.* Tirana: Mësonjëtorja e parë. 350 pp.

-       (2001), *Gjymtime dhe shëmtime të letërsisë së Arbëreshëve të Italisë.* Prishtina: Shpresa. 111 pp.

-       (2002), *Në mbretërinë poetike. Kritikë letrare për veprën e Anton Pashkut.* Zgjodhi dhe përgatiti për shtyp Anton Nikë Pashku. Prishtina: Shpresa, 286 pp.

-       (2003), *Vepër e qenies dhe e qenësisë sonë. Vëzhgime mbi artin poetik të Fishtës.* Prishtina: Shpresa & Faik Konica, 343 pp.

BERISHA, Anton & MUSLIU, Beqir (ed.)
       (1990), *Atë Gjergj Fishta. Me rastin e 50-vjetorit të vdekjes.* Jeta e re, revistë letrare, Prishtina, 11-12.

BIHIKU, Koço (ed.)
       (1978), *Historia e letërsisë shqiptare të realizmit socialist.* Tirana: Akademia e Shkencave. 424 pp.

-       (1981), *Studime për letërsinë shqiptare 1. Probleme të letërsisë shqiptare të Rilindjes Kombëtare.* Tirana: Akademia e Shkencave. 720 pp.

-       (1988), *Studime për letërsinë shqiptare 2. Probleme të letërsisë shqiptare të realizmit socialist.* Tirana: Akademia e Shkencave. 672 pp.

BIRGE, John Kingsley
       (1937), *The Bektashi order of dervishes.* London: Luzac. reprint 1965, 1982, 1994) 291 pp.

BOGDANI, Pjetër (= BOGDANO, Pietro, BOGDANUS, Petrus)
       (1685), *Cvnevs prophetarvm de Christo salvatore mvndi et eivs evangelica veritate, italice et epirotice contexta, et in duas partes diuisa* a Petro Bogdano Macedone, Sacr. Congr. de Prop. Fide alvmno, Philosophiae & Sacrae Theologiae Doctore, olim Episcopo Scodrensi & Administratore Antibarensi, nunc vero Archiepiscopo Scvporvm ac totivs regni Serviae Administratore. Padua: Typographia Seminarii. 418 pp.

-       (1691), *L'infallibile verità della Cattolica Fede, dimostrata sino all' evidenza ad ogni qualità di persone; cavata dall' alto fonte delle divine scrittvre,* per opera di Monsignor Pietro Bogdano Arcivescovo di Scopia, Et Amministratore di tutto il Regno di Servia, Dottor di Filosofia, e Sacra Theologia, in cui trattandosi della nullità delle tre primarie sette, Ebrea, Maomettana, e Pagana, si stabilisce l'unità della nostra Fede sotto il Romano Pontefice, confutandosi con l'Antiche Eresie, e le Moderne di Lutero, Calvino, e suoi seguaci; s'abbatte lo Scisma de Greci, e si estirpa l'Incredulità degli Ateisti. Opera vtilissima... Venice: Girolamo Albrizzi. reprint 1702. 418 pp.

- (1977), *Cuneus Prophetarum a Pietro Bogdano.* Patavii MDCLXXXV. Beiträge zur Kenntnis Südosteuropas und des Nahen Orients. Vol 24. Munich: Trofenik. 438 pp.
- (1990), *Çeta e profetëve, I. Cuneus prophetarum.* Transliterimin në gjuhën e sotme, përkthimet dhe parrathënien Dr. Engjëll Sedaj. Redaktimin krahasues të transliterimit në gjuhën e sotme Dr. Ibrahim Rugova. Prishtina: Rilindja. 563 pp.
- (1997), *Çeta e profetëve, II. Jeta e Jezu Krishtit.* Parathënie Imzot Mark Sopi. Transliterimi në gjuhën e sotme, hyrja, përkthimet dhe shënimet: Dr. Engjëll Sedaj. Prizren: Drita. 414 pp.
- (1997), *Letra dhe dokumente. Nga Arkivi i Kongregatës 'de Propaganda Fide' si dhe nga Arkivat Sekrete të Vatikanit.* Odette Marquet, ed. Shkodra: At Gjergj Fishta. 580 pp.
- (1999), Fjalimi i P. Bogdanit me rastin e vdekjes së Ndre Bogdanit. in: *Dardania sacra, revistë shkencore për çështje shoqërore, ekonomike dhe tekniko-teknologjike të Kosovës,* Prishtina, 1, p. 301-304.

BOMBACI, Alessio
- (1969), *La letteratura turca con un profilo della letteratura mongola.* Nuova edizione aggiornata. Florence & Milan: Sansoni/Accademia. 528 pp.

BORGIA, Nilo (Ieromonaco)
- (1930), *Pericope evangelica in lingua albanese del secolo XIV da un manoscritto greco della Biblioteca Ambrosiana.* Grottaferrata: Tip. Italo-Orientale S. Nilo. 35 pp.

BRAUN, Ludwig & CAMAJ, Martin
- (1972), Ein albanischer Satz aus dem Jahre 1483. in: *Zeitschrift für Vergleichende Sprachforschung,* Göttingen, 86, p. 1-6.

BROVINA, Flora
- (1999), *Thirrje e Kosovë. Poezi. Cry and Kosova. Poetry.* Translated by Fadil Bajraj, Nehat S. Hoxha, Sazana Çapriqi, Shaqir Shaqiri, Shinasi A. Rama. Prishtina: Buzuku. 155 pp.
- (2001), *Call me by my name. Poetry from Kosova in a bilingual Albanian-English edition.* Edited, introduced and translated from the Albanian by Robert Elsie. New York: Gjonlekaj Publ. 165 pp.

BUDI, Pjetër (= BUDI, Pietro)
- (1618), *Dottrina Christiana.* Composta per ordine della fel.me. Di Papa Clemente VIII. Dal. R. P. Roberto Bellarmino Sacerdote della Compagnia di Giesv. Adesso Cardinale di Santa Chiesa del Titolo di S. Maria in Via. Tradotta in lingua albanese. Dal Rever. Don Pietro Bvdi da Pietra Biancha. Rome: Bartolomeo Zannetti. 229 pp.
- (1621), *Cusc zzote mesce keto cafsce i duhete me scerbyem.* Rome: Bartolomeo Zannetti.
- (1621), *Ritvale Romanvm et Specvlvm Confessionis.* In Epyroticam linguam a Petro Bvdi Episcopo Sapatense & Sardanense translata. Sanctissimi Domini Nostri Gregorii XV liberalitate typis data. Rome: Bartolomeo Zannetti. 360 pp.

- (1621), *Rituale Romanum in epyroticam linguam à Pietro Budi episcopo sapatense e sardanense translatum.* Sanctissimi domini nostri Gregorii XV liberalitate typis datum. Rome: Bartolomeo Zannetti. 360 pp.

- (1664), *Dottrina Christiana.* Composta per ordine della fel.me. Di Papa Clemente VIII. Dal. R. P. Roberto Bellarmino. Tradotta in lingua albanese. Dal Don Pietro Budi. Rome: Propaganda Fide. 288 pp.

- (1868), *Dottrina cristiana composta per ordine della S. memoria di Papa Clemente VIII dal ven. cardinale Roberto Bellarmino d. c. d. G. Tradotta in lingua albanese dal R. Dom Pietro Budi da Pietra Bianca.* Terza edizione nuovamente corretta. Rome: Propaganda Fide. 207 pp.

- (1986), *Poezi (1618-1621).* Parathënia, tejshkrimi, komentet: Rexhep Ismajli. Prishtina: Rilindja. 289 pp.

BULO, Jorgo

  (1986), Një variant i ri i vjershës "Moj Shqypni" të P. Vasës. in: *Studime filologjike,* Tirana, 4, p. 209-216.

- (1992), Pashko Vasa dhe Rilindja kombëtare. in: *Studime filologjike,* Tirana, 1-4 p. 17-22.

- (1997a), Classificazione tipologica e cronologica delle liriche di Naim Frashëri. in: *Albanistica. Novantasette.* A cura di Italo Costante Fortino. Naples: Istituto Universitario Orientale. p. 261-268.

- (1997b), La letteratura albanese dell'epoca moderna fra Occidente e Oriente. in: *Albanistica. Novantasette.* A cura di Italo Costante Fortino. Naples: Istituto Universitario Orientale. p. 211-220.

- (1999), *Tipologjia e lirikës së Naim Frashërit. Monografi.* Tirana: Akademia e Shkencave. 199 pp.

BULO, Jorgo, HYSA, Enver, JORGO, Kristaq (ed.)

  (2001), *Naim Frashëri dhe kultura shqiptare.* Tirana: Akademia e Shkencave e Shqipërisë, 221 pp.

BULO, Jorgo, KODRA, Klara, JORGO, Kristaq, SMAQI, Laura (ed.)

  (2003), *De Radës. Në 100-vjetorin e vdekjes. Përmbledhje studimesh.* Tirana: Akademia e Shkencave, 425 pp.

BUSHATI, Gilmana (ed.)

  (2003), *Letërsia jashtë kopshteve tanë. Autorë shqiptarë.* Tirana: Ars, 150 pp.

BUXHOVI, Jusuf

- (2002), *Shënimet e Gjon Nikollë Kazazit.* Botim i plotësuar. Prishtina: Faik Konica, 256 pp.

- (2003), *Letra për kryeprincin. Prozë, që do të mund të merrej edhe si vazhdim i romanit Nata e Shekujve.* Prishtina: Faik Konica, 360 pp.

- (2004), *Vdekja e kolonelit. Prozë që mund të merret edhe si plotësim i trilologjisë "Prapë vdekja."* Prishtina: Faik Konica, 262 pp.

- (2004), *Vera e fundit e Gjin Bardhit. Mund të merret edhe plotësim i romanit Letrat për Kryeprincin.* Prishtina: Faik Konica, 244 pp.

BYRON, Janet Leotha

  (1979), Albanian nationalism and socialism in the fiction of Ismail Kadare. in: *World Literature Today,* Norman OK, 53.3 (Summer), p. 614-616.

- (1984), Albanian folklore and history in the fiction of Ismail Kadare. A review of two French translations. in: *World Literature Today,* Norman OK, 58.1 (Winter), p. 40-42.

ÇABEJ, Eqrem

   (1929), Mbi poezinë e Lasgush Poradecit. in: *Gazeta e re,* 22 shkurt 1929, p. 3. reprint in: *Studime filologjike,* Tirana, 1999, 3-4, p. 123-126.

- (1941), Der albanische Dichter Gjergj Fishta (1871-1940). Nachruf. in: *Südost-Forschungen,* Leipzig, 6, p. 635-647.

- (1966), Pjetër Budi dhe gjuha e tij. in: *Studime Filologjike,* Tirana, 4, p. 139-150.

- (1986-1989), *Studime gjuhësore.* Botim i dytë. Vol. 1-9. Prishtina: Rilindja.

ÇABEJ, Eqrem (ed.)

   (1968), *Meshari i Gjon Buzukut (1555). Botim kritik.* Pjesa e parë: Hyrje dhe transliterim, Pjesa e dytë: Faksimile dhe transkribim fonetik. 2. vol. Tirana: Universiteti Shtetëror i Tiranës, reprint Rilindja, Prishtina 1987.

ÇAJUPI, Andon Zako (= ZAKO, Andon)

   (1902), *Baba-Tomorri. Vjérsha préj A. Z... Chajup.* Cairo: reprint Tirana 1935. 192 pp.

- (1921), *Perralla te sgjedhura nga te vjérshtarit math La Fontaine.* Heliopolis. 212 pp.

- (1922), *Lulé te Hindit. Vjérsha sanskrité te shqiperuara préj A. Zako (Çajupi).* Cairo: Shoqeria Botonjesé Shqipetaré. 44 pp.

- (1937), *Burr' i dheut. Tragjedi me vjersha e ndarë ndë 5 pamje.* Cairo: Sofokli Çapi. 80 pp.

- (1937), *Pas vdekjes. Botim' i parë.* Cairo: Sofokli Çapi. 41 pp.

- (1962), *Père Tomor.* Tirana: Naim Frashëri. 94 pp.

- (1983a), *Vepra 1-6.* Prishtina: Rilindja. 140, 220, 232, 296, 172 + 528 pp.

- (1983b), *Vepra letrare 1-3.* Përgatitur dhe redaktuar nga Floresha Dado. Tirana: Naim Frashëri. 324, 268 + 352 pp.

ÇALI, Edmond

   (2003), *Romanet e Jakov Xoxës.* Tirana: Redona, 111 pp.

CAMAJ, Martin

   (1953), *Nji fyell ndër male.* Prishtina: Mustafa Bakija. 70 pp.

- (1954), *Kânga e vërrinit.* Prishtina: Mustafa Bakija. 55 pp.

- (1958), *Djella. Tregim në prozë e në vjerrshë.* Rome: Shêjzat / Le Pleiadi. reprint Prishtina 1964. 143 pp.

- (1964), *Legjenda. Vjerrsha.* Rome: Shêjzat / Le Pleiadi. 74 pp.

- (1967), *Lirika mes dy moteve.* Munich: Selbstverlag. reprint 1995. 87 pp.

- (1969), Jeronim de Radas "Scanderbeccu i pa-faan" (Der glücklose Skanderbeg). in: *Studia Albanica Monacensia in memoriam Georgii C. Scanderbegi.* Munich: Trofenik. p. 68-75.

- (1978), *Njeriu më vete e me tjerë. Poezi.* Biblioteka shqipe 2. Munich: Selbstverlag. 99 pp.

- (1978), *Rrathë. Roman.* Biblioteka shqipe 1. Munich: Selbstverlag. reprint Shkodra 2001. 317 pp.

- (1981), *Dranja. Madrigale.* Biblioteka shqipe 3. Munich: Selbstverlag. 103 pp.
- (1981), *Poezi 1953-1967.* Biblioteka shqipe 5. Munich: Selbstverlag. 255 pp.
- (1981), *Shkundullima. Proza.* Biblioteka shqipe 4. Munich: Selbstverlag. 295 pp.
- (1987), *Karpa.* Bibliotheka Shqipe Nr. 6. Rome. 205 pp.
- (1990), *Selected Poetry.* Translated from the Albanian by Leonard Fox. New York University Studies in Near Eastern Civilization XIV. New York: New York University Press. 220 pp.
- (1991), *Në hijen e gjarpnit.* Prishtina: Jeta e re. 71 pp.
- (1991), *Palimpsest.* Translated from the Albanian by Leonard Fox. Biblioteka shqipe 7. Munich & New York. 63 pp.
- (1991), *Pishtarët e natës. Novela.* Prishtina: Buzuku. 159 pp.
- (1996), *Vepra letrare.* 1-5. Tirana: Apollonia, 215, 265, 220, 299, 157 pp.
- (2000), *Lirika. Poezi.* Përgatitja, parathënia dhe shënimet Rexhep Ismajli. Peja: Dukagjini. 742 pp.

ÇAPALIKU, Alfred
- (1996), *At Vinçenc Prennushi. Jeta dhe veprat. Monografi.* Shkodra: Universiteti i Shkodrës.187 pp.
- (1999), *Bernardin Palaj. Jeta dhe veprat. Monografi.* Shkodra: At Gjergj Fishta. 100 pp.

ÇAPALIKU, Stefan
- (1995), *Fishta satirik. Studim.* Shkodra: Universiteti i Shkodres. 189 pp.
- (2002), *Quelqu'un de passage, Roman.* Tr. Edmond Tupja. Marseille: Éd. Albania-CCU, Corse, 100 pp.
- (2002), *Tregime për Anën.* Tirana: Onufri, 96 pp.
- (2003), *Pesë drama dhe një korn anglez.* Tirana: Ideart, 176 pp.

CASSIANO, Domenico
- (1977a), *Le comunità Arbresh nella Calabria del XV secolo.* Cosenza: Brenner. 123 pp.
- (1977b), *Poeti i Strigharit, Zep Serembe.* Strighari / San Cosmo Albanese: Editrice Amministrazione Comunale di S. Cosmo Albanese. 95 + 17 pp.
- (1981), *La cultura minoritaria arbëreshe in Calabria.* A cura di A. Piromalli. Saggi e testi di cultura calabrese. Cosenza: Brenner. 177 pp.

ÇAUSHI, Tefik
- (1993), *Universi letrar i Kadaresë.* s.l.[Tirana]: Evropa. 324 pp.
- (1995), *Kadare. Fjalor i personazheve.* Tirana: Enciklopedik. 401 pp.
- (2000), *Klubi i personazheve. (Shenime per personazhe te shquara te letersise shqipe).* Tirana: Dajti, 310 pp.
- (2001), *Erosi te Kadareja.* Tirana: Dajti 2000, 259 pp.
- (2002), *Kadareja përmes pasqyrave. Sprovë kritike.* Tirana: Onufri, 256 pp.

ÇAUSHI, Tefik & SHKURTAJ, Gjovalin
- (2004), *Kadareja dhe fjala shqipe.* Tirana: Albas, 184 pp.

ÇEFA, Kolec

(2003a), *Nëpër gjurmët e Fishtës*. Shkodra: Shtëpia e Botimeve Françeskane, 152 pp.

- (2003b), *Simpoziumi Fishta dhe françeskanët. Në 130-vjetorin e lindjes të At Gjergj Fishtës*. Shkodra:Botime Françeskane, 86 pp.

CHETTA, Nicola

(1992), *La creazione del mondo sino al diluvio. Editio princeps. Prolegomeni, trascrizione e apparato critico*. A cura di Giuseppe Schirò jun. Prefazione di Giuseppe Gradilone. Rome: Istituto di Studi Albanesi dell'Università degli Studi di Roma. 185 pp.

- (1993), Fragmentum lyricae sacrae. A cura di Matteo Mandalà. in: *Atti del XVI Congresso Internazionale di studi albanesi. Gli Albanesi d'Italia e la Rilindja Albanese. Linguistica, letteratura, storia, folclore. Il contributo degli albanesi di Sicilia e di Calabria*. Palermo.

CHOUBLIER, Maximilien

(1927), 'Les Bektachis et la Roumélie,' in: *Revue des Etudes Islamiques*, Paris, 1, p. 427-453.

CIPO, Kostaq

(1952), Vërejtje fonetike, morfologjike e sintaktike mbi 'Doktrinën e Kërshtenë' të Budit. in: *Buletin për Shkencat Shoqërore*, Tirana, 1, p. 5-32.

ÇIRAKU, Ymer

(2003), *Bota poetike e Martin Camajt*. Tirana: Albas, 95 pp.

ÇIRAKU, Ymer & GJINAJ, Maksim

(2001), *Letërsia shqiptare. Autorë dhe vepra. Bibliografi*. Tirana: Libri Universitar. 271 pp.

ÇIRAKU, Ymer & SHEHRI, Dhurata (ed.)

(2004), *Fenomeni i avanguardës në letërsinë shqiptare*. Aktet e seminarit shencor. Departamenti i Letërsisë, Fakulteti i Historisë dhe i Filologjisë, Universiteti i Tiranës. Tirana: Arbëria, 288 pp.

CLAYER, Nathalie

(1990), *L'Albanie. Pays des derviches. Les ordres mystiques musulmans en Albanie à l'époque postottomane (1912-1967)*. Balkanologische Veröffentlichungen 17. Berlin: In Kommission bei Otto Harrassowitz, Wiesbaden. 505 pp.

- (1993), 'Bektachisme et nationalisme albanais,' in *Bektachiyya, études sur l'ordre mystique des Bektachis et les groupes relevant de Hadji Bektach*. A. Popovic & G. Veinstein (ed.), *Revue des Etudes Islamiques* 60 (1992). Numéro spécial. Paris: Paul Geuthner, Paris (1993), Istanbul: Isis (1995), p. 271-300.

- (2003), *Religion et nation chez les Albanais: XIXe-XXe siècles*. Istanbul: Isis, 449 pp.

ÇOBANI, Tonin

(1988), *Kërkime letrare. Artikuj dhe studime*. Tirana: Naim Frashëri. 140 pp.

- (1999), *Miti dhe antimiti fishtjan. Dhjetë ese*. Lezha: Lisitan. 120 pp.

ÇOLLAKU, Shaban
(1985), *Mendimi iluminist i Sami Frashërit.* Tirana: Akademia e Shkencave.
315 pp.

CORNIS-POPE, Marcel & NEUBAUER, John (ed.)
(2004), *History of the literary cultures of East-Central Europe. Junctures and disjunctures in the 19th and 20th centuries.* Comparative Histories of Literatures of European Languages, XIX. Amsterdam: John Benjamins, xx + 648 pp.

CUCCI, Maria Franca
(1968), Giulio Variboba e la sua opera poetica. in: *Risveglio-Zgjimi,* Cosenza, 3, p. 19-26.

-        (1969), Le kalimere di G. Variboba e il loro valore poetico. in: *Risveglio-Zgjimi,* Cosenza 3, p. 38-40.

CUFAJ, Beqë
(2003), *Shkëlqimi i huaj.* Peja: Dukagjini, 285 pp.

DADO, Floresha
(1983), *A. Z. Çajupi. Jeta dhe vepra.* Tirana: Akademia e Shkencave. reprint Prishtina 1986. 284 pp.

DAGLIOGLU, Hikmet Turhan
(1934), *Şemsettin Sami. Hayati ve eserleri.* Istanbul. 72 pp.

DAIJA, Tonin
(2004), *Fjala, tingulli, metrika në Lahutën e Malcís.* Shkodra: Botime Françeskane, 78 pp.

DAKA, Palok
(1983), Frang Bardhi. Babai i leksiografisë shqiptare 1606-1643. in: *Gjuha jonë,* Tirana, 3, p. 104-110.

DAKO, Christo Anastas
(1922), *Liga e Prizrenit, e para lëvizje kombtare për të mprojtur tërësinë toksore të atdheut dhe për të fituar independencën e Shqipërisë. Shoqëruar me dokumenta zyrtare.* Bucharest: Socec & Co. 57 pp.

DARA, Gabriele (the Younger) (= DARA, Gavril)
(1906), *Kënka e sprasme e Balës. Viershë e pa ljecciturë. Gavriljit i Dharënjêvet. Il canto ultimo di Bala. Poema inedito di Gabriello Dara.* Catanzaro: Caliò. 278 pp.

-        (1967), *The last lay of Bala.* Rendered into English by Ali Cungu. Tirana: Naim Frashëri. 116 pp.

-        (1994), *Kënga e sprasme e Balës.* Transkribuar e përshtatur nga Shaban Demiraj. Tirana: Naim Frashëri. 227 pp.

DE MOOR, Piet
(1998), *Een masker voor de macht. Over Ismail Kadare.* Amsterdam: Van Gennep. 79 pp.

DE RADA, Girolamo
(1836), *Poesie albanesi del secolo XV. Canti di Milosao, figlio del despota di Scutari.* Naples: Guttenberg. 96 pp.

- (1839), *Canti storici albanesi di Serafina Thopia, moglie del principe Nicola Ducagino, tradotti in prosa italiana.* Naples: Bolziana. 64 pp.
- (1843), *Canti di Serafina Thopia, principessa di Zadrina nel secolo XV.* Naples: Capasso, reprint Cosenza: Brenner, 1964. 66 pp.
- (1846), *I Numidi, tragedia di Girolamo De Rada tradotta dall'albanese per l'autore.* Naples: Urania. 75 pp.
- (1847), *Poesie albanesi di Girolamo De Rada. Prima parte.* Naples: Fibreno. 136 pp.
- (1848), *Poesie albanesi di Girolamo De Rada. Seconda parte.* Naples: Fibreno. 405 pp.
- (1861), *Principii di estetica, estratti dalle considerazioni sulla vita e i fini di essa.* Naples: De Angelis. 105 pp.
- (1864), *Antichità della nazione albanese e sua affinità con gli Elleni e i Latini.* Naples: Stamp. dell'Industria. reprint Rossano Scalo: Guido, 1990, Cosenza: Brenner, 1997. 40 pp.
- (1866), *Rapsodie d'un poema albanese raccolte nelle colonie del Napoletano tradotte da Girolamo De Rada e per cura di lui e di Niccolò Jeno de' Coronei ordinate e messe in luce.* Florence: Bencini. reprint Cosenza: Casa del Libro 1964. 106 pp.
- (1873), *Poesie albanesi di Girolamo De Rada. Volume 1. Canti di Milosao figlio del despota di Scutari.* Corigliano Calabrese: Tip. Albanese. 144 pp.
- (1873), *Poesie albanesi di Girolamo De Rada. Volume 2. Scanderbeccu i pa faan. Storie del secolo XV.* Corigliano Calabrese: Tip. Albanese. 199 pp.
- (1873), *Poesie albanesi di Girolamo De Rada. Volume 3. Scanderbeccu i pa-faan. Storie del secolo XV. Libro 2.* Corigliano Calabrese. 176 pp.
- (1873), *Poesie albanesi di Girolamo De Rada. Volume 4. Scanderbeccu i pa-faan. Storie des secolo XV. Libro 3.* Corigliano Calabrese. 176 pp.
- (1877), *Poesie albanesi di Girolamo De Rada. Volume 5. Scanderbeccu i pa-faan. Storie des secolo XV. Libro 4.* Naples: Mormile. 192 pp.
- (1882), *Quanto di libertà ed ottimo vivere sia nello stato rappresentativo.* Naples: De Angelis. 98 pp.
- (1883-1887), *Fiamuri Arbërit. La Bandiera dell'Albania 1883-1887. Rapsodie e Lexicon.* reprint Sala Bolognese: Arnaldo Forni Editore 1978.
- (1884), *Poesie albanesi di Girolamo De Rada. Volume 6. Scanderbeccu i pa-faan. Storie des secolo XV. Libro 5.* Naples. 189 pp.
- (1892), *Sofonisba, dramma storico di Girolamo De Rada.* Naples: De Angelis-Bellisario. 75 pp.
- (1894), *Caratteri e grammatica della lingua albanese.* Corigliano Calabro: Popolano 100 pp.
- (1896), *Appendice alla grammatica. Antologia albanese tradotta fedelmente in italiano.* Naples. Morano. 82 pp.
- (1897), *Specchio di umano transito, vita di Serafina Thopia, Principessa di Ducagino.* Naples: Di Gennaro & Morano. 137 pp.
- (1898), *Autobiologia. Vol. 1, 4.* Consenza: Principe.
- (1899), *Autobiologia. Vol. 2, 3.* Naples: Di Gennaro & Morano.

- (1902), *Testamento politico.* Catanzaro: Caliò. 32 pp.
- (1939), *Milosaat. Pjesë të zgjedhura e të komentuara prej Dr. Namik Ressulit.* Tirana: Luarasi. 92 pp.
- (1965), *I canti di Milosao. Traslitterazione, varianti delle edizioni a stampa e traduzione a cura di Giuseppe Gradilone.* Studi Albanesi, Pubblicati dall'Istituto di Studi Albanesi dell'Università di Roma sotto la direzione del Prof. Ernesto Koliqi. Studi e Testi, vol 1. Florence: Olschki. 134 pp.
- (1980-1988), *Vepra 1-6.* Prishtina: Rilindja.
- (1981), *Les chants de Milosao.* Tirana. 8 Nëntori. 56 pp.
- (1987), *Vepra letrare 1-2.* Tirana. Naim Frashëri. 408 + 404 pp.
- (1988), *Vepra 6. Skanderbeku i Pafan. Histori i shekullit XV. Përshtatur në gjuhën e sotme nga Jup Kastrati.* Prishtina: Rilindja. 402 pp.
- (1988), *Vepra 7. Sofonizba, Diana, Parime të estetikës, Mendimi estetik, Autobiografia 1898-1899, Publicistika dhe letërkëmbimi.* Prishtina: Rilindja. 397 pp.
- (1998), *I canti premilosaici. Edizione critica e traduzione italiana a cura di Francesco Altimari.* Con edizione ipertestuale su CD-Rom realizzata in collaborazione con Franesco Iusi. Soveria Mannelli: Rubbettino. x + 401 pp.
- (2001), *Këngët e Milosaut. Bir i sundimtarit të Shkodrës.* Transkriptimin Françesko Altimari. Parathënien Anton Nikë Berisha. Poezi shqipe të shekullit XV [sic]. Prishtina: Shpresa. 135 pp.

DEMA, Benedikt
- (1941), Në dekë të Drejtorit t'onë, A. Gjergj Fishtës O.F.M. in: *Hylli i Dritës,* Shkodra, 17, 1-2, p. 1-7.
- (1942), Veprimi letrar i At. Gj. Fishta. Të gjitha veprat. in: *Hylli i Dritës,* Shkodra, 17, p. 433-451.

DEMA, Benedict (ed.)
- (1940), *At Gjergj Fishta 1871-1940.* (s.l., s.a.[1940?]) 575 pp.

DEMAÇI, Adem
- (1958), *Gjarpijt e gjakut.* Prishtina: Jeta e re. reprint New York 1983, Biel/Bienne 1984, Prishtina 1991. 87 pp.

DEMIRAJ, Bardhyl (ed.)
- (2004), *Kuvendi i Arbënit, 1703.* Në 300-vjetorin e mbajtjes së tij, Tubim kulturo-shkencor. Mynih, shtator, 2003. ISBN 9951-406-31-9. Prishtina: Shpesa, 190 pp.

DEMIRAJ, Shaban
- (1953), Disa shënime të krahasuara mbi gjuhën e Jul Varibobës. in: *Buletin për shkencat shoqërore,* Tirana, 1, p. 66-75; 2, p. 16-31; 3, p.39-50.
- (1956), Gjella e Shën Mëris Virgjër e Jul Varibobës rreth botimit të parë të 1762 dhe transkriptimit të saj prej V. Librandit. in: *Buletin i shkencave shoqërore,* Tirana 3, p. 262-270.
- (1958), Jul Variboba (1762). in: *Buletin i Univeritetit shtetëror të Tiranës. Seria shkencat shoqërore,* Tirana, 1, p. 125-144.
- (1986), Frano Bardhi - veprimtar i shquar i kulturës shqiptare. in: *Kultura popullore,* Tirana, 1, p. 141-146.

DESNICKAJA, Agnija Vasil'evna

(1985a), O poetičeskom stile klassika albanskoj literatura Jeronima De Rady. in: *Izvestija Akademij Nauk S.S.S.R. Serija literatury i Jazyka*, Mar.-Apr. 44 (2), p. 135-146.

- (1985b), Le style poétique de Jeronim de Rada. Remarques sur le texte du poème *Këngët e Milosaut* (Les chants de Milosao). in: *Recherches Albanologiques*, Prishtina, 2, p. 121-140.

- (1987), *Albanskaja literatura i albanskij jazyk.* Leningrad: Nauka. 293 pp.

DODONA, Efthim

(1996), *Noli i panjohur.* Tirana: Enciklopedike. 302 pp.

DOUGLAS, Norman

(1915), *Old Calabria.* London: Secker & Warburg, reprint 1928, 1955, 1993. 352 pp.

DESSART, Francis

(1984), Albanian ethnic groups in the world. An historical and cultural essay on the Albanian colonies in Italy. in: *East European Quarterly*, Boulder CO, 15.4, p. 469-489.

DIBRA, Ridvan

(2002), *Triumfi i dytë i Gjergj Elez Alisë. Roman.* Prishtina: Buzuku, 225 pp.

- (2003), *Em@il. Roman.* Tirana: Sejko, 148 pp.

- (2004), *Kumte dashurie. Roman.* Tirana: Dudaj, 260 pp.

DOMI, Mahir

(1966), Pjetër Budi (1566-1662). in: *Studime filologjike*, Tirana, 4, p. 11-19.

- (1967), Pjetër Budi (1566-1622). in: *Studia albanica*, Tirana, 1, p. 67-73.

DONES, Elvira

(1997), *Dashuri e huaj. Roman.* Tirana: Çabej. 234 pp.

- (1998), *Kardigan. Roman.* Tirana: Çabej. 248 pp.

- (1999), *Lule të gabuara. Tregime.* Tirana: Onufri. reprint 2000. 217 pp.

- (2000), *Yjet nuk vishen kështu. Roman.* Elbasan: Sejko. 256 pp.

- (2001), *Ditë e bardhë e fyer. Roman.* Tirana: Sejko. 322 pp.

- (2001), *Sole bruciato.* Tr. Elio Miracco. Milan: Feltrinelli, ca. 300 pp.

- (2002), *I love Tom Hanks: përralla moderne.* Elbasan: Sejko, 258 pp.

- (2004), *Më pas heshtja. Roman.* Elbasan: Sejko, 204 pp.

DORSA, Vincenzo

(1847), *Su gli Albanesi, ricerche e pensieri.* Naples: Trani, reprint Cosenza: Brenner 1985. 170 pp.

DRUON, Maurice

(1993), *Présentation d'Ismail Kadaré par Maurice Druon.* Les Colloques de LADELF, vol. 2. Paris: Sepeg International. 304 pp.

DUKA-GJINI, Pal (= GJEÇI, Daniel)

(1992), *Gjergj Fishta. Jeta dhe veprat [Jeta dhe veprat e Gjergj Fishtës].* S. Maria degli Angeli [Assisi]: Provinça Françeskane Shqiptare. 299 pp.

EJNTREJ, Gertruda Iosifovna

(1973), *Tvorčestvo Mid'eni.* Leningrad: Izdat. Leningradskogo Universiteta. 118 pp.

- (1999), *Fan Noli i realizm v literature Albanii XX veka (1900-1939 gody)*. Saint Petersburg: Izd. S.-Peterburgskogo Universiteta. 274 pp.

ELSIE, Robert

   (1984), The Albanian lexicon of Arnold von Harff, 1497. in: *Zeitschrift für Vergleichende Sprachforschung*, Göttingen, 97, 1, p. 113-122.

- (1986), *Dictionary of Albanian literature*. Westport CT, New York & London: Greenwood. 171 pp.

- (1987), *Migjeni, Freie Verse. Gedichte aus Albanien. Übertragen von Robert Elsie*. Idstein: Schulz-Kirchner Verlag. 70 pp.

- (1988), *Einem Adler gleich. Anthologie albanischer Lyrik vom 16. Jahrhundert bis zur Gegenwart.* Hildesheim: Olms. 303 pp.

- (1990), Modern Albanian literature. in: *Albanien in Umbruch. Eine Bestandsaufnahme. Untersuchungen zur Gegenswartskunde Südosteuropas.* Schriftleitung Franz-Lothar Altmann, Band 28. Munich: Südost-Institut. p. 247-292.

- (1991), Albanian literature in Greek script. The eighteenth- and early nineteenth century Orthodox tradition in Albanian writing. in: *Byzantine and Modern Greek Studies*, Birmingham, 15, p. 20-34.

- (1991), Albanische Literatur und Kultur nach sechsundvierzig Jahren Sozialismus. Ein Zustandsbericht. in: *Südosteuropa, Zeitschrift für Gegenwartsforschung*, Munich, 11-12, p. 600-613.

- (1991), The earliest references to the existence of the Albanian language. in: *Zeitschrift für Balkanologie*, Munich, 27.2, p. 101-105.

- (1991), Evolution and revolution in modern Albanian literature. in: *World Literature Today*, Norman OK., 65.2 (Spring), p. 256-263.

- (1991), Rezeption albanischer Literatur im deutschen Sprachraum. in: *Aspekte der Albanologie. Akten des Kongresses 'Stand und Aufgaben der Albanologie heute' 3.-5. Oktober 1988*, Universität zu Köln. BREU, Walter, KÖDDERITZSCH, Rolf & SASSE, Hans-Jürgen (ed.). Berlin: Balkanologische Veröffentlichungen, Band 18. In Kommission Harrassowitz, Wiesbaden. p. 167-174.

- (1991), The Scutarine Catholic contribution to the development of nineteenth-century Albanian literature. in: *Albanian Catholic Bulletin / Buletini Katolik Shqiptar*, San Francisco, 12, p. 91-97.

- (1992a), Albanian literature in English translation: a short survey. in: *The Slavonic and East European Review*, London, 70. 2 (April), p. 249-257.

- (1992b), Albanian literature in the Moslem tradition. Eighteenth and early nineteenth century Albanian writing in Arabic script. in: *Oriens, Journal of the International Society for Oriental Research*, Leiden, 33, p. 287-306.

- (1992c), Three poets of the golden age of Scutarine Catholic literature in Albania. in: *Albanian Catholic Bulletin / Buletini Katolik Shqiptar*, San Francisco, 13, p. 97-101.

- (1993), *Literature*. in: K. D. Grothusen (ed.), Südosteuropa-Handbuch VII. Albanien. Göttingen: Vandenhoeck & Ruprecht. p. 653-680.

Bibliography

- (1993), *Theatre.* in: K. D. Grothusen (ed.), Südosteuropa-Handbuch VII. Albanien Göttingen: Vandenhoeck & Ruprecht. p. 681-692.
- (1993), *Anthology of modern Albanian poetry. An elusive eagle soars. Edited and translated with an introduction by Robert Elsie.* UNESCO Collection of Representative Works. London & Boston: Forest Books. 213 pp.
- (1993), Benjamin Disraeli and Scanderbeg. The novel 'The Rise of Iskander' (1833) as a contribution to Britain's literary discovery of Albania. in: *Südost-Forschungen,* Munich, 52, p. 25-52.
- (1993), Gjergj Fishta. The voice of the Albanian nation. in: *Albanian Catholic Bulletin / Buletini Katolik Shqiptar,* San Francisco, 14, p. 104-113.
- (1993), Romani 'Ngritja e Skënderbeut' (*The rise of Iskander,* 1833), i shkrimtarit anglez Benxhamin Dizraeli-t. Një zbulim i ri albanologjik. in: *Hylli i Dritës,* Tirana, 2-3 (1993), p. 113-115.
- (1994), The Currents of Moslem and Bektash writing in Albania. in: *Albanian Catholic Bulletin / Buletini Katolik Shqiptar,* San Francisco, 15, p. 172-177.
- (1995), *History of Albanian literature.* East European Monographs 379. 2 volumes. Boulder: Social Science Monographs. Distributed by Columbia University Press, New York. xv + 1,054 pp.
- (1995), *Një fund dhe një fillim. Vëzhgime mbi letërsinë dhe kulturën shqiptare bashkëkohore.* Tirana: Globus R & Prishtina: Buzuku. 194 pp.
- (1995), Rruga e modernitetit dhe koha e artë e letërisë shqiptare. Kultura shqiptare e viteve 30. in: *Përpjekja, E përtremuajshme kulturore,* Tirana, 2, p. 33-39.
- (1996), *Studies in modern Albanian literature and culture.* East European Monographs, CDLV. Boulder: East European Monographs. Distributed by Columbia University Press, New York. 188 pp.
- (1997a), *Histori e letërsisë shqiptare.* Përktheu nga anglishtja Abdurrahim Myftiu. Tirana & Peja: Dukagjini. reprint 2001. 686 pp.
- (1997b), *Kosovo. In the heart of the powder keg.* East European Monographs, CDLXXVIII. Boulder: East European Monographs, Boulder, Distributed by Columbia University Press, New York. vi + 593 pp.
- (1999), Albanian literature since the Second World War. in: *Encyclopedia of World Literature in the 20th century.* Third Edition. Vol. 1: A-D. General Editor: Steven R. Serafin. Farmington Hills MI: St. James Press. p. 35-36.
- (1999), Introduction. in: *The truth on Albania and the Albanians. Historical and critical issues by Wassa Effendi. Introduction by Robert Elsie.* London: Centre for Albanian Studies. p. i-iii.
- (2000), *Who will slay the wolf. Selected poetry by Ali Podrimja. Translated from the Albanian with an introduction by Robert Elsie.* New York: Gjonlekaj Publishing Company. 268 pp.
- (2001a), *Albanian folktales and legends. Selected and translated from the Albanian by Robert Elsie.* Dukagjini Balkan Books. Peja: Dukagjini. 240 pp.
- (2001b), *A Dictionary of Albanian religion, mythology and folk culture.* London: Hurst & Company. 357 pp.

- (2001c), Die drei Frashëri-Brüder. in: *Albanien. Reichtum und Vielfalt alter Kultur.* ed.: Staatliches Museum für Völkerkunde. Munich: Museum für Völkerkunde. p. 147-152.
- (2001d), *Flora Brovina. Call me by my name. Poetry from Kosova in a bilingual Albanian-English edition.* Edited, introduced and translated from the Albanian by Robert Elsie. New York: Gjonlekaj Publ. 165 pp.
- (2001e), *Der Kanun. Das albanische Gewohnheitsrecht nach dem sogenannten Kanun des Lekë Dukagjini.* Kodifiziert von Shtjefën Gjeçovi, ins Deutsche übersetzt von Marie Amelie Freiin von Godin und mit einer Einführung von Michael Schmidt-Neke. Herausgegeben mit Vorwort und Bibliographie von Robert Elsie. Dukagjini Balkan Books. Peja: Dukagjini. 283 pp.
- (2001f), *Migjeni (Millosh Gjergj Nikolla). Free Verse. A bilingual edition translated from the Albanian and introduced by Robert Elsie.* Dukagjini Balkan Books. Peja: Dukagjini. 143 pp.
- (2002), *Handbuch zur albanischen Volkskultur. Mythologie, Religion, Volksglaube, Sitten, Gebräuche und kulturelle Besonderheiten.* Balkanologische Veröffentlichungen, Fachbereich Neuere Fremdsprachliche Philologien der Freien Universität Berlin, Band 36. Wiesbaden: in Kommission Harrassowitz. vii + 305 pp.
- (2003a), Albanian literature: an overview of its history and development. in: *Albanien: Geographie, historische Anthropologie, Geschichte, Kultur, postkommunistische Transformation.* Herausgegeben von Peter Jordan, Walter Lukan, Stephanie Schwandner-Sievers und Holm Sundhaussen. = *Österreichische Osthefte,* Vienna, 45 (2003), p. 243-276.
- (2003b), *Early Albania: a reader of historical texts. 11th-17th centuries.* Balkanologische Veröffentlichungen, Band 39. Wiesbaden: Harrassowitz. ix + 233 pp.
- (2003c), *Eqrem Basha. Neither a Wound nor a Song: poetry from Kosova in a bilingual Albanian-English edition.* With a foreword by Janice Mathie-Heck. Selected, translated from the Albanian and edited by Robert Elsie. New York: Gjonlekaj. xviii + 171 pp.
- (2003d), *Gjergj Fishta. The Highland Lute: the Albanian national epic. Cantos I-V. The cycle of Oso Kuka.* Translated from the Albanian by Robert Elsie. Dukagjini Balkan Books. Peja: Dukagjini. 167 pp.
- (2004a), *Historical dictionary of Albania.* New edition. European historical dictionaries, no. 42. Lanham, Maryland and Oxford: Scarecrow. xlv + 534 pp.
- (2004b), *Historical dictionary of Kosova.* European historical dictionaries, no. 44. Lanham, Maryland and Oxford: Scarecrow. lvi + 290 pp.
- (2004c), *Tales from old Shkodra: early Albanian short stories.* Edited by Robert Elsie. Dukagjini Balkan Books. Peja: Dukagjini. 178 pp.
- (2005), *Visar Zhiti. The Condemned apple. Selected poetry.* Translated by Robert Elsie. A bilingual edition. Green Integer 134. Los Angeles: Green Integer. 314 pp.

ELSIE, Robert & MATHIE-HECK, Janice
    (2001), Five emerging Albanian poets. Mimoza Ahmeti, Luljeta Lleshanaku, Visar Zhiti, Bardhosh Gaçe, Lindita Arapi. Presented and edited by Janice Mathie-Heck. Translated by Robert Elsie. in: *Filling station,* Calgary AL, 22, p. 52-63.
-     (2001), Mendime mesnate nga Kanadaja. Mbi poezinë e Ali Podrimjes. Robert Elsie & Janice Mathie-Heck. in: *Jeta e re, revistë letrare,* Prishtina, 2, p. 310-322.
-     (2004), *Songs of the Frontier Warriors: Këngë Kreshnikësh. Albanian epic verse in a bilingual English-Albanian edition.* Edited introduced and translated from the Albanian by Robert Elsie and Janice Mathie-Heck. Wauconda: Bolchazy-Carducci. xviii + 414 pp.
-     (2005), *The Highland Lute: the Albanian national epic.* Translated from the Albanian by Robert Elsie and Janice Mathie-Heck. forthcoming.

ERCOLE, Francesco
    (1941), Giorgio Fishta. in: *Rivista d'Albania,* diretta da Francesco Ercole. Anno II. Fasc. I. Marzo 1941. Reale Accademia d'Italia. Centro di Studi per l'Albania. Istituto per gli studi di politica internationale. Milano, p. 3-18.

FAENSEN, Johannes
    (1980), *Die albanische Nationalbewegung.* Osteuropa-Institut an der Freien Universität Berlin. Balkanologische Veröffentlichungen 4. Wiesbaden: in Komm. Harrassowitz. 195 pp.

FAYE, Eric
    (1991a), *Ismaïl Kadare. entretiens avec Eric Faye, en lisant en écrivant.* Paris: José Corti. 109 pp.
-     (1991b), *Ismaïl Kadaré. Prométhée porte-feu.* Paris: José Corti. 173 pp.

FERRARI, Giuseppe
    (1963), *Giulio Variboba e la sua opera politica albanese.* Bari: Cressati. 79 pp.

FETAHU-ABDIXHIKU, Emine
    (1997), *Bibliografia e Gjurmimeve Albanologjike, 1962-1996.* Prishtina: Instituti Albanologjik, 250 pp.
-     (2004), *Bibliografia e botimeve të veçanta të Institutit Albanologjik të Prishtinës, 1953-2003.* Prishtina: Instituti Albanologjik, 385 pp.

FETIU, Sadri, HALIMI, Mehmet, & LAJÇI, Lulëzim (ed.)
    (1997), *Faik Konica. Jeta dhe vepra. Sesion shkencor, mbajtur në Prishtinë, më 28 prill 1995.* Prishtina: Instituti Albanologjik. 260 pp.

FETIU, Sefedin
    (1984), *Vepra e Migjenit dhe kritika e saj.* Prishtina: Instituti Albanologjik. 160 pp.

FISHTA, Filip
    (1940), Muhamet Çami (qinvjeti XVIII). in: *Shkëndija,* Tirana, 6, p. 32-38.
-     (2002), *Kosova për historín e letërsín kombtare.* Përgatiti për shtyp Willy Kamsi. Prishtina: Shpresa, 127 pp.

FISHTA, Gjergj (= TOSKA, Gegë)

    (1905-1906), *Lahuta e Maltsiis. Kângë populloré. Blêe i pare.* Zadar. reprint Shkodra 1912. 48 pp.

- (1906), *Vierrsha i pershpirteshem t'kthyem shcyp.* Shkodra: Shtyp. t'Xoies zânun pa mkat t'rriédhshem. 94 pp.
- (1907), *Ânxat e Parnasit.* Sarajevo: Bosnische Post. 67 pp.
- (1907), *Komisiia e kléri katolik. Préjé gni méshtarit shcyptaar.* s.l. [Shkodra]: Bashkimi. 29 pp.
- (1909), *Pika voëset. Carmina proveniumt animo deducta sereno.* Zadar: Ernesto Vitaliani. 62 pp.
- (1912), *Lahuta e Malciis. Kângë populloré. E dyta dorë. Blêe i parë (-dytë).* Shkodra: Nikaj.
- (1912), *Melodram Vllaznii.* Shkodra.
- (1912), *Sh' Françesku i Asizit. Melodram.* Shkodra: Nikai. 99 pp.
- (1913), *Mrizi i zânavet.* Shkodra: Nikaj. reprint Shkodra 1941, Ljubljana 1990. 115 pp.
- (1923), *Gomari i Babatasit. Poem dramatik.* (Pseud. Gegë Toska). Shkodër. 104 pp.
- (1923), *Juda Makabe. Botue së dytit.* Shkodra: Shtypshkroja Françiskane. reprint Prishtina 1994, Lezha 1995. 31 pp.
- (1923), *Lahuta e Malcis.* Shkodra: Shtypshkroja Françeskane. 67 pp.
- (1924), *Mrizi i zânavet.* Biblioteka Shoqëria e Studenteve Shqipëtare në Rumani. Shkodra: Shtyp. e së Paperlyemes. 229 pp.
- (1925), Lahuta e Malcîs von Gjergj Fishta. Herausgegeben und übersetzt von Gustav Weigand. in: *Balkan-Archiv,* Leipzig 1, p. 173-265.
- (1925), *Vallja e Parrizit.* Shkodra: Shtypshkroja Françiskane, reprint 1941. 235 pp.
- (1927), *Anzat e parnasit. Botim i dytë.* Shkodra: Shtypskroja Françeskane. reprint 1928. 249 pp.
- (1927), *Gomari i Babatasit. Poem melodramatik . Pjesë 1,* Botim i tretë. [pseud. Gegë Toska]. reprint Tirana 1994. 77 pp.
- (1927), *Shna Ndou i Padues.* Shkodra: Shtypshkroja Françiskane. 54 pp.
- (1927), *Sh. Luigji Gonzaga. Melodram.* Shkodra: Shtyp. e Zojes se Paperlyeme. 76 pp.
- (1931), *I ligu per mend.* Komedi trí aktesh shkrue mbas Molière-it e pershtatë Instituteve Mashkullore të Shqypnís. Shkodra: Shtypshkroja Françeskane. 156 pp.
- (1931), *Lahuta e Malcís. Lidhja e Prizrenit.* Pjesa e dytë. Shkodra: Shtypshkroja Françiskane. 86 pp.
- (1931), *Odisea. Ifigenija n'Aullí.* Shkodra: Shtypshkroja Françeskane. 46 pp.
- (1937), *Lahuta e Malcís.* Shkodra: Shtypshroja françeskane, s.a. [1937]. reprint Rome 1958, Ljubljana 1990, Rome 1991, Prishtina 1997, Tirana 2000. 511 pp.
- (1941), *Jerina ase mbretnesha e luleve. Poem dramatik.* Shkodra: Shtypshkroja françeskane. 51 pp.

- (1941), *Mrizi i zânavet.* Komentuem prej A. Viktor Volaj OFM. Botim i katert. Shkodra: Shtypshkroja A. Gj. Fishta. 123 pp.
- (1958), *Die Laute des Hochlandes. Lahuta e Malcis. Übersetzt, eingeleitet und mit Anmerkungen versehen von Max Lambertz.* Südosteuropäische Arbeiten 51. Munich: Oldenbourg. 312 pp.
- (1968-1973), *Il liuto della montagna (Lahuta e Malcís). Prefazione, commento, traduzione e note di Papàs Ignazio Parrino.* Centro Internationale di Studi Albanesi presso l'Università di Palermo. 4 fasc. Palermo: Scuola grafica salesiana. xx + 83, lviii + 157, xxxii + 299, xl + 95 pp.
- (1973), *Jerina, regina dei fiori. Poema melodrammatico.* Traduzione con test a fronte. Introduzione e note di Luigi Marlekaj. Bari: Favia. 181 pp.
- (1997), *Dramatika.* Prishtina: Rilindja. 493 pp.
- (1997), *Lahuta e Malcís,* e pajisun me argumenta e sqarime fjalori. Prishtina: Rilindja.
- (1997), *Lirika.* Prishtina: Rilindja. 395 pp.
- (1997), *Satirika.* Prishtina: Rilindja. 493 pp.
- (1998), *Shqiptarët dhe të drejtat e tyne.* Përgatitur nga Tonin Çobani. Lezha: Lisitan. 32 pp.
- (2000), *Estetikë dhe kritikë.* Antologji përgatitur nga Persida Asllani. Tirana?: Hylli i dritës & Shtëpia e librit, s.l. s.a. [Tirana? 2000]. 221 pp.
- (2000), *Hajrija. Tragjedi.* Prishtina: Faik Konica. 75 pp.
- (2000), *Përndritje. Publicistike. Analiza, polemika, kronika.* Tirana: Lajmëtari. 325 pp.
- (2003), *The Highland Lute: the Albanian national epic. Cantos I-V. The cycle of Oso Kuka.* Translated from the Albanian by Robert Elsie. Dukagjini Balkan Books. Peja: Dukagjini. 167 pp.
- (2005), *The Highland Lute: the Albanian national epic.* Translated from the Albanian by Robert Elsie and Janice Mathie-Heck. forthcoming.

FLOQI, Kristo
- (1964), *Komedi të zgjedhuna.* Belgrade: Enti për botimin e teksteve. 177 pp.
- (1984), *Vëllazëri e interesë e komedi të tjera.* Prishtina: Rilindja.

FORTINO, Italo Costante
- (1986), L'opera poetica di Giulio Varibobba. in: *Recherches Albanologiques,* Prishtina, 3, p. 111-129.
- (1993), La letteratura contemporanea degli Albanesi di Calabria. in: *Ricostruzione delle origini albanesi. Atti del Convegno di Guardiafiera, 24 giugno 1989.* A cura del Centro Studi Molise 2000. Guardafiera. p. 2-18.

FORTINO, Italo Costante (ed.)
- (1997), *Albanistica. Novantasette.* Naples: Instituto Universitario Orientale. 335 pp.
- (2992), *Albanistica - duemiladue,* a cura di Italo Costante Fortino. Dipartimento di Studi dell'Europa Orientale. Naples: Università degli Studi di Napoli "L'Orientale," 454 pp.

FRASHËRI, Kristo

  (1955), Sami Frashëri (1850-1904). in: *Buletin për shkencat shoqërore,* Tirana, 4, p. 56-112.

- (1962), *Rilindja kombëtare shqiptare. Me rastin e 50-vjetorit të shpalljes së Pavarësisë Kombëtare 1912 - 28 nëndor 1962.* Tirana: Naim Frashëri. 120 pp.

- (1966), Şemseddin Sami Frashëri, idéologue du mouvement national albanais. in: *Studia Albanica,* Tirana, 1, p. 95-110.

- (1979), *Lidhja shqiptare e Prizrenit 1878-1881.* Tirana: 8 Nëntori, reprint 1989, 1997. 248 pp.

- (1984a), *Abdyl Frashëri (1839-1892).* [Albanian-language version] Tirana: 8 Nëntori. 328 pp.

- (1984b), *Abdyl Frashëri (1839-1892).* [French-language version] Tirana: 8 Nëntori, 330 pp.

FRASHËRI, Mehdi bey

  (1927), *Liga e Prizrenit dhe effektet dipllomatike të saj.* Tirana: Mrothësija. 60 pp.

- (2000), *Vepra. Nevruzi, Trathëtia.* Prishtina: Faik Konica. 279 pp.

FRASHËRI, Mid'hat bey

  (1901), *Naim Be Frashëri.* Sofia: Mbrothësia, reprint Tirana 1923, 1941. 39 pp.

- (1997), *Kthimi i Mid'hat Frashërit. Pjesë të zgjedhura nga vepra.* Përgatitur nga Uran Butka. Tirana: Phoenix, Tirana. 430 pp.

FRASHËRI, Naim bey

  (1871), *Kavâid-i fârisiyye dar tarz-i nevîn.* Constantinople Mühendisynn Matbaasi [1288 A.H.]. 64 pp.

- (1881-1882), *Ihtiraat ve keşfiyat.* Constantinople [1298 A.H.]. 79 pp.

- (1883), *Fusûli erbe'a. Francizcadan me'huzdur.* Cep Kütüphanesi aded 16. Constantinople: Mihran [1300 A.H.]. 127 pp.

- (1884), *Tahayyulat.* Constantinople: Mihran [1301 A.H.]. 66 pp.

- (1886), *Bagëti e bujqësija prej N.H.F.* Bucharest: Dritë. 23 pp.

- (1886), *E këndimit çunavet këndonjëtoreja copë e parë prej N.H.F.* Bucharest: Dritë. 55 pp.

- (1886), *E këndimit çunavet këndonjëtoreja copë e dytë prej N.H.F.* Bucharest: Dritë. 52 pp.

- (1886), *Ho alêthês pothos tôn skypetarôn hypo D.* Bucharest. reprint Tirana 2000. 19 pp.

- (1886), *Istori e përgjithëshme për mësonjëtoret të para prej N.H.F.* Bucharest: Dritë. 116 pp.

- (1886), *Vjersha për mësonjëtoret të para prej N.H.F.* Bucharest: Dritë. 96 pp.

- (1888), *Diturit ë për mësonjëtoret të para pej N.H.F.* Bucharest: Dituri. 212 pp.

- (1890), *Luletë e verësë. N.H.F.* Bucharest. Dituri. 80 pp.

- (1894), *Mësime prej N.F.* Bucharest.126 pp.

- (1894), *Parajsa dhe fjala fluturake. Vjersha të N.F.* Bucharest. reprint Korça: Dhori Koti, s.a. 76 pp.

Bibliography

- (1895), *Ho Erôs. Poiêmata prôtotypa eis asmata oktô met' eikonôn.* Constantinople: Gerardos. 32 pp.
- (1896), *Fletore e Bektashinjet.* Bucharest: Shtypëshkronjët të Shqipëtarëvet. reprint Thessalonika: Mbrothësia 1909. 32 pp.
- (1896), *Iliadë e Omirit. Këngë e parë kthyerë prej N.H.F.* Bucharest: Dituri. 76 pp.
- (1898), *Istori' e Skenderbeut.* Bucharest: Tipografi' e Shqipëtarëvet, 312 pp.
- (1898), *Qerbelaja prej N.H.F.* Bucharest: Dituri. 352 pp.
- (1902), *Shqipëria (vjershë). Prej Naim Be Frashërit.* Sofia: Mbrothësia. 6 pp.
- (1903), *Ho alêthês pothos tôn skypetarôn. Poiêma hypo Naêm Frassarê.* Sofia: Mbrothësia. 16 pp.
- (1904), *Dëshira e vërtetë e Shqipëtarëvet. Vjershë kombiare prej N.H.F. Shqipëruar nga greqishtja.* Sofia: Mbrothësia. 20 pp.
- (1921), *Istori e Shqipërisë.* Korça: Korça. 28 pp.
- (1926), Die Bektaschis. Herausgegeben und übersetzt von Norbert Jokl. in: *Balkanarchiv* 2, p. 226-256.
- (1942), *Bageti e bujqesia. I pascoli e i campi. Con testo a fronte.* Spoleto.
- (1980-1985), *Vepra të zgjedhura 1-2.* Tirana: Akademia e Shkencave. 495 + 376 pp.
- (1981), *Frasheri's song of Albania.* Anglicized by Ali Cungu. Smithtown NY: Exposition Press. 32 pp.
- (1986), *Vepra 1-7.* Prishtina: Rilindja.
- (1994), *Bagëti' e bujqësia. I pascoli e i campi.* Introduzione, edizione critica, traduzione italiana e concordanza a cura di Francesco Altimari. Studi e testi di albanistica 4. Rende: Centro Editoriale Librario dell'Università della Calabria. 355 pp.
- (1995-1996), *Vepra letrare 2, 3, 4, 5.* Tirana: Naim Frashëri. 195, 232, 355, 135 pp.

FRASHËRI, Sami bey (Şemsettin Sami)

- (1872), *Taaṣṣuk-u Tal'at ve Fitnat.* Constantinople. reprint Ankara 1979. 180 pp.
- (1875), *Besa yahud ahde vefa. Alti fasildan ibaret facia.* Muharriri S. Sami. Istanbul: Matbuat-i Ceyyide [1292 AH]. 176 pp.
- (1876), *Gave. Beş fasisdan îbaret faciâ.* Matbaati Ceyyide. Istanbul: Tasviri Efkar Matbaasi [1293A.H.]. 190 pp.
- (1882), *Kamûs-u fransevî, fransizcadan türkçeye lugat. Dictionnaire français-turc.* Constantinople: Mihran,[1299 A.H.]. 1,630 pp.
- (1885), *Kamûs-u fransevî, türkçeden fransizcaya lugat. Dictionnaire turc-français.* Constantinople: Mihran [1301 A.H.]. 1,208 pp.
- (1886), *Abetare e gjuhësë shqip prej S.H.F.* Bucharest: Dituri. 78 pp.
- (1886), *Shkronjëtore e gjuhësë shqip prej S.H.F.* Bucharest: Dritë. 141 pp.
- (1888), *Dheshkronjë prej S.H.F.* Bucharest: Dituri. 158 pp.
- (1889-1896), *Kamûs al-a'lâm. Dictionnaire universel d'histoire et de géographie par Ch. Samy-Bey Fraschery.* 6 vol. Constantinople: Mihran [1306-1313 A.H.].

239

Bibliography

- (1899), *Abetare prej S.H.F.* Sofia: Mbrodhesia. 16 pp.
- (1899), *Shqipëria - Ç'ka qënë, ç'është e ç'do të bëhetë? Mendime për shpëtimt të mëmëdheut nga reziket që e kanë rethuarë.* Bucharest. reprint Sofia: Mbrothësia 1907. 96 pp.
- (1900-1901) *Kamûs-u türkî.* 2 vol. Istanbul: Ikdam [1317 A.H.], reprint Istanbul 1979. 1,574 pp.
- (1901), *Besa. Drame me ghashte pamje, prej Sami Bej Frashërit.* Shqipëruar nga Turqishtja prej Ab. A. Ypi Kolonja. Sofia: Mbrothësia. 108 pp.
- (1913), *Was war Albanien, was ist es, was wird es werden? Gedanken und Betrachtungen über die unser geheiligtes Vaterland Albanien bedrohenden Gefahren und deren Abwendung. Verfaßt von Sch. Sami Bey Frasheri.* Aus dem Türkischen übersetzt von A. Traxler. Vienna & Leipzig: Alfred Hölder 1913. 69 pp.
- (1945), *Pledge of honor, an Albanian tragedy by Sami Bey Frasheri.* Translated and edited by Nelo Drizari. NewYork: S. F. Vanni. 118 pp.
- (1978-1984) Vepra 1-8. Prishtina: Rilindja.
- (1988), *Vepra 1-2.* Tirana: Akademia e Shkencave. 444 + 392 pp.
- (2000), *Kush e prish paqen në Ballkan. Publicistike e Sami Frashërit turqisht.* Përktheu nga turqishtja Dr. Abdullah Hamiti. Peja: Dukagjini. 361 pp.

FULLANI, Dhimitër (ed.)
- (1973), *Poetë të Rilindjes.* Poezia shqipe. Tirana: Naim Frashëri. 388 pp.

GALICA, Shyqri
- (1997), *Konica - moderniteti, eseistika, kritika.* Prishtina: Rilindja. 226 pp.

GANGALE, Giuseppe Tommaso
- (1973), *Kommentare von Dr. G. Gangale zur Albanischen Handschriftensammlung Kopenhagen.* 5.XI.1973. typescript. Copenhagen: Royal Library of Copenhagen. 167 pp.
- (1977), Verzeichnis zur albanischen Handschriftensammlung Kopenhagen. in: *Akten des Internationalen Albanologischen Kolloquiums. Zum Gedächtnis an Univ.-Prof. Dr. Norbert Jokl. Innsbruck, 28. September - 3. Oktober 1972.* Hermann Maria Ölberg (ed.). Innsbrucker Beiträge zur Kulturwissenschaft, Sonderheft 41. Innsbruck. p. 601-617.

GECI, Pashko
- (1965), Frang Bardhi dhe fjalori i tij latin-shqip. in: *Studime filologjike,* Tirana, 2, p. 121-128.
- (1970), Derivatet në fjalorin latin-shqip të Frang Bardhit. in: *Konferenca e dytë e studimeve albanologjike, Tiranë 12-18 Janar 1968* (Universiteti i Tiranës, Tirana), vol. 3, p. 153-158.

GIANCANE, Daniele (ed.)
- (1999), *Poesia dal Kossovo.* Nardò: Besa.163 pp.

GIBB, E. J. W.
- (1900-1909), *A History of Ottoman poetry,* Vol. 1-6. London: Luzac.

GJEÇOVI, Shtjefën
- (1933), *Kanuni i Lekë Dukagjinit. Vepër postume. Permbledhë e kodifikue prej A. Shtjefen Konst. Gjeçov. O.F.M.* Shkodra: Shtypshkroja Françeskane. reprint Prishtina (1972), Tirana (1993). 144 pp.
- (1989), *Kanuni i Lekë Dukagjinit. The code of Lekë Dukagjini. Albanian text collected and arranged by Shtjefën Gjeçov.* Translated with an introduction by Leonard Fox. New York: Gjonlekaj. 269 pp.

GJINAJ, Maksim
   (2003), *Letërsia shqiptare e përkthyer. Sprovë bibliografike.*Tirana: Ideart, 112 pp.

GJINAJ, Maksim & GJINAJ, Aleks
   (2003), *Dritëro Agolli. Bibliografi.* Tirana: Dritëro, 606 pp.

GJOKA, Behar
   (2002), *Poetika e Budit. Studim për veprën poetike.* Tirana: Albas, 202 pp.

GODO, Sabri
   (1970), *Ali Pashë Tepelena.* Tirana: Naim Frashëri. reprint Prishtina 1972. 411 pp.
- (1975), *Skënderbeu. Roman.* Tirana: Naim Frashëri.

GRAÇI, Virion
   (1998), *Le paradis des fous.* Roman traduit de l'albanais par Christiane Montécot. La Tour d'Aigues: Editions de l'Aube. reprint Paris: Gallimard 2000. 223 pp.

GRADILONE, Giuseppe
   (1960), *Studi di letteratura albanese.* Rome: Urbinati. 247 pp.
- (1969), Il 30° anno di ordinariato universitario del Prof. Ernesto Koliqi. in: *Shêjzat / Le Pleiadi,* Rome, 13, p. 21-23.
- (1974), *Altri studi di letteratura albanese.* Studi albanesi. Studi e testi Vol 6. Rome: Bulzoni. 301 pp.
- (1983), *La letteratura albanese e il mondo classico. Quattro studi.* Rome: Bulzoni. 177 pp.
- (1989), *Contributo alla critica del testo dei canti di Giuseppe Serembe.* Rome: Istituto di Studi Albanesi. 179 pp.
- (1997a), *Miscellanea di albanistica.* Rome: Istituto di Studi Albanesi. 265 pp.
- (1997b), *Studi di letteratura albanese contemporanea.* Rome: Istituto di Studi Albanesi. 321 pp.

GRASSI, Ennio & SPORTELLI, Rosangela (ed.)
   (2002), *Poeti della terra d'Albania.* A cura di Ennio Grassi, Rosangela Sportelli, e traduzione di Rosangela Sportelli. Anno ventiduesimo, La quarta serie. Numero secondo e terzo. Bologna: In Forma di Parole, 446 pp.

GRENDLER, P. F.
   (1977), *The Roman inquisition and the Venetian Press, 1540-1605.* Princeton: Princeton University Press. 374 pp.

GROOTE, E. von (ed.)
   (1860), *Die Pilgerfahrt des Ritters Arnold von Harff von Cöln durch Italien, Syrien, Ägypten, Arabien, Äthiopien, Nubien, Palästina, die Türkei,*

Frankreich und Spanien, wie er sie in den Jahren 1496 bis 1499 vollendet, beschrieben und durch Zeichnungen erläutert hat. Cologne: J. M. Heberle. 280 pp.

GUALTIERI, Vittorio Gaspare

(1930), *Girolamo de Rada poeta albanese. L'uomo, il clima storico-letterario, l'opera, caratteri romantici dell'opera.* Palermo: Sandron. 143 pp.

GURAKUQI, Karl (ed.)

(1941), *Shkrimtarët shqiptarë. Pjesa II. Prej Lidhjes së Prizrenit deri sot.* Punue nën kujdesin e Ernest Koliqit nga Karl Gurakuqi. Tirana: Botim Ministris s'Arsmit. 548 pp.

GURAKUQI, Luigj

(1905), *Versi.* Naples: Tocco & Salvietti. 40 pp.

- (1905), *Knnimé t'para per msojtoré filltaré t'Shcypniis. Libri i dyte.* Naples: Tocco & Salvietti. 96 pp.

- (1905), *Abétari per msoitoré filltaré t'Shcypniis. Libri i paré.* Naples: Tocco & Salvietti. 83 pp.

- (1906), *Abétar i vogel shcyp mas abévét t'Bashkimit é t'Stambollit mé trégimé n't'dy dhialéktet préj Lék Grudes.* Bucharest: Voicu. 28 pp.

- (1906), *Fjalorth shcyp-frângisht e frângisht-shcyp i fjalevé t'réja.* Naples: Tocco & Salvietti. 32 pp.

- (1906), *Vargenimi n'gjuhe shcypé me gni fjalorth shcyp-frângisht n'marim.* Naples: Tocco & Salvietti. 142 pp.

- (1940), *Vjersha. Me nji jetëshkrim të shkurtë prej Gjikam.* Bari: Laterza & Polo. 94 pp.

- (1988), *Vepra 1-3.* Prishtina: Rilindja. 283, 201 + 423 pp.

GURAKUQI, Mark

(1967), *Jeta dhe vepra e poetit të shquem demokrat Ndre Mjeda.* Tirana: Naim Frashëri. 182 pp.

- (1980), *Mbi veprën poetike të Mjedës. Studim.* Tirana: Naim Frashëri. 272 pp.

GURRA, Milto Sotir

(1938), *Plagët e kurbetit. Tregime.* Tirana: Luarasi. 150 pp.

- (1972), *Tregime të zgjedhura.* Tirana: Naim Frashëri. 160 pp.

GUZZETTA, Antonino

(1968), *Ernesto Koliqi, un poeta sociale.* Centro Internazionale di Studi Albanesi. Pubblicazione Nr. 15. Milan: Missioni estere.

HAJDARI, Gëzim

(1990) *Antologjia e shiut. Poezi.* Tirana: Naim Frashëri, 72 pp.

- (1993), *Ombra di cane. Hije qeni.* Frosinone: Dismisuratesti, 63 pp.

- (1995), *Sasso contro vento. Gurë kundër erës.* Integrazioni. Collana di poesia, 57. Milan: Laboratorio delle Arti, 59 pp.

- (1998), *Pietre al confine.* A cura di Massimiliano Martolini. Ancona: Associazione Culturale Essenza Metrica, 52 pp.

- (1999), *Corpo presente.* Tirana: Dritëro, 153 pp.

- (2000), *Antologia della pioggia.* Traduzione dell'autore. Santarcangelo di Romagna: Fara Editore, 79 pp.

- (2001), *Erbamara. Barihidhur.* Traduzione dell'autore. Santarcangelo di Romagna: Fara Editore, 71 pp.
- (2002), *Stigmate. Vragë. Poesie.* Prefazione di Cristina Benussi. Nardò/Lecce: Besa, 128 pp.
- (2004), *Spine nere, poesie. Gjemba të zinj, poezi.* Nardò/Lecce: Besa, 105 pp.

HAKKI, Ismail
  (1895), *Shemsedin Sami bey.* Constantinople [1311 A.H.]. 18 pp.

HALIMI, Kadri
  (1957), 'Derviški redovi i njihova kultna mjesta na Kosovu i Metohiji,' in: *Glasnik Muzeja Kosova i Metohije,* Prishtina, 2, p. 193-206.

HAMITI, Sabri
  (1983), *Arti i leximit. Sprova për një poetikë 3.* Prishtina: Rilindja. 339 pp.
- (1991), *Faik Konica: jam unë.* Prishtina: Rilindja. 196 pp.
- (1996), *Letra shqipe. Sprovë për një poetikë 5.* Peja: Dukagjini. 289 pp.
- (1999), *Lasgushi qindvjeçar.* Prishtina: Faik Konica. 174 pp
- (2000a), *Bioletra. Një teori e shkrimit dhe e leximit.* Prishtina: Faik Konica. 148 pp.
- (2000b), *Letërsia moderne shqiptare. Gjysma e parë e shek. XX.* Tirana: Alb-Aas. 320 pp.
- (2002), *Vepra letrare,* Vol. 1-10. Prishtina: Faik Konica.
- (2003), *Studime letrare.* Botime të veçanta XLIX. Seksioni i Gjuhësisë dhe i Letërsisë, Libri 21. Prishtina: Akademia e Shkencave dhe e Arteve e Kosovës, 744 pp.
- (2004), *Shkollat letrare shqipe. Ese.* Prishtina: Faik Konica, 96 pp.
- *Sympathia: testamente për urtakun.* Prishtina: Faik Konica, 146 pp.

HAMITI, Sabri (ed.)
  (1998), *Letërsia moderne shqipe. Për klasën e tretë të shkollave të mesme.* Prishtina: Libri shkollor. 373 pp.

HASANI, Hasan
  (2003), *Leksikoni i shkrimtarëve shqiptarë, 1501-2001.* Prishtina: Faik Konica, 493 pp.

HASLUCK, Frederick William
  (1929), *Christianity and Islam under the Sultans.* Edited by Margaret Hasluck. 2 vol. Oxford: Clarendon. Reprint New York: Octagon (1973) 770 pp.

HASLUCK, Margaret Masson Hardie
  (1925), 'The Nonconformist Moslems of Albania,' in: *Contemporary review,* London, 127, p. 599-606. Reprinted in *Moslem World* 15 (1925), p. 388-398.
- (1954), *The unwritten law in Albania. A record of the customary law of the Albanian tribes. Description of family and village life... & waging of blood-feuds.* Cambridge: Cambridge University Press. reprint Hyperion Conn. (1981). 285 pp.

HATIBI, Ervin
  (1995), *Ervin never dies. Poezi.* Tirana: Marin Barleti, 99 pp.
- (2004), *Pasqyra e lëndës. Poezi.* Tirana: Ora, 98 pp.

HAXHIADEMI, Etëhem

    (1931), *Akili. Tragedi me pesë akte.* Tirana: Luarasi. 64 pp.

-    (1931), *Aleksandri. Tragedi me pesë akte.* Tirana: Luarasi. 72 pp.

-    (1931), *Ulisi. Tragedi me pesë akte.* Tirana: Luarasi. 66 pp.

-    (1935), *Skenderbeu. Tragedi me pesë aktë.* Tirana: Luarasi. reprint Rome 1968. 84 pp.

-    (1936), *Diomedi. Tragjedi me pesë akte.* Tirana: Luarasi.

-    (1939), *Lyra.* Tirana: Dielli. 73 pp.

-    (2000), *Vepra 1-2.* Prishtina: Faik Konica. 302 + 283 pp.

HETZER, Armin

    (1981), Wie ist Arnold von Harffs Wörterverzeichnis (1496) zu lesen? Ein Beispiel für das Ineinandergreifen von albanischer und deutscher Sprachgeschichtsforschung. in: *Balkan-Archiv, Neue Folge,* Hamburg, 6, p. 227-262.

-    (1983), Die Wortschatz und die Orthographie der "Erveheja" von Muhamet Kyçyku-Çami. in: *Balkan-Archiv, Neue Folge,* Hamburg, 8, p. 199-289.

-    (1984), Die "Erveheja" von Muhamet Kyçyku (Çami). Eine Untersuchung zur albanischen Literatur in arabischer Schrift und deren Bedeutung im Rahmen der Nationalbewegung des 19. Jahrhunderts in: *Südost-Forschungen,* Munich, 43, p. 181-239.

-    (1985), *Geschichte des Buchhandels in Albanien. Prologomena zu einer Literatursoziologie.* Balkanologische Veröffentlichungen 10. In Kommission bei Otto Harrassowitz (Wiesbaden). Berlin. 212 pp.

-    (1991), Geschichte der albanischen Literatur bis zur Gewinnung der nationalen Unabhängigkeit (1912) (Vorüberlegungen zu einer Literaturgeschichte). in: *Zeitschrift für Balkanologie,* Berlin, 27.2, p. 106-132.

-    (2000), Shqipnia und Shqenia in Fishtas "Laute des Hochlandes." in: *Zeitschrift für Balkanologie,* Berlin, 36. 2, p.134-142.

HOTI, Rexhep

    (2002), *Tempulli i fjalës: studim mbi krijimtarinë e Ismail Kadaresë.* Tirana: Toena, 230 pp.

HOXHA, Fatbardha

    (1998), *Haki Stërmilli. Jeta dhe vepra.* Shkodra: Camaj-Pipa.138 pp.

-    (2001), *Fjala jonë. Autorë dhe vepra të traditës. Studime.* Shkodra: Camaj-Pipa. 152 pp.

HYSA, Mahmud

    (1987), *Krestomaci e letërsisë së vjetër shqiptare.* Prishtina: Enti i teksteve. 317 pp.

-    (1990), Vepra poetike e Nezim Frakullës. in: *Studime Filologjike,* Tirana, 4, p. 131-148.

-    (1993), *Autorë dhe tekste nga letërsia e vjetër shqiptare 1.* Skopje: Flaka e vëllazërimit, Skopje. 243 pp.

-    (1995), *Autorë dhe tekste nga letërsia e vjetër shqiptare, II.* Skopje: Flaka e vëllazërimit. 330 pp.

- (1996), Vendi i alhamiadës shqiptare në historinë e letërsisë. in: *Perla, revistë shkencore-kulturore tremujore*, Tirana, 3, p. 12-23.
- (2000), *Alamiada shqiptare. Studime letrare.* Skopje: Logos A. 331 + 249 pp.

IBRAHIMI, Nexhat
  (1997), *Kontaktet e para të Islamit me popujt ballkanike në periudhën paraosmane.* Skopje: Logos-A.100 pp.

IDRIZI, Rinush
  (1980), *Ndre Mjedja.* Tirana: 8 Nëntori. 288 pp.
- (1992), *Migjeni.* Tirana: Enciklopedike. 288 pp.

INALCIK, Halil
  (1960), Arnawutluk. in: *Encyclopedia of Islam.* Edited by H.A.R. Gibb et al. London: Luzac, Vol. 1. p. 650-658.

ISMAILI, Rifat
  (1999), *Historia e letërsisë shqipe, II.* Prishtina. 324 pp.

ISMAJLI, Rexhep
  (2000). *Tekste të vjetra.* Peja: Dukagjini. 427 pp.

ISMAJLI, Rexhep (ed.)
  (1978), *Rrënje e fortë. Poezia arbëreshe e ditëve tona.* Prishtina: Rilindja. 191 pp.
- (1990), *Poezia e sotme arbëreshe.* Prishtina: Rilindja. 321 pp.

JACQUES, Edwin E.
  (1938), 'Islam in Albania,' in: *Moslem World,* 28, p. 313-314.
- (1995), *The Albanians. An ethnic history from prehistoric times to the present.* Jefferson NC: McFarland & Co. 768 pp.

JAKU, Pjetër
  (2000a), *Fjalori fishtian. Fjalë dhe shprehje që kërkojnë shpjegime nga vepra poetike e Fishtës.* Lezha: Kuvendi. 87 pp.
- (2000b), *Vlerat letrare në Lahutën e Malcisë të Gjergj Fishtës.* Lezha: Kuvendi. 88 pp.

JANURA, Petro
  (1982), *Migjeni.* Skopje: Flaka e Vëllazërimit. 327 pp.

JARNIK, Jan Urban
  (1881), *Zur albanischen Sprachenkunde* von Dr. Johann Urban Jarník. Programm der Realschule in Wien. Leipzig: Brockhaus. 51 pp.

JASIQI, Ali D.
  (1968), Proza tregimtare e Mitrush Kutelit. in: *Jeta e re,* Prishtina, 5, p. 1009-1019.

JORDAN, Peter, LUKAN, Walter, SCHWANDNER-SIEVERS, Stephanie & SUNDHAUSSEN, Holm (ed.)
  (2003), *Albanien: Geographie, historische Anthropologie, Geschichte, Kultur, postkommunistische Transformation.* = Österreichische Osthefte, Vienna, 45 (2003). Österreichische Ost- und Südosteuropa-Institut. Vienna: Peter Lang, 416 pp.

JORGAQI, Nasho
  (1987), *Poetika e dokumentit. Studime, artikuj, ese.* Tirana: Naim Frashëri. 296 pp.
- (1996), Kontributi i Faik Konicës në zhvillimin e letërsisë shqiptare. in: *Studime albanologjike,* Tirana, 2, p. 167-173.
- (2000), *Fanoliana. Risi dokumentare, kujtime e studime për F. Nolin.* Tirana: Toena. 430 + 16 pp.
- (2001), *Për Fan Nolin e të tjerë.* Tirana: Dudaj, 330 pp.
JORGAQI, Nasho (ed.)
  (2001), *Antologji e poezisë bashkëkohore arbëreshe.* Tirana: Dudaj, 222 pp.
JORGAQI, Nasho, BULO, Jorgo, IDRIZI, Frida, BULO, Stefan, KODRA, Klara, BUÇPAPA, Skënder, CAKO, Niko (ed.)
  (1994a), *Antologjia e letërsisë shqiptare 1 (Për shkollat e mesme).* Tirana: Libri Shkollor. 408 pp.
- (1994b), *Historia e letërsisë shqiptare 1 (Për shkollat e mesme).* Tirana: Libri Shkollor. 190 pp.
JUBICA, Irhan (ed.)
  (2004), *Antologjia e prozës bashkëkohore shqiptare.* Tirana: Orana, 108 pp.
KABASHI, Emin
- (1997), *Lasgush Poradeci. Jeta dhe vepra.* Prishtina: Instituti Albanologjik. 252 pp.
- (1998), *Kadare. Mendësja shqiptare.* Prishtina: Instituti Albanologjik. 181 pp.
- (2003), *Jeronim de Rada: Poetika e poemave.* Tirana: Ombra GVG, 272 pp.
KADARE, Ismail
  (1961), *Shekulli im. Vjersha dhe poema* Tirana: Naim Frashëri.148 pp.
- (1963), *Gjenerali i ushtrisë së vdekur. Roman.* Tirana: Naim Frashëri. 167 pp.
- (1964), *Përse mendohen këto male. Vjersha dhe poema.* Tirana: Naim Frashëri. 116 pp.
- (1967), *Gjenerali i ushtrisë së vdekur. Roman.* Botimi i 2-të. Tirana: Naim Frashëri. 242 pp.
- (1968), *Dasma. Roman.* Tirana: Naim Frashëri. 224 pp.
- (1968), *The Wedding.* Rendered into English by Ali Cungu. Tirana: Naim Frashëri. reprint Gamma, New York 1972, 1974, 1982. 196 pp.
- (1969), *Vjersha dhe poema.* Prishtina: Rilindja. 217 pp.
- (1970), *Le général de l'armée morte. Roman.* Traduit de l'albanais. Préface par Robert Escarpit. Paris: Albin Michel. 288 pp.
- (1970), *Kështjella. Roman.* Tirana: Naim Frashëri. reprint Prishtina 1976. 244 pp.
- (1971), *The general of the dead army.* Novel translated from the French by Derek Coltman. London: W. H. Allen, & New York: Grossman. reprint Tirana 1983, New York 1986, 1991.
- (1971), *Kronikë në gur. Roman.* Tirana: Naim Frashëri. reprint Prishtina 1972. 229 pp.
- (1973), *Dimri i vetmisë së madhe. Roman.* Tirana: Naim Frashëri. 496 pp.

- (1974), *The castle. A novel.* Translated by Pavli Qesku. Tirana: 8 Nëntori. 259 pp.
- (1975), *Nëntori i një kryeqyteti. Roman.* Tirana: Naim Frashëri. 223 pp.
- (1977), *Dimri i madh. Botim i tretë. Roman.* Tirana: Naim Frashëri. 620 pp.
- (1977), *Emblema e dikurshme. Tregime e novela.* Tirana: Naim Frashëri. 444 pp.
- (1978), *Ura me tri harqe. Triptik me një intermexo.* Tirana: Naim Frashëri. 512 pp.
- (1980), *Gjakftohtësia. Novela.* Tirana: Naim Frashëri. 544 pp.
- (1981-), *Vepra letrare.* 12 vol. Tirana: Naim Frashëri.
- (1986), *Koha e shkrimeve. Tregime novela përshkrime.* Tirana: Naim Frashëri. 408 pp.
- (1987), *L'année noire. Le cortège de la noce s'est figé dans la glace.* Traduit de l'albanais par Jusuf Vrioni et Alexandre Zotos. Paris: Fayard. 239 pp.
- (1987), *Chronicle in stone.* Translated from the Albanian. London: Serpent's Tail & New York: Meredith. 277 pp.
- (1988), *Doruntine. A novel.* Translated by Jon Rothschild. New York: New Amsterdam & London: Saqi. 168 pp.
- (1988), *Koncert në fund të dimrit. Roman.* Tirana: Naim Frashëri. 556 pp.
- (1990), *Broken April.* New York: New Amsterdam & London: Saqi. 216 pp.
- (1990), *Dosja H. Roman.* Tirana: Naim Frashëri & Prishtina: Rilindja. 232 pp.
- (1990), *Ftesë në studio.* Tirana: Naim Frashëri & Prishtina: Rilindja. 328 pp.
- (1990), *Migjeni ose uragani i ndërprerë.* Prishtina: Pena. 84 pp.
- (1990), *Viti i mbrapshtë.* Prishtina: Rilindja. 110 pp.
- (1991), *Ardhja e Migjenit në letërsinë shqipe.* Tirana: Naim Frashëri. 116 pp.
- (1991), *Ëndërr mashtruese. Tregime e novela.* Tirana: Naim Frashëri. 364 pp.
- (1991), *Nga një dhjetor në tjetrin. Kronikë, këmbim letrash, persiatje.* Paris: Fayard. 262 pp.
- (1991), *Përbindëshi.* Prizren: Vreber & Tirana: Lidhja e Shkrimtareve. 119 pp.
- (1991), *Pesha e kryqit.* Paris: Fayard. 213 pp.
- (1993), *The palace of dreams.* A novel written in Albanian and translated from the French of Jusuf Vrioni by Barbara Bray. New York: William Morrow & Co. & London: Harvill. 205 pp.
- (1993-2004), *Oeuvres, 1-12.* Paris: Fayard. 575, 635, 511, 592, 645, 782, 652, 635, 668, 692, ca. 500 pp.
- (1993-2004), *Vepra, 1-12.* Parathënie dhe shënime prezantuese nga Eric Faye. Paris: Fayard. 519, 566, 454, 521, 582, 685, 570, 542, 570, 604, 539 pp.
- (1994), *Albanian spring. The anatomy of tyranny.* London: Saqi. 240 pp.
- (1994), *The Concert.* A novel written in Albanian and translated from the French of Jusuf Vrioni by Barbara Bray. New York: William Morrow & Co. & London: Harvill. reprint New York: Arcade 1998. 444 pp.
- (1995), *Albanie. Visage des Balkans. Ecrits de lumière.* Photographies de Pjetër, Kel et Gegë Marubi. Texte de Ismail Kadaré. Traduit par Jusuf Vrioni et Emmanuelle Zbynovsky. Paris: Arthaud. 143 pp.

- (1995), *La légende des légendes*. Traduit de l'albanais par Yusuf Vrioni. Paris: Flammarion. 277 pp.
- (1995), *Piramida. Roman.* Tirana: Çabej/MÇM. 139 pp.
- (1996), *Dialog me Alain Bosquet.* Elbasan: Onufri. 189 pp.
- (1996), *Legjenda e legjendave.* Peja: Dukagjini. 169 pp.
- (1996), *Pallati i ëndrrave. Versioni përfundimtar.* Peja: Dukagjini. reprint: Tirana: Onufri. 203 pp.
- (1996), *The pyramid.* Translated by David Bellos from the French version of the Albanian by Jusuf Vrioni. London: Harvill & New York: Arcade Publ. 129 pp.
- (1996), *Shkaba. Roman.* Tirana: Çabej, & Peja: Dukagjini. 100 pp.
- (1996), *Spiritus. Roman me kaos, zbulesë dhe çmërs.* Elbasan: Onufri, 259 pp.
- (1997), *The file on H.* Translated by David Bellos from the French version of the Albanian by Jusuf Vrioni. London: Harvill Press. 171 pp.
- (1997), *Poèmes, 1957-1997.* Version française établie par Claude Durand et l'auteur avec la collaboration de Mira Meksi, Edmond Tupja et Jusuf Vrioni. Préface de Alain Bosquet. Paris: Fayard. 153 pp.
- (1997), *The three-arched bridge.* Translated from the Albanian by John Hodgson. London: Harvill. 184 pp.
- (1997), The Wedding procession turned to ice. Translated from the Albanian by Robert Elsie. in: *Kosovo. In the heart of the powder keg.* ed: Robert Elsie. East European Monographs, CDLXXVIII. Boulder: East European Monographs, Boulder, Distributed by Columbia University Press, New York. p. 105-192.
- (1998), *Kombi shqiptar në prag të mijëvjeçarit të tretë.*Tirana: Onufri. 47 pp.
- (1998), *Tri këngë zie për Kosovën. Novela.* Tirana: Onufri. 89 pp.
- (1999), *Ikja e shtergut.* Tirana: Onufri. 97 pp.
- (1999), *Qorrfermani.* Tirana: Onufri. 90 pp.
- (1999), *Ra ky mort e u pamë. Ditar për Kosovën, artikuj, letra.* Tirana: Onufri. 249 pp.
- (1999), *Vjedhja e gjumit mbretëror. Tregime.*Tirana: Onufri. 213 pp.
- (2000), *Kohë barbare. Nga Shqipëria në Kosovë. Biseda.* Tirana: Onufri. 298 pp.
- (2000), *Lulet e ftohta të Marsit. Roman.* Tirana: Onufri. 180 pp.
- (2000), *Three elegies for Kosovo.* Translated from the Albanian by Peter Constantine. London: Harvill Press. 87 pp.
- (2001), *Përballë pasqyrës së një gruaje: tre romane të shkurtër.* Tirana: Tirana, 156 pp.
- (2001), *Qyteti pa reklama. Roman.* Tirana: Onufri. 166 pp.
- (2001), *Unaza në kthetra. Sprova letrare, shkrime të ndryshme, intervista.* Tirana: Onufri. 175 pp.
- (2002a), *Jeta, loja dhe vdekja e Lul Mazrekut. Roman.* Tirana: Onufri. 246 pp.
- (2002b) *Spring flowers, spring frost.* Translated from the French by David Bellows. New York: Arcade Publ.

Bibliography

- (2002c), *Stinë e mërzitshme në Olimp. Tragjedia e Prometeut dhe e një grupi hyjnash në 14 dukje.* Tirana: Onufri. 200 pp.
- (2003a), *Ca pika shiu ranë mbi qelq. Dyzet poezi të zgjedhura.* Tirana: Onufri. 112 pp.
- (2003b), *Pasardhësi. Roman.* Tirana: Shtëpia Botuese 55. 163 pp.
- (2003c), *Vajza e Agamemnonit. Roman.* Tirana: Shtëpia Botuese 55. 114 pp.
- (2004) *Kristal: 60 poezi të zgjedhura.* Tirana: Onufri, 128 pp.
- (2004), *Poshtërimi në Ballkan. Sprovë.* Tirana: Onufri. 97 pp.

KADARE, Ismail & MALCOLM, Noel
    (1998), In the palace of nightmares, an exchange. in: *New York Review of Books,* New York, 45, 1 (January 15), p. 59-60.

KADARE, Ismail & RECATALÀ, Denis Fernàndez
    (2003), *Les quatres interprètes.* Paris: Editions Stock, 212 pp.
- (2004), *Katër përkthyesit.* Përktheu nga frëngjishtja Haki Shtalbi. Tirana: Onufri, 205 pp.

KALESHI, Hasan
    (1956), Prilog poznavanju arbanaške knjizevnosti iz vremena preporoda. Arbanaska knjizevnost na arapskom alfabetu. in: *Godišnjak Balkanološkog Instituta u Sarajevu,* Sarajevo, 1, p. 352-388.
- (1958), Mevludi kod Arbanasa. in: *Zbornik Filozofskog Fakulteta u Univerziteta Beogradu,* Belgrade, 4, p. 349-358.
- (1964), Arnavut edebiyatinda türk etkileri. in: *X. Türk Dil Kurultayinda Okunan Bilimsel Bildiriler 1963'ten ayribasim.* Ankara: Türk Tarih Kurumu. p. 61-74.
- (1966-1967), Albanska aljamiado knjizevnost. in: *Prilozi za orijentalnu filologiju,* Sarajevo, 16-17, p. 49-76.
- (1968), Sami Frashëri në letërsinë dhe filologjinë turke. in: *Gjurmime Albanologjike,* Prishtina, 1, p. 33-116.
- (1970), Le rôle de Chemseddin Sami Frachery dans la formation de deux langues littéraires, turc et albanais. in: *Balcanica* 1, p. 197-216.
- (1971), Burimet lidhur me studimin e Sami Frashërit. in: *Zbornik Filozofskog Fakulteta u Prištini,* Prishtina, 8, p. 35-54.
- (1975), 'Das türkische Vordringen auf dem Balkan und die Islamisierung. Faktoren für die Erhaltung der ethnischen und nationalen Existenz des albanischen Volkes,' in: *Südeuropa unter dem Halbmond. Prof. Georg Stadtmüller zum 65. Geburtstag gewidmet.* Peter Bartl & Horst Glassl (ed.). Munich, p. 125-138.
- (1991), *Kontributi i shqiptarëve në diturité islame.* Prizren, reprint Riyadh, 1992. 112 pp.

KALLAJXHI, Xhevat
    (1964), *Bektashizmi dhe teqeja shqiptare n'Amerikë.* Parathënie e Hirësisë së Tij Baba Rexhebit. E boton Teqeja me rastin e 10-vjetorit të themelimit të saj. Detroit: s.e. 75 pp.

Bibliography

KAMSI, Kolë
(1956), Frangu i Bardhë (1606-1643). in: *Buletin për Shkencat Shoqërore,* Tirana, 4, p. 104-114.

KAMSI, Vili (= KAMSI, Willy)
(1962), Cuneus Prophetarum i Pjetër Bogdanit. Të dhëna rreth botimit të veprës. in: *Shkodra,* Shkodra, 1, p. 157-168.
- (1997), Gjon Buzuku dhe Koncili i Trentit. in: BECI, Bahri, RRAHMANI, Zejnullah, YLLI, Xhelal (ed.), *Seminari XVII ndërkombëtar për gjuhën, letërsinë dhe kulturën shqiptare. Përmbledhje e ligjëratave, referimeve, kumtesave dhe e diskutimeve.* Tiranë 16-31 gusht 1995. Akademia e Shkencave, Instituti i Gjuhësisë dhe Letërsisë. Universiteti i Prishtinës, Fakulteti i Filologjisë (Tirana: Eurorilindja). p. 381-389.

KARJAGDIU, Abdullah
(1993), *Me Konicën në Evropë. 'Albania' dhe sensibilizimi i çështjes shqiptare në kapërcyellin e shek. XX.* Tirana: Lidhja e Shkrimtarëve. 227 pp.

KASTRATI, Jup
(1962), *Jeronim De Rada. Jeta dhe veprat.* Tirana: Naim Frashëri, reprint 1979. 72 pp.
- (1975), Pashko Vasa. in: *Nëntori,* Tirana, 9, p. 164-180.
- (1995), *Faik Konica. Monografi.* New York: Gjonlekaj Publ. 236 pp.
- (2000), *Historia e Albanologjisë (1497-1997). Vëllimi i parë (1497-1853).* Tirana: Argeta LMG. 832 pp.
- (2003), *Studime për De Radën.* Botohet me rastin e 100 vjetorit të vdekjes së De Radës. New York: Gjonlekaj Publishing Company, 375 pp.

KELMENDI, Shpëtim (ed.)
(2004), *Antologji e prozës bashkëkohore shqiptare.* Tirana: Ombra GVG. 404 pp.

KHAIR, Antoine A.
(1973), *Le moutaçarrifat du Mont-Liban.* Beirut: Université Libanaise. 195 pp.

KISSLING, Hans-Joachim
(1962), 'Zur Frage der Anfänge des Bektašitums in Albanien,' in *Oriens, Journal of the International Society for Oriental Research,* Leiden, 15, p. 281-286.

KLOSI, Ardian
(1991), *Mythologie am Werk: Kazantzakis, Andrić, Kadare. Eine vergleichende Untersuchung am besonderen Beispiel des Bauopfermotivs.* Slavistische Beiträge 227. Munich: Sagner. 183 pp.

KOÇA, Vangjel
(1999), *Në udhën e shqiptarizmës.* Pergatitur nga Ndriçim Kulla. Tirana: Phoenix. 300 pp.

KODRA, Klara
(1970), Zef Serembeja dhe folklori. in: *Studime filologjike,* Tirana, 2, p. 117-130.
- (1971), Vlera ideo-artistike e poezisë së Zef Serembes. in: *Studime filologjike,* Tirana, 1, p. 29-55.

- (1975), *Vepra poetike e Zef Serembes. Monografi.* Tirana: Naim Frashëri. 190 pp.
- (1987), Poezia e F. A. Santorit. in: *Studime filologjike,* Tirana, 1, p. 175-200.
- (1988), *Poezia e De Radës.* Tirana: Akademia e Shkencave. 311 pp.
- (1991a), Santori - poet dramatik dhe humorist. in: *Studime filologjike,* Tirana, 2, p. 5-16.
- (1991b), Santori, poète de la satire et de l'humour. in: *Studia albanica,* Tirana, 1-2. p. 109-122.
- (1996), Santori fabulist. in: *Studime filologjike,* Tirana, 1-4, p. 19-32.
- (1997), 'I Canti di Milosao,' un'opera poetica profondamente albanese e ad un tempo europea. in: *Albanistica. Novantasette.* A cura di Italo Costante Fortino. Naples: Istituto Universitario Orientale. p. 269-278.
- (2000), *Tipologjia e poemës arbëreshe.* Tirana: Shkenca. 130 pp.

KODRA, Masar
- (1989), *Fan Noli në rrjedhat politike të shoqërisë shqiptare (1905- 1945).* Prishtina: Rilindja. 219 pp.

KODRA, Ziaudin
- (1954), Dy vjersha lirike fort të rralla të Francesk Anton Santorit. in: *Nëndori,* Tirana, 7, p. 69-73.

KOKALARI, Musine
- (1941), *Naim Frashëri (1846-1900).* Tesi di laurea in Letteratura Albanese. Anno Accademico 1940-1941. R. Università degli Studi di Roma. Facoltà di Belle Lettere. Rome. 148 pp.
- (1941?), *Siç më thotë nënua plake.* Tirana: Gutenberg, s.a. reprint Livonia MI, 1984; Prishtina: Buzuku 1996. 80 pp.
- (1944), *Rreth vatrës.* Tirana: Mesagjeritë shqiptare. 144 pp.
- (1944), *...sa u-tunt jeta.* Tirana: Nikaj. reprint Tirana 1995. 302 + xlvi pp.
- (2000), *Si lindi Partia Socialdemokrate. Artikuj, shrime, esse, kujtime.* Përgatitur dhe botuar nën kujdesin e Platon Salim Kokalarit. Tirana: Naim Frashëri. 128 pp.
- (2004), *Vepra.* Prishtina: Faik Konica. 439 pp.

KOKOJKA, Mali
- cf. FRASHËRI, Mid'hat bey

KOLA, Gjovalin
- (1997), *Ndoc Nikaj dhe burimet e romanit shqip.* Tirana: Apollonia. 149 pp.

KOLEVICA, Petraq
- (1988), Entretiens avec Lasgush Poradeci. Extraits. in: *Lettres Albanaises,* Tirana, 1, p. 142-163.
- (1992), *Lasgushi më ka thënë. Shënime nga bisedat me Lasgush Poradecin.* Tirana: 8 Nëntori. 240 pp.
- (1997), *Me Mitrushin.* Tirana: Toena. 95 pp
- (2002), *Autobiografia e Ismail Kadaresë në vargje: studim kritik.* Tirana: Marin Barleti, 95 pp.

KOLIQI, Ernest
- (1924), *Kushtrimi i Skanderbeut. Poemth dramatik.* Tirana: Nikaj. 41 pp.

- (1929), *Hija e maleve. Novela.* Zadar: E. De Schonfeld, reprint Livonia MI 1984, Shkodra 1999. 208 pp.
- (1932), *Poetët e mëdhej t'Italis. Vellim i parë. Me një parathënje nga At Gjergj Fishta.* Tirana: Nikaj. 280 pp.
- (1933), *Gjurmat e stinve.* Tirana: Shkodra. 92 pp.
- (1935), *Tregtar flamujsh.* Tirana. reprint Harper Woods MI 1988, Prishtina 1991, Shkodra 2000) 216 pp.
- (1936), *Poetët e mëdhej t'Italis. Vellim i dytë.* Tirana: Nikaj 241 pp.
- (1937), *Epica popolare albanese. Tesi di laurea in lingua e letteratura albanese di Ernesto Koliqi.* Relatore: Prof. Carlo Tagliavini. Padua: Gruppo universitario fascista. 221 pp.
- (1941), *Symfonija e shqipevet.* Tirana. reprint Rome 1970. 42 pp.
- (1957), *Poesia popolare albanese a cura di Ernesto Koliqi. Vjerrsha popullore shqipe.* Edizioni Fussi. Florence: Casa Editrice Sansoni, reprint 1986? 111 pp.
- (1959), *Kangjelet e Rilindjes. I canti della Riniscita. Poemth me përkëthim italisht.* Rome: Shêjzat / Le Pleiadi. 85 pp.
- (1960), *Shija e bukës së mbrûme. Rromanx.* Rome: Shêjzat / Le Pleiadi. reprint: Shkodra: Camaj-Pipa 1996. 173 pp.
- (1962), Giuseppe Schirò, poeta della fratellanza Pan-Albanese. in: *Shêjzat / Le Pleiadi,* Rome 6, Nr. 3-4, p. 118-137.
- (1963a), *Antologia della lirica albanese.* Versioni e note a cura di Ernesto Koliqi. Milan: All' Insegna del Pesce d'Oro. 318 pp.
- (1963b), *Pasqyrat e Narçizit.* Rome: Shêjzat / Le Pleiadi. reprint Shkodra 2001. 32 pp.
- (1967), Faik Konica. in: *Shêjzat / Le Pleiadi,* Rome, 11. 5-8, p. 240-246.
- (1972a), *Saggi di letteratura albanese.* Studi albanesi. Studi i testi 5. Florence: Olschki. 260 pp.
- (1972b), *The symphony of eagles. Translated and with an introduction by Anesti Andrea.* Rome: Shêjzat / Le Pleiadi. 21 pp.
- (1995), *Ernest Koliqi. 1903-1975. Simpozium me rastin e 20 vjetorit të vdekjes së Koliqit Shkodër, 16 qershor 1995.* Studime Shqiptare 3. Shkodra: USH Luigj Gurakuqi. Departamenti i Letërsisë. 103 pp.
- (1995), *Hanë gjaku. Tregime dhe novela të zgjedhura.* Tirana: Apollonia. 200 pp.
- (1996), *Vepra 1, 2.* Prishtina: Rilindja. 281 + 474 pp.
- (2001), *Pasqyrat e Narçizit. Tregime.* Shkodra: Camaj-Pipa. 68 pp.
- (2003), *Vepra, 1-6.* Prishtina: Faik Konica, 279, 407, 295, 355, 587, 652 pp.

KOLIQI, Ernest (ed.)
- (1941), *Gjergj Fishta. Nën kujdesin e revistës 'Shkëndija'.* Tirana: Luarasi, s.a. [1941?]) 185 pp.

KONGOLI, Fatos
- (1978), *Tregime.* Tirana: Naim Frashëri. 247 pp.
- (1992), *I humburi. Roman.* Tirana: Dituria. 211 pp.
- (1994), *Kufoma. Roman.* Tirana: MÇM. 210 pp.

- (1997), *Le paumé*. Traduit de l'albanais par Christiane Montécot et Edmond Tupja. Paris: Rivages. 187 pp.
- (1998), *L'ombre de l'autre*. Traduit de l'albanais par Edmond Tupja. Paris: Rivages. 258 pp.
- (1999), *Dragoi i fildishtë*. Tirana: Çabej. 200 pp.
- (2000). *Le dragon d'ivoire*. Roman traduit de l'albanais par Edmond Tupja. Paris: Rivages. 257 pp.
- (2002), *Le rêve de Damoclès*. Roman traduit de l'albanais par Edmond Tupja. Paris: Rivages 280 pp.
- (2003), *Die albanische Braut*. Roman. Aus dem Albanischen von Joachim Röhm. Frankfurt: Fischer Taschenbuch Verlag, 240 pp.
- (2003), *Lëkura e qenit*. Roman. Tirana: Toena, 288 pp.
- (2005), *Peau de chien*. Roman traduit de l'albanais par Edmond Tupja. Paris: Rivages. 262 pp.

KONITZA, Faik (= KONICA, Faik)
- (1915), *L'Allemagne et l'Albanie. Lettre ouverte à M. le professeur Dr. Hans Delbrück*. Lausanne. 15 pp.
- (1918), *The Albanian question*. London: Williams, Lea & Co. 27 pp.
- (1924), Dr. Gjëlpëra zbulon rënjët e dramës së Mamurrasit. Prallë. in: *Dielli*, Boston, from 16.08.1924.
- (1924), *Në hien e hurmave. Pralla t'Arabisë*. I shqipërój F.K. Shtypur me Harxhet e Përkthénjësit. Boston: s.e. reprint Tirana 2000. 80 pp.
- (1929), Shqiperia si m'u-duk. serialized in: *Dielli*, Boston.
- (1957), *Albania. The rock garden of southeastern Europe and other essays*. Edited and amplified by Gerim M. Panarity, with an introduction by Fan Noli. Boston: Vatra. 175 pp.
- (1990), *Shqipëria. Kopshti shkëmbor i Evropës juglindore*. Përktheu nga anglishtja Prof. Dr. Abdullah Karagdiu. Prishtina: Buzuku. 195 pp.
- (1993a), *Shqipëria. Kopshti shkëmbor i Evropës juglindore*. E përktheu nga origjinali anglisht Ferdinand Leka. Tirana: Marin Barleti. 201 pp.
- (1993b), *Vepra*. Mbledhur dhe përgatitur nga N. Jorgaqi dhe Xh. Lloshi. Tirana: Naim Frashëri. 536 pp.
- (1995), *Vepra 1-2*. Prishtina: Rilindja. 359 + 316 pp.
- (1998), *Vepra e zgjedhur. Katër përrallat e Zullulandit, Shqipëria si m'u duk, Doktor Gjëlpera zbulon rrënjët e dramës së Mamurrasit*. Tirana: Naim Frashëri. 143 pp.
- (2000), *Selected correspondence 1896-1942. Edited by Bejtullah Destani. Introduction by Robert Elsie*. London: The Centre for Albanian Studies. 185 pp.
- (2001) *Vepra 1-5*. Zgjedhur e përgatitur nga Prof. Nasho Jorgaqi. Tirana: Dudaj, Tiranë. 403, 430, 456, 292, 460 pp.

KONUSHEVCI, Abdullah
- (1987), *Loja e strucit*. Prishtina: Rilindja, 83 pp.
- (1990), *Të qenët të mosqenë*. Prishtina: Rilindja, 71 pp.
- (2002), *Pikat AD. Poezi*. Prishtina: Papyrus, 98 pp.

KOSTA, Koço
  (1986), Ata të dy e të tjerë. Novelë. in: *Nëntori,* Tirana, 4, p. 112-162; 5,
  p. 107-149. reprint as *Ata të dy e të tjerë. Novelë... e thyer.* Tirana:
  Enciklopedike. 1994. 155 pp.

KOSTALLARI, Androkli, MANSAKU, Seit, YLLI, Xhelal (ed.)
  (1991), *Pjetër Bogdani dhe vepra e tij.* Tirana: Akademia e Shkencave.
  172 pp.

KRAJA, Mehmet
- (2004), *Edhe të çmendurit fluturojnë. Roman.* Tirana: Onufri, 174 pp.

KRAJA, Musa
  (1973), *Migjeni mësues.*Tirana: 8 Nëntori. 127 pp.

KRASNIQI, Gazmend
  (2002), *Skodrinon.* Botimi i ripunuar dhe i plotësuar. Shkodra: Camaj-Pipa,
  60 pp.
- (2003), *Alfabeti i fshehtë. Tregime.* Tirana: s.e. 150 pp.
- (2003), *Fund i botës. Një verë në Paris.* Shkodra: Camaj-Pipa, 180 pp.

KRASNIQI, Gazmend (ed.)
  (2003), *Sprovë antologjike.* Tirana: Naim Frashëri, 160 pp.

KRASNIQI, Nysret
  (2003), *Rrëfimi dhe shkrimi: Lahuta e Malcís e Gjergj Fishtës.* Prishtina:
  Asociacioni për Integrime Kulturore dhe Demokratike, 88 pp.

KUÇUKU, Bashkim
  (2001), *Kadare në gjuhët e botës. Ismail Kadare në tridhjetë e tri gjuhë.*
  Tirana. Onufri. 476 pp.

KUTELI, Mitrush (= PASKO, Dhimitër)
- (1938a), *Nete shqipëtare. Rrëfime.* Bucharest: Albania. reprint: Tirana 1944.
  177 pp.
- (1938b), Poetika e Lasgush Poradeci-t. in: *Përpjekja shqiptare,* Tirana, 3 (17),
  p. 243-252.
- (1943), *Ago Jakupi e të tjera rrëfime.* Tirana: Botim' i Autorit. 157 pp.
- (1944), *Kapedan Gardani me shokë. Novela edhe pralla.* E këtheu shqip M.
  K. Letërsi Rumune. M. Beza, L. Rebreanu, I. Creanga, P. Ispirescu. Tirana:
  Luarasi. 87 pp.
- (1944), *Kapllan Aga i Shaban Shpatës. Rrëfime - Rrëfenja.* Tirana: Botim' i
  autorit. 111 pp.
- (1944), *Këngë e brithma nga qyteti i djegur.* I mblodhi M. Kuteli. Tirana:
  Botim i mbledhësit. 148 pp.
- (1944), *Shënime letrare.* Tirana: Shtypshkronja e shtetit. 179 pp.
- (1944), *Sulm e lotë. Me një fjalë prej Dr. Pas.* Tirana: Nikaj. repirnt Prishtina
  1997. 79 pp.
- (1945), Fan Noli, shqipëronjës dhe kritik letrar. in: *Bota e re,* Tirana, 1,
  p. 17-22.
  (1965), *Tregime të moçme shqiptare.* Tirana. Naim Frashëri. 1987, 1998)
  254 pp.

- (1972), *Tregime të zgjedhura. Vjeshta e Xheladin beut dhe rrëfime të tjera.* Tirana: Naim Frashëri. 355 pp.
- (1979), *Poemë kosovar.* Ribot. P. Ktona New York: Baldwin, vi + 69 pp.
- (1989), *Vepra letrare 1-5.* Tirana: Naim Frashëri.
- (1992), *L'autunno di Geladyn Bey.* Traduzione dall'albanese Eugenio Scalabrino. Lecce: Argo. 71 pp.
- (1993), *Fiabe e leggende albanesi.* Traduzione Eugenio Scalambrino. Milan: Rusconi.185 pp.
- (1995), *El otoño de Xheladin Bey y otros relatos.* Selección, presentación y traducción del albanés de Ramón Sánchez Lizarralde. Guadarrama: Ediciones del Oriente y del Mediterráneo, 256 pp.
- (2001), *Prozë dhe vargje të zgjedhura, 1.* Tirana: Mitrush Kuteli. 296 pp.

KUTELI, Mitrush (ed.)
- (1943), *Fan S. Noli. Mall e brengë. Vjersha. Me një vështrim kritik prej Mitrush Kuteli-t.* Tirana: Botim' i Mitrush Kutelit. 94 pp.

KYÇYKU, Ardian Christian (= KUCIUK, Ardian-Christian)
- (2003), *Un alfabet al poeziei albaneze. Antologia 101 autori.* Prezentare, traducere, aparat critic de Ardian-Christian Kuciuk. Bucharest: Privirea, 181 pp.
- (2003), *Kristali dhe hienat. Roman.* Prishtina: Buzuku, 150 pp.
- (2004), *Sy. Roman.* Bucharest: Arvin Press, 138 pp.

KYÇYKU, Muhamet (= ÇAMI, Muhamet)
- (1888), *Erveheja vjershuarë prej Muhamet Çamit, mbaruarë prej Hajdar Argjirokastritit edhe qëruarë fjalët' e huaja prej I. Vretosë.* Bucharest: Dituri, Bucharest.
- (1992), *Jusufi e Zylejhaja. Dashuri përvëluese.* Tirana: Hasan Tahsini. 136 pp.
- (2002), *Muhamet Çami. Jeta dhe vepra. Erveheja.* Skopje: Vatra, 74 pp.

LA PIANA, Marco
- (1912), *Il catechismo albanese di Luca Matranga (1592), da un manoscritto Vaticano.* Grottaferrata: Tip. Italo-Orientale S. Nilo. 53 pp.
- (1912), Il catechismo albanese di Luca Matranga (1592), da un manoscritto Vaticano. in: *Roma e l'Oriente,* 2, vol. 3, p. 271, 395-411; vol. 4, p. 23-32, 151-160, 303-314.

LACAJ, Henrik
- (1959), Luigj Gurakuqi (1879-1925), shënime mbi jetën dhe veprën e tij letrare. in: *Buletin i Universitetit Shtetëror të Tiranës. Seria Shkencat Shoqërore,* Tirana, 4, p. 162-176.
- (1963), Dom Ndoc Nikaj (1864-1951). Shënime mbi jetën dhe veprat. in: *Buletin i Universitetit Shtetëror të Tiranës. Seria Shkencat Shoqërore,* Tirana, 1, p. 184-197.

LAÇO, Teodor
- (2003), *Trokitje në shpirt. Tregime.* Tirana: Mësonjëtorja, 242 pp.

LAHOLLI, Ferdinand
- (2003), *Antologji e poezisë moderne shqipe. Zgjodhi dhe përktheu nga shqipja në gjermanisht Ferdinand Laholli. Anthologie der modernen albanischen*

Lyrik. Ausgewählt und aus dem Albanischen übersetzt von Ferdinand Laholli. Holzminden: Doruntina, 435 pp.

LALAJ, Meri

    (1995), *Lasgushi në Pogradec. Ditar.* Elbasan: Onufri. 194 pp.

LAMBERTZ, Maximilian

    (1943), Das Werden der albanischen Literatur. in: *Leipziger Vierteljahrsschrift für Südosteuropa,* Leipzig, 7, p. 160-174

-    (1948), *Albanisches Lesebuch mit Einführung in die albanische Sprache. I. Teil: Grammatik und albanische Texte. II. Teil: Texte in deutscher Übersetzung.* Leipzig: Harrassowitz. 387 + 302 pp.

-    (1949), *Gjergj Fishta und das albanische Heldenepos Lahuta e Malcís, Laute des Hochlandes. Eine Einführung in die albanische Sagenwelt.* Leipzig: Harrassowitz. 76 pp.

-    (1956a), *Albanien erzählt. Ein Einblick in die albanische Literatur.* Übersetzt und herausgegeben. Literatur der Volksdemokratien. Berlin: Volk und Welt. 191 pp.

-    (1956b), Giulio Variboba. in: *Zeitschrift für Vergleichende Sprachforschung,* Göttingen, 74, p. 45-122, 185-224.

    (1958), Zur albanischen Literaturgeschichte. Forschungsbericht. in: *Südost-Forschungen,* Munich, 17, p. 237-243.

-    (1960), Das Drama im albanischen Theater von heute. in: *Südost-Forschungen,* Munich, 19, p. 316-325.

LAMPROS, Spyridôn P.

    (1906), To Christos anestê albanisti. in: *Neos Hellênomnêmôn. Trimêniaion periodikon syggramma,* Athens 3, p. 481-482.

LANKSCH, Hans-Joachim

    (1992), Von Felsen, Wölfen und Flüssen. Dichtung aus Kosova. in: *Literatur und Kritik,* Salzburg, September 1992, 267/268, p. 49-55.

-    (1994), Die einen... und die anderen... Albanische Lyrik nach 1945. in: *Neue Literatur, Zeitschrift für Querverbindungen,* Bucharest, 3, 1994. Supplement Dokumentationen. 26 pp.

-    (2000), Bin Kristall zersprungen. Albanische Lyrik und Prosa aus der Schweiz. in: *Metaphorà, Zeitschrift für Literatur und Übertragung,* Munich, 6, March 2000. p. 1-213.

LAUDONE, Cosmo

    (1981), *Omaggio di Mbuzati (S. Giorgio Albanese) al suo cittadino (Giulio Variboba sacerdote italo-greco) nel 190 anniversario della morte.* Grottaferrata. 82 pp.

LEKA, Vangjel

    (1999), *La poudrerie.* Roman traduit de l'albanais par Anila Poher-Vaso et Catherine Leka. Avant-propos d'Ismaïl Kadaré. Paris: La différence. 359 pp.

LEMAHIEU, Daniel (ed.)

    (2004), *Voyage en Unmikistan. Udhëtim në Unmikistan.* Doruntina Basha, Ilirjan Bezhani, Visar Fejzullahu, Mentor Haliti, Sabri Hamiti, Jeton Neziraj, Kujtim Paçaku & Albena Reshitaj. Sous la direction de Daniel Lemahieu, avec la collaboration de Dominique Dolmieu et Véronique Marco. Traduction franco-albanaise d'Irena Rambi, avec la collaboration de Sophie Daull. Préface de Dominique Dolmieu. Paris: Editions L'Espace d'un Instant, 117 pp.

LETTS, Malcolm Henry Ikin

(1946), *The pilgrimage of Arnold von Harff, knight, from Cologne, through Italy, Syria, Egypt, Arabia, Ethiopia, Nubia, Palestine, Turkey, France and Spain, which he accomplished in the years 1496 to 1499.* Translated from the German and edited with notes and an introduction by Malcolm Letts. Works issued by the Hakluyt Society. Second series, No. XCIV. London: Hakluyt Society, reprint 1967. 325 pp.

LEVEND, Agâh Sirri

(1969), *Şemsettin Sami.* Türk Dil Kurumu Tanitma Yayinlari. Türk Diline Emek Verenler Dizisi 13. Ankara: Ankara Üniversitesi Basimevi. 216 pp.

LEVY, Michele

(2001), Brotherly wounds. Representations of Balkan conflict in contemporary Balkan literature. in: *World Literature Today,* Norman OK, 75. 1 (Winter 2001), p. 66-75.

LIBRANDI, Vincenzo

(1897), *Grammatica albanese con le poesie rare di Variboba.* Milan. Hoepli. reprint 1928. 198 pp.

LIÇO, Eduard, ed. (= LICHO, Edward)

(1982), *Flamurtar i kombit. Theofan S. Noli 1882-1982. Seminar studimesh me rastin e njëqindvjetorit të lindjes së Theofan S. Nolit.* Worcester MA: Vatra. reprint 1984. 177 pp.

LIZARRALDE, Ramón Sánchez

(2004), *Problemas de iluminación. Antologia poética de Agron Tufa, Ervin Hatibi y Gentian Çoçoli.* Trad. por Sánchez Lizarralde. Malaga: Maremoto.

- (2004), *La prueba de la tierra. Prova e tokës. Tres jóvenes poetas albaneses.* Editión y traducción de Ramón Sánchez Lizarralde. Edición bilingue. Agron Tufa, Ervin Hativi, Gentian Çoçoli. Málaga: Maremoto. 156 pp.

LLESHANAKU, Luljeta

(2002), *Fresco. Selected poetry of Luljeta Lleshanaku.* Edited with an afterworrd by Henry Israeli. Introduction by Peter Constantine. Translated, with Henry Israeli and Joanna Goodman, by Ukzenel Buçpapa, Noci Deda, Alban Kupi, Albana Lleshanaku, Lluka Qafoku, Shpresa Qatipi, Qazim Sheme, Daniel Weissbort; and the author. New York: New Directions. 80 pp.

LLUNJI, Ali

(1990), *Migjeni. Filiz i epokës sonë (Kujtime).* Prishtina: Enti i teksteve. 146 pp.

LUBONJA, Fatos

(2004), *Intervista sull' Albania. Dalle carceri di Enver Hoxha al liberalismo selvaggio.* A cura di Claudio Dazzochio. Prefazione di Dacia Maraini. Bologna: Il Ponto, 176 pp.

LUBONJA, Fatos & HODGSON, John

    (1997), *Përpjekja / Endeavour. Writing from Albania's critical quarterly.* Translated by John Hodgson. Tirana: Përpjekja. 154 pp.

MAKSUTOVICI, Cristia

    (1995), *Confluente culturale romanoalbaneze.* Cuvint inainte de N. Ciachir. Bucharest: Kriterion, 191 pp.

MAKSUTOVICI, Gelcu

    (1992), *Istoria comunității albaneze din România.* Bucharest: Kriterion, 103 pp.

-    (1995), *Despre Albania și albanesi.* Volum aparut cu ocazia aniversării a 400 de ani de atestare documentara albanezilor pe teritorul României. Bucharest: Ararat, 287 pp.

MALCOLM, Noel

    (1998), *Kosovo, a short history.* London: MacMillan. 491 pp.

MALËSHOVA, Sejfulla (= KODRA, Lame)

    (1945), *Vjersha.* Tirana. reprint 1994. 71 pp.

-    (1998), *Lame Kodra. Vepra letrare. 1-3.* Tirana: Argeta. 199, 321, 495 pp

MALOKU, Krist

    (1938), A asht poet Lasgush Poradeci? in: *Përpjekja shqiptare,* Tirana 3 (18), p. 333-350.

MANDALÀ, Matteo

    (1990), *La diaspora e il ritorno. Mito, storia, cultura tradizionale nell'opera di Giuseppe Schirò.* Istituto di Lingua e Letteratura Albanese e Centro Internazionale di Studi Albanesi. Palermo: Università di Palermo. 500 pp.

-    (1992), L'opera di Nicolò Chetta e la cultura albanologica italo-albanese nel XVIII secolo. in: *Dialetti italo-albanesi e letteratura. Atti del XV congresso internazionale di studi albanesi, Palermo, 24-28 novembre 1989.* A cura di Antonino Guzzetta. Palermo: Istituto di Lingua e Letteratura Albanese. Facoltà di Lettere e Filosofia di Palermo. p. 87-149.

-    (2000), Jeta dhe vepra e Lekë Matrëngës. in: *Studime filologjike,* Tirana, 1-2, p. 79-116.

-    (2003), *Nicolò Chetta. Nel bicentenario (1803-2003).* Albanica 14. Collana di albanistica fondata da Antonino Guzzetta, diretta da Matteo Mandalà. Palermo: A.C. Mirror, 126 pp.

MANN Stuart E.

    (1955), *Albanian literature. An outline of prose, poetry and drama.* London: Quaritch. 121 pp.

MARCHIANÒ, Michele

    (1902), *L'Albania e l'opera di Girolamo De Rada.* Trani: V. Vecchi, reprint Sala Bolognese: Arnaldo Forni 1979. 380 pp.

-    (1903), *Poemi albanesi di Girolamo de Rada. Scelti, tradotti e illustrati con prefazione.* Trani: V. Vecchi. 327 pp.

-    (1906a), *Canto inedito di Girolamo de Rada nella traduzione juxtalineare italiana.* Publicato con prefazione ed illustrazione da Michele Marchianò. Foggia: Tip. Francesco Paolo de Nido. 54 pp.

- (1906b), *La Rondinella. Carme nuziale albanese inedito con parafrasi pubblicato da un manoscritto del secolo XVIII.* Con prefazione e traduzione justalineare. Foggia: Tip. Francesco Paolo de Nido. 38 pp.
- (1908a), *Canti popolari albanesi delle colonie d'Italia. Publicati da un manoscritto della prima metà del secolo XVIII con traduzione iuxtalineare, introduzione, note e un facsimile in autotipia de Michele Marchianò.* Foggia: Francesco Paolo de Nido, reprint Sala Bolognese: Arnaldo Forni Editore 1986. lxx + 94 pp.
- (1908b), *Poesie sacre albanesi. Con parafrasi italiana e dialettale la più parte inedite, pubblicate da un codice manoscritto della 1ª metà del sec. XVIII, con traduzione, introduzione, note e facsimile... parte 1.* Naples: R. Università.143 pp.
- (1909), *Un autografo inedito del poeta albanese Girolamo de Rada intorno la sua vita.* Trani: V. Vecchi. 34 pp.

MARINAJ, Gjekë
    (2000) *Infinit. Poezi.* Richardson Texas: Marinaj, 128 pp.

MARKO, Petro
    (1958), *Hasta la vista.* Tirana: Ndërm. Shtetërore e Botimeve. reprint Prishtina 1972, 1987, Tirana 1991) 470 pp.
- (1960), *Qyteti i fundit. Roman.* Tirana: Naim Frashëri, reprint Prishtina 1972, Tirana 2000. 380 pp.
- (1964), *Rrugë pa rrugë. Tregime dhe skica.* Tirana: Naim Frashëri. 204 pp.
- (1973), *Një emër në katër rrugë.* Tirana: Naim Frashëri.
- (1989), *Nata e Ustikës. Roman* Tirana: Naim Frashëri. 360 pp.
- (2002), *Një natë dhe dy agime. Roman.* Tirana: Omsca-1, 562 pp.
- (2002), *Ultimatumi. Roman.* Tirana: Omsca-1, 308 pp.
- (2003), *Tregime të zgjedhura.* Tirana: Omsca-1, 342 pp.

MARLEKAJ, Luigj
    (1989), *Pietro Bogdano e l'Albania del suo tempo con la riproduzione fotografica di centotrentadue documenti.* Palo del Colle BA: Liantonio Editrice. 729 pp.

MARQUET, Odette
    (1989), Bogdani në dritën e disa dokumenteve të rishqyrtuara. in: *Gjurmime albanologjike, seria e shkencave filologjike,* Prishtina, 19, p. 119-126.
- (1991), Bogdani à la lumière des documents réexaminés. in: *Zeitschrift für Balkanologie,* Berlin, 27.1, p. 26-44.

MARQUET, Odette (ed.)
    (1997), *Pjetër Bogdani. Letra dhe dokumente. Nga Arkivi i Kongregatës 'de Propaganda Fide' si dhe nga Arkivat Sekrete të Vatikanit.* Shkodra: At Gjergj Fishta. 580 pp.

MATO, Tomi
    (2000), *Të vërteta të pathëna për Lasgushin.* Tirana: Gazeta 55. 208 pp

MATOSHI, Hysen
    (2000), *Poezia e Lasgush Poradecit në kontekstin e poezisë evropane.* Prishtina: Instituti Albanologjik. 196 pp.

MATRËNGA, Lekë (= MATRANGA, Luca)

  (1592), *Embsuame e chraesterae. Baeaera per tae Vrtaenae Atae Ladesmae sciochiaeriet Iesusit.* E prierrae laetireiet mbae gluchae tae arbaeresciae paer Lecae Matraengnae. Imbsuam i Cullegit Graec tae Romaesae. Dottrina Christiana. Composta dal Reuerendo P. Dottor Ledesma della Compagnia di Giesù. Tradotta di lingua Italiana nell'Albanese per Luca Matranga alumno del Collegio Greco in Roma. Rome: Guglielmo Facciotto. 28 pp.

MEDIUS, Thomas (= DE MEZZO, Tommaso)

  (1483), *Thomae Medii, patricii veneti. Fabella Epirota.* Venice: Bernardinus Celerius, reprint Leipzig 1514, Oppenheim 1516, Mainz 1547.

MEHMETI, Din

  (2002), *Klithmë është emri im. Poezi të zgjedhura.* Zgjodhi e përgatiti Agim Vinca. Tirana: Toena, 308 pp.

- (2004), *Antologjia personale. Poezi.* Tirana: Ora, 178 pp.

MEHMETI, Kim

  (1998), *Fshati i fëmijve të mallkuar. Roman.* Peja: Dukagjini, 144 pp.

- (2000), *Fshati pa varreza.* Peja: Dukagjini, 191 pp.

- (2002), *Atje dhe dikur.* Peja: Dukagjini, 156 pp.

- (2002), *Das Dorf der verfluchten Kinder. Roman.* Aus dem Albanischen von Joachim Röhm. Klagenfurt: Drava Verlag, 160 pp.

- (2004), *Ritet e Nishanes. Roman.* Peja: Dukagjini, 184 pp.

MEKULI, Esad

  (1955), *Për ty.* Prishtina: Mustafa Bakija. reprint 1963, 1967. 100 pp.

- (1989), *Drita që nuk shuhet.* Prishtina: Rilindja. 96 pp.

MIGJENI (= NIKOLLA, Millosh Gjergj)

  (1936), *Vargjet e lira.* Tirana: Gutenberg, Tirana. 84 pp.

- (1944), *Vargjet e lira.* Tirana: Ismail Mal' Osmani. 94 pp.

- (1957), *Veprat. Mbledhur dhe përgatitur nga Skënder Luarasi.* Tirana: Naim Frashëri.

- (1961), *Oeuvres choisies.* Comité des relations culturelles avec l'Etranger. Unesco. Traduit de l'albanais par K. Luka. Introduction par Skender Luarasi. Paris: UNESCO.

- (1963), *Selected works [Selected Albanian songs and sketches].* Translated by Ali Cungu. Tirana: Naim Frashëri. 143 pp.

- (1965), *Poèmes.* Autours du monde. Paris: Pierre Seghers. 82 pp.

- (1980), *Vepra 1-4.* Botim i dytë. Prishtina: Rilindja.

- (1987), *Freie Verse. Gedichte aus Albanien übertragen von Robert Elsie.* Idstein: Schulz-Kirchner. 70 pp.

- (1988), *Vepra.* Tirana: Naim Frashëri. 448 pp.

- (1989), *Der Selbstmord des Sperlings und andere Prosaskizzen.* Aus dem Albanischen von Joachim Röhm. Karlsruhe: Info-Verlag. 80 pp.

- (1990), *Chroniques d'une ville du Nord, précédé de: L'irruption de Migjeni dans la littérature albanaise par Ismaïl Kadaré.* Traduit de l'albanais par Jusuf Vrioni. Paris: Fayard, 298 pp.

- (1991), *Free verse. Translated from Albanian by Robert Elsie.* Tirana: 8 Nëntori. 117 pp.
- (2000), *Free Verse. A bilingual edition translated from the Albanian and introduced by Robert Elsie.* Dukagjini Balkan Books. Peja: Dukagjini. 143 pp.
- (2002), *Vepra.* Mbledhur dhe redaktuar nga Skënder Luarasi. Tirana: CetisTirana, 304 pp.

MINISCI, Teodoro
  (1959), La poesia di Giulio Variboba. in: *Shêjzat / Le Pleiadi,* Rome, 3-4, p. 89-95.

MITCHELL, Anne-Marie
  (1990), *Un rhapsode albanais: Ismail Kadaré.* Marseille: Temps parallèle. 113 pp.

MJEDA, Ndre
  (1887), *Scahiri Elierz Do beita ci kaa cit N.M. i S.J. Vaji i Bylbylit.* Shkodra: Sctyp. e Zojs zanun pa kurr lece. 32 pp.
- (1888), *Jeta e sceitit sc' Gnon Berchmans, t' scocnis Jezu Krisctit, kthye sccyp prei Nnrek Mjeds gezuitit sckodran.* Rome: Propaganda Fide. 151 pp.
- (1892), *T' perghjamit e zojs bêkume kththye sccyp, prej Nnrek Mdjeds, Gezuitit Sckodran.* Rome: Me sctamp t'Kuvennit S. t'Propagands. 102 pp.
- (1904), De pronuntiatione palatalium in diversis albanicae linguae dialectis. in: *Verhandlungen des 13. Internationalen Orientalistenkongresses zu Hamburg,* Sept. 1902. Leiden: Brill.
- (1911), *Këndimet për shkollat e para të Shqypnisë.* Shkodra?/Vienna?.
- (1917), *Juvenilia.* Vienna: Vernay, reprint Shkodra 1928; Prishtina 1990. 79 pp.
- (1928), *Lissus.* Shkodra: Typ. Zoja e Paperlyeme. 12 pp.
- (1934), *Vrejtje mbi artikuj e prêmna pronës të giûhës shqipe. Prei Ndré Mjedës.* Shkodra: Zoja e paperlyeme. 31 pp.
- (1966), *Poesie e poemi. Versione dall'originale a cura di Jolanda Kodra.* Tirana: Naim Frashëri. 96 pp.
- (1982), *Vepra 1-3.* Prishtina: Rilindja. 166, 195, + 238 pp.
- (1988), *Vepra letrare 1-2.* Tirana: Naim Frashëri, 204 + 164 pp.

MORELLI, Tommaso
  (1842), *Cenni storici sulla venuta degli Albanesi nel Regno delle Due Sicilie.* Naples: Guttemberg. 40 pp.

MORINA, Irfan
  (1987), *Priştineli mesihi, hayati, sanati ve eserleri.* Prishtina: Tan. 304 pp.

M'RAIHI, Miriam
  (2004), *Ismail Kadaré ou l'inspiration prométhéenne.* Paris: L'Harmattan. 213 pp.

MUSTAFAJ, Besnik
  (1989), *Vera pa kthim. Tregime dhe novela.* Tirana: Naim Frashëri. 376 pp.
- (1992), *Un été sans retour.* Roman traduit de l'albanais par Christiane Montécot. Arles: Actes Sud. 202 pp.

- (1993), *Les cigales de la canicule*. Roman traduit de l'albanais par Christiane Montécot. Arles: Actes Sud. 165 pp.
- (1994), *Gjinkallat e vapës. Roman*. Tirana: Arbri. reprint Peja: Dukagjini 1995. 110 pp.
- (1994), *Petite saga carcérale*. Roman traduit de l'albanais par Elizabeth Chabuel. Arles: Actes Sud. 214 pp.
- (1995), *Një sagë e vogël. Roman*. Tirana: Arbri.179 pp.
- (1998), *Boshti. Roman*. Tirana: Onufri. 123 pp.
- (1999), *Le vide. Roman*. Traduit de l'albanais par Elisabeth Chabuel. Paris: Albin Michel. 249 pp.

MYDERRIZI, Osman
- (1951), Erveheja e M. Çamit [Erveheja dhe Muhamet Çami]. in: *Buletin i Institutit të Shkencavet,* Tirana, 1, p. 72-82.
- (1954), Nezim Frakulla (1690?-1759). in: *Buletin për shkencat shoqërore,* Tirana, 4, p. 56-75.
- (1955a), Hasan Zyko Kamberi. in: *Buletin për shkencat shoqërore,* Tirana, 1, p. 93-109.
- (1955b), Letërsia fetare e bektashive. in: *Buletin për shkencat shoqërore,* Tirana, 3, p. 131-142.
- (1955c) Letërsia shqipe në alfabetin arab. in: *Buletin për Shkencat Shoqërore,* Tirana, p. 148-155
- (1957), Erveheja. in: *Buletin për shkencat shoqërore,* Tirana 1, p. 253-278.
- (1959), Dorëshkrime të vjetra shqip të panjohura të Gjirokastrës. in: *Buletin i Universitetit Shtetëror të Tiranës. Seria Shkencat Shoqërore,* Tirana, 13. 2, p. 159-189.
- (1965), Tekstet e vjetra shqip me alfabetin arab. in: *Konferenca e parë e studimeve albanologjike,* Tirana, p. 287-291.
- (1996), Letërsia fetare e bektashinjve. in: *Perla, revistë shkencore-kulturore tremujore,* Tirana, 4, p. 71-79.
- (2000), Meshari i Gjon Buzukut në vështrimin fetar në Shqipëri. in: *Studime historike,* Tirana, 3-4, p. 37-46.

MYFTIU, Abdyrrahim
- (2002), *Nga letërsia te filmi. Filmi artistik shqiptar dhe çështje të ekranizimit.* Tirana: Akademia e Shkencave, 304 pp.

MYRTAJ, Faruk
- (2003), *Luftëtarët vriten në paqe. Tregime.* Peja: Dukagjini, 243 pp.

MYZYRI, Hysni
- (1978), *Shkollat e para kombëtare shqipe (1887-Korrik 1908).* Botim i dytë me plotësime e ndryshime. Tirana: 8 Nëntori. 250 pp.
- (1979), *Shoqëria e të shtypurit shkronja shqip.* Tirana: 8 Nëntori. 113 pp.

MYZYRI, Hysni (ed.)
- (1994), *Historia e popullit shqiptar për shkollat e mesme.* Tirana: Libri shkollor. 263 pp.

NAUNI, Enea
- (1993), *Kadareja i panjohur. Laokonti filloi të flasë.* Tirana: Evropa. 207 pp.

NEKAJ, Zef

(1981), Remembering Gjergj Fishta, the Albanian national poet on the occasion of his 110th anniversary. in: *Albanian Catholic Bulletin,* Santa Clara, 2, p. 73-79.

NIKAJ, Ndoc (= NIKAJ, Dom Anton)

(1888), *Vakinat e scêites kisc, t'cituna n'ghiuhe sccyptare prej Giakonit D. Nnoz Njkai, e t'kusctuume n'émen t'nneruuscmit zotni, Pieter Dodmassei, n'scêi t'itaatit e t'gymertiis tii.* Rome: Propaganda Fide. 320 pp.

- (1892), *Marzia o ksctenimi n'files t'vet, e citi n'ghiuh sccyptare D. Nnoz Njkai, prift skodran n'famulii t'sckrelit.* Shkodra: Typ. Immaculatae Conceptionis. 70 pp.

- (1899), *Bleta nner lulé t'Parrixit.* Shkodra: Me sctamp t'Kolegs Papnore. 504 pp.

- (1902), *Historia é Shcypniis ch' me fillése e déri me kohe ku ra ne dore te turkut préj N.D.N.* Perlindia é Shcypetarevé. Brussels: Imprimé pour P. 'Albania' par E. Kumps. reprint Shkodra 1917. 416 pp.

- (1902), *Historia e Turkiis é diftuemé Ghinnvé t'Shcypniis. Préi N.D.N.* London: Perlindia é Shcyptarevé. 106 pp.

- (1904), *Bléta e ree nner lulé t'Parrixit.* Shkodra: Shtyp. t'Xojes zânun pa mkat t'rriédhshem. 398 pp.

- (1913), *Fejesa n'djep ase Ulqini i mârrun.* Shkodra: Shtypshkroja Nikaj. 137 pp.

- (1913), *Tak-tuk: tak-tuk a se Shkodra e Rrethueme.* 1-2. Shkodra: Shtypshkroja Nikai, 123, 163 pp.

- (1915), *Zêmer nanet a Tivari i mârrun. E dyta dorë.* Shkodra: Shtypshkroja Nikaj. 112 pp.

- (1918), *Bukurusha. Diftim historiak i vietve 1478-79.* Shkodra: Shtypshkroja Nikai, 126 pp.

- (1920), *Burbuqja. Diftim historian i vjetve 1815-17.* Shkodra: Shtypshkroja Nikaj. 146 pp.

- (1920), *Lulet në thes. Diftim historik i vjetëve 1830-33.* Shkodra: Shtypshkroja Nikai. 90 pp.

- (1921), *Motra per vllàn. Shfaqtime teatrore per varza.* Shkodra: Shtypshkroja Nikaj. 54 pp.

Një grup studentësh t'Austrisë

(1925), *Naim Frashërit. Vjershëtorit dh'edukatorit kombëtar. Kushtuar me rrastin e mbushjes së 25 vjetve pas vdekjes së tija (20.X.1900).* Graz: Hans Bertschinger. 110 pp.

NOLI, Fan Stylian

(1907), *Israilitë dhe Filistinë. Dramë me 3 akte.* Boston: Kombi. reprint Prishtina 1968. 48 pp.

- (1908), *Sherbes' e javes se madhe. Kethyér nga grécishtja prej priftit orthodox Fan S. Nolit.* Boston: Kombi. 104 pp.

- (1909), *Librë e shërbesave të shënta të kishës orthodoxe. Kthyer nga gërqishtia prej priftit orthodox Fan S. Noli.* Boston. 244 pp.

- (1911), *Libre é te krémtevé te medha te kishes orthodoxe. Kthyér nga greqishtia préj priftit orthodox Fan S. Noli.* Boston: Boston. 315 pp.
- (1921), *Historia e Skënderbeut (Gjerq Kastriotit), mbretit të Shqipërisë 1412-1468,* prej Peshkopit Theofan (Fan S. Noli). E botuar prej Shoqërisë Korchare 'Arësime'. Boston: Dielli. reprint Boston 1950. 285 pp.
- (1924), *Storia di Scanderbeg (Giorgio Castriotta), re d'Albania (1412-1468), pel vescovo Fan S. Noli.* Versione di Francesco Argondizza. Rome: V. Ferri. reprint Rome: Maglione e Strini 1927. 196 pp.
- (1941), *Uratore e kishës orthodokse. E përktheu Imzót Fan S. Noli.* Boston: Peshkopata e Amerikës. 600 pp.
- (1943), *Mall e brengë. Vjersha.* Me një vështrim kritik prej Mitrush Kuteli't. Tirana: Botim' i Mitrush Kutelit. 94 pp.
- (1947), *Beethoven and the French revolution.* New York: International Universities Press. reprint Tirana 1991. 126 pp.
- (1947), *George Castrioti Scanderbeg (1405-1468).* New York: International Universities Press. 240 pp.
- (1947), *Kremtore e kishës orthodokse. E përktheu Imzót Fan S. Noli.* Boston: Peshkopata e Amerikës. 818 pp.
- (1948), *Albumi dyzetvjeçar në Amerikë 1906-1946. I Hirësisë tij Peshkop Fan S. Noli.* Boston: Vatra. reprint Prishtina: Rilindja 1990. 110 pp.
- (1960), *Fiftieth anniversary book of the Albanian Orthodox Church in America (1908-1958).* Boston: Albanian Orthodox Church in America. 265 pp.
- (1968), *Vepra të plota.* Prishtina: Rilindja.
- (1988-1996), *Vepra 1-6.* Tirana: Akademia e Shkencave.
- (1990), *Eroica. Das heftige Leben des Ludwig van Beethoven.* Aus dem Amerikanischen von Paridam von dem Knesebeck. Kiel: Neuer Malik. 96 pp.
- (1992), *Rubairat e Omar Khajam-it. I shqipëroi: Fan. S. Noli.* Tirana: s.a. [1992]. 71 pp.
- (1993), *Scanderbeg.* Traduzione dall'Albanese Alessandro Laporta, Halil Myrto. Lecce: Argo. 184 pp.
- (1994), *Autobiografia.* E përktheu nga origjinali anglisht Abdullah Karjagdiu. Tirana: Elena Gjika. 119 pp.
- (1998), *Poezi të zgjedhura, përkthime, introdukta.* Tirana: Dituria. 142 pp.
- (2002), *Faqe të panjohura të Nolit. Artikuj dhe shënime publicistike, 1915-1919.* Tirana: Albin, 328 pp.
- (2003), *Ligjerime.* Tirana: Dudaj, 484 pp.

NORRIS, Harry Thirlwall
- (1993), *Islam in the Balkans. Religion and society between Europe and the Arab world.* London: C. Hurst & Co. 304 pp.

OSEKU, Shqiptar
- (2001), *Nutida albansk poesi, på svenska. I urval och översättning av Shqiptar Oseku. Poezia bashkëkohore shqipe, suedisht. Zgjodhi dhe përktheu Shqiptar Oseku. Poezia suedeze, shqip. Zgjodhi dhe përktheu Shqiptar Oseku. Svensk poesi på albansk. I urval och översättning av Shqiptar Oseku.* Trelleborg: Drita. 149 + 199 pp.

OSMANI, Shefik

    (1996), *Pjetër Bogdani.* Tirana: Idromeno. 246 pp.

PALAJ, Bernardin

    (1969), *Opere. Volume 1. Poesie.* A cura di Angela Cirrincione. Rome: Dario Detti. 313 pp.

PAPLEKA, Anton (ed.)

    (1999), *Poetë shqiptarë. Nga shek. XII deri në shek. XIX. Antologji.* Tirana: Mësonjëtorja e parë. 387 pp.

PASHKU, Anton

    (1961), *Tregime.* Prishtina: Jeta e re.

-     (1971), *Oh.* Prishtina: Rilindja. reprint 1979, 1986. 159 pp.
-     (1973), *Kjasina. Tregime të zgjedhura.* Prishtina: Rilindja. 201 pp.
-     (1976), *Gof.* Prishtina: Rilindja. 60 pp.
-     (1978), *Lutjet e mbrëmjes.* Prishtina: Rilindja. 83 pp.
-     (2000), *Fièvre.* Traduit de l'Albanais (Kosovo) par Eqrem Basha et Christiane Montécot. Nantes: Edition du Petit Véhicule. 53 pp.

PETERS, Markus W. E.

    (2003), *Geschichte der katholischen Kirche in Albanien, 1919-1993.* Albanischen Forschungen, 23. Wiesbaden: Harrassowitz, viii + 340 pp.

PETROTTA, Gaetano

    (1931a), *Popolo lingua e letteratura albanese.* Palermo: Tip. Pontifica. 571 pp.

-     (1931b), *Saggio di bibliografia albanese 1500-1930.* Palermo: Tip. Pontificia. 40 pp.
-     (1932), *Popolo lingua e letteratura albanese.* 2a tiratura con aggiunte e correzioni. Palermo: Tip. Pontificia. 528 pp.
-     (1939), *Letteratura albanese e italo-albanese.* Venice: Carlo Ferrari. 40 pp.
-     (1942), Svoglimento storico della letteratura albanese. in: *Rivista d'Albania,* Milan, 3, p. 214-224.
-     (1950), *Svoglimento storico della cultura e della letteratura albanese.* Palermo: Boccone del Povero. 251 pp.

PIPA, Arshi

    (1941), Fishta, njeriu dhe vepra. in: *Shkëndija, botim i veçantë,* Tirana.

-     (1944a), Faik Konica. in: *Kritika,* Tirana, 1.2, p. 41-46.
-     (1944b), Historija e dhimbshme e shpirtit të ri [Migjeni]. in: *Kritika,* Tirana, 1.3, p. 112-120; 1.4, p. 147-160.
-     (1944c), *Lundërtarë. Vargje.* Tirana: Tirana. 86 pp.
-     (1945), Përkujtim i Migjenit. in: *Bota e re,* Tirana, 5, p. 33-45.
-     (1959a), Komunizmi dhe shkrimtarët shqiptare. in: *Shqiptari i lirë,* New York, 28.02.1959, p. 3; 31.03.1959, p. 2-3.
-     (1959b), Libri i burgut. Rome: Apice. 246 pp.
-     (1968), Rusha. Munich: Logos. 75 pp.
-     (1969a), Meridiana. Munich: Logos. 60 pp.
-     (1969b), Milosao and its three editions. in: *Südost-Forschungen,* Munich, 28, p. 182-198.

- (1969-1970), Panorama of contemporary Albanian literature. in: *Zeitschrift für Balkanologie,* Berlin, 7, p. 110-117.
- (1970a), Fasi e caratteristiche della letteratura italo-albanese. in: *Rivista di letteratura moderne e comparata,* Florence, vol. 23.3 p. 176-178.
- (1970b), For a critical appraisal of Albanian literature. in: *Përpjekja jonë,* 1 Jan. p. 44-57.
- (1970c), Milosao, a popular and classical 'lyrical romance'. in: *Comparative Literature* 7.3, p. 336-353.
- (1970d), Modern and contemporary Albanian poetry. in: *Books abroad,* Norman OK, 44.1 (winter 1970), p. 51-54.
- (1971), Le mythe de l'occident dans la poésie de Migjeni. in: *Südost-Forschungen,* Munich, 30, p. 142-175.
- (1973), The genesis of Milosao. in: *Revue des études sud-est européennes,* Bucharest, 4, p. 711-739.
- (1975), Albanian metrics. in: *Südost-Forschungen,* Munich, 34, p. 217-221.
- (1977), Calabro-Albanian romanticism. in: *Zeitschrift für Balkanologie,* Berlin, 13, p. 113-124.
- (1978a), *Albanian folk verse, structure and genre.* Albanische Forschungen 17. Trilogia Albanica 1. Munich: Dr. Dr. Rudolf Trofenik. 191 pp.
- (1978b), *Hieronymus de Rada.* Albanische Forschungen 18, Trilogia Albanica 2. Munich: Dr. Dr. Rudolf Trofenik. 319 pp.
- (1978c), *Albanian literature, social perspectives.* Albanische Forschungen 19, Trilogia Albanica 3. Munich: Dr. Dr. Rudolf Trofenik. 292 pp.
- (1978d), Gli Italo-Albanesi e la tradizione greco-bizantina. in: *Revue des Etudes Sud-Est Européennes,* Bucharest 16.2, p. 239-251. reprint in: *8 Convegno internazionale di studi albanesi.* Palermo: Centro internazionale di studi albanesi, 1978, p. 57-75.
- (1980), Albanian literature. in: *Columbia Dictionary of Modern European Literature.* ed. Jean-Albert Bede & William A. Edgerton. New York: Columbia University Press, p. 12-13, 252-253, 335.
- (1981), Typology and periodization of Albanian literature. in: *Serta Balcanica-Orientalia Monacensis in honorem Rudolphi Trofenik septuagenarii.* ed. Peter Bartl. Munich.p. 245-253.
- (1982), Classical and Byzantine elements in a romantic Calabro-Albanian poem. in: *Zeitschrift für Balkanologie,* Berlin, 18, 2, p. 143-158.
- (1983-1984), Subversion gegen Konformismus. Das Phänomen Kadare. in: *Münchner Zeitschrift für Balkankunde,* Munich, 5, p. 165-178.
- (1984), Fan Noli as a national and international figure. in: *Südost-Forschungen,* Munich, 43, p. 241-270.
- (1987), Subversion vs. conformism. The Kadare phenomenon. in: *Telos,* 73, fall, p. 47-77.
- (1991), *Contemporary Albanian literature.* East European Monographs 305. New York: Columbia University Press. 175 pp.
- (1992), Conformisme et subversion. Le double jeu de Kadare. in: *Autre Europe* 24-25, p. 138-151.

- (1993), Albanian poetry. in: *The new Princeton encyclopedia of poetry and poetics.* Edited by Alex Preminger and I.V.F. Brogan. Princeton: Princeton University Press. p. 27-28.
- (1994), De Rada's 'Milosao'. in: *Südost-Forschungen,* Munich, 53, p. 131-148.
- (1998), *Poezi. Vepra poetike.* Përgatiti Rexhep Ismajli. Peja: Dukagjini. 471 pp.
- (1999), *Subversion drejt konformizmit. Fenomeni Kadare.* Përktheu Bardhyl Shehu. Tirana: Phoenix.77 pp.
- (2000a), *Vepra 1. Lundërtarë, Libri i dashunís dhe i fatit. Vargje.* Tirana: Phoenix. 142 pp.
- (2000b), *Vepra 2. Autobiography.* Tirana: Phoenix. 104 pp.
- (2000c), *Vepra 3. Lirika latine.* Tirana: Phoenix. 296 pp.
- (2000d), *Vepra 4. Lirika evropiane moderne.* Tirana: Phoenix. 148 pp.

PIRRAKU, Muhamet
- (1979-1980), Gjurmë të veprimtarisë letrare shqipe me alfabetin arab në Kosovë. in: *Gjurmime albanologjike, seria e shkencave filologjike,* Prishtina, 9, p. 203-236; 10, p. 203-224.
- (1988), Në gjurmë të kulturës dhe të sugjerimeve shqipe fetare moralizuese të provoniensës islame në shek. XVII-XVIII. in: *Gjurmime albanologjike, seria e shkencave filologjike,* Prishtina, 18, p. 205-224.
- (1995), *Albania e Konicës.* Prishtina: s.e., Prishtina, 135 pp.

PLASARI, Aurel
- (1991), Trembëdhjetë infraksionet e Dom Ndoc Nikajt. in: *Shqipëria zgjim i dhimbshëm. Albania painful awakening.* ed. Ardian Klosi. Tirana. p. 82-93.
- (1995), *Kuteli. Midis të gjallëve dhe të vdekurëve.* Tirana: Apolonia, Tirana. 123 pp.
- (1996a), *Fishta i dashuruari. Një aventurë i kritikës.* Tirana: Marin Barleti. 107 pp.
- (1996b),Qasje tregimit të Koliqit. in: *Hylli i dritës,* Tirana, 3-4, p. 10-20.
- (1997), Për një histori 'të re' të letërsisë shqipe. in: BECI, Bahri, RRAHMANI, Zejnullah, YLLI, Xhelal (ed.), *Seminari XVII ndërkombëtar për gjuhën, letërsinë dhe kulturën shqiptare. Përmbledhje e ligjëratave, referimeve, kumtesave dhe e diskutimeve. Tiranë 16-31 gusht 1995.* Akademia e Shkencave, Instituti i Gjuhësisë dhe Letërsisë. Universiteti i Prishtinës, Fakulteti i Filologjisë. Tirana: Eurorilindja. p. 265-270.
- (1997), *Përballë një kulture të vdekjes.* Tirana: Hylli i Dritës, 67 pp.
- (2000), *Dhjetë ditë, që nuk trondilën botën. Arlekinadë.* Tirana: Korbi, 112 pp.
- (2002), *Lufta e Trojës vazhdon. Shënime nga kthimi.* Tirana: Sejko, 90 pp.

PLASARI, Aurel (ed.)
- (1996), *Hylli i dritës.* Numër i posaçëm [Gjergj Fishta]. Tirana. 293 pp.

PODRIMJA, Ali
- (1961), *Thirrje.* Prishtina: Jeta e re. reprint Tirana 1972, Prishtina 1973. 63 pp.
- (1981), *Drejtpeshimi.* Prishtina: Rilindja. 245 pp.
- (1982), *Lum Lumi.* Prishtina: Rilindja. reprint 1986. 107 pp.

267

- (1994), *Buzëqeshje në kafaz*. Peja: Dukagjini. 106 pp.
- (2000), *Défaut de verbe. Edition bilingue.* Traduit de l'albanais et préfacé par Alexandre Zotos. Le Chambon-sur-Lignon: Cheyne. 109 pp.
- (2000), *Who will slay the wolf. Selected poetry by Ali Podrimja.* Translated from the Albanian with an introduction by Robert Elsie. New York: Gjonlekaj Publishing Company. 268 pp.

PODRIMJA, Ali (ed.)
- (2000), *Take të larta. Antologji e shkrimtareve shqiptare.* Prishtina: Sfinga. 229 pp.
- (2002), *Dritaren lëre hapur. Gjashtë poetë të Kosovës.* Prishtina: Rozafa, 196 pp.
- (2003), *E frikshme dhe e bukur. Sprovë për një antologji.* Perpiloi Ali Podrimja. Prishtina: Rozafa, 300 pp.
- (2003), *I kujt je, atdhe. Sprovë për një antologji, 2.* Përpiloi Ali Podrimja. Prishtina: Rozafa, 246 pp.
- (2004), *Eni vjen pej Çamërie.* Përpiloi Ali Podrimja. Mesazhi Ismail Kadare. Prishtina: Rozafa, 152 pp.

POLLO, Stefanaq
- (1979), Luigj Gurakuqi, un éminent démocrate révolutionnaire. in: *Studia Albanica,* Tirana, 16, 1, p. 3-17.

POPOVIC, Alexandre
- (1986), *L'Islam balkanique. Les musulmans du sud-est européen dans la période post-ottomane.* Balkanologische Veröffentlichungen Nr 11. Berlin: in Kommission Harrassowitz, Wiesbaden. 478 pp.

POPOVIC, Alexandre & VEINSTEIN, Gilles (ed.)
- (1986), *Les ordres mystiques dans L'Islam. Cheminements et situation actuelle.* Paris: Editions de l'Ecole des Hautes Etudes en Sciences Sociales. 324 pp.
- (1993), *Bektachiyya, études sur l'ordre mystique des Bektachis et les groupes relevant de Hadji Bektach. Revue des Etudes Islamiques* 60 (1992). Numéro spécial. Paris: Paul Geuthner, (1993) / Istanbul: Isis (1995), xii + 598 pp.
- (1996), *Les voies d'Allah. Les ordres mystiques dans l'Islam des origines à aujourd'hui.* Sous la direction de Alexandre Popovic. Paris: Fayard. 711 pp.

PORADECI, Lasgush
- (1933), *Vallja e yjve.* Edituar nënë kujdesin e M. Kutelit. Constanza: Albania. 117 pp.
- (1937), *Ylli i zemrës.* Edituar nënë kujdesjen e M. Kutelit. Bucharest 1937. reprint 1939, Prishtina 1990. 182 pp.
- (1986), *Vdekja e nositit.* Botim i dytë i plotësuar. Prishtina: Rilindja, 278 pp.
- (1990), *Vepra letrare.* Tirana: Naim Frashëri. 534 pp.
- (1999), *Vepra 1-3.* Tirana: Onufri. 370, 381 + 235 pp.

POSTOLI, Foqion P.
- (1943), *Për mprojtjen e atdheut. Romancë.* Korça: Dhori Koti. 304 pp.
- (s.a.), *Lulja e kujtimit. Dramë me 6 pamje.* Korça: Dhori Koti. reprint Tirana 1957, 1959, 1961, Prishtina 1985. 71 pp.

- (1990-1991), *Vepra letrare 1-2.* Tirana: Naim Frashëri. 348 + 300 pp.

PRENNUSHI, Vinçenc

    (1911), *Visari komtaar. I. Kângë popullore. Blêe i parë. Kângë popullore gegnishte.* Mledhë e rreshtue prejë P. Vinçenc Prênnushit O.F.M. Zur Kunde der Balkanhalbinsel. II. Quellen und Forschungen. Herausgegeben von Dr. Carl Patsch. Heft 1. Sarajevo: Daniel A. Kajon. 172 pp.

- (1918), *Grueja shqiptare. Rromanzë.* Shkodra. 8 pp.
- (1924), *Gjeth e lule.* Shkodra. reprint Shkodra 1931, Prishtina 2000. 181 pp.
- (1993), *Foglie e fiori. Poesie.* Trad. a cura di Amik Kasoruho. Bari: Quaderni del Centro Solidarietà della Caritas, Diocesana di Bari-Bitonto. 116 pp.

PRIFTI, Peter Rafael

    (2002), *Land of Albanians: a crossroads of pain and pride.* Tirana: Horizont, 362 pp.

- (2003), *Mozaik shqiptar. Publicistikë, portretë, studime, recensione, pjesë teatrale.* Prishtina: Gjon Buzuku, 292 pp.

PUTO, Arben

    (1990), *Demokracia e rrethuar. Qeveria e Fan Nolit në marrëdhëniet e jashtme, qershor-dhjetor 1924.* Tirana: 8 Nëntori. 320 pp.

QOSJA, Rexhep

    (1968), *Dialogje me shkrimtarët.* Prishtina: Rilindja. reprint 1979. 295 pp.

- (1972), *Asdreni, jeta dhe vepra e tij. Monografi.* Prishtina: Instituti Albanologjik. reprint 1987. 463 pp.
- (1974), *Vdekja më vjen prej syvë të tillë. Trembëdhjetë tregime që mund të bënin një roman.* Prishtina: Rilindja. reprint Prishtina 1986, Tirana 1998. 295 pp.
- (1984-1986), *Historia e letërsisë shqipe. Romantizmi. Vol. 1-3.* Prishtina: Rilindja. 441, 489, 589 pp.
- (1986), *Porosia e madhe. Monografi mbi krijimtarine e Naim Frashërit. (=* Frashëri, Vepra 7). Prishtina: Rilindja. 606 pp.
- (1994), *La mort me vient de ces yeux-là. Treize contes qui peuvent faire un roman.* Traduit de l'albanais par Christian Gut. Préface de Ismaïl Kadaré. Paris: Gallimard. 321 pp.

QUKU, Mentor

    (1990), Ndre Mjeda, personnalité remarquable et complexe de notre culture nationale. in: *Lettres Albanaises,* Tirana, 4, p. 72-85.

- (2004), *Mjeda. Rinia (1866-1888).* Tirana: Ilar. 639 pp.

RADI, Lazër

    (1998), *Një verë me Migjenin. Kujtime, shënime.* Tirana: Liria. 240 pp.

RAIFI, Mensur

    (1975), *Fan S. Noli dhe Migjeni.* Prishtina: Rilindja. 192 pp

- (1977), *Mbi poezinë bashkëkohose shqiptare.* Prishtina: Rilindja. 127 pp.
- (1978), *Mbi prozën bashkëkohore shqiptare.* Prishtina: Rilindja. 135 pp.
- (1986), *Lasgushi Noli Migjeni.* Prishtina: Rilindja. 162 pp.
- (1987), *Tri moderna albanska pesnika.* Prishtina: Društvo Knjizevnih Prevodilaca Kosova. 152 pp.

- (1995), *Fan Noli dhe çështja e Kosovës*. Prishtina: Shoqata e përkthyesve letrare të Kosovës. 112 pp.

RAIFI, Mensur (ed.)

    (1988), *Roads lead only one way. A survey of modern poetry from Kosova*. Prishtina: The Kosova Association of Literary Translators. 235 pp.

- (1990), *The Angry cloud. An anthology of Albanian stories from Yugoslavia*. Translated from the Albanian by John Hodgson. Prishtina: Kosova Association of Literary Translators. 112 pp.

RAMA, Luan

    (1999), *Le long chemin sous le tunnel de Platon. Le destin de l'artiste sous la censure en Albanie (1945-1990)*. Nantes: Editions du Petit Véhicule. 228 pp.

- (2002), *Francë-Shqipëri, France-Albanie: krushq të largët [Krushq të largët: Francë-Shqipëri, France-Albanie]*. Tirana: Argeta LMG, 409 pp.

RESO, Esad

    (1962), *Sami Frashëri, pikëpamjet filozofike, shoqërore dhe politike*. Tirana. 72 pp.

RESSULI, Namik

    (1987), *Albanian literature*. Edited by Eduard Liço. Boston: Vatra. 108 pp.

RESSULI, Namik (ed.)

    (1941), *Shkrimtarët shqiptarë. Pjesa I (1462-1878)*. Botim i Ministris s'Arsimit. Mbledhë e punue nën kujdesin e Ernest Koliqit, nga Namik Ressuli. Tirana: Shypshkroja Gurakuqi. 367 pp.

- (1958), *Il "Messale" di Giovanni Buzuku*. Riproduzione e trascrizione. Studi e testi 199. Vatican City: Biblioteca Apostolica Vaticana. 407 pp.

REXHEBI, Baba

    (1970), *Misticizma Islame dhe Bektashizma*. New York: Waldon Press. 389 pp.

- (1984), *The mysticism of Islam and Bektashism*. Naples: Dragotti. 173 pp.

RIZA, Selman

    (1962), Disa teza mbi tre dorëshkrimet e katekizmit të Matrëngës. in: *Buletin i Universitetit Shtetëtor të Tiranës, Seria shkencat shoqërore*, Tirana, 2, p. 76-82.

- (1965a), Dy versionet e veprës së Pjetër Bogdanit. in: *Konferenca e parë e Studimeve Albanologjike*, Tirana, p. 278-286.

- (1965b), Thèses sur les trois manuscrits du Catéchisme de Lekë Matrënga. in: *Studia Albanica*, Tirana, 1, p. 125-130.

- (1979), *Studime albanistike*. Prishtina.

- (1996), *Vepra. 1*. Botime të veçanta XXII. Seksioni i gjuhësisë dhe i letërsisë. Libri 11. Redakcia: Idriz Ajeti, Besim Bokshi, Rexhep Ismajli. Prishtina: Akademia e Shkencave dhe e Arteve e Kosovës. 566 pp.

- (2002), *Pesë autorët më të vjetër në gjuhën shqipe. Vepër postume e Selman Rizës*. Tirana: Toena, 400 pp.

RIZAJ, Skënder

    (1985), The Islamization of the Albanians during the XVth and XVIth centuries, in *Studia Albanica*, Tirana, 2, p. 127-131.

ROQUES, Mario Louis

(1932a), *Le dictionnaire albanais de 1635, édité et avec index complet.* Paris: Paul Geuthner. 222 pp.

-       (1932b), *Recherches sur les anciens textes albanais. Avec huit facsimilés.* Paris: Paul Geuthner. 47 pp.

ROSSI, Ettore

(1942), 'Saggio sul dominio turco e l'introduzione dell'Islam in Albania,' in *Rivista di Albania,* Milan, 3, p. 200-213.

-       (1946), Notizia su un manoscritto del canzionere di Nezim (Secolo XVII-XVIII) in caratteri arabi e lingua albanese. in: *Rivista degli Studi Orientali,* Rome, 21, p. 219-246.

-       (1948), La fonte turca della novella poetica albanese "Erveheja" di Muhamet Çami (Sec. XVIII-XIX) e il tema di "Florence de Rome" e di "Crescentia". in: *Oriente Moderno,* Rome, 28, p. 143-153.

ROTELLI, Claudio (ed.)

(1988), *Gli Albanesi in Calabria. Secoli XV-XVIII. 1.* Cosenza: Edizione Orizzonti Meridionali, reprint 1990. 113 pp.

RRAHMANI, Kujtim

(2002), *Intertekstualiteti dhe oraliteti. E, Koliqi, M. Kuteli, A. Pashku.* Prishtina: Asociacioni për Integrime Kulturore dhe Demokratike, 282 pp.

RRAHMANI, Zejnullah

(1996), Faik Konica për kritikën. in: *Studime Albanologjike,* Tirana, 1, p. 54-58.

RROTA, Justin

(1930), *Monumenti mâ i vjetri i gjûhës shqype. D. Gjon Buzuku 1555.* Copa të zgjedhuna e të komentueme per shkolla të mjesme. Shkodra: Shtypshkroja Françeskane, reprint Shkodra 1938. 57 pp.

-       (1939), *Shkrimtari mâ i vjetri i Italo-Shqyptarvet: Lukë Matranga. 1592.* Copa të zgjedhuna e të komentueme per shkolla të mjesme. Botim i dytë. Shkodra: Shtypshkroja Françeskane. 29 pp.

RUBERTO, Roberto

(1966), An Albanian poet from Italy: Girolamo De Rada (1814-1903). in: *Italian Quarterly,* 10, 38 (fall 1966), p. 45-56.

RUGOVA, Ibrahim

(1982), *Vepra e Bogdanit 1675-1685.* Prishtina: Rilindja. 313 pp.

SALIHU, Hajdar

(1987), *Poezia e Bejtexhinjve.* Prishtina: Rilindja. 511 pp.

SANTORI, Francesco Antonio

(1848), *Il prigionero politico libero e reduce per la costituzione del 1848. Novella.* Naples: Trani.

-       (1855), *Cryshtèu i shẏityrùory me ty θẏnnuryn e parcalhèssavet çy lhipsen ca dhitta gkiθ gnerìu po ty truhet t'iny Zhotti... Marrura ca za lhìvyre shpirtulhòre lhitalìre e prierrura mby gkugyn alhbyrèshe ca vlau Ntôny Santori ca Pizzilhia.* Naples: Gaetano Nobile. 230 pp.

-       (1855), *Krýšten i šyityruory.* Naples: Galtani. 230 pp.

- (1959), *Emira dhe disa vjersha. Teksti në origjinal dhe i vënë në gjuhën e sotme.* Me një hyrje rreth jetës dhe veprave të autorit nga Ziaudin Kodra. Tirana: Naim Frashëri. 148 pp.
- (1975), *Il canzoniere albanese.* Trascrizione, traduzione italiana e note a cura di Francesco Solano. Corigliano Calabro: Quaderni di Zjarri. 50 pp.
- (1977), *Romanci i tretë. Brisandi Lletixja e Ulladheni. Transkriptim i tekstit origjinal të pabotuar dhe ndryshimet e redaktimit të parë.* Me një hyrje dhe një fjalorth nga Ital Konstant Fortino. Cosenza: Biondi. 257 pp.
- (1979), *Panaini e Dellja (Panaino e Delia), Fëmija pushtjerote (La famiglia campestre)* a cura di G. Gradilone. Rome, Bulzoni. 316 pp.
- (1980), *Këngëtorja arbërore.* Poemë përshtatur në gjuhën e sotme nga Andrea Varfi. Tirana: Naim Frashëri. 112 pp.
- (1983), *Alessio Ducagino. Melodramma.* Edizione del testo albanese con traduzione e note a cura di Francesco Solano. Castrovillari: Quaderni di Zjarri. 63 pp.
- (1984), *Emira.* Edizione del testo albanese con traduzione e note a cura del prof. Francesco Solano. Commune di Cerzeto/Qana. Biblioteca communale. Grottaferrata: Scuola Tip. Italo-Orientale 'S. Nilo'. 291 pp.
- (1985), *Tre novelle.* A cura di Italo Costante Fortino, Carmine Stamile, Ernesto Tocci. Cosenza: Brenner.
- (1993-1994), *Vepra 1 & 2.* Prishtina: Rilindja, 409 + 375 pp.
- (1995), *Tri novelle.* Cosenza. 380 pp.
- (1998), *Satira.* Transliteruar dhe pajisur me shënime nga Karmell Kandreva dhe Gjovalin Shkurtaj. Tirana: Dituria. 80 pp
- (2000), *Neomenia. Tragjedia e parë shqipe.* Prishtina: Shpresa. 145 pp.

SCAGLIONE, Pietro
- (1921), *Historia e Shqipëtarëvet t'Italisë, me parathënie prej Prof. Josef Kadikami e me përhyrje prej Lumo Skendo.* New York: Emporium, 104 pp.

SCHIRÒ, Giuseppe Jr.
- (1944), Arte e lingua di Giulio Variboba. in: *Rivista d'Albania,* Rome, anno V, fasc. 1, p. 24-40.
- (1959), *Storia della letteratura albanese.* Florence: Nuova Accademia Editrice. 267 pp.
- (1969), Nicola Chetta e il poemetto inedito sulla creazione del mondo. in: *Studia Albanica Monacensia in memoriam Georgii C. Scanderbegi.* Munich. Trofenik, p. 76-86
- (1970), Një poem i pabotuar i Nikollë Ketës. in: *Konferenca e dytë e studimeve albanologjike, Tiranë 12-18 Janar 1968.* Tirana: Universiteti i Tiranës, vol. 3, p. 89-100.

SCHIRÒ, Giuseppe Sr.
- (1887), *Rapsodie albanesi, testo traduzione note...* Palermo: Amenta. reprint Palermo: Lauriel 1892. 350 pp.
- (1888-1889), Saggi di letteratura popolare della colonie albanese di Piana dei Greci. in: *Archivio per le tradizioni popolari,* Palermo, 7 (1888), p. 31, 517; 8 (1889), p. 73, 233, 521.

- (1890), Canti religiosi e morali delle colonie albanesi di Sicilia. in: *Archivio albanese*, Palermo III.
- (1890), Canti tradizionali delle colonie albanesi di Sicilia. in: *Archivio albanese*, Palermo I.
- (1891), *Mili e Haidhia, idillio.* in: *Archivio delle tradizioni popolari*, Palermo.
- (1891), *Milo e Haidhee. Idillio.* Palermo: Spinnato.
- (1897) *Kënkat e luftës (I canti della battaglia). Con note e osservazioni sulla questione d'oriente.* Palermo: Sandron. 192 pp.
- (1900), *Te Dheu i huaj (Nella terra straniera), poema. Mili e Haidhia, idillio.* Palermo: Spinnato. 136 pp.
- (1901), *Canti popolari dell'Albania.* Palermo: Marsala. 78 pp.
- (1904), *Gli Albanesi e la questione balcanica.* Naples: Ferd. Bideri. 603 pp.
- (1907), *Canti sacri delle colonie albanesi di Sicilia.* Naples.
- (1907), *Mili è Haidhia. Idhyll nde gjuhe shcypé i perkethyér édhè italísht fjale pas fjalé.* Shpállejé é tréte. Naples: Tocco & Salvietti, Naples s.a. [1907]. xv + 65 pp.
- (1907), *Kaenka tae paershpyrtaeshme tae Shjyptàraevet tae Sikjilis. Canti sacri delle colonie albanesi di Sicilia.* Naples. reprint Palermo 1991. 160 pp.
- (1923), *Canti tradizionali ed altri saggi delle colonie albanesi di Sicilia.* Naples: Pierro & figlio. reprint Piana degli Albanesi: Amministrazione Communale 1986. 535 pp.
- (1926), *Kënkat e litorit.* Palermo 1926.
- (1940), *Te Dhéu i húaj. Poema in lingua albanese con traduzione letterale italiana dell'autore.* Palermo: Boccone del Povero. 403 pp.
- (1965), *Këthimi. Il ritorno.* Poema postumo con introduzione a cura di Giuseppe Schirò junior. Studi albanesi, pubblicati dall'Istituto di Studi Albanesi dell'Università di Roma. Studi e testi 2. Florence: Olschki. 262 pp.
- (1994), *Mili e Haidhia. Idil.* Poema është përshtatur në shqipen e sotme, pajisur me shënime dhe me një studim hyrës nga Dr. Ali Xhiku. Tirana: Dituria. reprint 1999. 118 pp.
- (1994), *Mili e Hajdhia. Idil.* Vënë edhe në shqipen e sotme nga Dhimitër Shuteriqi. Sipas botimit III të Napolit, 1907. Prishtina: Gjon Buzuku. 119 pp.
- (1997), Opere, I. Kroja, Rapsodie Albanesi. A cura di Matteo Mandalà. Provincia regionale di Palermo. Comune di Piana degli Albanesi. Biblioteca Comunale G Schirò. Soveria Mannelli: Rubbettino Editore. xcv + 242 pp.
- (1997), Opere, II. Milo e Haidhe. A cura di Matteo Mandalà. Provincia regionale di Palermo. Comune di Piana degli Albanesi. Biblioteca Comunale G Schirò. Soveria Mannelli: Rubbettino Editore. xix + 375 pp.
- (1997), Opere, III. Vistari, Te dheu i huaj (ed. del 1940 [sic] (1900)). A cura di Matteo Mandalà. Provincia regionale di Palermo. Comune di Piana degli Albanesi. Biblioteca Comunale G Schirò. Soveria Mannelli: Rubbettino Editore. xxvi + 235 pp.
- (1997), Opere, IV. Te dheu i huaj (ed. del 1940). A cura di Matteo Mandalà. Provincia regionale di Palermo. Comune di Piana degli Albanesi. Biblioteca Comunale G Schirò. Soveria Mannelli: Rubbettino Editore. xv + 401 pp.

273

- (1997), Opere, V. Këthimi, Mino, Opere teatrali, Mantner. A cura di Matteo Mandalà. Provincia regionale di Palermo. Comune di Piana degli Albanesi. Biblioteca Comunale G. Schirò. Soveria Mannelli: Rubbettino Editore. xxxii + 409 pp.

- (1997), Opere, VI. Prose e canti sacri. A cura di Matteo Mandalà. Provincia regionale di Palermo. Comune di Piana degli Albanesi. Biblioteca Comunale G Schirò. Soveria Mannelli: Rubbettino Editore. xviii + 441 pp.

- (1997), Opere, VII. Liriche sparse, Canti della Battaglia, Canti del Littorio. A cura di Matteo Mandalà. Provincia regionale di Palermo. Comune di Piana degli Albanesi. Biblioteca Comunale G Schirò. Soveria Mannelli: Rubbettino Editore. 1997) xii + 324 pp.

- (1997), Opere, VIII. Saggi. A cura di Matteo Mandalà. Provincia regionale di Palermo. Comune di Piana degli Albanesi. Biblioteca Comunale G Schirò. Soveria Mannelli: Rubbettino Editore. xvii + 392 pp.

- (1998), Opere, IX. Gli Albanesi e la Questione Balcanica. A cura di Matteo Mandalà. Provincia regionale di Palermo. Comune di Piana degli Albanesi. Biblioteca Comunale G Schirò. Piana degli Albanesi: Biblioteca Comunale G Schirò, Piana degli Albanesi. vi + 563 pp.

SCHIRÒ, Giuseppe & PETROTTA, Gaetano

(1932), Il più antico testo di lingua albanese. Trascrizione fonetica con note e osservazioni grammaticali di Mons. P. Schirò e riproduzione del testo dell'Editio Princeps con introduzione di G. Petrotta. in: *Rivista Indo-Greco-Italica* (RIGI) 16 (1932).

SCHMIDT-NEKE, Michael

(2002), Die Roten Paschas: Ismail Kadares Rolle im Hoxha-System. in: *Albanische Hefte,* Bochum, 2, p. 10-18.

SCHWANDER-SIEVERS, Stephanie & FISCHER, Bernd J. (ed.)

(2002), *Albanian identities: myth and history.* London: C. Hurst, London / Bloomington & Indianapolis: Indiana University Press, xvii + 238 pp.

SCHWARTZ, Stephen

(1992), Ernest Koliqi. An Appreciation. in: *Albanian Catholic Bulletin,* San Francisco, 13, p. 91-94.

- (2000), *Intellectuals and assassins. Writings at the end of Soviet Communism.* Preface by Roger Kimball. London: Anthem Press. 188 pp.

SCIAMBRA, Matteo

(1964), *La 'Dottrina cristiana' albanese di Luca Matranga. Riproduzione, trascizione e commento del Codice Barberini Latino 3454.* Studi i testi 240. Vatican City: Bibl. Apost. Vaticana. 256 pp.

- (1965), *Bogdanica - studi su Pietro Bogdano e l'opera sua. Volume II. Saggio sul lessico scientifico e culturale del Bogdani.* Bologna: Prof. Riccardo Pàtron. 68 pp.

SEDAJ, Ëngjell

(1997), *Tradita dhe letërsia. Autorë dhe vepra.* Prishtina: Shoqata e shkrimtarëve të Kosovës. 293 pp.

SEGEL, Harold B.
(2003), *The Columbia guide to the literatures of Eastern Europe since 1945.*
New York: Columbia University Press, 641 pp.
SEREMBE, Giuseppe (= SEREMBE, Zef)
(1883), *Poesie italiane e canti originali tradotti dall'albanese.* Cosenza:
Avanguardia. 101 pp.
- (1895), *Il reduce soldato. Ballata lirica.* Shtypur prej Vincent Selvaxhi.
Corigliano Scalo: Sybaris & New York: Italiana.
(s.a.), *Sonetti vari.* Naples: Eugenio. 4 pp.
- (1926), *Vjershe,* a cura con prefazione e note dell'avv. Cosmo Serembe.
Milan. Grandi Edizione. 132 pp.
- (1985), *Vepra 1-4.* Prishtina: Rilindja.
- (1986), *Zonjës madhe perëndeshë Elenës Gjika (Canto a Dora d'Istria).*
Edizione (Introduzione, trascrizione e apparato critico) a cura di Giuseppe
Gradilone. Rome: Istituto di Studi Albanesi. 71 pp.
- (1994), *Këngëtori i dashuruar. Poezi erotike.* Skopje: Vatra. 81 pp.
- (1999), *Më të bukurës në Strigari. Vjersha, poema, balada, letërkëmbimi i*
Serembes, poezi kushtuar Serembes, ese, studime, refleksione. Përgatiti për
botim Perikli Jorgoni. Tirana: Toena. 408 pp.
SHALA, Kujtim M.
(2002a), *Shinimet e Fishtës.* Prishtina: Asociacioni për Integrime Kulturore
dhe Demokratike, 111 pp.
- (2002b), *Vox-i i Anton Pashkut.* Prishtina. Buzuku, 110 pp.
- (2004), *Fishta përballë Fishtës.* Prishtina: Gjon Buzuku, 92 pp.
SHEHU, Bashkim
(1994), *L'automne de la peur. Récit.* Traduit de l'albanais de Isabelle
Joudrain-Musa. Préface d'Ismaïl Kadaré. Paris: Fayard, 203 pp.
- (1993), Vjeshta e ankthit. Esse. Me parathënie të Ismail Kadaresë. Tirana:
Albin, 174 pp.
- (1995), *Le dernier voyage d'Ago Umeri.* Traduit de l'albanais par Anne-Marie
Autissier. Paris: L'Esprit des Péninsules, 157 pp.
- (1995), *Rrugëtimi i mbramë i Ago Ymerit. Roman.* Prishtina: Buzuku, 157 pp.
- (2001), *El último viaje de Ago Ymeri.* Tahona de letras, 5. Transl. Ramón
Sánchez Lizarralde. Barcelona: Meteora, 217 pp.
- (2003), *Udhëkryqi dhe humnerat. Roman.* Tirana: Toena, 102 pp.
- (2004), *Mulliri që gëlltiste shpirtra. Novela.* Tirana: Toena, 176 pp.
SHEMA, Isak
(1995), *Vrojtime letrare dhe artistike.* Prishtina: Rilindja. 277 pp.
- (1996), *Vlerësime të letërsisë shqiptare.* Prishtina: Rilindja. 212 pp.
- (1999), *Procedime letrare.* Prishtina: Rilindja. 197 pp.
SHEMA, Isak & RUGOVA, Ibrahim
(1976), *Bibliografi e kritikës letrare shqiptare 1944-1974.* Prishtina: Instituti
Albanologjik. reprint 1997. 448 pp.

Bibliography

SHKRELI, Azem
   (1960), *Karvani i bardhë. Roman.* Prishtina: Rilindja. reprint Prishtina 1980, Tirana 1996. 117 pp.
- (1965), *Sytë e Evës.* Prishtina: Rilindja. reprint 1973, 1985. 135 pp.
- (1984), *Poezi.* Tirana: Naim Frashëri. 216 pp.
- (1986), *Kënga e hutinit.* Prishtina: Rilindja. 87 pp.
- (1989), *The call of the owl.* Translated from the Albanian by John Hodgson. Prishtina: Kosova Association of Literary Translators. 84 pp.
- (2001), *Zjarr i fjetur. Poezi të zgjedhur.* Tirana: Toena. 175 pp.
- (2005), *Blood of the quill: selected poetry from Kosova in a bilingual, English-Albanian edition.* Edited and translated by Robert Elsie and Janice Mathie-Heck. forthcoming.

SHPUZA, Gazmend
   (1988), *Bibliografi për Rilindjen kombëtare shqiptare. Shkrime të botuara në RPSSh 1945-1978.* Tirana: Akademia e Shkencave. 251 pp.
- (1997), *Në vazhdim e gjurmimeve për epokën e Rilindjes Kombëtare. Përmbledhje shëndimesh historike dhe historiografike.* Tirana: Toena. 343 pp.

SHTYLLA, Behar
   (1997), *Fan Noli, siç e kam njohur. Kujtime.* Tirana: Dituria. 191 pp.

SHUTERIQI, Dhimitër
   (1961), Mbi jetën e krijimtarinë e Zef Serembes. in: *Buletin i Universitetit Shtetëror të Tiranës. Seria Shkencat Shoqërore,* Tirana, 4, p. 69-195.
- (1963), Të dhëna të reja mbi jetën dhe krijimtarinë e Ndre Mjedës. in: *Nëntori,* Tirana, 3, p. 98-122.
- (1974), *Gjurmime letrare.* Tirana: (Naim Frashëri. 325 pp.
- (1976), *Shkrimet shqipe në vitet 1332-1850.* Tirana: Akademia e Shkencave. reprint Prishtina 1978. 316 pp.
- (1977), *Autorë dhe tekste.* Tirana: Naim Frashëri. 423 pp.
- (1982), *Naim Frashëri. Jeta dhe vepra.* Tirana: 8 Nëntori. 236 pp.
- (1987), *Marin Beçikemi dhe shkrime të tjera.* Tirana: Naim Frashëri. 348 pp.
- (1989), Mbi Pjetër Bogdanin dhe veprën e tij. in: *Nëntori,* Tirana, 12, p. 17-33.

SHUTERIQI, Dhimitër (ed.)
   (1983), *Historia e letërsisë shqiptare që nga fillimet deri te lufta antifashiste nacionalçlirimtare.* Tirana: Akademia e Shkencave. reprint Prishtina 1990. 629 pp.

SHUTERIQI, Dhimitër, BIHIKU, Koço & DOMI, Mahir (ed.)
   (1959-1960), *Historia e letërsisë shqipe, 1-2.* Tirana: Universiteti Shtetëror i Tiranës. reprint Prishtina 1975.

SINETI, Paul de (ed.)
   (2000), Entretiens avec Ismail Kadaré et une nouvelle inédite. in: *L'Oeil de Boeuf, revue littéraire trimestrielle,* Paris, 20 (Mai 2000). 89 pp.

SINANI, Shaban
   (2005), *Një dosje për Kadarenë.* Tirana: Omsca-1. 395 pp.

SINISHTA, Gjon

(1976), *The fulfilled promise. A documentary account of religious persecution in Albania.* Santa Clara CA. 247 pp.

SKENDI, Stavro

(1953a), Beginnings of Albanian nationalist and autonomous trends. The Albanian league 1878-1881. in: *American Slavic and East European Review* 12. 2 (Apr.), p. 219-232.

- (1953b), Beginnings of Albanian nationalists trends in culture and education (1878-1912). in: *Journal of Central European Affairs* 12. 4 (Jan.), p. 356-367.
- (1954), Albanian political thought and revolutionary activity 1881-1912. in: *Südost-Forschungen,* Munich, 13, p. 159-199.
- (1956), 'Religion in Albania during the Ottoman rule,' in: *Südost-Forschungen,* Munich, 15, p. 311-327. reprint in *Balkan Cultural Studies.* New York (1980) p. 151-166.
- (1967), *Albanian national awakening (1878-1912).* Princeton: Princeton University Press. 498 pp.

SOPAJ, Nehas (ed.)

(2002), *Antologjia e poezisë së pastër shqipe.* Kumanova: Jehona e Karadakut, 178 pp.

SPAHIU, Xhevahir

(2003), *Rreziku. Poezi.* Botimi dytë i plotësuar. Tirana: Ideart, 160 pp.

SPASSE, Sterjo

(1935), *Nga jeta në jetë - Pse!?.* Me parathënie nga Vangjo Nirvana. Korça: Drita. reprint Prishtina 1968, 1986; Tirana 1995. 193 pp.

- (1944), *Afërdita. Roman.* Tirana: Luarasi. reprint Prishtina 1956, 1968) 191 pp.
- (1968), *Kompleti, 1-8.* Prishtina: Rilindja. 222, 202, 333, 327, 278, 151, 336, 308 pp.
- (1980-1985), *Vepra letrare 1-9.* Tirana: Naim Frashëri.

STADTMÜLLER, Georg

(1942a), Die 'Berglaute', das albanische Nationalepos. in: *Stimmen aus dem Südosten. Zeitschrift des Südost-Ausschusses der Deutschen Akademie.* Herausgegeben von Gustav Fochler-Hauke. Munich, p. 171-180.

- (1942b), Gjergj Fishta (1871-1940), der albanische Nationaldichter. in: *Stimmen aus dem Südosten. Zeitschrift des Südost-Ausschusses der Deutschen Akademie.* Herausgegeben von Gustav Fochler-Hauke. Munich, p. 133-135.
- (1955), 'Die Islamisierung bei den Albanern,' in: *Jahrbücher für Geschichte Osteuropas N.F.* 3, p. 404-429.
- (1971), 'Der Derwischorden der Bektaschi in Albanien,' in: *Serta slavica in memoriam Aloisii Schmaus.* W. Gesemann et al. (ed.). Munich: Trofenik. p. 683-687.

STAROVA, Luan (ed.)

(1995), *Librat e babait.* Skopje: Flaka e vëllazërimit. 176 pp.

- (1998a), *Faïk Konitza et Guillaume Apollinaire, une amitié européenne.* Edition établie et présentée par Luan Starova. Ouvrage publié avec le soutien du Centre National du Livre. Paris: L'Esprit des péninsules. 236 pp.
- (1998b), *Le livre de mon père. Roman.* Traduit du macédonien et de l'albanais par Clément d'Içartéguy. Paris: Fayard. 302 pp.
- (1999), *Le musée de l'athéisme. Roman.* Traduit du macédonien par Harita Wybrands. Paris: Fayard, 310 pp.
- (1999), *Zeit der Ziegen.* Aus dem Makedonischen von Roberto Mantovani. Zürich: Unionsverlag, 196 pp.
- (2001), *Kthimi i Faik Konicës.* Skopje: Flaka, 359 pp.
- (2003), *Le rivage de l'exil.* Roman traduit du macédonien par Clément d'Içartéguy. Préface d'Edgar Morin. Paris: L'Aube, 283 pp.
- (2004), *Koha e dhive.* Skopje: Logos-A, 266 pp.

STASSIJNS, Koen (ed.)
- (2001), *Klaagzang van een vogel. De mooiste moderne poëzie uit Kosova en Albanië.* Samengesteld en vertaald door Koen Stassijns. Antwerp: Lannoo. 171 pp.

STAVILECI, Masar
- (2000), Iluminizmi shqiptar. Botim i dytë i rishikuar. Tirana: Toena. 231 pp.

STËRMILLI, Haki
- (1936), *Sikur t'isha djalë. Roman.* Tirana: Ora. reprint 1938, Prishtina 1976, 1985, Tirana 1995. 310 pp.
- (1982-1983), *Vepra letrare 1-3.* Tirana: Naim Frashëri, 525, 358, + 386 pp.

STRATICÒ, Alberto
- (1896), *Manuale di letteratura albanese.* Milan: U. Hoepli. 280 pp.

SULEJMANI, Fadil
- (1979), *E mbsuame e krështerë e Lekë Matrëngës.* Prishtina: Instituti Albanologjik i Prishtinës. 295 pp.

SULEJMANI, Hivzi
- (1959), *Era dhe kolona.* Prishtina: Rilindja.
- (1969), *Fëmijët e lumit tim. Roman.* Prishtina: Rilindja. reprint 1989.

SVANE, Gunnar
- (1980), How to read Budi's Speculum Confessionis. in: *Studia Albanica,* Tirana, 1, p. 121-183
- (1982a), The formation of the literary language as reflected in Budi's 'Mirror of Confession' (1621). in: *Studia Albanica,* Tirana, 2, p. 193-211
- (1982b), Formimi i gjuhës letrare shqipe siç paraqitet në 'Pasqyrën e të Rrëfyemit' të Budit (1621). in: *Studime filologjike,* Tirana, 3, p 115-132.
- (1985a), *Pjetër Budi, Dottrina Christiana (1618).* With a transcription into modern orthography and a concordance prepared by Gunnar Svane. Text. in: Sprog og Mennesker 9, Institut for Lingvistik, Århus. 552 pp.
- (1985b), *Pjetër Budi, Dottrina Christiana (1618). Concordance 1-2.* in: Sprog og Mennesker 10, Institut for Lingvistik, Århus. 1,068 pp.

- (1986a), *Pjetër Budi, Speculum Confessionis (1621)*. With a transcription into modern orthography and a concordance prepared by Gunnar Svane. Text. in: Sprog og Mennesker 11, Institut for Lingvistik, Århus. 445 pp.
- (1986b), *Pjetër Budi, Speculum Confessionis (1621). Concordance 1-3*. in: Sprog og Mennesker 12, Institut for Lingvistik, Århus. 3,021 pp.
- (1986c), *Pjetër Budi, Rituale Romanum (1621)*. With a transcription into modern orthography and a concordance prepared by Gunnar Svane. Text. in: Sprog og Mennesker 13, Institut for Lingvistik, Århus. 398 pp.
- (1986d), *Pjetër Budi, Rituale Romanum (1621). Concordance 1-2*. in: Sprog og Mennesker 14, Institut for Lingvistik, Århus. 1,442 pp.
- (1986?), *Pjetër Budi, Speculum Confessionis (1621). Concordance 4*. in: Sprog og Mennesker, Institut for Lingvistik, Århus.

TAJANI, Filippo
- (1969), *Albanesi in Italia*. Cosenza: Casa del Libro/Brenner. 166 pp.

TAKO, Piro
- (1975), *Fan Noli në fushën politike dhe publicistike. Monografi*. Tirana: Naim Frashëri. 295 pp.
- (1988), *Luigj Gurakuqi. Jeta dhe vepra*. Prishtina: Rilindja. 423 pp.

TEFERIÇI, Parid
- (1996), *Bërë me largësi. Poezi*. Tirana: Albin, 174 pp.
- (2003), *Meqenëse sytë*. Tirana: Aleph, 87 pp.

TERPAN, Fabien
- (1992), *Ismaïl Kadaré*. Encyclopédie Universitaire. Paris: Editions Universitaires. 176 pp.

TREBESHINA, Kasëm
- (1991), *Stina e stinëve. Novela*. Prishtina: Buzuku, 303 pp.
- (1994), *Der Esel auf dem Mars. Eine Liebesgeschichte*. Aus dem Albanischen übersetzt von Hans-Joachim Lanksch. Klagenfurt: Wieser, 108 pp.
- (1994), *Lirika dhe satira. Shfletim i paqëllimtë kujtimesh*. Tirana: Marin Barleti, 116 pp.
- (1995), *Historia e atyre që s'janë*. Prishtina: Buzuku, 63 pp.
- (1996), *Hijet e shekujve. Novela*. Tirana: Eurorilindja, 291 pp.
- (1999), *Nata para apokalipsit. Triptik*. Tirana: Phoenix, 111 pp.
- (2001), *Kënga shqiptare: roman*. 1-5. Tirana: Globus R.
- (2004), *Më përtej kohërave*. Tirana: Ars, 152 pp.

TRIX, Frances
- (1993), *Spiritual discourse. Learning with an Islamic master*. Philadelphia: University of Pennsylvania Press. 189 pp.

TUFA, Agron
- (1996), *Aty te portat skee. Poezi*. Elbasan: Onufri, 105 pp.
- (2002), *Dueli. Roman*. Tirana: Ora, 145 pp.
- (2002), *Rrethinat e Atlantidës*. Tirana: Aleph, 133 pp.
- (2004), *Fabula rasa: histori e një wunderkind-i. Roman*. Tirana: Ideart, 224 pp.

UÇI, Alfred

(2003), *Pesë të mëdhenjtë e letërsisë shqipe në optikën e një rileximit. N. Frashëri, Gj. Fishta, F. Konica, M. Kuteli, Migjeni.* Skopje: Vatra, 247 pp.

VALENTINI, Giuseppe

(1964), Girolamo De Rada nella letteratura e nella storia albanese. in: *Shêjzat / Le Pleiadi,* Rome, 7-10, p. 234 sq.

- (1968), *Legge delle montagne albanesi nella relazioni della Missione Volante (1880-1932).* Studi albanesi. Studi i testi, 3. Florence: Olschki. xvi + 288 pp.

VARFI, Andrea

(1981), Të dhëna të reja për jetën dhe veprimtarinë e Gavril Darës (të Riut). in: *Studime për letërsine shqiptare 1. Probleme të letërsisë shqiptare të Rilindjes kombëtare.* ed. K. Bihiku, Tirana, p. 343-375.

VARIBOBA, Giulio

(1762), *Ghiella e S. Mëriis Virghiër scruar mbë viers Arbërist caa gnë prift puru i Arbëres për ndeert asaj Regin e par spass të atire divotrave, cia së duan të chëndognën chënch' namurije; ma duan të theen chënch' Spirituaal. mbë trij manerës: mbë Calimeer, mbë canghiell' e mbë gn' atër sort chëndimmi Lëtist: Vergine Bella.* Rome.

- (1984), *La vita di Maria. Prolegomeni, trascrizione, traduzione, glossario e note di Italo Costante Fortino.* Biblioteca degli Albanesi d'Italia, 1. Cosenza: Brenner. 357 pp.

VASA, Pashko

(1850), *La mia prigionia, episodio storico dell'assedio di Venezia di Pasco Wassa da Scutari d'Albania* Constantinople: A. Domenichini. 151 pp.

- (1865) *La Bosnie et l'Herzégovine pendant la mission de Djevdet Efendi par Pasco Wassa Efendi.* Constnatinople: Courrier d'Orient. 216 pp.

- (1872), *Esquisse historique sur le Monténégro d'après les traditions de l'Albanie par Pasco Wassa.* Constantinople: Courrier d'Orient. 81 pp.

- (1873), *Rose e spine per P. Wassa Effendi.* Constantinople: A. Coromila. 80 pp.

- (1879a), *Albanien und die Albanesen. Eine historisch-kritische Studie von Wassa Effendi,* Beamter der Kaiserlich Türkischen Regierung, Christlich-Albanischer Nationalität. Berlin: Julius Springer. 68 pp.

- (1879b), *Etudes sur l'Albanie et les Albanais par Wassa Effendi.* Constantinople: La Turquie. 113 pp.

- (1879c), *The truth on Albania and the Albanians: historical and critical. By Wassa Effendi,* an Albanian Christian functionary. Translation by Edward Saint John Fairman. London: National Press Agency. 48 pp.

- (1879d), *La vérité sur l'Albanie et les Albanais: étude historique et critique par Wassa Effendi, fonctionnnaire chrétien albanais.* Paris: Société Anonyme de Publications Périodiques. 103 pp.

- (1887), *Grammaire albanaise à l'usage de ceux qui désirent apprendre cette langue sans l'aide d'un maître par P. W.* Trübner's Collection of Simplified Grammars of the Principal Asiatic and European Languages. Ludgate Hill: Trübner & Co. 169 pp.

- (1890), *Bardha de Témal, scènes de la vie albanaise.* Paris: Albert Savine. 335 pp.
- (1987), *Vepra letrare 1-2.* Tirana: Naim Frashëri. 400 + 276 pp.
- (1989), *Vepra 1-4.* Prishtina: Rilindja.
- (1999), *The truth on Albania and the Albanians: historical and critical issues by Wassa Effendi.* Introduction by Robert Elsie. London: Centre for Albanian Studies. 46 pp.

(1999), *Bardha e Temalit. Roman.* Tirana: Mësonjëtorja. 266 pp.

VEHBIU, Ardian

(1989), Orientalizmat në poemën 'Erveheja' të M. Kyçykut-Çamit. in: *Studime Filologjike,* Tirana, 3, p. 101-112.

VELO, Maks

(2002), *Zhdukja e "Pashallarëve të kuq" të Kadaresë. Anketim për një krim letrar.* Tirana: Onufri, 156 pp.

- (2004), *La disparition des "Pachas rouges" d'Ismail Kadaré. Enquête sur un "crime littéraire."* Traduit de l'albanais par Tedi Papavrami. Paris: Fayard, 221 pp.

VINCA, Agim

(1977), *Aspekte të kritikës sonë,* Prishtina: Rilindja. 237 pp.
- (1985), *Struktura e zhvillimit të poezisë së sotme shqipe (1945-1980).* Prishtina: Rilindja. reprint 1997. 499 pp.
- (1990), *Orët e poezisë.* Prishtina: Rilindja. 561 pp.
- (1995), *Alternativa letrare shqiptare.* Skopje: Shkupi. 331 pp.
- (1996), Vepra letrare e Mitrush Kutelit. in: *Studime,* Prishtina, 3, p. 121-136.
- (2002), *Panteoni i ideve letrare.* Shkodra: Camaj-Pipa, 276 pp.

VLORA, Eqrem bey (= VLORA, Ekrem bey)

(1911), *Aus Berat und vom Tomor. Tagebuchblätter.* Zur Kunde der Balkanhalbinsel I. Reisen und Beobachtungen, 13. Sarajevo: D. A. Kajon. 168 pp.

- (1968-1973), *Lebenserinnerungen 1-2.* Südosteuropäische Arbeiten, 66, 67. Munich: Oldenbourg. 275 + 301 pp.

VRIONI, Jusuf

(1998), *Mondes éffacés, souvenirs d'un Européen.* Avec Eric Faye. Paris: JC Lattès. 318 pp.

VUÇANI, Petro

(1995), Jeta dhe veprat e Koliqit. in: *Ernest Koliqi 1903-1975, Studime shqiptare,* Shkodra, 3, 1995, p. 97-103.

WEIGAND, Gustav

(1927), Cuneus prophetarum von Peter Bogdan. in: *Balkan-Archiv,* Leipzig, 3, p. 173-207.

XHELILI, Vaxhid

(2001), *Sehnsucht nach Etleva. Malli për Etlevën. Ausgewählte Gedichte Albanisch und Deutsch.* Wegspuren von Marianna Leupi. Herausgegeben und aus dem Albanischen übersetzt und mit einem Nachwort versehen von Hans-Joachim Lanksch. Zürich: Limmat. 95 pp.

281

Bibliography

XHIKU, Ali
> (2002), *Romantizmi arbëresh.* Botim i tretë. Tirana: Dituria, 111 pp.

XHOLI, Zija
> (1962), *Naim Frashëri. Jeta dhe idetë.* Tirana. reprint Prishtina: Rilindja. 83 pp.
> - (1978), *Sami Frashëri. Nga jeta dhe vepra.* Tirana: 8 Nëntori. 187 pp.
> - (1986a), Pjetër Bogdani, son époque et son oeuvre. in: *Studia Albanica,* Tirana, 2, p. 35-46.
> - (1986b), Pjetër Bogdani, koha dhe vepra e tij. in: *Studime Filologjike,* Tirana, 1, p. 51-60.
> - (1987), *Mendimtare të Rilindjes kombëtare.* Tirana: 8 Nëntori. 383 pp.
> - (1990), Pjetër Bogdani, éminent humaniste albanais. in: *Studia albanica,* Tirana, 2, p. 155-170.
> - (1998), *Naim Frashëri midis së kaluarës dhe së sotmes. Studime naimjane.* Tirana: Luarasi. 213 pp.
> - (2003), *Pesë mendimtarët më të vjetër të kulturës sonë kombëtare. M. Barleti, Gj. Buzuku, P. Budi, F. Bardhi, P. Bogdani.* Tirana: Akademia e Shkencave, 202 pp.

XHUNGA, Rudina
> (2003), *Preja e një martese të lodhur: roman.* Tirana: Ombra GVG, 114 pp.

XHUVANI, Dhimitër
> (1966), *Tuneli. Roman.* Tirana: Naim Frashëri. 190 pp.
> - (1986), *Përsëri në këmbë. Roman.* Tirana: Naim Frashëri. reprint Prishtina 1986. 257 pp.

XOXA, Jakov
> (1965), *Lumi i vdekur. Roman.* 3 vol. Tirana: Naim Frashëri, reprint Tirana 1967, 1970, Prishtina 1971, 1987) 253, 256 + 320 pp.
> - (1983), *Vepra letrare 1-6.* Tirana: Naim Frashëri.

YOUNG, Antonia
> (1997), *Albania. Revised edition.* World bibliographical series, Volume 94. Oxford, Santa Barbara & Denver: Clio Press. 295 pp.

YZEIRI, Ana
> (2001), *Lirizmi i Fishtës tek "Lahuta e Malcís."* Tirana: Mokra. 82 pp.

ZAMPUTI, Injac
> (1954), Shënime mbi kohën dhe jetën e Pjetër Bogdanit. in *Buletini për Shkencat Shoqërore,* Tirana, 3, p. 39-75.
> - (1956), Relacioni i Frang Bardhi mbi Zadrimën, drejtue Kongregacionit të Propagandës në Romë në shek. XVII. in: *Buletini për Shkencat Shoqërore,* Tirana, 2, p. 163-192.
> - (1958), Shënime mbi rrethanat e vdekjes së Pjetër Budit. in: *Buletin i Universitetit Shtetëror të Tiranës. Seria Shkencat Shoqërore,* Tirana, 12, 2, p. 67-94.
> - (1963), Qëmtime mbi Pjetër Bogdanin. in: *Buletin i Universitetit Shtetëror të Tiranës. Seria Shkencat Shoqërore,* Tirana, 2, p. 199-206.
> - (1965), Koha dhe veprimtaria e Pjetër Budi. in: *Nëndori,* Tirana, 9, p. 123-142

-    (1985), Qëmtime për Budin e Bardhin. in: *Studime historike,* Tirana, 1, p. 165-176.

-    (1986), Mbi rrëthanat historike të botimit të 'Mesharit' të Gjon Buzukut dhe vendin e tij në letërsinë e vjetër shqiptare. in: *Studime filologjike,* Tirana, 3, p. 185-204.

-    (1988), Les circonstances historiques de la parution du 'Missel' de Gjon Buzuku et sa place dans la littérature ancienne albanaise. in: *Studia albanica,* Tirana, 1, p. 83-104.

-    (1993a), *Ekskursion në dy vepra të Kadaresë.* Tirana: Dituria. 235 pp.

-    (1993b), *Fishta. Koha, njeriu, vepra.* Tirana: Pasqyra. 175 pp.

ZAMPUTI, Injac (ed.)

    (1963-1965), *Relacione mbi gjendjen e Shqipërisë veriore e të mesme në shekullin XVII.* Teksti origjinal dhe përkthimi nga Injac Zamputi. Burime dhe materiale për historinë e Shqipërisë, 3. Vëllimi I (1610-1634), Vëllimi II (1634-1650). Tirana: Universiteti shtetëror i Tiranës. 540 + 525 pp.

ZANGARI, Domenico

    (1940), *Le colonie italo-albanesi di Calabria. Storia e demografia. Secoli XV-XIX.* Naples: Casella. 174 pp.

ZEKAJ, Ramiz

    (1997), *Zhvillimi i kulturës islame te shqiptarët gjatë shekullit XX.* Tirana: Instituti shqiptar i mendimit dhe qytetrimit islamik. 403 pp.

ZHEJI, Gjergj

    (1966), *Andon Zako-Çajupi, jeta dhe vepra.* Tirana. reprint Prishtina: Rilindja 1969. 95 pp.

ZHITI, Visar

    (1993), *Kujtesa e ajrit. Poezi.* Tirana: Lidhja e Shkrimtarëve. 209 pp.

-    (1994), *Hedh një kafkë te këmbët tuaja. Poezitë e burgut (1979-1987).* Tirana: Naim Frashëri. 167 pp.

-    (1994), *Mbjellja e vetëtimave.* Skopje: Flaka e vëllazërimit. 99 pp.

-    (2000), *Si shkohet në Kosovë. Poezi.* Tirana: Toena. 117 pp.

-    (2001), *Rrugët e ferrit. Burgologji.* Tirana: Onufri. 478 pp.

-    (2002), *Ferri i çarë. Roman i vërtetë.* Tirana: Omsca-1, 453 pp.

-    (2003), *Funerali i pafundmë. Roman.* Tirana: Omsca-I, 180 pp.

-    (2004), *Perëndia mbrapsht dhe e dashura. Roman.* Tirana: Omsca-1. 283 pp.

-    (2005), *The Condemned apple. Selected poetry.* Translated by Robert Elsie. A bilingual edition. Green Integer 134. Los Angeles: Green Integer. 314 pp.

ZOTOS, Alexandre

    (1997), *De Scanderbeg à Ismail Kadaré. Propos d'histoire et de littérature albanaises.* Saint-Etienne: Université de Saint-Etienne. 205 pp.

ZOTOS, Alexandre (ed.)

    (1984), *Anthologie de la prose albanaise présentée par Alexandre Zotos.* Paris: Fayard. 554 pp.

-    (1998), *Anthologie de la poésie albanaise.* Chambéry: La Polygraphe, Edition Comp'Act. 388 pp.

11. Index

ABOUT THE AUTHOR

Robert Elsie (Vancouver, Canada, 1950) is a leading specialist in Albanian affairs. He is the author of over forty books, primarily on Albania and its culture, including literary translations from Albanian, and of many articles and research papers. Elsie studied at the University of British Columbia, graduating in 1972 with a degree in classical studies and linguistics. In the following years, he did postgraduate research at the Free University of Berlin, the Ecole Pratique des Hautes Etudes and the University of Paris IV in Paris, the Dublin Institute for Advanced Studies in Ireland and the University of Bonn, where he finished his doctorate in 1978 at the Linguistics Institute. From 1982 to 1987, he was employed by the German Ministry of Foreign Affairs in Bonn. Since that time he has worked as a freelance writer and conference interpreter, primarily for Albanian and German. He lives in the Eifel Mountains of Germany, not far from the Belgian border. *See* www.elsie.de and www.albanianliterature.com.